CHRISTIAN INTERCULTURE

WORLD CHRISTIANITY

Dale T. Irvin and Peter Phan, Series Editors

ADVISORY BOARD:
Akintunde E. Akinade
Adrian Hermann
Leo D. Lefebure
Elaine Padilla
Yolanda Pierce

Moving beyond descriptions of European-derived norms that have existed for hundreds of years, books in the World Christianity series reflect an understanding of global Christianity that embodies the wide diversity of its identity and expression. The series seeks to expand the scholarly field of world Christianity by interrogating boundary lines in church history, mission studies, ecumenical dialogue, and interreligious dialogue among Christians and non-Christians across geographic, geopolitical, and confessional divides. Beyond a mere history of missions to the world, books in the series examine local Christianity, how Christianity has been acculturated, and how its expression interacts with the world at large. Issues under investigation include how Christianity has been received and transformed in various countries; how migration has changed the nature and practice of Christianity and the new forms of the faith that result; and how seminary and theological education responds to the challenges of world Christianity.

OTHER BOOKS IN THE SERIES:

Krista E. Hughes, Dhawn B. Martin, and Elaine Padilla, eds., *Ecological Solidarities: Mobilizing Faith and Justice for an Entangled World*

Aminta Arrington, *Songs of the Lisu Hills: Practicing Faith in Southwest China*

CHRISTIAN INTERCULTURE

Texts and Voices from Colonial and Postcolonial Worlds

Edited by Arun W. Jones

The Pennsylvania State University Press
University Park, Pennsylvania

Library of Congress Cataloging-in-Publication Data

Names: Jones, Arun W., editor.
Title: Christian interculture : texts and voices from colonial and postcolonial worlds / edited by Arun W. Jones.
Other titles: World Christianity (University Park, Pa.)
Description: University Park, Pennsylvania : The Pennsylvania State University Press, [2021] | Series: World Christianity | Includes bibliographical references and index.
Summary: "A collection of essays exploring how scholars can discern the voices, thoughts, activities, and motivations of indigenous Christians of Asia, Africa, and the Americas in texts produced in the context of European domination from 1500 to the present"—Provided by publisher.
Identifiers: LCCN 2020050644 | ISBN 9780271087795 (hardback) | ISBN 9780271087801 (paper)
Subjects: LCSH: Christianity and culture—History. | Africa—Church history. | America—Church history. | Asia—Church history.
Classification: LCC BR115.C8 C44425 2021 | DDC 270.089—dc23
LC record available at https://lccn.loc.gov/2020050644

Copyright © 2021 The Pennsylvania State University
All rights reserved
Printed in the United States of America
Published by The Pennsylvania State University Press,
University Park, PA 16802–1003

The Pennsylvania State University Press is a member of the Association of University Presses.

It is the policy of The Pennsylvania State University Press to use acid-free paper. Publications on uncoated stock satisfy the minimum requirements of American National Standard for Information Sciences—Permanence of Paper for Printed Library Material, ANSI Z39.48–1992.

Contents

Acknowledgments VII

Introduction 1
ARUN W. JONES

Methodological Reflections

chapter 1 Beyond Troublemakers and Collaborators: Historical Research into Newly Evangelized African Catholics 17
PAUL KOLLMAN

chapter 2 Completing the Line of Communication: On Hearing the Voice of the "Native Christian" 39
MRINALINI SEBASTIAN

chapter 3 In Search of the Women in the Archival Sources: The Case of Maria Maraga 63
ESTHER MOMBO

Early Colonial Catholicism

chapter 4 In Search of Kirishitan Women Martyrs' Voices in the Early Modern Jesuit Mission Literature in Japan 81
HARUKO NAWATA WARD

chapter 5 Native Christianity and Communal Justice in Colonial Mexico: An Ambivalent History 107
YANNA YANNAKAKIS

chapter 6 Ocaña's Mondragón in the "Eighth Wonder of the World" 130
KENNETH MILLS

Christian Nationalism

chapter 7 They Talk. We Listen? Native American Christians in Speech and on Paper   165
CHRISTOPHER VECSEY

chapter 8 Native Christians Writing Back? The Periodicals of the Iglesia Filipina Independiente in the Early Twentieth-Century Philippines   189
ADRIAN HERMANN

chapter 9 "For You, Most Reverend Father, and for Our Archives": Recovering the Voice of Bishop Aloys Bigirumwami in Late Colonial Rwanda   214
J. J. CARNEY

Conclusion   233
ARUN W. JONES

List of Contributors   241
Index   245

Acknowledgments

I am grateful to a number of persons who have been instrumental in the preparation and publication of this volume. First, I would like to thank the authors who originally contributed papers to the 2014 conference at Emory University that provided the genesis of this book. It was certainly gratifying to have their enthusiastic assent when I asked them to participate in a consultation on the historiography of non-Western Christianity, and then to have them agree to turn their papers into essays for an edited collection. Given that most of the chapters here came out of that conference, I am especially thankful to Esther Mombo for agreeing to write an essay for this volume when she did not participate in that original event.

The conference itself was sponsored wholly by Emory University, to which I am thankful for its generous aid. Dean Jan Love of the Candler School of Theology enthusiastically encouraged me to pursue the project from its inception, and facilitated the school's sponsorship of the conference. Emory's Halle Institute for Global Research, and its previous director Holli Semetko, also supported the conference as well as a preliminary gathering of scholars. The bulk of the funding for the conference came from the Emory Conference Center Subvention Fund, and Allison Adams of the university's Center for Faculty Development and Excellence gave expert advice on how to navigate the requirements of the grant request.

The editorial staff at Penn State University Press have been most patient and reassuring as I endeavored to bring this volume to completion. In particular, Kathryn Yahner was excited about the project from the first time I talked with her about it, and gently encouraged me to keep working on it over the years. She directed me to the new series on World Christianity that the Press was initiating, and the work has benefited much from being included in the series.

Peter Phan and Dale Irvin, the editors of the World Christianity series at Penn State Press, offered very helpful suggestions and advice for the collection of essays. I am also grateful to the outside reviewers of the volume for their attentive examination of each essay as well as the work as a whole.

Finally, I would like to offer a personal word of thanks to my colleague Yanna Yannakakis in Emory's history department. On several occasions

ACKNOWLEDGMENTS

I have called on Yanna to provide wisdom and timely advice on how to proceed with this project. Not only has she always answered the call, but she has done so with much graciousness and goodwill, setting aside precious time in her extremely busy schedule to help me deal with my questions and conundrums. To me, she exemplifies not only the best of Emory, but also of the larger community of scholars of which I am fortunate to be a part.

INTRODUCTION

Arun W. Jones

Christianity and Culture

Since its inception in the first century CE, Christianity has been a cross-cultural and a culturally pluralistic religion. Already in its earliest writings there is evidence that the first generation of adherents came from both Jewish and gentile backgrounds. The impetus to expand beyond one people and one geographical location dates back, according to the Christian scriptures, to the resurrection of Jesus of Nazareth from the dead. Modern historians may find the origins of Christianity's expansive nature in the first followers of Jesus, some of whom traveled rather extensively in the Roman Empire, and perhaps beyond, with a desire to spread their faith. In any case, within the first two centuries after its founding, various incarnations of the faith had quickly appeared in parts of Asia, Africa, and Europe. Most important, each cultural incarnation of the faith was not only allowed but expected—within certain intensely contested and negotiated boundaries—to express the faith in its own linguistic and cultural idiom. This principle had been established in the earliest council of the church, the Council of Jerusalem, during which the first leaders of what we may call the Jewish "Jesus is the Messiah" movement decided that Greek followers did not have to adopt Jewish religious and cultural norms in order to join the movement (Acts 15). In fact, according to the biblical witness, it was precisely when the faith passed beyond its Jewish cultural milieu into the cultural world of pagan adherents that the followers became known as "Christians" (Acts 11:26). Christianity, as a religious tradition, was marked by cross-cultural movement and cultural pluralism at its birth.

Christianity, however, has not only been cross-cultural and culturally pluralistic; it has also always been intercultural. So, while Christian communities have differed in significant ways from one another, they have also held that interaction and intercommunion with Christian communities from other cultures was a vital element of their own self-understanding. This has led to both severe disagreements and deep intercommunion between different incarnations of the Christian faith. Christians have argued (and too often fought) among themselves about the purportedly correct views on everything from theological understandings to liturgical practices to social behavior. Given the wide variety and innumerable disagreements within the religion, it is easy to forget that Christians across time, culture, and geography have also agreed on certain basic doctrines; shared common rituals and scriptures; borrowed various ideas, liturgies, and quotidian practices from one another; committed themselves to helping one another across human and natural boundaries; and made concerted efforts to be in touch with fellow believers in other parts of the world. This last characteristic is well exemplified in the ancient churches of Ethiopia and South India, both established by the fourth century CE, whose leaders until the modern age have insisted that the head of their churches come from Egypt (in the case of the Ethiopian Orthodox Church) or Mesopotamia (in the case of the South Indian Syrian Orthodox Church). The cross-cultural expansion of Christianity, therefore, has yielded not only a culturally pluralistic but also an intercultural church.

Christianity is intercultural in yet another way. Behind the fact of Christian pluralism lies a sometimes unacknowledged but absolutely inescapable reality: Christian communities have always relied on other religious and theological traditions, on other conceptual worlds, on other rituals and social practices for their own identities and self-expressions. Repeatedly cast by church leaders as antagonists and grave dangers to the faith, proximate communities of other religious, social, and cultural backgrounds have been vital for Christian self-understanding. Sometimes these other communities have acted as foils and negative examples of what it means to be a faithful follower of Christ in a particular context. Yet more often than the acknowledged guardians of the faith have admitted, these neighbors have provided cultural and religious scripts and models to be adopted and adapted for Christian thought, action, and affections. The essays in this volume explore both types of intercultural interactions of various Christian traditions beginning in the sixteenth century.

Christian Expressions since 1500

The year 1500 marks a significant moment in the history of Christian cultural expansion and expression. From its inception until the eighth century CE, the religion had expanded from its origins in Palestine into Asia at least as far as China and India, into Africa as far as Ethiopia, into the whole Mediterranean basin, and into Europe as far as France and England. Dogmatic and institutional conflicts and controversies between different groups within the worldwide church, the destruction of the Western Roman Empire by pagan barbarians beginning in the fifth century, and the rise of Islam beginning in the eighth century checked the growth of Christianity in Europe, Asia, and Africa—although the interaction between the various religions was certainly neither simple nor straightforward. From the fifth to the fifteenth century there was a slow accession to the Christian faith of the tribal peoples who had settled down in what is known as Europe, and a slow recession of the faith among the populations of Asia and Africa, so that by the end of the fifteenth century, Christianity was more European than it had ever been before or would be again, and Europe was more Christian than it ever had been before or would be again.[1]

This geographical and cultural constriction of the faith to Europe—with notable exceptions in Asia and Africa—had a highly deleterious effect on its cross-cultural and intercultural feature. While there was no doubt variety among them, over the course of approximately four centuries European Christians generally assumed—both implicitly and explicitly—that in comparison to any other possible incarnations of the tradition, theirs was the norm in terms of both theology and practice. To prove this rule, as it were, there were always exceptional minority voices, often connected with the church's missionary movements, that kept insisting to European Christians that the religion was culturally and ideologically heterogenous rather than uniform.

The general limitation of Christianity to Europe was broken by the military and commercial expansion of European nations into the world beginning in the fifteenth century. This development was accompanied by a new phase of Christian expansion, one in fact that was unprecedented due to the invasion and conquest of the Americas. As in the case of the relationship between Islam and Christianity in Africa and Asia, and between Christianity and the tribal religions and cultures of the people who settled down in the Western Roman Empire, the relationships between the political, economic, and religious dimensions of Europe's expansion into the world from the fifteenth century onward were complex.[2]

While the fact of Christian expansion, contraction, and communication over the course of two millennia is well known, far less understood are the processes by which the faith was appropriated in new cultural and religious domains, and thereby took on new expressions of itself in conversation with the existing cultures and religions. It is true that the historian can identify a number of different factors, ranging from individual personalities to global forces, that have affected the ways in which the Christian religion has expanded into cultures once alien to it. One of the important factors has been the relative political, military, and economic strength of the missionizing Christians vis-à-vis the receiving groups. During the sixteenth and seventeenth centuries, for example, while the Roman Catholic Church and the Iberian kingdoms were simultaneously Christianizing and conquering the Americas and the Philippines, the same church's missions to Japan and China were at the mercy of local Asian rulers and empires. Radical adaptation of Christianity to Japanese and Chinese cultures therefore was not simply an experiment in mission theory and practice: it was also a practical necessity if the Christian mission was to succeed.

However, on the whole, the cultural processes involved in the reception and incarnation of the religion have remained relatively obscure. What people apprehended when they came to know about Christianity in any particular historical context, why certain people did or did not identify themselves as Christians, how they understood that identity to apply to themselves, and how they viewed and related to people (whether Christian or not) outside their cultural and religious group has often been more a matter of historical speculation and supposition than actual historical examination. So, to return to the examples above, even though we know quite a bit about the missionary thinking and the political forces involved in the expansion of Christianity in sixteenth-century Mexico and Japan, how Mesoamerican and Japanese Christians understood their adoption and living out of a Christian identity has, until recently, been more assumed than investigated.

Grappling with the Histories of Christians of Africa, Asia, and the Americas

It was to address the challenges of writing histories of Christians from non-Western cultures and contexts that in May of 2014 a conference was held at Emory University with the title "Can the Native Christian Speak? Discerning the Voices of Indigenous Christians in Missionary and Colonial Archives." The conference's title purposely evoked the title of Gayatri Chakravorty Spivak's well-known essay "Can the Subaltern Speak?"[3] Like Spivak, the conference was grappling with issues of representation of non-Western people in Western academic writing. And in echoing Spivak, the conference organizer assumed that indigenous Christians, at least in colonial contexts, were in most cases among the subaltern of society.

The essays in this volume, with the exception of that by Esther Mombo, originated as papers delivered at that conference. They all deal with the history of Christians in Africa, the Americas, and Asia. The historians contributing to this volume are seasoned scholars who have studied the religious traditions of non-European populations. They were asked to reflect on a problem that seems endemic to the study of the history of Christianity in non-Western contexts: namely, that so much of what we know of Christian persons and communities outside the West comes from materials produced and archived by Westerners. The "West" here, as in many other academic contexts, refers to people and cultures with their origins in Europe, as opposed to other parts of the world (Africa, the Americas, Asia, and Oceania). The contributors were encouraged to include self-conscious, partly autobiographical reflections on how they have dealt with historiographical problems arising from the study of Christianity in non-Western cultures, in eras when European empires were either dominating or were attempting to dominate the globe.

Once the papers were assembled, it became clear that they called into question (though did not render completely irrelevant) two of the underlying assumptions that went into the organization of the conference. First, the idea that indigenous Christians have been unable to leave a historical record of their voices and activities is simply not true in many instances. The essays by Carney, Hermann, Yannakakis, Vecsey, and Ward, for example, deal with material that was produced or coproduced by indigenous Christians, and these materials are available to historians today. The important question for many contemporary historians, then, is not how to discover and uncover native Christian voices but whether one is willing to look at materials produced by indigenous Christians and other persons, and work with these materials. As Chris Vecsey's essay title aptly puts it, "They Talk. We Listen?"

A second assumption that was shown to be quite (although again, not completely) mistaken was that indigenous Christians have been, for the most part, in the position of dependence and relative weakness with respect to European power—both secular and religious. The essays in this volume describe the lives of persons from across the social spectrum: from humble low-class Bible Women in South India, to African Christian leaders mediating Christianity between converts and missionaries, to highly educated nationalist revolutionaries in the early twentieth-century Philippines. Natives, whether Christian or not, were by no means necessarily "subalterns," even in colonial situations.

Rather than addressing old complaints, the contributions to this volume take up new challenges of studying some of the cross-cultural and intercultural processes involved in the expansion of Christianity into non-Western cultural areas from the sixteenth to the twentieth century. They build on and further the historical project of understanding the enculturation of Christian traditions in contexts where expansive and aggressive Western Christian cultures had given rise to non-Western varieties of the faith. The essays accomplish this in two distinct yet interrelated ways.

First and foremost, the essays tackle the historiographical problems of reconstructing local religion, from the individual to the communal level, when such religion has emerged in the shadow of Western Christianity. The problems involved in historical reconstruction are many, and actually vary significantly according to context, as the essays demonstrate. In contexts where Christianity was adopted in oral rather than literary cultures, written and material evidence produced by local Christians is scarce, if it exists at all. A number of essays deal with this reality and chart some ways forward in cases where the existing evidence from oral cultures prove problematic for reconstructing their histories. For example, Paul Kollman's essay provides helpful principles for evaluating Western missionary sources describing the lives of East African Christians.

In some contexts (including those involving oral cultures), European Christian missionaries and other foreigners were highly privileged in relation to local people. Indigenes were often (but certainly not always) deemed inferior in one or more ways, and their lives either not worth commenting on much or viewed in a deprecating manner. Foreigners could then leave behind significantly distorted records and impressions of the native population. For example, Kenneth Mills explores the distorted representations of colonial American life by a traveling Spanish Dominican friar in the first years of the seventeenth century. Yet Mills demonstrates how such strongly biased Western accounts are not useless for reconstructing histories of the indigenous; when used with appropriate caution and care, they can reveal important aspects and dimensions of the lives of local persons.

In still other cases, local and foreign voices were inextricably intertwined and blended in existing sources produced by Western Christians. Haruko Ward deals with the case of sixteenth- and seventeenth-century documents produced by Jesuit missionaries and local Christian women in Japan. She warns us not to dismiss these joint productions as simply authored by Jesuit males, for in the writings she discerns a distinct Japanese Christian woman martyr's communal theology. Chris Vecsey confronts the problems of trying to guess from Western Christian accounts what Native American Christians thought, said, and did, even in the case of such a putatively authentic work such as *Black Elk Speaks*. He urges historians to take with utmost seriousness the voices of contemporary Native American Christians, with all their great variety and variability.

Finally, rhetoric to the contrary notwithstanding, sometimes it is contemporary Western scholarship that has too often failed to take an interest in local productions of Christian (and other religious) thought and activity. Jay Carney writes about the life of the Rwandan bishop Aloys Bigirumwami, who left behind a considerable record of writings that are generally neglected and unexplored in the histories of late colonial Rwanda. Adrian Hermann discusses newspapers published by local Christian elites such as the founders of the Iglesia Filipina Independiente, an indigenous Catholic church that emerged in the Philippines around the turn of the twentieth century in the midst of the Filipino-Spanish-American War. Yanna Yannakakis uses extant but generally neglected archives that preserve records of local Zapotec Christian thought and action, while Mrinalini Sebastian reveals writings by indigenous Indian Christians that historians have ignored because they are found only in mission archives.

While the primary task of the essays in this volume is to engage problems related to the historiography of non-Western Christianity, a second feature is that, in the process of discussing these problems, they also produce history. In other words, they narrate the lives of Christians from cultures indigenous to Africa, Asia, and the Americas. And so we start to learn about the lives of obscure and unknown persons such as the silver merchant Pedro de Mondragón who lived in early seventeenth-century Potosí, Bolivia, and of Maria Maraga, a pillar of the East African Quaker communities in the first half of the twentieth century.

Common Themes

The essays in this volume, then, focus on certain historiographical problems and issues when it comes to writing the history of Christians in non-European contexts, and they also narrate some of that history for us. Diverse as the essays are, certain themes keep reoccurring in them, which indicates the importance of these themes in the history and historiography of non-European Christianity and religion. One of the most prevalent motifs in this collection is the power of translation. As Andrew Walls and Lamin Sanneh have argued, translation is essential to Christianity, and of course, it both transmits and transmutes.[4] A number of essays demonstrate the necessity of paying close attention to the process of translation, as it obscures and reveals, acts as liberator and oppressor, and is manipulated by various segments of society, from the very weak to the very powerful, for their particular ends.

Tony Stewart has helpfully described translation in the realm of religion as a "search for equivalence," and he has enumerated four different ways it takes place.[5] The first is "formal literary equivalence," where the translator seeks an exactly equivalent idea or concept from the Source Language (SL) in the Receptor Language (RL). However, such translation is both misguided and frustrating, since "perfect one-to-one correspondences" of religious ideas and practices rarely—if ever—exist in two languages and cultures.[6] A second mode of translation is mirroring and refraction. In this process, there is no attempt to translate terms exactly from one language into another. Rather, "a translation *reflects* the original idea but *refracts* it in the process; that is, it does not capture the identical semantic field but approximates it, often with distortions, the latter being key."[7] Mirroring works well when a term has a rough equivalent in both languages. However, this technique reaches its limits when the two different communities using two different languages regard apparently equivalent religious practices or expressions quite differently. To deal with such cases, a third translation technique, that of dynamic equivalence, is employed: "Dynamic equivalence not only accounts for overlapping semantic domains but also gives priority to cultural context, which can begin to account for the different values ascribed to equivalent terms."[8] So the translator shifts her concern for finding as similar a term as possible in the receptor language and instead gives priority to how the expression or concept is used in the target language and culture. The translation then is dynamic with respect to context.

There is one more level of translation that goes beyond simply translating particular words and ideas and practices from one language and culture to another. Such translation occurs in the realm of the "intersemiotic," where whole metaphoric worlds are involved. At this level of translation in the sphere of religion, there is "an interchange and interpolation of ideas" among mythologies, rituals, and even parts of theological systems: "At this stage, which is the most vexing type of translation—a cultural translation—an entire conceptual world is understood in terms of another, not just in its single terms or phrases."[9]

To these four categories of translation, some of the essays allude to one other kind of translation that has taken place and continues to take place in the realm of religion—and that is willful mistranslation. Paul Vecsey recounts the life of George Copway, an Ojibwa Protestant, who ended up presenting himself to the public in patently false ways, while Paul Kollman reveals how a missionary passed off the fictional account of an East African woman named Suema as historical truth.

The essays in this volume deal with translation—and sometimes willful mistranslation—occurring at various levels, sometimes several levels simultaneously. For instance, while the essays of Haruko Ward and Yanna Yannakakis deal most explicitly with the complexities of translation, all the others also delve into the problems and possibilities of moving between languages, cultures, and worldviews.

A second theme that emerges in the essays collected in this volume is what I call polyvalent identities.[10] In colonial and postcolonial contexts, persons with origins in disparate communities (converts are a prime example) often found themselves grappling with the fact that their identities encompassed more than one religious tradition, more than one culture, and more than one social location. Jay Carney describes how Bishop Bigirumwami understood himself as both Hutu and Tutsi, as loyal to both the Catholicism introduced by French missionaries and to the Christian identity of Rwandans, while Chris Vecsey details the sometimes agonizing struggle for Native American Catholics to hold on to both their Native American and Christian identities.

The polyvalent identities of Christians and others worked themselves out in a number of different ways. There were complex negotiations within local religious communities, where Christians from different backgrounds—African and American, Brahmin and Billava—found themselves belonging to one religious community. Such experiments did not always end well. Adrian Hermann reminds us that the intracommunal negotiations were not restricted to one region or country but spanned continents, as rising classes of educated native Christian elites in Asian and African societies started using newspapers and other print media to communicate with one another and with the larger world. The polyvalent identities could also result in highly complex struggles and negotiations between locals and foreigners of the same faith community, as the cases from colonial Peru, the Philippines, and Rwanda demonstrate.

The multifaceted identities also could lead to unexpected allegiances and resistances, as well as to interesting confluences and divergences. In Japan, Jesuits whose constitution barred women from their order found themselves working closely with Japanese Christian women to produce reading materials that would support their community during severe persecution from the Japanese government. On the other hand, the East African Quaker leader Maria Maraga used her position to defy traditional dietary taboos for African women in her community of origin.

One important consequence of polyvalent identities is that Christians, again especially indigenous ones, took on or were thrust into the role of intermediaries in negotiations between various antagonistic parties. The same qualities that made for intermediaries could also make for misfits, another role that native Christians inherited, often unwittingly, as communities from different social, cultural, and religious backgrounds came into contact and conflict with one another. A number of negotiators and misfits—such as Carlos Chichimecateuctli and Juan Ramos in colonial Mexico—are described and examined in this volume.

Besides translation and polyvalent identities, a third theme that recurs in the collected essays is that it is of vital importance to understand European sources in order to discern non-European voices. While the knowledge of the distorting and suppressing effects of powerful alien perspectives and sources may lead historians to try and avoid the foreign in search of the "true" indigenous voice, it is only when the social and intellectual patterns and proclivities of European actors are well comprehended that historians can begin to interpret with some integrity the various sources on which we depend. Reductionist views of Europeans do not produce more accurate apprehensions of the autochthonous. This theme is well investigated in the contributions by Paul Kollman, Mrinalini Sebastian, and Yanna Yannakakis, where the authors carefully describe the mindset of Christians in and from Europe in order to shed light on the history of East African, South Indian, and Mexican Christians at various periods of time.

Finally, the essays implicitly or explicitly warn us always to keep in mind the existence of the great variety, in terms of race, gender, and social location, of the actors in colonial and postcolonial contexts. The authors focus on particular persons and strata in society: common and elite, women and men, ruler and ruled, clergy and laity, missionary and colonial official. The picture that emerges from the essays is kaleidoscopic rather than neatly composed. The similarly confident voices of upper-caste Indian Christian converts and *illustrado* Filipino Christian elites certainly do not convey similar messages. These disparate religious experts had their own particular concerns, their own particular challenges, their own particular fulfillments. In our eagerness and commitment to uncover and distinguish "the indigenous voice," historians are liable to forget that no such thing exists, as Paul Kollman reminds us. Instead, what we have are distinctive voices, with their own emphases and modulations, their own assertions of truth and falsehood, their own revelations and deceptions. This does not mean that there are no common concerns of Christian and other religious communities in various times, places, and cultures. Rather, it means that our moves between the particular and the general need to be made with careful deliberation, if we are to embrace the full plenitude of Christian and other voices in colonial and postcolonial worlds.

Organization of the Volume

The nine essays in this volume are grouped in three sections. The first three essays concern themselves largely with methodological issues. Paul Kollman discusses various strategies for weighing and dealing with historical evidence. Mrinalini Sebastian highlights the importance of knowing the frameworks that missionary authors used when they wrote of "native Christians." And Esther Mombo explores the difficulties and possibilities of writing African Christian women's histories, using the case of the Quakers in Kenya.

The second group of essays takes us back to the first generations of Roman Catholics in Latin America and Asia. Haruko Ward argues that Japanese translations of European Catholic source material give us insight into the communal mindset of Japanese Christian women working with

Jesuit missionaries. Yanna Yannakakis tackles the issue of translation from a different perspective, demonstrating how it was manipulated by political contestants in Oaxaca, Mexico, as they struggled for power in their localities. Lastly, Kenneth Mills examines and cross-examines the often-unreliable accounts of a Spanish visitor to South America to understand some aspects of emerging indigenous Christianity in Peru.

The third set of essays brings us to the nineteenth and twentieth centuries, as formerly colonized Christians joined in their people's struggles to liberate themselves from European rule and control. Christopher Vecsey details the difficulties that native peoples in North America have faced in getting European Christians in both Europe and North America to take seriously their multiple articulations of Native American Christianity. The Philippines, on the other side of the globe, is the site of Adrian Hermann's investigations into the publishing activities of Catholics seeking independence from both Spain and Rome at the beginning of the twentieth century. Finally, Jay Carney narrates the life of the Rwandan Roman Catholic bishop Aloys Bigirumwami, to reveal—among other things—how the late twentieth-century genocide was not an inevitable trajectory of the country's history.

All the essays suggest how official, or orthodox, lines of thought and action developed in the West have been challenged and shaped by non-Western actors whose claim to legitimacy rested on their identity as Christians. So, the great reversal between the colonial and postcolonial periods is not simply that the colonized began to claim power but that the very Christianity that so often authorized the colonizing movement was used to authorize decolonization.

Furthermore, all the essays suggest, in one way or another, that in writing the history of Christianity in Africa, Asia, and the Americas, historians need to pay careful attention to the multiple cultures and religions that are interacting with one another in all sorts of ways: in other words, to understand how Christianity is intercultural. These interacting cultural and religious traditions may be easy to discern in historical sources, but they may also be obscured, hidden, and effaced. As Clifton Crais commented at the end of the Emory conference, "We work with silences, not simply the absence of evidence but the hard fact that all evidence—a record, a letter, some document—exists only by a simultaneous creation of silence. Something is there and something else isn't. Presence and absence, memory and forgetting, remain inextricably intertwined."[11] Part of the historian's task is to decide which cultural and religious silences, absences, and forgotten pasts need to be disturbed for new intercultural histories to emerge, and which voices need to be temporarily quieted to make this emergence a possibility.

Notes

1. Andrew F. Walls, "Eusebius Tries Again: Reconceiving the Study of Christian History," *International Bulletin of Missionary Research* 24, no. 3 (July 2000): 105.

2. For example, see the essay of Yanna Yannakakis in this volume; Andrew N. Porter, *Religion versus Empire? British Protestant Missionaries and Overseas Expansion, 1700–1914* (Manchester, UK: Manchester University Press, 2004); and Dana L. Robert, ed., *Converting Colonialism: Visions and Realities in Mission History, 1706–1940* (Grand Rapids, MI: Eerdmans, 2008).

3. Gayatri Chakravorty Spivak, "Can the Subaltern Speak?," in *Marxism and the Interpretation of Culture*, ed. Cary Nelson and Lawrence Grossberg (Urbana: University of Illinois Press, 1988), 271–315.

4. Andrew F. Walls, *The Missionary Movement in Christian History: Studies in the Transmission of the Faith* (Maryknoll, NY: Orbis Books, 1996); and Lamin O. Sanneh, *Translating the Message: The Missionary Impact on Culture*, 2nd ed. (Maryknoll, NY: Orbis Books, 2009).

5. Tony Stewart, "In Search of Equivalence: Conceiving Muslim-Hindu Encounter through Translation Theory," *History of Religions* 40, no. 3 (February 2001): 278–86.

6. Ibid., 278–79.

7. Ibid., 279; italics added.

8. Ibid., 280.

9. Ibid., 282–83.

10. See Devaka Premawardhana, "Conversion and Convertibility in Northern Mozambique," in *What Is Existential Anthropology?*, ed. Michael Jackson and Albert Piette (New York: Berghahn, 2015), 30–57; Premawardhana, *Faith in Flux: Pentecostalism and Mobility in Rural Mozambique* (Philadelphia: University of Pennsylvania Press, 2018), esp. chap. 4; and Alexander Chow and Emma Wild-Wood, eds., "Christianity and Multiple Identities," special issue, *Studies in World Christianity* 25, no. 1 (April 2019).

11. I am deeply indebted to Clifton Crais's response to the nine presentations at the conference for raising interesting questions and suggestions about them.

Works Cited

Chow, Alexander, and Emma Wild-Wood, eds. "Christianity and Multiple Identities." Special issue, *Studies in World Christianity* 25, no. 1 (April 2019).

Porter, Andrew N. *Religion versus Empire? British Protestant Missionaries and Overseas Expansion, 1700–1914*. Manchester, UK: Manchester University Press, 2004.

Premawardhana, Devaka. "Conversion and Convertibility in Northern Mozambique." In *What Is Existential Anthropology?* edited by Michael Jackson and Albert Piette, 30–57. New York: Berghahn, 2015.

———. *Faith in Flux: Pentecostalism and Mobility in Rural Mozambique*. Philadelphia: University of Pennsylvania Press, 2018.

Robert, Dana L., ed. *Converting Colonialism: Visions and Realities in Mission History, 1706–1940*. Grand Rapids, MI: Eerdmans, 2008.

Sanneh, Lamin O. *Translating the Message: The Missionary Impact on Culture.* 2nd ed. Maryknoll, NY: Orbis Books, 2009.

Spivak, Gayatri Chakravorty. "Can the Subaltern Speak?" In *Marxism and the Interpretation of Culture*, edited by Cary Nelson and Lawrence Grossberg, 271–315. Urbana: University of Illinois Press, 1988.

Stewart, Tony. "In Search of Equivalence: Conceiving Muslim-Hindu Encounter through Translation Theory." *History of Religions* 40, no. 3 (February 2001): 260–87.

Walls, Andrew F. "Eusebius Tries Again: Reconceiving the Study of Christian History." *International Bulletin of Missionary Research* 24, no. 3 (July 2000): 105–11.

———. *The Missionary Movement in Christian History.* Maryknoll, NY: Orbis Books, 1996.

METHODOLOGICAL REFLECTIONS

Chapter 1

BEYOND TROUBLEMAKERS
AND COLLABORATORS

Historical Research into Newly Evangelized African Catholics

Paul Kollman

My historical work and accompanying archival research have explored Catholic evangelization in eastern Africa over the past century and a half. I began with the experiences of the earliest African Catholics in the region beginning in the nineteenth century,[1] most of whom were onetime slaves. My current research examines later evangelization, with slaves less a central part of the story. Throughout, emphasis has fallen not on missionaries per se but on believers and communities arising due to evangelization—that is, native Christians. This essay will explore historical practices and insights that advance understanding of their experiences.

Admittedly, the term "native Christians" carries lingering racist connotations in some uses,[2] and stereotypical depictions of newly evangelized African Christians are easy to find. Mindful of the way the term "native Christians" can recapitulate these stereotypes, discursively effacing the individuality of converts, I use it here rarely and tentatively—with apologies implied—as a shorthand for those who have undergone missionary evangelization, often in situations of incipient or full-blown colonial overrule, and who joined the faith of their evangelizers at least for a short time.

Yet the problematic connotations of the term "native Christians" represent only part of the historical challenge. Subjects like newly evangelized Christians in Africa, most of whom left little by way of recoverable self-representation, raise other thorny issues for historical practice—issues posed pointedly by Gayatri Spivak. As noted in the introduction, Spivak famously questioned the historical practice of the important movement of subaltern studies. In their efforts to represent the experiences of those overlooked in the past—"subalterns"—Spivak detected in subalternist historians' efforts paternalistically unhelpful projections from well-meaning but inextricably clouded, presentist vantages.

Spivak's challenge to apparently benevolent but misguided historical practice and instinct also applies to attempts to grasp the historical experiences of the newly evangelized, or native Christians. Like those subalterns whose attempted ventriloquism by sophisticated theorists Spivak questioned, native Christians, too, can be easily homogenized and thereby effaced by well-meaning scholars. In addition, new Christians have always acted as agents of their own history and continue to represent themselves without assistance, acting in complex and nuanced ways. Nonetheless, historical access to such Christians of the past and their own capacities for self-representation have both changed over time. Moreover, the challenge of historical understanding always exists, especially when sources are scant or multifaceted. Seeking to be wary in representing such people, but nonetheless trying to do so responsibly, I want to take Spivak's challenge seriously. Here I will suggest ways to approach archival materials in particular, as well as other historical sources, in order to respond with appropriately critical historical practice.

Mission history as a field occupies a rather dubious position these days, caught between an earlier hagiographical approach—mostly past, though one still sees traces of the hagiographical, especially in popular descriptions of missionaries—and occasional postcolonial dismissal that can find religion historically irrelevant and/or missionary-carried Christianity inimical to national or broader human flourishing.[3] In a 2012 podcast, historian Brian Stanley spoke about the need for so-called mission history to "interbreed" if it is to survive—that is, it needs to draw on many other disciplines since the actions of European missionaries themselves do little to interest professional historians.[4] Regardless of the appeal of mission history itself, however, serious historians of all sorts find missionary activity historically interesting in shaping the present, which makes the historical study of Christian missions important even if mission history in its traditional form remains untenable.[5] And certainly, any understanding of native Christians requires an appreciation of Christian mission, with a critical approach to mission archives a necessary precondition for serious research.

Two trends highlight the importance of a critical approach to such archives. First, increasingly sophisticated scholarship analyzes colonial archives—for example, in Ann Stoler's *Along the Archival Grain*, a study of the written descriptive habits of colonial governance in the nineteenth-century Dutch Indies, today Indonesia. Second, historians attend more and more to so-called memory work, trying to render more self-conscious and self-critical the social and individual processes by which the past becomes available to consciousness in the present.[6] With only a few exceptions,[7] the interpretation of missionary archives has not been subject to serious study like colonial archives, nor has it benefited from insights into critical memory studies.

This essay will first examine some of the stereotypes around native Christians. Then it will describe two dangers to be avoided when trying to overcome those stereotypes: first, to aspire to discern the "authentic" voice and, second, to draw on missionary archives mistakenly. To illustrate this second possibility, the essay will show the problematic nature of a frequently cited historical resource, a cautionary tale designed to urge the need for careful use of archival materials. This example will be followed by discussion of two historical practices that have personally helped me in my own archival research in seeking to understand new African Catholic converts. The most important strategy—and the one to be more extensively addressed here—lies in developing a critical and sophisticated understanding of the complex forces shaping various sorts of missionary discourse, since such forces also helped determine how those evangelized are portrayed. Such writings include original documents found in missionary archives, as well as reports produced with reference to such original documents, along with other materials produced to record the results of missionary activity. Second, great value comes from personal visits to the early missions themselves. This is so for two reasons. On the one hand, visits to the actual sites where missionary evangelization took place generate historical insights due to simple physical proximity. "Being there" matters. In addition, present-day Catholics who live near the early missions remain important sources of information about those who came before them. Many historical insights into native African Catholics can be gleaned only in conversation with those who remember them.

Depicting Native Christians

The most extensive and popularly disseminated depictions of native Christians appear in mission-sponsored magazines, begun in the early modern period and later read by millions of Catholics and Protestants in Europe and the United States as such journals expanded in number and scope beginning in the nineteenth century. Popular portrayals draw on narrative conventions developed over time, conventions often shaped by racist and other stereotypes. Articles and drawings in such periodicals usually arose through the efforts of editors who combed missionary reports and letters, selecting material to appeal to their readership, from whom they sought financial and perhaps other sorts of support. At times, too, editors and mission-agency writers drew on other sources, including their own imaginations. These descriptions resemble other missionary discourse, but they have also undergone extensive editing; they are, as Anna Johnston puts it, "the end result of a well-oiled and efficient production machine run by missionary societies and their supportive evangelical publishers."[8]

This popular discourse in describing African Christian converts has often utilized categories traceable at least to the so-called *Jesuit Relations* of the seventeenth and eighteenth centuries, mostly originally French-language accounts of Jesuit missionary exploits in North America and elsewhere.[9] Typical stereotypes among First Nations Amerindian converts—and, two centuries afterward, African converts—include the category of "loyal co-workers" or "collaborators" who work closely with missionaries as personal assistants, for example, or as catechists, teachers, and translators. There are also "troublemakers" who, despite their alleged Christian loyalty, in fact stand in the way of evangelization or manipulate missionaries for their own ends. These were often local healers, or other political or religious authorities. Finally, when narratives of a mission's history develop, there appear "backsliders," who raise and then frustrate missionary hopes by falling away from onetime loyalty. In addition, of course, there appear those who belong but are indifferent, those actively and openly hostile, and usually some hopeful converts who simply belong without being deeply involved like the loyal co-workers. The vivid characters, however, often fall into defined categories.

Historical practitioners have long recognized such problematic stereotypes, and scholars have sought to discern the biases that shape these and similar depictions. At times, such efforts have pursued the putative "authentic" voice of native Christians and other overlooked past historical agents, imagining the recovery of such a voice—an occluded self-revelation reflecting deeper desires and connections to a future imagined nation-state or an oppressed class or ethnic identity. Spivak's criticism finds such efforts inevitably to be extensions of the scholar's own predilections, and she emphasizes the elusive nature of something like *the* "authentic" voice of oft-silenced historical agents such as "native Christians." All, she believes, have been subject to what certain philosophical perspectives would deem "historical interpellation"—the fact that ideological shaping occurs prior to consciousness and indeed constitutes it—and her criticism suggests wariness in pursuing "the authentic."

Of course, reluctance to pursue an authentic voice or identity does not mean giving up on efforts to appreciate the subjective experiences of those in the past. In the effort to understand such experiences, scholars delve deeply into recoverable traces to glean whatever they can. In so doing, however, they need to equip themselves with the best critical-historical skills available. Allowing indigenous Christians to speak means, then, avoiding both an unrealistic self-imposed expectation of there being a "true African Catholic" voice, a voice always desirable in historical pursuit even if never quite graspable, as well as an uncritical reliance on missionary records—since, as the example to follow shows, missionaries had their own reasons for describing African believers.

The Origins of the Stirring Narrative of a Slave Girl Who Became a Catholic Nun

In 1983, an article by Edward Alpers, distinguished historian of eastern Africa and the Indian Ocean at UCLA, appeared in the edited volume *Women and Slavery in Africa*. Alpers's piece, titled "The Story of Swema: Female Vulnerability in Nineteenth-Century East Africa," concerns a mission-produced narrative about a slave girl, Suema (or Suéma, in some spellings), that had first been published in French in 1870 by Catholic missionaries in Zanzibar.[10] For the past three decades, Alpers's article about this tale of a slave girl who becomes free and joins the church has been a common resource in courses in African history and the history of slavery.[11] And understandably so, for it is an interesting article about a compelling tale.

Alpers begins his article by explaining why he trusts the genuineness of this mission-preserved story, which he learned about from a Catholic archivist in France, and which was penned by a missionary whose other accounts have great historical value. The story's reliability defended, Alpers then proceeds to describe the light *Suéma* sheds both on contemporaneous slave practices and gender relations among the ethnic/linguistic group into which the girl was born. The 1983 Alpers piece concludes with the original French text of the story.

Suéma itself touches a reader's emotions. The young girl from what is today southern Tanzania or northern Mozambique falls into slavery with her mother when taken by slave raiders, who force them and others on a harrowing trek to the coast. The expedition's leader murders Suema's mother when, exhausted by the journey, she cannot continue. A ship takes Suema to the island of Zanzibar, where eastern Africa's largest slave market existed until 1873. Instead of being sold, however, Suema is thrown into a garbage heap by a slave trader disgusted by her ill health. There a man from the Catholic mission rescues her. She enters the care of the nuns and gets well.

Despite their preparation for her to become Catholic through catechesis, the mission delays Suema's baptism because she cannot—to quote the Our Father prayer—"forgive those who trespassed against her," namely the Arab slave-caravan leader who murdered her mother. One day, as Suema volunteers in the sisters' hospital, that leader arrives after having been mortally wounded by the British. Recognizing him, Suema recoils. Prodded by the sisters, however, she finally cares for his wounds. He dies, and later in prayer Suema feels herself bathed in life-giving water as she pardons her mother's murderer. Baptized, she becomes Madeleine and later enters the sisters' congregation as a postulant herself.

Alpers's article has become widely recognized for its value in revealing nineteenth-century slave experiences in eastern Africa, especially those of women.[12] Suema's internal feelings and emotions feature prominently, suggesting she dictated it to a transcriber. And at face value, there are no reasons to doubt its veracity, for the tale represents something described elsewhere by Catholic missionaries and other eyewitnesses, in both eastern Africa and other locales.

The Zanzibar mission began in 1860 under the direction of diocesan priests from nearby Réunion, and three years later it passed into the hands of the Congregation of the Holy Ghost, or Spiritans, a Catholic religious order that served as colonial clergy for the French. The missionary writer in this case, Father Antoine Horner, CSSp, was the first Spiritan superior at Zanzibar's Catholic mission. I agree with Alpers that Horner usually is a reliable witness, and his accounts of Zanzibar itself and journeys to the continent of eastern Africa retain significant historical importance.

Yet the archives also contain evidence that cast significant doubt on the story's historicity. Letters show that Horner self-consciously prepared *Suéma* as part of a planned volume of thirty stories designed for fundraising and edifying European youth. In correspondence regarding the volume's preparation, he never mentioned that it was a true story. More damning still to his later claims of veracity are comments by two of his confreres after *Suéma* appeared. One attributed what he called *le roman* (the novel) *Suéma* to a French consular official at Zanzibar, then mentioned his repugnance at Horner's farce and charlatanism, regarding such behavior as undignified for the head of a mission—presumably, to claim a fictional tale as true. Another fellow Spiritan also found Horner's assertions about the story's veracity ludicrous. He wrote to a friend that Suema's mother—who, according to the story, had been killed by the ruthless caravan master whom Suema eventually forgave, and whose body Suema allegedly saw picked at by crows—lived at the sisters' house at the mission. "What a sham!" Horner's colleague and confrere wrote.[13]

Missionaries' rivalries can color their epistolary depictions of one another, yet it seems clear that Horner began the story of Suema as a work of fiction for didactic and/or fundraising purposes, then affixed a real person to it. That a certain Suema, later named Madeleine, existed is beyond doubt, for she wrote several letters in the 1870s and appears in other missionary records. *Suéma*, as an account in her name, however, represents more a creation of Horner (or others) than a firsthand account.[14]

My point here is not to dismiss the story itself—which I find interesting regardless of its veracity. Like many contemporary African historians, Alpers appropriately appreciated a story with something important to reveal, in this case insights into African gender relations, the slave trade, and nineteenth-century slave-caravan practices in particular, and he published it following sound historical practice. Nor is there any reason to suspect that the Spiritan archivist who pointed the story out to him knew the circumstances under which it was produced. Relevant Spiritan missionary correspondence in the period amounts to thousands of cramped and handwritten pages, many in a poor state of repair. Even if Alpers's assumption about the story's historicity were misplaced, this does not undermine its value as a window on slaves' and women's experiences in eastern Africa. Still, it might say more about what the missionaries like Horner wanted their native Christians to be like than what they actually were.

Engaging Missionary Archives and Interpreting Missionary Discourse

This account of the story of Suema and its reception in Africanist and slave-studies historical circles raises a number of issues surrounding research into African Catholic converts. In particular, Alpers's understandable misconception about the story's veracity invites a consideration of the challenges implicit in engaging missionary archives and in analyzing the nature of missionary discourse itself as a way to understand native Christians.

All historical sources require critical analysis, and the historical evidence for understanding early African converts, which consists of many forms, is no exception. Missionary discourse represents an invaluable resource and itself comprises a variety of media; missionaries produced not only a variety of texts but also photos, drawings, charts, maps, and other forms of representation like medals and statues. Archives, when interpreted with care, disclose a variety of different ways of responding to the missionary message, shaped by particular historical circumstances. And such responses create important windows on the experiences of "native Christians." I have come to believe that close attention to archival materials reveals much about the evangelized that missionaries themselves might not have wanted self-consciously to disclose.

My early research on onetime slaves who were evangelized has yielded few written traces by such converts. Consequently, missionary records were always the best and usually almost the only historical sources. Even now, with the compass broadened to include later developments when slaves moved away from the center of missionary strategy, discerning the voices of the earliest African Catholics has only rarely meant discovering their own writings, which remain comparatively few. Even after the strategy of slave evangelization eased, missionaries wrote by far the most about those who joined the church. Thus, even if the focus remains on African individuals and collectivities arising due to evangelization—that is, in native Christians—missionary writings remain unavoidable historical sources.

Missionary biases certainly exist, so missionary writings are inevitably a "tainted" source. That said, such bias can be discerned, easing historical interpretation of their writings, as important research on historical and anthropological topics linked to African Christianity has shown.[15] The skills required, however, can elude many historians: "Reading mission archives and publications requires skills that differ from those used in the examination, translation and deconstruction of the official discourse of colonial power," as David Arnold and Robert Bickers put it.[16] Ann Stoler writes that instead of seeing colonial archival records simply as "skewed and biased sources," she prefers to see them as "condensed sites of epistemological and political anxiety" in need of well-informed interpretive care.[17] Missionary records contain similar complexities, since missionaries, too, faced confusing circumstances and their own idealism as they described their settings and their work. Moreover, their anxieties can be most revealing, and they can be discerned in their language.[18]

Of course, ordinary historical skills also help in interpreting missionary records, such as attempts at corroboration with other sources. And, fortunately, missionary-produced writings on their work can often be checked for accuracy with others' accounts. In the case of my research, it helps that eastern Africa grew in European awareness at the time of its modern-era evangelization beginning in the nineteenth century, capturing the European imagination as a remaining site of the slave trade, as a place of physical remoteness and beauty, and eventually as a setting in which European countries could compete with one another for colonial territory as their empires expanded overseas. The current researcher wanting to interrogate the history of Christianity in the region, therefore, must consult missionary archives but also can draw on other sources to balance the missionary perspective—explorer accounts and colonial records, for example.

One of the boons of studying early Catholic missionary activity in eastern Africa is the large amount of written material. Missionaries themselves produced most of it, and they followed clear instructions in their writing, for most Catholic missionary orders by the mid-nineteenth century had stipulated guidelines for reporting. Expectations mandated careful observation, regular writing of reports, and scheduled sending of written accounts to Europe, and these were reinforced by reference to the vow of obedience. Many such missionaries also knew they were starting the church in a new place and thus had a strong sense of the historical importance of their efforts.

The nineteenth-century groups who founded the Catholic Church in eastern Africa followed Catholic precedents in their literary production. The Jesuits had pioneered the standardization of missionary writing shortly after their founding, and later groups followed their lead. Beginning in the mid-sixteenth century, accounts from the Jesuit missions, their founder Ignatius of Loyola urged, ought to pursue "the service and glory of God, [and] the common good and assistance to the Company [the Society of Jesus]." Besides the spiritualizing of the writing process, two of their principles became standard among later groups. First, Ignatius specified that the writing should cover four points—"the king and the nobles, the common people, the Company and yourself"[19]—generating ethnographic descriptions and dramatic portrayals, as well as self-reflection. Nineteenth-century reports followed a similar set of expectations. Second, Ignatius also specified that such writings ought to begin with text prepared with the broader public in mind and then also contain, in a later section, private reflections meant only for internal Jesuit consumption, and sometimes only for Jesuit leadership. Missionary reports from nineteenth-century eastern Africa also often follow this structure.

One important difference, however, between the first Jesuit writings and those of the later period consists in the growing diversity of audiences for which missionaries wrote in the nineteenth century. The Jesuits in the early modern missionary field wrote mainly for their superiors, who took it on themselves to share what was deemed suitable to the broader public or the Vatican. Over the next few centuries, however, three other audiences arose for missionary writings, with missionaries themselves self-consciously producing discourses for each.

First, starting in the seventeenth century, the Vatican sought to centralize missionary activity in the office of Propaganda Fide, which began to request reports for itself in fulfillment of its role in organizing missionary activity. Second, the nineteenth century saw the appearance of lay-led mission support organizations that gathered funds to support missionary activity and, on the Protestant side, even recruited missionaries. Consequently, missionary publications began to reach a wider reading public in Europe and North America—sometimes linked to particular missionary societies, sometimes to lay mission-support organizations, occasionally to the Vatican itself. Third, as European nations began to encroach on places like Africa, which eventuated in colonial overrule in eastern Africa as in so many other places, colonial authorities showed considerable interest in missionary activity, which sometimes was seen to advance national interests, at other times to undermine them. Colonizers also requested reports. Besides internal documents for their own religious congregations, therefore, modern Catholic missionaries had to prepare reports for the Vatican, lay-led agencies, and colonial offices. In addition to these institutionalized audiences, many missionaries also wrote to numerous personal correspondents among friends, family, and benefactors, using postal services nonexistent several centuries earlier.

This set of audiences naturally meant that the writings of missionaries took different genres in response to expectations embedded in the process of preparation. Four genres constitute the bulk of pertinent missionary writings in my research into early eastern African Catholics.[20] First, each mission kept a journal on-site to recount the day-to-day events, and missionaries were required by the vows of obedience to keep these faithfully. In fact, however, they often were a burden easily overlooked, and even if not ignored for long stretches, the responsibility to maintain the journal often fell to the most recently arrived religious, whose writings often lack context that could fill in historical understanding. Second, each mission also produced sacramental records, keeping track of baptisms and other sacraments like marriage, as well as deaths. Third, missionaries wrote reports for a number of different audiences, which varied depending on whether they were prepared for their own mission society, a mission-support agency, the Vatican, or some other designee like a colonial office. Finally, there were the aforementioned letters to various people. These, too, took different forms depending on whether they were addressed to family members, fellow missionaries, benefactors, religious superiors, or Vatican or colonial officials.

A great deal of the historical work describing the Catholic Church in eastern Africa—as elsewhere—depends on published reports. Often historians have had nothing else to rely on, since archives can be inaccessible. Yet, writings that appeared in public had inevitably passed through complex, sometimes hard-to-decipher editorial processes before their publication. The story of Suema, for instance, raised money for the Spiritan mission in the 1870s. Three editions were published in French, the last one illustrated, and one in English. A play based on the story was prepared and performed by a woman in Grenoble. And the uses for the story have not ceased. Since 2000 it has become a stage play performed in Kiswahili in Tanzania, which also became the basis for a video. Given the history and current state of relations between Muslims and Christians in contemporary Tanzania—generally peaceful, with moments of tension in the recent past—Suema's story has new audiences, and new potential effects. In addition, the work's appeal continues to be seen for the global church, since a conservative Catholic publisher in 2012 reissued the English translation, originally published in Dublin in 1871.[21]

Given these diverse genres and audiences, as well as the complex processes of their production, those seeking to do research in missionary archives need to work with tools not dissimilar to those employed by scholars of scripture. In the variety of historical-critical methods commonly used to study the Bible, several seem especially important. For instance, *form criticism* examines the literary form of a given piece of writing, and the four different genres just identified as constituting most missionary discourse from eastern Africa create different challenges for discerning how to interpret them. What scripture scholars call *text criticism* seeks to identify the earliest version of a given piece of discourse when several different editions exist of similar writing with slight variations among versions.

Missionary accounts often were rewritten and edited, so determining the original version of a particular story or episode means comparing dates, writing, and other factors like handwriting and mailing practices. *Source criticism* seeks to understand the prior materials from which a given piece of writing might have been drawn. Reports appearing in public especially drew on numerous sources, often from several different missionaries. Finally, *redaction criticism* stresses the editorial processes that texts undergo before they appear as finished products, something that happened both in the mission field and, even more extensively, back in Europe in the preparation of formal reports.

Another important facet of the historical-critical methods applicable to missionary texts examined to discern the voices and experiences of native Christians concerns grasping larger historical contexts in which missionaries acted. In general, historians have been better at situating missionary writings in relation to the large-scale social traumas—colonial and civil wars, uprisings among colonized peoples, and the world wars of the twentieth century—that overlapped with the foundations of Christianity in eastern Africa as in much of the colonized world.

More elusive for historians have been internal debates about missionary practice itself that were ongoing in Europe especially. Quite often missionaries discuss their strategies mindful of the Christians they seek to produce through evangelization, and they do so with reference to contemporary debates in their homes that have relevance for their missionary work. For instance, the French Catholic missionaries I have studied considered the best processes for forming Catholics in eastern Africa by arguing about nineteenth-century French educational and penitential theories, for they thought of the onetime slaves they evangelized like children—and especially the juvenile delinquents—with whom they had worked at home.[22] German Catholic missionaries, who came later to eastern Africa, argued about their missionary methods in relationship to contemporaneous controversies over Catholic catechetical technologies in post-Kulturkampf Germany.[23]

Presence and Absence in Missionary Archives

Missionary writings that were published nearly always draw on original texts found in archival collections of various sorts. Most of the larger, male Catholic missionary societies and religious orders have well-organized and well-staffed archives of their own. These are usually open to qualified researchers, with help given generously by local archival assistants.[24] Archival records that lie outside a given missionary group's official archives are often in a more perilous state. Those in dioceses or parishes in Africa itself, for example, are often disregarded, bundled haphazardly, or stacked helter-skelter in closets. In some places they go years without being consulted, years during which worms and dust mites and humidity, dry rot and silverfish and mice, can do profound damage. Not all local bishops and pastors show care to preserve such records. I have heard doleful older missionaries tell of how the records preserving the fruit of years of their labor were undone by the one who followed them into the role. As a scholar, too, I wince, though with less poignant sadness.

Despite the care with which many groups tend their archives, missionary archives are never "complete." Some of the frustrating absences are explicable. Already in the early twentieth century, for example, there was a complaint about a missing journal volume from the first major Catholic mission station in eastern Africa, at Bagamoyo on Tanzania's coast, founded by the Holy Ghost missionaries from France in 1868. It was to Bagamoyo in 1873 where David Livingstone's desiccated body was brought after being carried thousands of miles by his African assistants, and it was from Bagamoyo that it began its journey to London and Westminster Abbey, where it lies with other British luminaries. Apparently, the journal with the date describing the body's arrival was lost as Livingstone's story became well known and his heroic status was forged.

Mysterious disappearances of descriptions of famous events are only one problem. Another missionary society active in eastern Africa had as one of their early superiors general a man wary of how posterity might view him. He thus burned a great many of his private papers, not a few of which dealt with nineteenth-century missionary work in what are today Uganda and Kenya. I have cursed him many times and likely will continue to do so.

In addition, different kinds of Christian missionaries depict native Christians differently, depending on their particular Christian orientation. Speaking broadly, for example, Protestant and Catholic missionaries differ in how they describe native Christians. Such differences reflect varying theological assumptions that shaped their missionary practices and discourses, for over the past few centuries Catholics and Protestants tended to prioritize different virtues and values in those they evangelized. For example, while there are exceptions, Catholics tended to pay less attention to the subjective experiences of native Christians than do Protestants. One reason might be because Catholic missionaries usually did not approach belonging to the church through the metaphor of conversion, at least in the voluntaristic, individualized, and subjective approach to conversion that is foregrounded in much Protestant theological anthropology visible in missionary writings. For Catholics, belonging was considered differently, more in a sacramental way, with certain practices—liturgical as well as moral-social—marking how one became and remained Catholic.[25]

Given these differences, it is not surprising that the most impressive discussions of native Christians in Africa have tended to be about Protestants rather than African Catholics. Examples include John Peel's remarkable work on Yoruba converts evangelized by the Church Missionary Society, Terence Ranger's explorations of Zimbabwean Christians, and Stephen Volz's more recent discussion of Tswana catechists.[26]

Comparable studies of Catholic native Christians in Africa are not so easy to find. The most thorough study of the development of a formidable Catholic presence in eastern Africa remains a 1976 history dissertation by the late Ugandan priest John Waliggo.[27] Waliggo's work, a publication only available at a few archives in the United Kingdom until its publication in book form in 2010, tells the story of the church's growth in Buddu county, Uganda, today the diocese of Masaka. There Catholics were constricted by the colonial regime, but their church grew considerably in the forty-six years covered by the dissertation—between 1879 and 1925. Every serious student of Uganda's late nineteenth- and early twentieth-century history with an interest in the religious aspects of that history—which were central—has drawn on Waliggo's superb scholarship.

The dissertation closes its introductory chapter with a short section on "the sources" (which is not unusual for the field). There, Waliggo identifies four categories of written archival sources—in Europe and Africa—that he drew on in his work. He then names four categories of "oral sources," comprising different kinds of older people whom he interviewed.[28] Thirty-six years after the appearance of Waliggo's masterful dissertation, what is striking is the absence of any discussion about *how* he interpreted those sources, which must have created an immense amount of potential historical material. He does not describe how he compared them with one another, or which he relied on when there were contradictions, or other factors that shaped his interpretations. Nor does he mention the state of the various written archives in which he worked. Waliggo offers his most self-conscious comment in relation to his oral interviews, writing, "Having several times tried to interview groups of old men or husbands and wives together, I found group interviews stimulated quarrels while producing less information, and I abandoned them."²⁹ Those of us who have done oral interviews likely know this experience! Yet Waliggo's lack of any discussion of his interpretive methods—his hermeneutics—suggest that he found unproblematic the sifting, comparing, and cross-referencing of the different sorts of evidence he amassed. In practice, however, my guess is that he found it very difficult.

Early Mission Stations and Their Current Residents

Besides using the best historical-critical tools for texts (not to mention photos, videos, and other materials) found in missionary archives, another lesson I have learned about how to understand "native Christians" concerns visits made to the sites where such people were first evangelized—early mission stations. Certain details at such sites, despite the passage of time, invigorate the historical imagination.

For example, the relative proximity of some of the earliest mission sites to present-day roads speaks to missionary struggles to find suitable locations for their mission stations in a precolonial situation. In Tanzania, for instance, some of the earliest Catholic missions—at the time of their nineteenth-century establishment representing huge investments—still lie in remote settings, evidence of the uncertainty about the land that would become German East Africa, then Tanganyika, now Tanzania. In Uganda, by contrast, the earliest Catholic foundations, like their Anglican counterparts, established missions in a region with a well-established centralized political order—the Kingdom of Buganda—which, though soon ruling indirectly under the thumb of British colonial overrule, nonetheless had an established road system. Their missions, therefore, are strategically located in ways the earliest Tanzania missions are not. That said, one recognizes in even the currently somewhat isolated locations reasons they were attractive to the missionaries: proximity to water, dense population, arable land.

Mission stations also usually continue to house records of important historical interest. Cemeteries, for example, if well maintained, sometimes are the only ways to determine when native Christians died. Missions also have documents available nowhere else. Certainly many Catholic religious orders have sought to preserve the missions' journals by transferring them to formal archives prepared for historical preservation, usually in Europe. Missionary correspondence also has often been removed. Yet copies often remain of the journals on-site. In addition, there are sacramental records that, in line with the expectations of Catholic canonical law, have to remain at the site of the parish itself.

As mentioned above, sacramental records keep track of the reception of sacraments by converts and parishioners. When well kept, they allow one to see the progression of individual Christians from birth to baptism, through marriage to death. Such books are themselves not always clear—they have their own arcane language, sometimes Latin, and often are coded for insiders' consumption only. (As an example, the notation *Hannibal ad portas* [Hannibal at the gates] on a marriage notation meant that the bride was pregnant at the time of the wedding. This was placed there to expedite an annulment later should that be requested.)

Finally, visiting old missions themselves often means meeting people who knew someone who knew someone whose story you are interested in. I vividly recall asking two older women in Tanzania about their memories of their childhoods as students in an early mission school. They drew on an unusual Swahili word for "enclosure" to describe their education—and it made me think about other ways that the early missionaries fretted about protecting their charges from contagion from outside. Zeal for such protection motivated their missionary strategy, captured in the French word *clôture*. That kind of language also featured in the discourse in French educational and penitential discussions of the nineteenth century. The fact that local Christians knew other French words—*les dortoirs* for the students' dormitories, and *les mariés* for the once-enslaved married couples who founded the missions—testified to their memories of their Catholic forebears.[30]

Conclusion

In a telling admission, Keith Thomas, the distinguished historian of early modern Europe, a few years ago made this comment about methodology in the discipline of history:

> It never helps historians to say too much about their working methods. For just as the conjuror's magic disappears if the audience knows how the trick is done, so the credibility of scholars can be sharply diminished if readers learn everything about how exactly their books came to be written. Only too often, such revelations dispel the

impression of fluent, confident omniscience; instead, they suggest that histories are concocted by error-prone human beings who patch together the results of incomplete research in order to construct an account whose rhetorical power will, they hope, compensate for gaps in the argument and deficiencies in the evidence.[31]

Thomas's candor about the nonsystematic way that most historical research and writing proceeds was, to me at least, quite refreshing. As someone who has spent much of the last three decades striving to understand the history of Christian communities in eastern Africa, I appreciate the subjective embarrassment Thomas acknowledges as he admits the "gaps in the argument and deficiencies in the evidence" of his work. In his frankness one detects almost a methodological shrug: What, after all, are we to do? Historical understanding somehow happens *despite* such felt inadequacy—at least so we hope.

New historical understanding comes in different ways. Sometimes one finds more or less unknown historical material and analyzes it for the first time. One example of such a "new discovery" inspired Carlo Ginzburg's 1976 masterpiece *The Cheese and the Worms*, which reads a heretic's trial record to reconsider assumptions about the worldviews of early modern Europeans. At other times, historical insights come from bringing new interpretive frameworks and comparative perspectives to existing and already well-known records—what might be called "new historical relationship." Ira Berlin's celebrated, generation-based studies of Africans brought to North America over several centuries, for example, not only unearthed new data but more importantly put known facts about the lives of African Americans over several centuries into new patterns, thereby enriching our understanding of the vastness and diversity of the African American historical experience.

Missionary archives can sometimes generate previously unknown writings, such as the letters casting doubt on the veracity of Suema's tale, discussed above. Other letters I discovered were penned by nineteenth-century African seminarians complaining about their treatment by European missionaries. Placing previously known but not consciously connected historical materials in a single historical frame has also helped me gain new insights. Comparing missionary writings, colonial archives, explorers' accounts, baptismal and other records found in church rectories, and the fading etchings on cemetery tombstones has allowed me to chart anew an African Christian family's historical transformations.

Today there are a number of efforts underway to preserve the history of "native Christians," in Africa and elsewhere. The most important rely on what might be called crowdsourcing. Data collection efforts like the *Dictionary of African Christian Biography* (or *DACB*) welcome those who want to tell the story of an African Christian to preserve it for posterity. These accounts are then saved in an accessible format at a website anyone can visit.[32] In addition, there is an organized effort sponsored by the International Association of Mission Studies called the Documentation, Archives, Bibliography, and Oral History Group (or DABOH), which seeks to work together to catalog and preserve records of Christians around the world. Over time, one hopes that institutional arrangements like the *DACB* and DABOH will accumulate new historical insights, helping us hear native Christians even more clearly.

Notes

I thank organizer Arun Jones for the invitation to present previous versions of this paper at the 2012 meeting of the American Academy of Religion and at the conference "Can the Native Christian Speak? Discerning the Voices of Indigenous Christians in Missionary and Colonial Archives" held at Emory University in Atlanta on May 28, 2014. Both he and other colleagues present improved this essay by their kind remarks on those occasions and afterward. Part of this chapter condenses material found in my book *The Evangelization of Slaves and Catholic Origins in Eastern Africa* (Maryknoll, NY: Orbis Books, 2005), 128–32.

1. Paul V. Kollman, *Evangelization of Slaves and Catholic Origins* (Maryknoll, NY: Orbis Books, 2005). There had been an earlier time of Portuguese occupation and limited missionary work in eastern Africa from the sixteenth to eighteenth centuries, but nineteenth-century missionaries found no African Christian communities when Christianity returned to the region.

2. Judging from the unapologetic deployment of the term in some references to Amerindian Christians—for example, in the excellent collection of essays in Aparecida Vilaça and Robin M. Wright, eds. *Native Christians: Modes and Effects of Christianity among Indigenous Peoples of the Americas* (Burlington, VT: Ashgate, 2009)—not all uses raise such qualms.

3. Jeffrey Cox sees these two options and elaborates what he calls the "Saidian master narrative" (after Edward Said) and the "providentialist master narrative." See Jeffrey Cox, *Imperial Fault Lines: Christianity and Colonial Power in India, 1818–1940* (Stanford, CA: Stanford University Press, 2002), 9–13.

4. See Stanley's reflections in "Mission Studies and Historical Research: Past Trends and Future Trajectories," History Spot (blog), November 1, 2012, https://ihrprojects.word press.com/2012/11/01/mission-studies-and -historical-research-past-trends-and-future -trajectories.

5. This is especially true of the study of Christianity itself since, as two scholars of Amerindian native Christians put it in their introduction to their edited volume, "given its missionary and inclusive nature, Christianity has always been refined by the social groups in contact with it. Cultural openness is an indissociable part of any missionary religion" (Vilaça and Wright, *Native Christians*, 3). For an earlier groundbreaking set of essays in this area, see Steven Kaplan, ed., *Indigenous*

Responses to Western Christianity (New York: New York University Press, 1995).

6. Ann Laura Stoler, *Along the Archival Grain: Epistemic Anxieties and Colonial Common Sense* (Princeton, NJ: Princeton University Press, 2009). For an important collection on memory with regard to European history, see Karin Tilmans, Frank van Vree, and Jay Winter, eds. *Performing the Past: Memory, History, and Identity in Modern Europe* (Amsterdam: Amsterdam University Press, 2010). A helpful overview of this field can be found at the Leiden University Institute for History website, accessed May 4, 2020, http://www.hum.leiden.edu/history/talesoftherevolt/approach/approach-1.html.

7. For example, see J. D. Y. Peel, *Religious Encounter and the Making of the Yoruba* (Bloomington: Indiana University Press, 2000), 9–22, which builds on J. D. Y. Peel, "Problems and Opportunities in an Anthropologist's Use of a Missionary Archive," in *Missionary Encounters: Sources and Issues*, ed. Robert A. Bickers and Rosemary Seton (Surrey, UK: Curzon Press, 1996), 70–94. See also Kollman, *Evangelization of Slaves and Catholic Origins*, 22–32.

8. Anna Johnston, *Missionary Writing and Empire, 1800–1860* (Cambridge, UK: Cambridge University Press, 2003), 6. For another discussion of such production among British Protestant missionary societies, drawing on Johnston's work and others, see Jeffrey Cox, *The British Missionary Enterprise since 1700* (New York: Routledge, 2009), 114–42.

9. *The Jesuit Relations and Allied Documents* (Cleveland: Burrows Brothers, 1896–1901) appeared in seventy-three volumes in the English translation organized by Reuben G. Thwaites. For a summary of the *Relations* and the strengths and weaknesses of the Thwaite edition, see Allan Greer, ed., *The Jesuit Relations: Natives and Missionaries in Seventeenth-Century North America* (Boston: Bedford / St. Martin's, 2000), v–vi. Greer's edited collection also presents a larger discussion of the Jesuit missionary efforts and consists mostly of a representative set of texts organized thematically. The English version is based on the prior *Lettres édifiantes et curieuses*, a popular compilation of edited letters on Jesuit missionary activity in New France (Canada) that was published in thirty-four volumes between 1703 and 1776.

10. Edward Alpers, "The Story of Swema: Female Vulnerability in Nineteenth-Century East Africa," in *Women and Slavery in Africa*, ed. Claire Robertson and Martin Klein (Madison: University of Wisconsin Press, 1983), 185–219. Regarding the 1870 French version, Alpers cites it in his article as follows: Mgr. Gaume, *Suéma, ou La Petite Esclave Africaine enterée vivante: Histoire contemporaine dediée aux jeunes chrétiennes de l'ancien et du nouveau monde* (Paris, 1870).

11. A number of Africanist and other colleagues have told me they have used it in their courses. Also, it is listed in the online "Slavery Reading List," Department of History, University of Wisconsin-Madison, updated May 2017, https://history.wisc.edu/wp-content/uploads/sites/202/2017/05/prelim_slavery_pierce.pdf.

12. All references to Suema I uncovered have treated it as a true story. The narrative was regarded as nonfictional in an article about the original publisher of the piece, Bishop Gaume, and in a late 1990s radio broadcast of the story in Tanzania prepared by the Holy Ghost priests at Bagamoyo. See Daniel Moulinet, "Mgr. Gaume, l'oeuvre apostolique et le rachat des esclaves," *Mémoire Spiritain* 7 (1998): 108–26; and personal communication from Joseph Healey, MM, and Daniel Bouju, CSSp. A video has also been produced from a stage play based on Suema performed at Bagamoyo. Others who aver to Alpers's article assuming its veracity include Kirk Hoppe, "Whose Life Is It, Anyway? Issues of Representation in Life Narrative Texts of African Women," *International Journal of African Historical Studies* 26, no. 3 (1993): 623–36; and Pier Larson, *History and Memory in the Age of Enslavement: Becoming Merina in Highland Madagascar, 1770–1822* (Oxford, UK: James Currey, 2000), 19–20. Alpers himself refers to his piece again in a later publication, "The Other Middle Passage: The African Slave Trade in the Indian Ocean," in *Many Middle Passages: Forced Migration and the Making of the Modern World*, ed. Emma Christopher,

Cassandra Pybus, and Marcus Rediker (Berkeley: University of California Press, 2007), 20–22, describing it as "the earliest . . . freed-slave narrative" from the Indian Ocean slave trade.

13. As I have written elsewhere, in Kollman, *Evangelization of Slaves and Catholic Origins*, 132:

> Suéma was one of several stories the Spiritans produced for popular consumption in the mission support journals in France in the nineteenth century. Such stories revealed how the missionaries wanted their ideals to be embodied in the freed slaves they sought to evangelize. Suéma in this story represents the ideal missionary product, the former slave who becomes a committed Christian, the proper outcome of the missionary evangelization carried out in Zanzibar. Suéma, baptized Madeleine . . . showed herself a hard-working and pious girl, desiring to become a nun in order to evangelize her brothers and sisters who remained in darkness. Her gratitude to the mission and her dependence upon it were obvious. She prayed often in the story and forgave the one who had harmed her. These actions proved that she had been effectively evangelized, justifying the missionary enterprise. No wonder Horner was so keen to claim her story as real.

14. As recounted in Moulinet, "Mgr. Gaume, l'oeuvre apostolique et le rachat des esclaves," 117–19. Other writings about the Spiritan mission at Zanzibar also wrote about Suema/Madeleine.

15. See Peel, "Problems and Opportunities."

16. David Arnold and Robert A. Bickers, "Introduction," in *Missionary Encounters*, ed. Bickers and Seton, 3.

17. Stoler, *Along the Archival Grain*, 20.

18. See Kollman, *Evangelization of Slaves and Catholic Origins*, 1–9.

19. Ines G. Županov, *Disputed Mission: Jesuit Experiments and Brahmanical Knowledge in Seventeenth-Century India* (New Delhi: Oxford University Press, 1999), 7. For her fuller discussion of Jesuit epistolary practices, see 6–16.

20. Kollman, *Evangelization of Slaves and Catholic Origins*, 24–28.

21. Mgr. Gaume, *Suema: A Little African Slave, a Tale for Our Times* (Dublin, 1871).

22. See Kollman, *Evangelization of Slaves and Catholic Origins*, 65–67, 112–14, 157–66, and 276–78.

23. Paul V. Kollman, "Generations of Catholics in Eastern Africa: A Practice-Centered Analysis of Religious Change," *Journal for the Scientific Study of Religion* 51, no. 3 (2012): 418.

24. I have never faced insurmountable challenges in consulting them—at least those of the six major male missionary groups that more or less founded the Catholic Church in eastern Africa. That said, such collections are not always unrestrictedly open to researchers, something overcome in my case usually because I am a Catholic priest. Occasionally, however, I have been cautioned when I was perceived to be photocopying "too much," though I never understood where such a limit could be identified. In addition, some materials are held in remote locations away from the major archival center, which is usually in Europe, and this can make research expensive and time-consuming.

25. For a fuller discussion, see Kollman, *Evangelization of Slaves and Catholic Origins*, 58–67 and 274–79.

26. Peel, *Religious Encounter*; Terence Ranger, *Are We Not Also Men? The Samkange Family and African Politics in Zimbabwe, 1920–64* (London: James Currey, 1995); Terence Ranger, *Voices from the Rocks: Nature, Culture and History in the Matopos Hills of Zimbabwe* (Oxford, UK: James Currey, 1999); Stephen Volz, *African Teachers on the Colonial Frontier: Tswana Evangelists and Their Communities during the Nineteenth Century* (New York: Peter Lang, 2001).

27. John Mary Waliggo, *The Catholic Church in the Buddu Province of Buganda, 1879–1925* (Kampala, Uganda: CACISA, 2010).

28. Ibid., 13–15.

29. Ibid., 15.

30. Kollman, *Evangelization of Slaves and Catholic Origins*, 106.

31. Keith Thomas, "Diary," *London Review of Books* 32, no. 11 (2010): 36.

32. *Dictionary of African Christian Biography*, accessed May 4, 2020, http://www.dacb.org.

Works Cited

Alpers, Edward A. "The Other Middle Passage: The African Slave Trade in the Indian Ocean." In *Many Middle Passages: Forced Migration and the Making of the Modern World*, edited by Emma Christopher, Cassandra Pybus, and Marcus Rediker, 20–38. Berkeley: University of California Press, 2007.

———. "The Story of Swema: Female Vulnerability in Nineteenth-Century East Africa." In *Women and Slavery in Africa*, edited by Claire Robertson and Martin Klein, 185–219. Madison: University of Wisconsin Press, 1983.

Arnold, David, and Robert A. Bickers. "Introduction." In *Missionary Encounters: Sources and Issues*, edited by Robert A. Bickers and Rosemary Seton, 1–10. Surrey, UK: Curzon Press, 1996.

Cox, Jeffrey. *The British Missionary Enterprise since 1700*. New York: Routledge, 2008.

———. *Imperial Fault Lines: Christianity and Colonial Power in India, 1818–1940*. Stanford, CA: Stanford University Press, 2002.

Gaume, Mgr. *Suema: A Little African Slave, a Tale for Our Times*. Dublin, 1871.

———. *Suéma, ou La Petite Esclave Africaine enterée vivante: Histoire contemporaine dediée aux jeunes chrétiennes de l'ancien et du nouveau monde*. Paris, 1870.

Greer, Allan, ed. *The Jesuit Relations: Natives and Missionaries in Seventeenth-Century North America*. Boston: Bedford / St. Martin's, 2000.

Hoppe, Kirk. "Whose Life Is It, Anyway? Issues of Representation in Life Narrative Texts of African Women." *International Journal of African Historical Studies* 26, no. 3 (1993): 623–36.

Johnston, Anna. *Missionary Writing and Empire, 1800–1860*. Cambridge, UK: Cambridge University Press, 2003.

Kaplan, Steven, ed. *Indigenous Responses to Western Christianity*. New York: New York University Press, 1995.

Kollman, Paul V. *The Evangelization of Slaves and Catholic Origins in Eastern Africa*. Maryknoll, NY: Orbis Books, 2005.

———. "Generations of Catholics in Eastern Africa: A Practice-Centered Analysis of Religious Change." *Journal for the Scientific Study of Religion* 51, no. 3 (2012): 412–28.

Larson, Pier M. *History and Memory in the Age of Enslavement: Becoming Merina in Highland Madagascar, 1770–1822*. Oxford, UK: James Currey, 2000.

Moulinet, Daniel. "Mgr. Gaume, l'oeuvre apostolique et le rachat des esclaves." *Mémoire Spiritain* 7 (1998): 108–26.

Peel, J. D. Y. "Problems and Opportunities in an Anthropologist's Use of a Missionary Archive." In *Missionary Encounters: Sources and Issues*, edited by Robert A. Bickers and Rosemary Seton, 70–94. Surrey, UK: Curzon Press, 1996.

———. *Religious Encounter and the Making of the Yoruba*. Bloomington: Indiana University Press, 2000.

Ranger, Terence. *Are We Not Also Men? The Samkange Family and African Politics in Zimbabwe, 1920–64*. London: James Currey, 1995.

———. *Voices from the Rocks: Nature, Culture and History in the Matopos Hills of Zimbabwe*. Oxford, UK: James Currey, 1999.

Stoler, Ann Laura. *Along the Archival Grain: Epistemic Anxieties and Colonial Common Sense*. Princeton, NJ: Princeton University Press, 2009.

Thomas, Keith. "Diary." *London Review of Books* 32, no. 11 (2010): 36–37.

Thwaites, Reuben G., ed. *The Jesuit Relations and Allied Documents*. 73 vols. Cleveland: Burrows Brothers, 1896–1901.

Tilmans, Karin, Frank van Vree, and Jay Winter, eds. *Performing the Past: Memory, History, and Identity in Modern Europe*. Amsterdam: Amsterdam University Press, 2010.

Vilaça, Aparecida, and Robin M. Wright, eds. *Native Christians: Modes and Effects of*

Christianity among Indigenous Peoples of the Americas. Burlington, VT: Ashgate, 2009.

Volz, Stephen. *African Teachers on the Colonial Frontier: Tswana Evangelists and Their Communities during the Nineteenth Century*. New York: Peter Lang, 2011.

Waliggo, John Mary. *The Catholic Church in the Buddu Province of Buganda, 1879–1925*. Kampala, Uganda: CACISA, 2010.

Županov, Ines G. *Disputed Mission: Jesuit Experiments and Brahmanical Knowledge in Seventeenth-Century India*. New Delhi: Oxford University Press, 1999.

Chapter 2

COMPLETING THE LINE OF COMMUNICATION

On Hearing the Voice of the "Native Christian"

Mrinalini Sebastian

> How, in this assemblage of official notes and documents, might one recover the voice, conscience, and experience of its ostensible subject, of what we might metaphorically describe as the "original writing"—the subjectivity of the convert Ananda Row? Wherein do its traces lie, if at all, and to what—and how—does it give way?
> —GAURI VISWANATHAN, *OUTSIDE THE FOLD*

> For Echo is obliged to echo everyone who speaks. Her desire and performance are dispersed into absolute chance rather than an obstinate choice, as in the case of Narcissus. If the ever-renewed narcissus flower is a "natural monument" to the fulfillment of Narcissus's desire-as-punishment out of this world, the lithography of Echo's bony remains merely points to the risk of response. It has no identity proper to itself.
> —GAYATRI CHAKRAVORTY SPIVAK, "ECHO"

> Hear: perceive with the ear the sound (made by someone or something).
> —*OXFORD ENGLISH DICTIONARY*

Texts from the past have a way of speaking to us in the present. They reveal to us something of the subjectivity of the writer. However, if the subjectivity that we seek to construct is not that of the writer but of the individuals about whom the text is written, would the text lend itself to such an exercise? Can we discover the voice of the "native Christian" in the missionary archives? Do missionary documents from the past reveal to us anything at all about the subjectivity of those who converted to Christianity during the nineteenth century in different regions of South Asia? Can the "native Christian" really speak?[1] Or, are the local voices available to us as unintentional echoes from the past, not because they chose to speak but simply by chance? If echoes of their voices get unintentionally included in historical documents, can we hear them today? These questions remind us of the difficulty in recapturing the agency of the early generation of Protestant Christians, and it gets even more complicated if we remember that in the Indian context, even though there are some written testimonials and autobiographies of individual converts, most of the narratives about them are written by others. Since the "native Christians" were rarely the authors of texts that told stories about them, it is a challenge to uncover the "life writings" of the Christian community that came into existence because of the efforts of the nineteenth-century Protestant missions in India.[2]

The opening epigraph reminds us of this challenge that a historian of nineteenth-century conversions to Christianity is likely to face in her reading of the archival material.[3] According to Gauri Viswanathan, conversion to Christianity in the Indian context was both transgressive and transformative in nature because it dramatically altered the communal life of an individual. In the community of birth, an individual's conversion to Christianity would amount to her civil and ritual death: civil death, because the converted individual would lose all rights prescribed by the religiously distinct code of personal laws;[4] and ritual death, because by converting, the individual had lost caste and would be considered dead by the community.[5] A controversial conversion could even lead to litigation. It is in the context of her analysis of an 1844 court case related to the conversion of a young Brahmin man in Mangalore, South India, that Viswanathan asks, "How, in this assemblage of official notes and documents, might one recover the voice, conscience, and experience of its ostensible subject, of what we might metaphorically describe as the 'original writing'—the subjectivity of the convert?"[6]

Viswanathan uses the colonial British governmental archives related to the court case filed by the family of this young man who had become

Christian. His family had questioned the authenticity of this conversion. Several of his relatives, including his wife, had very persuasively petitioned the court to intervene in this matter of conversion because, in their view, he was not in his right mind when he joined the Christians. Among all the court documents related to the conversion of this young man called Ananda Row, Viswanathan does not find any personal account of it by the convert himself. This conspicuous absence of Ananda Row's testimonial in the official documents is what makes her ask if one could ever find the "original writing" of this young man. Had he written something, Viswanathan seems to suggest, we would have had some insight into his own thoughts about this life-changing step taken by him.

I discuss Viswanathan's work, as well as this particular case of conversion, in a previously published essay, where I had underlined the importance of making a critical shift in the ways mission history is studied and analyzed, especially taking the agency of the local people into consideration.[7] In 1844, a Swiss-German missionary organization called the Basel Mission had its main station in Mangalore, and this young convert had been a student in one of the mission schools. In my essay, I argue that if Viswanathan had access to the reports and letters of the Basel Mission that were written, printed, and circulated around this time, she would actually have read accounts of this conversion by Ananda Row himself. In the mission documents he is called Anandrao Kaundinya. After his conversion, he was known as Hermann Anandrao Kaundinya. Kaundinya was one of the most articulate among the Indian Christians of this region and has left behind a number of written testimonials,[8] reports,[9] translations,[10] handwritten letters,[11] and notebooks.[12] After his conversion, he was sent to the headquarters of the Basel Mission in Switzerland to be trained in the mission seminary, following which he returned to India as the first Indian missionary of the Basel Mission in the Mangalore area and beyond.[13] Much has been written about him by those who were able to consult the Basel Mission documents,[14] but there is still much more to be explored in terms of the innumerable textual traces that he has left behind that are now preserved in the mission archives.[15]

Kaundinya's was an unusual case of conversion. Perhaps, when Gauri Viswanathan spoke about the need to recover the voice of the convert, she had in mind a more predictable representative of converts to Christianity. Unlike Anandrao Kaundinya, most of the other converts came from communities that did not have skills in reading or writing. They were not from those communities that were traditionally seen as the custodians of scriptural knowledge in the Indian society. These converts belonged to communities that we would now recognize as the subaltern.[16] Even though the Basel Mission established schools and made the education of the new converts a priority, the kind of intentional writing that Viswanathan seems to allude to is hard to come by in the archives of the Mission. This fact makes us wonder if the "native Christian" could ever speak. Yet, the question "Can the Native Christian Speak?" is as complicated as the now-famous question asked by Spivak, "Can the Subaltern Speak?"[17] Without denying the subaltern subject her agency, Spivak in her exploration of the above question reminds us of the many obstacles that come in the way of the subaltern voice from being heard. Unlike Anandrao Kaundinya, most of the other converts to Christianity came from communities that were "already socially or spiritually alienated" in this "highly integrated, caste-based society."[18] The Basel Mission placed a great emphasis on imparting literacy so that the new convert could read the Bible by him- or herself, but this does not seem to have resulted in a historical paper trail for most of the newly converted native Christians. If this is indeed the case, then the question "Can the Native Christian Speak?" raises an important methodological issue.[19] Given the seeming lack of sources authored by Indian Christians, how does one gain an understanding of the aspirations—spiritual or otherwise—of those who became Christians? How does one write their communal biography or assemble their "life writings"?

This essay will use some of the available historical material pertaining to the work of the Basel Mission in southwestern India during the nineteenth and early twentieth centuries and explore the possibility of discerning Indian Christian voices in these texts. It will make the argument that a careful reading of these documents from the past, even if they are not written by the "native Christian," can provide insights into the negotiating abilities and the agency of the early generations of Protestant Christians in this region. The premise on which it will make this argument is that even when there might not be intentional articulations by native Christians, an attentive reading of the missionary documents can help us "hear" the voices of these early Christians, especially in situations where they collectively and strategically negotiate with the missionaries. According to the definition in the *Oxford English Dictionary*, to "hear" is to be perceptive to the sound made by someone; in other words, it would be correct to argue that to "hear" is to be cognizant of the fact that those sounds are already there. Echoes from the past can tell us more about the desire of some individuals and groups for a social configuration that is framed by a different kind of theological vision than the traditional one that was familiar to them. In order to further nuance our understanding of the echoing of voices from the past, which is not the same as the "recovering of the voice" as this work hopes to demonstrate, we can now turn to the second epigraph that appears at the beginning of this essay. This epigraph is from Spivak's article "Echo," where she analyzes the symbolic implications of the story of Narcissus and Echo.[20] Spivak draws our attention to the story of Echo narrated by Ovid in his *Metamorphoses* and reminds us that the voice of the nymph Echo remains even after she is dead. We will turn to the story and its use by Spivak to elaborate her own point about the representation of the subaltern.

The Subaltern and Echo

Before we can turn to the story of Echo, we must remind ourselves of the two important lessons we can take away from Spivak's other essay under discussion, "Can the Subaltern Speak?" Spivak, first of all, wants to remind us that historiographical projects about the subaltern people usually overlook the figure of the gendered subaltern. Second, Spivak's subaltern is not incapable of speaking, but she is unable to complete the "line of communication" because she is outside the "circuits of citizenship and institutionality."[21] For Spivak, the objective in raising the question "Can the Subaltern Speak?" is less about denying people who are outside the "circuits of citizenship and institutionality" their own agency but more about questioning our agency in presuming to speak on their behalf. If this questioning of "speaking on behalf" of the subaltern sounds like a theoretical dead end for historiographical projects that seek to "recover the voices" of the subaltern, she nevertheless offers us a glimpse of an answer in her analysis of the story of Echo.

Without going into the details of the complex argument that Spivak makes about psychoanalysis and the gendered use of the symbolic meaning of Narcissus in psychoanalytical theories and practices, I want to discuss her interpretation of the one who falls in love with Narcissus, the nymph Echo. Jupiter gives Echo the task of keeping his wife, Juno, engaged in a conversation when he goes around flirting with the other nymphs. When Juno becomes aware of this ploy, she places a curse on Echo, rendering her inarticulate. All that she can do, by way of speaking, is to repeat the last part of the sentence uttered by another person. The curse complicates matters for Echo when she falls in love with Narcissus because she is not able to express her love to him through her own speech. She can only repeat his words and hence must wait for the opportune moment when the words that she repeats are likely to communicate her meaning to him. Finally, when she thinks that she has managed to convey her emotions to Narcissus, she puts her arms around him from behind, only to be spurned by him. Narcissus, who has fallen in love with his reflection, does not care for anyone. His self-love makes him plunge into the reflective pool in pursuit of his own image. Humiliated by this rejection, Echo recedes to the forest where she wastes away, and only her "boney remains"[22] prevail because she turns into a rock. However, her echoing voice persists, even though her body is not there anymore. But this voice is not the "original voice" that Gauri Viswanathan longs to see in the assemblage of documents from the past. It is an echoed voice, one that depends on the "absolute chance"[23] of being heard rather than on the "obstinate choice"[24] made by someone with the freedom to speak; the choice that was available to Narcissus is denied to Echo. Echo could not make a choice about what she spoke; she had to leave everything to chance and hope that through the act of echoing she would be heard. Her voice communicates without intending to complete the "line of communication," and only those who have ears that have been attuned to hear would detect her voice.

In a way, the current volume of essays also makes us think about speaking and hearing. It is about the voice and agency of the indigenous Christians. Can these voices be discerned in missionary and colonial archives? We can respond to the question in two possible ways. We can argue that it is possible to recover and extract the voices of the indigenous Christians in the missionary documents. Or we can say that the native Christian has no voice. The first answer would place the burden of recovery of this voice on the historian and the future representative of the "native Christian," whereas the second answer would deny the "native Christian" any agency in self-determination. The second answer does not leave us with sufficient reasons for undertaking a project on discerning the voices of indigenous Christians in missionary or colonial archives.

On the other hand, when researchers from later generations seek to discern the voice of the ancestors of their community in the historical resources, they are likely to slip into some kind of cultural narcissism. Perhaps they will be eager to "speak for, speak to, and listen to"[25] the voices of the first-generation Christians, but such efforts give importance to the agency of the researchers rather than to what is already there in the documents of the past. It might also prompt the future researchers to focus more on the "obstinate choice" of these first-generation Christians than on the "absolute chance" of a combination of factors—both metaphysical and social—that made them open themselves up to the "risk of response"[26] when they heard the message of the missionaries. Such "obstinate choice" could not be always exerted by most of the first-generation Protestant Christians who, for the most part, came from the subaltern sections of society.

Spivak's arguments in "Echo" are, in a way, supplementary to her argument in "Can the Subaltern Speak?" As mentioned above, in Spivak's view, the truly subaltern has no access to regular institutional structures that will make her voice heard: "In her own separate enclosure, the subaltern still cannot speak as the subject of a speech act."[27] It is this impossibility for the subaltern to complete the speech act that makes her ask the famous question "Can the subaltern speak?" The answer is not "Yes, she has agency, and hence she can speak for herself," nor is it "No, she cannot, because she is denied her agency." The question asks us to contemplate whether, when the subaltern speaks, she can complete the process of communication. Can she be heard even when she speaks?

In "Echo," we discern a possible resolution for this difficulty in representing the subaltern who was not stitched into the Protestant missions' communication networks. The story of Narcissus can provide new insights to anyone interested in writing the autobiography of one's own community, about its beginnings and its narratives. The story embodies a warning: "you disappear if you act on your knowledge" and spurn others as Narcissus did.[28] Fortunately, Spivak directs us from Narcissus to Echo. She attunes her ears so that she can hear the voice of Echo and thus asks us to be perceptive to the echoed voices from the past, even as we remember that Echo has no control over the words she echoes: "For Echo is obliged to echo everyone who speaks. Her desire and performance are dispersed into absolute chance rather than an obstinate choice, as in the case of Narcissus. . . . The lithography of Echo's bony remains merely points to the risk of response. It has no identity proper to itself."[29] We can learn much more about the first generation of Protestant Christians if we learn to let echoes from the past reach us. These echoes bounce off the texts of the European missionaries and the indirect accounts of the Indian Christians. They connect the fledgling Indian congregations with the other local communities. The historiographic project then becomes a process that enables echoes from the past to reach our present. These echoes are not created in an intentional manner but flit through the missionary narratives, almost as if by chance. But in order to acquaint ourselves of the spaces where we can hear the echoed voices of Indian Christians, we must first turn to the missionary records and identify discernible patterns in their accounts of the local Christians.

The "Native Christian" in Different Genres of Missionary Narratives

The mission magazines and the periodical reports of the missionary societies regularly carried stories about local Christians. A look at the annual reports of the Basel Mission for the early years of its work in southwestern India indicates that the mission was steadily expanding its realm of activities since its arrival there and also that within years of its arrival in these parts, a growing number of non-Christians were in one way or the other connected with the activities of the mission stations. For example, the census printed in the 1848 Basel Mission report[30] reveals that, of the 3,050 locals associated with the work of the Basel Mission in the various mission stations of southwestern India, only 762 were congregation members. The rest belonged to other local communities. We also learn from this report that the local employees of the mission—both Christian and non-Christian—were double the number of the Europeans. Another report published in 1850 indicates that during the reporting year, only about a quarter of the schoolteachers were Indian Christians.[31] These are interesting statistical details that reveal important factors about the mission stations' field of influence. Over the years, the institutions of the mission, especially its schools, were generating jobs for a small number of local non-Christian individuals and attracting a significant number of students from the other communities. Within two decades of the mission's arrival in southwestern India, its educational work had been deemed important by the surrounding communities. They sent their children to mission schools despite the fear of conversion. There was a degree of demand for the educational credentials that could be gained by going to such schools.

The reports and magazines of the mission can, in this manner, give us a broad sense of the time and the context within which the Basel Mission missionaries were working. The information that we can gather about the context is often in the form of description of locations, summaries of oral histories of temples and towns, or narratives about specific practices witnessed by the missionaries. These narratives are often framed by the theological perspectives of the missionaries. And yet, as the historian of the Catholic Jesuit mission in India, Ines Županov, reminds us, the "fragments of information" that the missionary accounts generate are important sources that give us an insight into "indigenous religious practices and cognitive categories."[32] Even when the reports and other periodicals of the mission agency follow specific modes of narration and description, they are full of such "fragments of information." In the next sections, I will identify some genres of writing where we can learn more about the subjectivity of the "native Christian" and the intercultural context within which they lived. Even when they are not direct accounts by the local Christians, if we are careful listeners, we are likely to hear their voices.

Testimonials and Conversion Narratives

The one genre of writing where the authorial presence of Indian Christians is clearly visible is when they write a testimonial about the moment of conversion. It is a document that attests to the spiritual transformation of an individual. Even though the narrative itself may be formulaic, it seeks to demonstrate the spiritual transformation of the convert. In fact, Judith Becker argues that this moment of spiritual change is not to be confused with what is generally seen as conversion to a new way of life.[33] Gauri Viswanathan's question about the subjectivity of the convert also reflects this concern about the easy conflation of whatever is transformative at the level of the individual with whatever is transgressive at the level of the birth community. In the Basel Mission reports, the autobiographical accounts and testimonials usually begin with an account of an individual's life before conversion, dwell on the recognition of her sinfulness, elaborate the phase when she becomes aware of the offer of forgiveness of sins, and finally proclaim her acceptance of that offer of grace and everlasting life.[34] This genre of writing is more readily viewed as writing that reveals the subjectivity of the convert even though it often catered to specific expectations from its intended readership.

Categorical Narratives

The printed reports of the different missionary organizations—not just the Basel Mission—carried short statements on the work of different categories of mission workers. These categorical narratives are about specific groups of local Christians such as Catechists and Bible Women. Local Catechists were the first Indian Christians to be mentioned by name in the mission documents. Sometimes, we also get to know the names of the Bible Women who were attached to the local mission stations. Often, under the category of

"Women's Work for Women," we read narratives about the everyday experiences of these individuals who were among the first female employees of the Protestant missions in India.[35] The Bible Women went from house to house selling small portions of the Bible and talking to the women of the household about Jesus, sin, and salvation. These women were not very successful in getting converts to Christianity, but they were important links between the communities of local women and the European female missionaries.

Descriptions of the work of the Catechists, the Bible Women, and, less prominently, the schoolteachers, are part of the annual and quarterly reports of the Basel Mission. I call narratives about their work "categorical narratives" because their reports were based on their category of employment. Categorical narratives can be easily overlooked as narratives that simply highlight some of the important moments in the professional life of the indigenous co-workers of the European missionaries. However, if we contextualize their work within the organizational structures of the mission and also within the hierarchies of the broader society in which they operated, we can glean the "indirect voices" of the Indian Christians and other local people, especially women, from these narratives. In an earlier essay on the Bible Women, I tracked the biography of one Bible Woman called Sanjivi who worked for the Wesleyan Mission for several years.[36] Even though there is a general desire for a Bible Woman from the "respectable classes," the work done by Sanjivi is affirmed because of the special significance of her work to people from the lower rungs of society.[37] Her work is also affirmed by the local women who believe that she does not speak of caste but only of Christ. The biography of Sanjivi gleaned from the annual reports of the mission provides a number of snapshots about contemporary conversations of women belonging to different religious and caste backgrounds; moreover, it gives us a chance to understand the transformative and transgressive elements in her own life.

Exemplary Narratives

There is a special place in the missionary reports for narratives about exemplary lives and deaths. Suffering and death were seen by the missionaries of the Basel Mission as occasions that provided opportunities for testimonies about the Christian disciples' unwavering faith in the goodness of God. Occasionally, such narratives also offer advice to their European readers. In one annual report of the Basel Mission, there is an account of the exemplary behavior of a local Christian woman called Christine and the exemplary death of another woman who became a Christian through Christine's witness:

> Among the Canarese people in these parts we cannot as yet report any conversion, but we have had the pleasure of admitting by baptism into the church of Christ, five adults and four children, of Tamil and Telugu extraction, who have been residing here for some time. The first was an old, infirm woman, the story of whose conversion will show, that there is here and there a native Christian to be found who so lets his light shine before men that they see his good works, and glorify the Father who is in heaven. This old woman unable to earn her bread and totally unbefriended, was obliged to beg. Christine, an elderly widow and a member of our native congregation, though poor and earning a livelihood by her own hands, seeing the helpless creature, took compassion on her, offered her a corner in her straw hut and provided her with food and clothes.[38]

Christine succeeds in her "earnest endeavour to lead her to the Saviour." The narrative concludes as follows: "Under the influence of the Holy Spirit she yielded to Christine's exhortations, forsook the idols, believed in Christ, was baptized, and died in the faith a month after her baptism. To those who from the acknowledged weakness of faith in many native Christians, are apt to look with suspicion on them all, we may say, European Brother or Sister, 'Go and do thou likewise.'"[39] For the missionary who wrote this report, two things seem to be important: that the individual in question died "in the faith," and that this should be presented as a case of exemplary behavior by a poor, old, widowed "native Christian" woman. This exemplary narrative comes with the admonition that the "European brother and sister" who are "apt to look with suspicion" on all "native Christians" because of their "acknowledged weakness of faith" would do well to emulate such behavior. Even though we do not hear the voice of the "native Christian" directly in this account, such narratives often come with descriptions of place and conversations that in turn offer us valuable insights into the lives of those very "native Christians."

Anecdotal Narratives

Most often, however, all that a researcher gets from these reports are anecdotes about the local people. The following anecdote, which appears in the fifth annual report of the Basel Mission, is drawn from the journal of one of the elders of the Mangalore congregation who was a native Christian.[40] It describes a difficult confrontation that he has had as an itinerant preacher and gives us a sense of the challenges that Indian Christians faced as members of a new and fledgling religious community:

> We went through the Bazar and passed a brook. When we measured our shade to know the time of the day, we found that it was about 3 o'clock in the afternoon. Being exceedingly thirsty we entered the house of a farmer. The master of the house sat upon a bench, writing. He looked at us for a moment, and asked: Who are you? Whence have you come? We replied: Please to finish your business, then we shall inform you of the purpose of our visit. Titus was exceedingly thirsty, and asked for water. The man enquired a second time: Who are you? We replied: We are men of Mangalore. He continued: and what is the purpose of your visit? We said, You know the purpose for which the Padres have come into this country: you have yourself heard the glad tidings which they proclaim. We have now come to make known unto you the same word. He asked with the air of astonishment: What! Do you belong to the padres? Yes, was our reply. I know their whole story, he said, go in peace. We answered: If you know, as you say, all they teach, you would not thus speak with us. The words which the padres and we speak are not our own, but God's; in these words is the salvation of men. Suddenly he cried full of rage. Will you go in peace, or shall I seize you by the throat and cast you out? We said: why do you get so angry? We have not come to stay here. However he called his people and cried aloud, Take them by the throat and cast them out; throw away the mat upon which they have sat, and the brass vessel out of which they have drunk. He set a guard of his own people over us.[41]

This telling recounting of the encounter between the Indian Christians and a local farmer,[42] though fascinating, may not give us sufficient clues to draw any sweeping conclusions. However, placed within the context of other similar anecdotes and other significant events that happened around the same time, this single anecdote can also tell us much about the particular context within which this incident takes place. This extract from the journal of the elder of the congregation, Simeon, appears in the report published in 1845, a year after Mangalore had witnessed turmoil around the conversion of Anandrao Kaundinya in early 1844. Kaundinya's conversion was an exceptional event for the missionaries in Mangalore because the small congregation there had been otherwise constituted by people mostly drawn from the non-elite sections of the population. This was also a remarkable event for the people of Mangalore, because a member of the local elite had lost caste by becoming a Christian. The harsh reaction of the farmer to Simeon, the elder of the Mangalore congregation, could have been a reaction to the well-known conversion of Anandrao. Simeon's journal also records that in the next village, the prominent landlord of the village asked him, "What are the words of your Padre? Is he able to mix all castes into one?"[43]

If we remember that the Basel Mission had forbidden the practice of maintaining caste among the newly converted people, we will understand the intensity of the emotions behind this question. As those who had lost caste through conversion, these native Christians had little social power in the larger societal context. At the same time, as non-European Christians, they did not have much power within the organizational structures of the mission agencies. It is in this space that was neither fully European-Christian, nor fully Indian-Hindu, that the new minority community of the Indian Protestant Christians takes shape. Anecdotal narratives can dramatize this unique societal space occupied by the new Christian communities within the small towns of southwestern India.

Exceptional Narratives

There are times when specific events, life stories, or conversations appear as being exemplary and highlighted in the publications of the Basel Mission. Much of my research and writing is about the life and work of Hermann Anandrao Kaundinya. If the subaltern is someone who stands outside the institutional and communicational networks of a given society, then it would be hard to call Anandrao Kaundinya a subaltern Christian. He was stitched into the institutional structures of the Basel Mission and was an indispensable participant in the translation and other literary works undertaken by the scholarly missionaries of the Basel Mission: Herrmann Mögling, Gottfried Weigle, and Pauline Bacmeister.[44] However, this does not mean that he never had moments of doubt about his status in Basel Mission. He openly expressed his desire for an apostolic model of governance of the Indian congregations by the mission committee.[45] His accounts of life in the Nilgiris, written well before the place was fully transformed into a hill resort, are "thick descriptions," full of what we now call ethnographic details.⁴⁶ He was a man who was well versed in local histories and the oral narratives. In one such representation of the collective memory of the city of Mangalore, we get a stunning spatial description of the living quarters of the different communities.⁴⁷ If we ask the question "Can the Native Christian Speak?" with reference to the life of Anandrao Kaundinya, and if we mean it in a simplistic literal sense, we can answer unequivocally "Yes, he can!" However, it is in the context of this narrative about and by this exceptional native Christian that we learn more about the "subaltern" Christians.

Echoes of the Desire to Be Free: The Christian Community in Anandapur

A remarkable chapter in the history of the work of the Basel Mission in southwestern India is related to its Coorg Mission, or the mission to the people of the Coorg district (Coorg is the anglicized version of the name Kodagu, which is now part of the state of Karnataka). The story of the Coorg Mission is also the story of a rebellion by the Basel missionary Herrmann Mögling. He had come to this region along with a native of Coorg called Somaya, who, after going through different phases in his search for religious enlightenment, including the phase where he became a sannyasi, or a holy ascetic, had finally declared to Mögling his intention to become a Christian. Somaya belonged to the landowning Kodava community.⁴⁸ On the suggestion of Somaya, Mögling had started the Coorg Mission despite the refusal of the Basel Mission to support the endeavor. In the ensuing conflict between the missionary Mögling and the mission headquarters in Basel, Anandrao Kaundinya decided to cast his lot with the mission, even though Mögling, his spiritual mentor, parted ways for a period of time with the Basel Mission and formed the Coorg Mission. The Coorg Mission was eventually taken over by the Basel Mission, but it is in the early years of its work in the region that we learn about the extraordinary negotiations made by a group of daily laborers who were agricultural workers.

A letter signed by a schoolteacher, Christian Kamsika, in 1856 tells us that a group of agricultural laborers in Coorg had "long felt inclined to send their boys to School, but they allowed themselves to be discouraged by their neighbours and masters."⁴⁹ The expectation from the school would be that such children attend classes regularly even during the monsoon season, when the community is busily engaged in agricultural work. Thus, attending school would deprive the landowners of field hands. In another instance, Pauline Mögling remarks in a letter that the children of the laborers are "almost without clothing" but acknowledges that she spends some of the "loveliest hours" of the day with them.⁵⁰

These field workers are identified in the missionary documents as being part of the "slave castes," as many of them belonged in perpetuity to the household of the former king of Coorg and were "freed" when the kingdom was taken over by the British administration in 1834. Even after they were freed, many of them served as laborers who were hereditarily attached to the land on which they worked and thereby belonged to the landlord; if the land was transferred to another family or owners, these laborers were also transferred to the new landlords. In a letter written by Herrmann Mögling to the Mission Committee in Basel on April 18, 1859, we learn that some laborers from a neighboring area had approached him and told him that they had decided to break with their village community; they wanted to become Christians and asked Mögling to accept them for baptism. The missionary rejected their request because he wanted them to know that the preparation for baptism was a long process that involved his getting to know them as individuals, and he emphasized that the desire for this should come to them "from above."⁵¹ But the missionary had no objection to their attending the Sunday services regularly or taking catechetical classes that would eventually lead to their baptism as Christians. However, given the nature of their strenuous work, leaving their huts early in the morning and returning only at dusk, it would have been impossible for them to attend baptismal classes. Hence, on the suggestion of Somaya (who had by then become a Christian and was known as Stephanas), Mögling looked for the possibility of settling them in a different location, where they could set up a Christian village.

The first offer came from an expatriate owner of a coffee estate who was willing to take them as workers and pay for the catechist who would have ministered to them. However, when Mögling told the laborers about this offer and asked them to take time to think it over, they rejected this proposal because they did not want to leave the area where their ancestors were born and buried, and they did not want to give up their ancestral profession of agricultural labor. It was their intention to settle somewhere else as free tenants: "It would be the best for them, even when difficult, to settle somewhere else as agriculturists. Even if they had to work very hard the rest of their lives to repay the interest and the capital, which they would begin to bear, their children could have ownership of the land and an independent life."⁵² In this reported interaction between the missionary and the local subaltern community, we hear echoes of their desire to be free of a relationship of absolute and inherited dependence on their landlords and to become independent tenants. Eventually it was suggested that they should be settled in a place that had lain uncultivated and uninhabited for a long time, and was therefore overgrown with trees, even though an old road ran through it. Hermann Anandrao Kaundinya bought this piece of land on their behalf in 1858, using his own funds. He then made parcels out of it and leased them to about thirty-four families as free tenants.

We learn about the founding of this new village in a quarterly report of Kaundinya written in 1860.[53] He gives us this history of the community while reporting on the first "mass" conversion of the people who had settled down in this village. On April 17, 1859, forty-two individuals from this community, nearly three years after they first approached the missionaries with their desire to become Christians, actually received their baptism. The place that until then was known as Mukkati came to be known as Anandapur from that year onward.[54] It continues to be known by that name today.

It would be easy to speak of these converts as Rice Christians, or those who became Christians because of a promise of material gain. However, it is only when we read the text carefully and respond to the echoed desire of the people who were completely powerless in a rigid structure of social hierarchy, that we appreciate their collective articulation of the desire to provide education to their children and to become free tenants. Unlike the dominant communities in this region, these poor daily workers who were from the lowest rungs of society had nothing to lose when they became Christians except a traditional model of bonded labor. Theirs was the very first group to settle in a Christian village in this region.[55] Their argument about the freedom of their children in material terms also suggests that they were perhaps indeed in search of a freedom of a different kind, a freedom of the spirit, a freedom to be considered unfettered human beings. One might always argue about the true ramifications and the worldly manifestations of this desire for freedom, but the attractiveness of this worldview and this theological perspective at that point in time in the lives of these poor people can only be denied by denying their humanness and their agency in choosing what they felt was a better option for their own and their children's lives. We hear in their negotiations with the missionaries their own voice, even if this voice is barely audible from across the valleys of time and in the dusty texts of the past.

This story of the fledgling Christian community in Coorg cannot be read in isolation but must be told along with those of the others who had compelling reasons to become Christians, not least of which was the theological view of being valued for who they were as human beings. Those who had traditionally been denied access to a life of dignity felt deeply attracted to an alternative vision of freedom from enslavement, both metaphorically and literally. In retrospect, we know that the vision did not necessarily translate as material freedom for many Christians, especially Christians from Dalit communities, or Christians from communities that were formerly known as the "untouchable" communities. But the glimpse of freedom that they had then was convincing enough for these communities to seek what they thought was transformative about Christianity.

The noticeable fact that new Christians were gaining the ability to read and write, seems to have been an attractive prospect even for the other communities that lived around the Basel Mission stations. In our next example, once again, we see the extraordinary negotiating skills of a community that had very little power in the contemporary social hierarchy and was not necessarily networked into the emerging institutions of the British administrative structures—and yet saw a way out of the social status quo through the educational mission of the Basel Mission. In this account of the petition submitted by the villagers in a fishing community, we witness the great appeal that the educational institutions of the Basel Mission had for people belonging to other communities who lived beside the newly formed Protestant Christian communities. In this instance, we do have access to the writing of the subaltern, and this time not metaphorically but literally. In this account from the past, we hear how not just "native Christians" but other subaltern communities persuasively sought educational opportunities for their own children.

Can the Subaltern Write? The Story of a Facsimile and a Picture in a Mission Magazine

A May 1909 issue of *Der evangelische Heidenbote* (a magazine of the Basel Mission that had numerous subscribers in the German-speaking parts of Europe) published a reproduction of a facsimile showing part of a document that carried signatures in Malayalam and Latin scripts.[56] The facsimile was printed along with a photograph of a fishing village. The accompanying story illustrates something that is usually assumed but not clearly documented: the desire of those communities that were not named as "respectable" or "learned" to secure access to education, especially for their children.

The text that accompanies these two images talks about budget cuts that had forced the Basel Mission in India to close some of its schools. In one instance, however, they had to rescind the decision because the local Muslims and fisherfolk had submitted a petition to the Basel Mission requesting them not to take this drastic step. Their petition stated that the school that had been started by the missionary Samuel Hebich (perhaps in the mid-nineteenth century) had catered to a good number of girls and boys from that area. It argued that those who had studied there had gone on to occupy positions of importance and also that these former students were now staunch supporters of the Christian religion. Finally, the letter had reminded the missionaries that it should not be forgotten that Jesus Christ himself had great affinity toward people of the fisher caste. One hundred fifty-seven members of the local Muslim and fisher communities had signed this document. The report concludes with the information that after such a persuasive case was made for the continuation of the school, the Basel Mission had decided to keep the school going.

These visual pieces of evidence that tell us how local communities came to terms with the rapid transformations in a colonial society are valuable because there are not too many records on the basis of which a history of the fishing community during this period can be written. This report in *Der evangelische Heidenbote* demonstrates that collective choices were being made and asserted by local communities, even when they did not become Christians.

What we see here is not a straightforward case of educational charity but a humanitarian gesture on the part of the missionaries that had been realized only because the initiative had come from the other side. A poor, marginalized community of fisher people had collectively negotiated with the local missionaries and the administrators in Basel for schooling and education; they seemed to have recognized that if one wished to be part of the new realities that were emerging, one had to have "modern" schooling of some kind.

Conclusion

We have barely answered the question "Can the Native Christian Speak?" but the discussion above demonstrates that this does not have to be answered in the affirmative or the negative. Voices of the first-generation Christians, especially those who converted from the subaltern communities, and voices of those who chose to remain in those very communities abound in the missionary documents. Caught in our reading habits that search for the most obvious and straightforward narratives, we have difficulty hearing those voices because they appear randomly, all across the documents, sometimes in indirect narrations, and often in the form of reported incidents and speeches. Even though their *intention* to speak across time cannot always be ascertained, their *desire* for the freedom of the spirit and their *claim* to be accorded dignity is clearly discernable in the missionary archives.

If we are indeed interested in discerning the voices of local Christians, we need to pay attention to what we can "hear" in those missionary texts. We need to pay attention to those who could not make resolute choices in the same way that Anandrao Kaundinya could. The subaltern people in the Coorg area and the fishing community from the Malabar area[57] took the risk of responding to an "absolute chance" that had come their way in the form of the message of the missionaries. Some of them became Christians not just because of material benefits, as it is often argued, but also because they were searching for an alternative vision that in turn was premised on a profound understanding of equality and dignity before God and in human society. Unlike the nymph Echo whose "desire and performance are dispersed into absolute chance rather than an obstinate choice," the two communities discussed in this essay demonstrate that these subaltern groups simply responded to what came their way, by *chance*, but saw in that chance their first opportunity to make a *choice* for a different order of things, both material and metaphysical, and resolutely opted for that order of things. Can we not *indeed* "hear" and perceive in the missionary archives this echoed desire of the subalterns who responded to the Christian message and sought to assert their human dignity by collectively and persuasively negotiating with the forces of their times?

Notes

Much of the research for this essay was undertaken during 2013–14 when I was at the Leibniz Institute of European History, Mainz, Germany, as the fellow-in-residence for the junior research group on "Europabilder der Missionare." The research group was supported by the Federal Ministry for Education and Research, Germany.

1. This essay was originally presented at the conference "Can the Native Christian Speak?" sponsored by Emory University, Atlanta, May 28, 2014. Since the title of the conference alludes to Gayatri Chakravorty Spivak's essay "Can the Subaltern Speak?" I seek to relate the two questions in a more deliberate manner throughout this essay.

2. In recent years, "life writings" is the term used for a broader genre of narratives and factual information about individuals, communities, and even objects. According to the Oxford Center for Life-Writing, "Life-writing includes autobiography, memoirs, letters, diaries, journals (written and documentary), anthropological data, oral testimony, and eye-witness accounts." "What Is Life-Writing?," Wolfson College, accessed May 4, 2020, https://oxlifewriting.wordpress.com/what-is-life-writing.

3. By "archival material," I mean to include all historical material, including the digitized reports and journals. My primary concern here is about the historiographical challenge of learning more about the new Christian communities in southwestern India during the nineteenth and early twentieth centuries, even when the only sources we have are the reports and narratives of the Protestant missionaries of those times.

4. In British India, civil matters were determined by the exclusive personal laws of a specific religious community. The decision of an individual to join a different faith community would amount to that individual's "civil death" because the laws of the community of birth would not be available anymore to settle conflicts related to inheritance, marriage, adoption, and other such civil matters. The matter of a Uniform Civil Code continued to be a challenge even in post-independence India.

5. Conversion of an individual from one of the upper-caste communities was often marked by the performance of the rituals of death.

6. Gauri Viswanathan, *Outside the Fold: Conversion, Modernity, and Belief* (Princeton, NJ: Princeton University Press, 1998), 90. I have used this particular citation in my earlier essays because both the case that she discusses and the argument she makes are quite central to my own work. The archival sources that we use are completely different. My reading of the Basel Mission documents complements rather than contradicts her reading.

7. Mrinalini Sebastian, "Mission without History? Some Ideas for Decolonizing Mission," *International Review of Mission* 93, no. 368 (2004): 75–96.

8. For example, see the autobiographical account given by him at the time of his ordination at the Leonberg Church in Württemberg on July 20, 1851, in Hermann Anandrao Kaundinya, "Lebensgeschichte des H. Anandraja Kaundinja, eines ehemaligen Braminen, nunmehrigen Predigers an der deutsch-evangelischen Gemeinde und zweiten Lehrers an der Katechistenschule zu Mangalur, Provinz Canara, Westküste von Ostindien: Von ihm selbst niedergeschrieben und vorgetragen bei seiner Ordination zum Missionar am 20. Juli 1851 in der Stadtskirche zu Leonberg (Württemberg)" (Basel, 1853). In an English letter to the head of the Basel Mission, signed simply as "I am your obedient, Hermann," he gives a short account of his conversion. See Basel Mission Archives (hereafter BMA) C-1.3 Mangalore 1844, 13 e. In 2013 and 2014, I spent six months as the fellow-in-residence for the junior research group "Missionaries' Images of Europe" at the Leibniz Institute of European History, Mainz, Germany. Some of the material that I have used here comes from my archival visits to the Basel Mission Archives, Basel, Switzerland, during this period and some from the shared resources of the project. I am grateful to the archivist and staff of the Archives of the Basel Mission, Mission 21, and Judith Becker, the lead researcher for "Missionaries' Images of Europe" for giving me access to this material.

9. As the missionary in charge of a mission station, Anandrao Kaundinya also submitted periodical reports that were edited and published in the printed reports of the Basel Mission.

10. For example, see BMA C-1.c 391 for his translation of the Kannada reader prescribed by the Madras Presidency of British India, H. A. Kaundinya, *Second Reader* (Madras: Director of Public Instruction, 1890).

11. See BMA C-10.39 for letters written by Kaundinya to his second wife, Maria, who had come from Germany (like most other missionary brides of the time) and lived in India till after his death toward the end of the nineteenth century.

12. BMA C-10.33b, 2 contains his notebooks with draft versions of his letters on various day-to-day matters, providing a glimpse into his life as a missionary in the Coorg district (now in the state of Karnataka).

13. Mrinalini Sebastian, "The Scholar-Missionaries of Basel Mission in Southwest India: Language, Identity, and Knowledge in Flux," in *Cultural Conversions: Unexpected Consequences of Christian Missionary Encounters in the Middle East, Africa, and South Asia*, ed. Heather Sharkey (Syracuse, NY: Syracuse University Press, 2010), 176–202; Mrinalini Sebastian, "Localised Cosmopolitanism and Globalised Faith: Echoes of 'Native' Voices in Eighteenth- and Nineteenth-Century Missionary Documents," in *European Missions in Contact Zones: Transformation through Interaction in a (Post-)Colonial World*, ed. Judith Becker (Göttingen: Vandenhoeck & Ruprecht, 2015), 47–64.

14. For a detailed analysis of the conversion and death of his first wife, see J. Jayakiran Sebastian, "The Baptism of Death: Rereading the Life and Death of Lakshmi Kaundinya," *Mission Studies* 28, no. 1 (2011): 26–53. Katrin Binder has written on him in Albrecht Frenz and Stefan Frenz, eds., *Zukunft im Gedenken / Future in Remembrance* (Norderstedt: Books on Demand, 2007), 419–24.

15. For a new and detailed analysis of conversion as a spiritual transformation that was in fact inspired by the case of Anandrao Kaundinya, see Judith Becker, *Conversio im Wandel: Basler Missionare zwischen Europa und Südindien und die Ausbildung einer Kontaktreligiosität, 1834–1860* (Göttingen: Vandenhoeck & Ruprecht, 2015). See also Parinitha Shetty, "Conversion, Contestation and Community: Missionary Dialogues," in *Zukunft im Gedenken / Future in Remembrance*, ed. Albrecht Frenz and Stefan Frenz (Norderstedt: Books on Demand, 2007), 132–52.

16. Even though the word "subaltern" is routinely used in academic writing to indicate the marginalized sections of society, in its earliest use in the context of Indian historiography it simply meant those who could not be counted as the elite of the land. For further discussion on the use of the term, see Ranajit Guha, ed., *Subaltern Studies I: Writings on South Asian History and Society* (Delhi: Oxford University Press, 1994), vii–viii. In this understanding of the term, any nondominant group in a given locality could be termed "subaltern." However, this does not mean that there is no diversity among the subaltern.

17. Gayatri Chakravorty Spivak, "Can the Subaltern Speak?," in *Can the Subaltern Speak? Reflections on the History of an Idea*, ed. Rosalind C. Morris (New York: Columbia University Press, 2010), 21–78. The title of my essay is also inspired by Spivak's comment about "establishing the line of communication between a member of subaltern groups and the circuits of citizenship or institutionality" (65).

18. John C. B. Webster, *A Social History of Christianity: North-West India since 1800* (Oxford, UK: Oxford University Press, 2007). See also the assertion of Sathianathan Clarke that in regions like Tamil Nadu, conversions to Christianity "had to do with the movement of Dalit and not-so-pure (*asat*) Shudra communities away from their traditional regions." Sathianathan Clarke, "Conversion to Christianity in Tamil Nadu: Conscious and Constitutive Community Mobilization toward a Different Symbolic World Vision," in *Religious Conversion in India: Modes, Motivations, and Meanings*, ed. Rowena Robinson and Sathianathan Clarke (Oxford, UK: Oxford University Press, 2003), 327.

19. This methodological concern has been raised by Webster and others working on the history of Dalit Christianity. See George Oommen and John C. B. Webster, eds., *Local Dalit Christian History* (Delhi: ISPCK, 2002).

20. Gayatri Chakravorty Spivak, "Echo," in *The Spivak Reader: Selected Works of Gayatri Chakravorty Spivak*, ed. Donna Landry and Gerald MacLean (New York: Routledge, 1996), 175–202.

21. Spivak, "Can the Subaltern Speak?," 65.
22. Spivak, "Echo," 185.
23. Ibid., 185.
24. Ibid., 185.
25. Ibid., 186.
26. Ibid., 185.
27. Ibid., 188.
28. Ibid., 183.

29. Ibid., 185.

30. *The Eighth Report of the German Evangelical Mission in South-Western India* (Bangalore: Wesleyan Mission Press, 1848), 8.

31. *The Tenth Report of the German Evangelical Mission, in the Canara, Southern Mahrattha, and Malayalam Provinces; and on the Nilagiris* (Bangalore: Wesleyan Press, 1850), 25.

32. Ines Županov speaks of "fragments of information about indigenous religious practices and cognitive categories" in the context of her discussion of the dispute between Roberto de Nobili and his fellow Jesuit missionary Gonçalo Fernandes in her book *Disputed Mission: Jesuit Experiments and Brahmanical Knowledge in Seventeenth-Century India* (New Delhi: Oxford University Press, 1999), 48.

33. Becker, *Conversio im Wandel*, 98–128.

34. The testimonials and conversion narratives in the Basel Mission archives, including that of Anandrao Kaundinya, share similar characteristics with the spiritual autobiography, "a well-known and often-used genre of Methodist writing." Arun W. Jones, *Missionary Christianity and Local Religion* (Waco: Baylor University Press, 2017), 141–51.

35. For an extensive study of the Indian Bible Women in the Telugu-speaking areas of South India, see James Elisha Taneti, *Caste, Gender, and Christianity in Colonial India* (New York: Palgrave Macmillan, 2013).

36. Mrinalini Sebastian, "Reading Archives from a Postcolonial Perspective: 'Native' Bible Women and the Missionary Ideal," *Journal of Feminist Studies in Religion* 19 (Spring 2003): 5–25.

37. Ibid., 19–20.

38. *The Fifth Report of the German Mission in the Canara, Southern Mahratta, and Malabar Provinces* (Bangalore: Wesleyan Mission Press, 1845), 20.

39. Ibid.

40. The elders of the congregation were elected members who had specific responsibilities such as visiting the congregation members or assisting the catechist and the missionaries during the church service and also in making visits to the neighborhood. See "Extract from a Journal of Simeon, an Elder of the Mangalore Congregation, Translated from the Tulu Original," in ibid., 15.

41. Ibid., 18.

42. In all probability, this was no regular farmer because when the two Indian Christians approached him, the former was writing something. If we read the anecdote carefully, we realize that the farmer had actually given them a mat on which to sit and shared water in a brass vessel, both of which suggest that he accepted them as his social equals. It is only when he realized that they were Christians that he gets angry and finds them "polluting." His anger further confirms that he is from the upper rungs of the caste hierarchy; it also indicates that the upward mobility of the Christian converts, especially in terms of their clothing, education, and profession, did not, in any way, make them more "acceptable" in terms of the existing caste practices.

43. *Fifth Report of the German Mission*, 19.

44. Pauline was first married to Gottfried Weigle and after his death married his colleague Herrmann Mögling. See also Veena Maben, "Pauline Mögling: An Exceptional Mission Woman," in *Zukunft im Gedenken / Future in Remembrance*, ed. Albrecht Frenz and Stefan Frenz (Norderstedt: Books on Demand, 2007), 324–43.

45. See Sebastian, "Mission without History?," 95–96.

46. An account of Kaundinya's experience in the Nilgiris in 1844 was sent to the director of the Basel Mission. In these pages written in English, Kaundinya reports the local accounts about the history of the different communities of people who lived in this hill station. See Kaundinya, BMA C-1.3, no. 27, 1844.

47. Anandrao Kaundinya provides an exceptional description and local history of the city of Mangalore in the first two quarterly reports of the Basel Mission for the year 1858. This original source is reprinted in Albrecht Frenz, *Freiheit hat Gesicht: Anandapur—eine Begegnung zwischen Kodagu und Baden-Württemberg* (Stuttgart: Staatsanzeiger Verlag, 2003), 15–16.

48. In the documents of the colonial times, they are also known as the Coorgis.

49. BMA C-1, 21 Mercara 1856. I am grateful to Judith Becker for sharing the transcript of this document with me.

50. Excerpt from Pauline's letter to Barth written on February 23, 1857, cited in Frenz, *Freiheit hat Gesicht*, 32.

51. Herrmann Mögling's letter from Anandapur to the mission committee in Basel, dated April 18, 1859, Basel Mission Archive, C-1.25.99, transcribed and reprinted in ibid., 228–32.

52. Mögling's letter to the mission committee in Basel, dated April 18, 1859, cited in ibid., 229. Translated from the German by Mrinalini Sebastian.

53. Hermann Anandrao Kaundinya, second quarterly report written on July 16, 1860, in Anandapur and sent to the mission committee in Basel, printed in full in German in ibid., 269–72.

54. Ibid., 9.

55. In 1841, a Christian colony was founded in Malasamudra in the then North Mahratta region of South India to settle a group of people called the Kalagnanis who believed that their community had predicted and anticipated the arrival of the messengers of Christ. From the reports, though there was a mission station in this region, the experiment to settle the Kalagnani community here seems to have been unsuccessful. For more, see the translations of the reports on and from Malasamudra in Paul and Jennifer Jenkins, "Journeys and Encounters: Religion, Society and the Basel Mission in Northern Karnataka, 1837–1850," *Documents on the Basel Mission in North Karnataka, Missions-Magazin*, October 2007, revised July 2013, http://divinity-adhoc.library.yale.edu/BaselMissionKarnataka/Section%203%20N%20Karnataka%201842.pdf. Sections 4–7 also have information on the Christian colony in Malasamudra.

56. *Der evangelische Heidenbote*, no. 5 (May 1909): 39.

57. The school founded by the missionary Samuel Hebich was located in the Malabar region, which is now in the Indian state of Kerala.

Works Cited

Becker, Judith. *Conversio im Wandel: Basler Missionare zwischen Europa und Südindien und die Ausbildung einer Kontaktreligiosität, 1834–1860*. Göttingen: Vandenhoeck & Ruprecht, 2015.

Clarke, Sathianathan. "Conversion to Christianity in Tamil Nadu: Conscious and Constitutive Community Mobilization towards a Different Symbolic World Vision." In *Religious Conversion in India: Modes, Motivations, and Meanings*, edited by Rowena Robinson and Sathianathan Clarke, 323–50. Oxford, UK: Oxford University Press, 2003.

The Eighth Report of the German Evangelical Mission in South-Western India. Bangalore: Wesleyan Mission Press, 1848.

The Fifth Report of the German Mission in the Canara, Southern Mahratta, and Malabar Provinces. Bangalore: Wesleyan Mission Press, 1845.

Frenz, Albrecht. *Freiheit hat Gesicht: Anandapur—eine Begegnung zwischen Kodagu und Baden-Württemberg*. Stuttgart: Staatsanzeiger Verlag, 2003.

Frenz, Albrecht, and Stefan Frenz, eds. *Zukunft im Gedenken / Future in Remembrance*. Norderstedt: Books on Demand, 2007.

Guha, Ranajit, ed. *Subaltern Studies I: Writings on South Asian History and Society*. Delhi: Oxford University Press, 1994.

Jones, Arun W. *Missionary Christianity and Local Religion*. Waco: Baylor University Press, 2017.

Kaundinya, H. A. *Second Reader*. Madras: Director of Public Instruction, 1890.

Maben, Veena. "Pauline Mögling: An Exceptional Mission Woman." In *Zukunft im Gedenken / Future in Remembrance*, edited by Albrecht Frenz and Stefan

Frenz, 324–43. Norderstedt: Books on Demand, 2007.

Oommen, George, and John C. B. Webster, eds. *Local Dalit Christian History*. Delhi: ISPCK, 2002.

Sebastian, J. Jayakiran. "The Baptism of Death: Rereading the Life and Death of Lakshmi Kaundinya." *Mission Studies* 28, no. 1 (2011): 26–53.

Sebastian, Mrinalini. "Localised Cosmopolitanism and Globalised Faith: Echoes of 'Native' Voices in Eighteenth- and Nineteenth-Century Missionary Documents." In *European Missions in Contact Zones: Transformation through Interaction in a (Post-)Colonial World*, edited by Judith Becker, 47–64. Göttingen: Vandenhoeck & Ruprecht, 2015.

———. "Mission without History? Some Ideas for Decolonizing Mission." *International Review of Mission* 93, no. 368 (2004): 75–96.

———. "Reading Archives from a Postcolonial Perspective: 'Native' Bible Women and the Missionary Ideal." *Journal of Feminist Studies in Religion* 19 (Spring 2003): 5–25.

———. "The Scholar-Missionaries of Basel Mission in Southwest India: Language, Identity, and Knowledge in Flux." In *Cultural Conversions: Unexpected Consequences of Christian Missionary Encounters in the Middle East, Africa, and South Asia*, edited by Heather Sharkey, 176–202. Syracuse, NY: Syracuse University Press, 2010.

Shetty, Parinitha. "Conversion, Contestation and Community: Missionary Dialogues." In *Zukunft im Gedenken / Future in Remembrance*, edited by Albrecht Frenz and Stefan Frenz, 132–52. Norderstedt: Books on Demand, 2007.

Spivak, Gayatri Chakravorty. "Can the Subaltern Speak?" In *Can the Subaltern Speak? Reflections on the History of an Idea*, edited by Rosalind C. Morris, 21–78. New York: Columbia University Press, 2010.

———. "Echo." *New Literary History* 24, no. 1 (Winter 1993): 17–43.

———. *The Spivak Reader: Selected Works of Gayatri Chakravorty Spivak*. Edited by Donna Landry and Gerald MacLean. New York: Routledge, 1996.

Taneti, James Elisha. *Caste, Gender, and Christianity in Colonial India*. New York: Palgrave Macmillan, 2013.

The Tenth Report of the German Evangelical Mission, in the Canara, Southern Mahrattha, and Malayalam Provinces; and on the Nilagiris. Bangalore: Wesleyan Press, 1850.

Viswanathan, Gauri. *Outside the Fold: Conversion, Modernity, and Belief*. Princeton, NJ: Princeton University Press, 1998.

Webster, John C. B. *A Social History of Christianity: North-West India since 1800*. Oxford, UK: Oxford University Press, 2007.

Županov, Ines. *Disputed Mission: Jesuit Experiments and Brahmanical Knowledge in Seventeenth-Century India*. New Delhi: Oxford University Press, 1999.

Chapter 3

IN SEARCH OF THE WOMEN IN THE ARCHIVAL SOURCES

The Case of Maria Maraga

Esther Mombo

> When I was a girl, I used to long to go to the school too. I could hear the boys singing and reciting but my parents forbid me to go. Finally, after weeks, I determined I could just go anyway. So I rushed down and sat there on the earthen floor and tried to sing with them. Other girls joined me after that and even though our parents beat us we continued to go.
> —ALTA HOYT, WE WERE PIONEERS

African Women in the Mission Archives

Implicit in the philosophy of colonization and the Western missionary movement of the nineteenth and twentieth centuries was the assumption that other cultures were inferior to theirs. The role of Europeans was perceived as that of civilizing these cultures by introducing education and Christianity. The ideological, theological, and cultural consequences on the ways in which the other cultures were portrayed in the writings of the time are many and cannot be covered in one essay. For this work I set out to discuss the ways in which African women's voices were drowned out in mission history, and how the things that were written about them were interpretations by missionaries for their own purposes. The essay looks at two of the implications of such a history and uses the story of one Quaker woman to recover the identity and agency of this woman. The first implication concerns the ways in which African women were perceived and portrayed in the mission literature of the time. One of the perceptions of Western missions was that African women were helpless and downtrodden as a result of cultural customs of diet, initiation, marriage, and death rites, and that the role of the missionaries was that of rescuing the poor African women who lacked agency to make choices for themselves. The second concerns the dearth of information about African women in the growth and development of the church.

That lack of data concerning African women's agency in the mission of the church in the nineteenth and twentieth centuries is slowly being addressed. The information still lies in the archives that have not yet been sufficiently used for research; such archival materials include magazines, mission reports, monographs, pictures, and narratives. Adrian Hastings observes, "All in all African society was apparently so male-dominated that the impact of Christianity upon it has been treated overwhelmingly in male terms. But this also derives from the nature of nineteenth-century Western Christianity. It allowed almost no public role to women in the main Churches. . . . A largely male-dominated missionary church encountered a largely male-dominated traditional Africa. Two forms of patriarchy appeared to fit together well enough."[1] The dearth of information can also be attributed to the ways sources of writing the story about women have been neglected due to researchers' biases: "Unless researchers have been interested in a topic that happens to be relevant to the experience of women, they seem to have disregarded them as useful informants, presuming them to be uninterested in and unaware of larger questions relating to political or economic change or structural patterns. In most cases this record of neglect seems to have been unconscious; only that part of society that happened to be male were considered when researchers established the pools of informants."[2] Jan Vansina has expressed similar views when discussing informants in oral tradition. He notes that in some traditions it is believed that "women cannot know much about tradition because of their sex, which excludes them from taking part in public affairs."[3] Writing about women and missionary establishments, Fiona Bowie has noted that "in being seen as adjuncts to men, rather than as historical protagonists in their own right, women have been systematically written out of historical records and anthropological records."[4] Lack of documentary evidence is at times "equated with historical passivity or, even worse, with historical insignificance."⁵ Mercy Amba Oduyoye argues that writing about women and their role in the establishment of the church in Africa is about "recreating and retrieving women's stories so that they can become an integral part of the story of the church and of Africa as a whole."⁶

While the body of literature on women in African Christianity is slowly increasing, the challenges of using archival material remains. In some locales, archives are nonexistent, or material is stored in dilapidated places. Where the archives are well kept, the expense of reaching them and spending time in them is prohibitive for many who really wish to access them.

Both the portrayal of African women and the lack of adequate source materials serve as the basis of this essay, which addresses the question of African women's agency in making choices about joining the mission stations for learning just as men of the same period did. This is in the light of postcolonial studies on the question of whether the African woman can speak to be heard, rather than being voiceless, as she is portrayed in missionary literature. Can her voice be heard rather than nuanced to fit the missionary image for the purposes of mission work among and with women?

In the context of such difficult conditions, this essay aims to locate women and their voices among Quakers in East Africa, with special reference to Western Kenya. By using the narrative of one woman, Maria Maraga, the strength, agency, and power of women is realized, retrieved, and acknowledged.

This essay is divided into four parts. The first is a brief overview of the Quakers and their history in Africa, especially in Western Kenya. The second part discusses my search for sources for the story of Maraga. Next comes the story of Maraga herself from the archives and other sources and the different interpretations given to her story that drown out her voice. Finally, the essay provides an analysis and a conclusion.

Quakers in Africa

The Religious Society of Friends (i.e., the Quakers) traces its origins to England in the sixteenth century, and it has a rich history both in the United Kingdom and in the United States. This essay, however, is about Quakers in East Africa, Kenya in particular, studied with a focus on the invisibility and presentation of women in Quaker mission literature. I zero in on the nineteenth- and twentieth-century Quaker work in Kenya, which was similar to the work of other mission agencies of the same period.

We begin with some information about the Quakers in East Africa. Statistics show that half the Quakers in the world live in Africa. Most of them live in East and Central Africa, although there are a small number in Southern and West Africa. The estimated number of Quakers in the world is six hundred thousand. Africa houses the various Quaker traditions: unprogrammed, programmed, and Evangelical. The majority of Quaker traditions in Africa are programmed and Evangelical. Programmed meetings are aligned to the Friends United Meeting, and Evangelical meetings to the Evangelical Friends Church International. These two groups are headquartered in the United States. Both the programmed and Evangelical Quaker meetings in Africa emphasize the centrality of Christ and obedience to the teachings of scripture. Moreover, the meetings employ pastors.

The first Quakers in East Africa settled in Pemba in the coastal region of Tanzania and worked with freed slaves. They were followed by American missionaries from Indiana who arrived in Kenya in 1902. The American Quakers—namely Edgar Hole, Willis Hotchkiss, and Arthur and Edna Chilson—founded the first Quaker mission station in Kaimosi, in Western Kenya. Over the next sixty years the number of Quakers grew substantially, and schools and hospitals were established. Friends Theological College was set up in 1942 to train pastors to work in the growing Quaker communities. Among the first women students at the college was Rasoah Mutua, who became a key preacher and leader of women in Kenya. As noted at the beginning of this essay, while women were among the first people to join the mission stations, their stories remain hidden or untold. It was the knowledge that a woman was among the first trainees in pastoral ministry that led me to my inquiry of women's voices in African Quaker traditions.

Those who converted to the Christian faith were known as readers, because literacy was equated with being a Christian, and the Bible was used as a textbook in schools. Literacy also included schooling in arithmetic and writing. In setting up mission stations, Quakers and other mission agencies used a fourfold form of ministry that included evangelism, education, industrial training, and medical work. The aim of the four ministries in each mission station was to lead people to conversion and to help them formulate a strong self-supporting and self-propagating church.[7]

Some of the mission work carried out by the Quakers took place among women. The work was based on the notion of the rescue and liberation of women. The language used about women indicates Quaker missionaries' perspectives on African women. Most notable is Willis Ray Hotchkiss's book *Sketches from the Dark Continent*, which describes African women of this period in various degraded ways: "[She is] practically a slave, a beast of burden, reckoned as just so much 'Mali' (property)"; "Womanhood is reduced to servitude, doomed to drudgery as mere beasts of burden"; "The women [are] bulwarks of superstition"; "Womanhood in Africa is womanhood without God."[8] These and other similar writings make it difficult to hear the voices of women, and when you try to hear such voices they are filtered through the missionary interpretations of their situations. How does one delineate the voices of women as agents of their own changes, as individuals who made choices based on the context of their lives at the time? It is within this context that we search for Maria Maraga.

Searching for Maria Maraga in the Archives

In researching the lives of Quaker women in Western Kenya I was faced with the challenge of locating sources and developing a workable methodology. If history is a reconstruction of the past, silence and omissions have been part of the historical work related to Quaker women in Western Kenya. In order to fill some of those silences and omissions, I needed to go to the sources of historical reconstruction, namely archives. I started to look for information in various archives in different parts of the country as well as outside Kenya, locating the places of origin for the different Quakers who worked in East Africa, especially Western Kenya.

The first archival sources I consulted were in the United Kingdom: The Friends House Library in London and Woodbrooke College Library in Birmingham. While these libraries house information on British Quakers, the Friends House also holds mission records of the American Friends Board of Foreign Missions, which became Friends United Meeting. It also has major journals such as the *American Friend*, *African Record*, *Missionary Advocate*, and *Quaker Life*, all of which were avenues of communication for the Quaker missionaries. The *African Record* especially was a valuable source for early missionary views and work among women. Special articles by women missionaries provided me with substantial information on the attitudes that formed the notion of mission work among women. The *Missionary Advocate* was particularly important because it focused on mission work and was written by and for women. This gave me useful information about the ways in which mission work among women was supported.

The next archival sources I consulted were the government records at the Kenya National Archives in Nairobi. The National Archives house a wide range of documents, among which the following were explored: district files for North Nyanza, Elgon Nyanza, Kakamega, and Bungoma districts; provincial files for Nyanza province and Western province; the records of the Friends Africa Mission in microfilm; and the files of Maendeleo ya Wanawake (Women's Development). In addition to being properly cataloged, the material there was well preserved and provided me with some basic and background information. The National Archives documents were important because they shed light on the social, economic, and political situations within which the Quaker missionaries worked. With regard to women's work, both the government of the time and the missions shared the same philosophy, which was that women were to be prepared for good motherhood.

The third archives consulted were at St. Paul's Theological College in Limuru, Kenya, which houses interview transcripts, especially on the churches in Western Kenya. The transcribed oral interviews include those of Rasoah Mutua, the first Quaker woman to train as a pastor, whom I had met and interviewed, even though she was frail. The interview recorded at St. Paul's was from the mid-sixties, when she was more alert, and most of the information was confirmed from what has been written about her. The fourth archival source I consulted was the Friends' Kaimosi Office; Kaimosi was the first mission station established by the Friends Africa Mission (later East Africa Yearly Meeting of Friends) in 1902. These archives were housed in a small windowless room with heaps of papers on the floor; it was not open to anyone. The materials were kept under lock and key, secured by a dedicated staff member. It took some negotiation and confirmation that I was a researcher to gain access. The reason for this situation was that the East Africa Yearly Meeting was embroiled in internal power struggles among different groups, and those in Kaimosi tried to guard any files with information, especially those that contained financial details. It was believed that the archives contained important materials that the Kaimosi group could use against those they considered outsiders. There was no effort to organize the material for use by anyone. Despite the poor state of these records, by sifting through the materials I was able to find some voices of women like Rasoah Mutua, whose story has been told in various publications. She was the first woman to be theologically trained and a pastor whose ministry among women contributed immensely to the growth and development of the Quaker movement in East Africa.⁹ This essay, however, is about Maria Maraga, herself an important woman in the establishment of East African Quaker meetings.

The Story of Maria Maraga (Lungaho)

Maria Maraga, later known as Maria Maraga Lungaho, was the first woman reader in the first mission station of Kaimosi, founded by the Quakers in 1902. According to the information in the archives, Maria Maraga was *wamagumba*, the daughter of Magumba. She came from Bumbo, a village adjacent to the Kaimosi mission station, in November 1902, three months after the establishment of the outpost. She came to the Kaimosi station because she wanted to learn. Later she recalled, "When I was a girl, I used to long to go to the school too. I could hear the boys singing and reciting but my parents forbid me to go. Finally, after weeks, I determined I could just go anyway. So I rushed down and sat there on the earthen floor and tried to sing with them. Other girls joined me after that and even though our parents beat us we continued to go."¹⁰

This testimony indicates that she was a strong girl determined to follow her heart's desire to learn. She was intellectually keen and able to disobey her parents and join the boys in learning. Her testimony as to why and how she joined the mission station was confirmed through her eulogy, read at her funeral on November 19, 1956, along with some of the speeches that were given at that time.¹¹ Maria was determined to break with the tradition that kept the women home while the boys went to explore and learn with the missionaries. Seeing and hearing the boys' recited numbers and words, she chose to be part of the new community. The first literacy classes were not given to the girls because it was believed they did not require such knowledge.

Although Maria, according to her eulogy and other testimony at the funeral, joined the mission to learn, other sources say that she came to the mission because she was running away from a forced marriage.¹² This perspective on the reason for Maraga joining the mission fits well with the reasons that mission stations became rescue centers for both men and women who chose to break with the traditions of the time. While the reasons given for Maraga coming to the mission station depend somewhat on the perspectives of those who recorded the testimonies, both perspectives could be true. The first one depicts her agency and interest, while the second one fits the narratives of the time that record that the mission stations served as rescue centers for girls who were running away from their communities in order to escape initiation or marriage rites. The second reason appears to downplay women's agency: it ignores their desire and capacity to choose or be interested in coming to the mission center to learn to sing and recite—as in the case of Maria—just like the boys. It ignores the agency of women in following their passion and interest.

Maraga's life was both a testimony to and positive influence on other girls who joined her at the mission and became readers like her. Some of the girls found in archival records are Khahombi, the daughter of Namudeya; Jindia, daughter of Mahajikha; and Murini, daughter of Magumba.[13] The fact that other girls followed Maraga raises questions regarding the second reason above, because not all these girls were running away from marriage.

The archives do not provide much information about the first women readers, but the ones who are named served in the houses of the missionaries. Maraga worked in the house of Mr. and Mrs. Edgar Hole. This was before Maraga was married to Daudi Lungaho, in 1903, a year after the Kaimosi mission station was started and a few months after she arrived. While we do not know if she was running away from a forced marriage, she was soon married to a fellow reader. The union took place before the two were admitted into membership.

In 1905 Maraga and Lungaho were accepted as members of the Quaker meeting in Kaimosi and became the first readers. Each of them came from different Luyia communities: Maraga from the Tiriki, Lungaho from the Isukha. Maraga became the first convert from the Tiriki language group and the first woman convert to Quakerism in East Africa.[14] Maraga and Lungaho were the first African Quaker family in the Kaimosi mission, and they became key leaders not only at Kaimosi but in the entire region covered by Quakers. They took leadership roles both as individuals and as a family. Maraga was a key leader in founding the women's meetings, training girls and women in the roles of motherhood. Lungaho was a key leader for the meetings, advising the missionaries who worked in the region. Maraga and Lungaho were a first family in terms of interpreting mission work for their fellow Africans, as well as interpreting the African ways to the missionaries. The roles they played as individuals and as a family formulated most of the Kenyan Quaker ethos of the time. As a couple, they were an example of the African Christian family structure; as first Christians, others relied on them to interpret the new ways to the people; as community leaders, they influenced the decisions that were taken and the policies that were formulated to serve the early converts.

Both Maraga and Lungaho served as teachers and evangelists of the faith. The first family had nine children of their own, and they also cared for orphans from the community. Maria served in the mission station as a teacher to the girls who came to read. She trained them in Christian motherhood, and they got married to the first readers as she had done. Most of the first African Quaker men met their wives in the house of Maraga and Lungaho.[15] Notable among the new couples were Maraga's sisters Mariamu Inyanje, who married chief Paul Amiani, and Labeka Amigidzi, who married Yohana Amugune. Both couples were prominent in the spread of Quakerism in the pioneer years. With her sisters marrying prominent leaders in the community, the Quaker movement was identified with family ties crossing ethnic barriers and creating a new society through marriage. In later years the fact that the leadership was closely tied with family through marriage became a breeding ground for tensions, because of perceived nepotism.

Maria's home became the first dormitory for women in mission centers. The dormitories served the mission community in various ways, but two of them were significant. First, they were used as places to introduce the Christian faith to the girls, as Hoyt reports:

> The young girls, who want to be Christians, are asking the mission to provide a house where they can come each evening before dark to sleep, then go home to help their parents in the early morning. About twice a week I take a lantern and join them for half an hour, visiting with them. They tell me some of their folklore tales, and I tell them some Bible story. We sing together and have prayer. As time goes on, first one then another expresses her heart's desire to become Christian; then later they really say a prayer that their hearts may be clean. It may be months before they are really born again Christians as it takes time for them to understand the Gospel story. But ultimately they do accept Christ.[16]

The girls were not able to read like the boys, who had the time and freedom to do so. The girls only had nights to know the Bible. Becoming a Christian involved a process, as girls raised questions about this faith before accepting it.

Second, the dormitories acted as schools for preparing young women for "Christian marriage," as we see that the first leaders found their wives in Maraga's house. Marriage and Christianity were closely tied, a theme that warrants further study. According to available literature, marriage was central because it created units or clusters of families to grow the church. Through marriage women learned new aspects of motherhood in a different community. Training girls and marrying them off to Christian men created a clique of Quaker leaders related to one another by marriage. Moreover, the first Quaker communities were families, and knowledge and power circulated among these relatives through marriage.

In his report, Hoyt described Maraga as an exemplary mother with a gift for evangelism, her whole life serving as testimony of her faith to the people around her.[17] She understood her community well and was able to demonstrate what it meant to be a woman reader during her time. Maraga led the women in challenging traditions, like those regarding diet, that did not affirm them. An example is the taboo on eating chicken, which was reported throughout the reports and correspondence of missionaries and African converts. A mission article from 1920 states, "There is a custom among the natives, which forbids a woman to eat chicken. Recently this has become a test as to a woman's willingness to do that that has been considered a disgrace for generations and we are sure she will grow more in her Christian life since she has made the sacrifice and broken the custom that bind so many of the women. Often the husband is unwilling for his wife to eat this meat but again the husband will encourage his wife to do it."[18] Isaac Shinadira, a missionary on leave, wrote in a letter, "My friend, many greetings to you and your wife. But we ourselves we are well together with our wives. Also the women of Kaimosi they ate chicken on May the 3rd. Angu she ate and Kerangis and Maraga and the wife of Minamo and Mudonyi the wife of Chahali and Krindulu all these they are really [sic]."[19]

Rasoah Mutua, the first woman pastor, confirmed that breaking with the taboo was a challenge to the women in her community as well: "We ate chicken on the 14th of September 1926. It was a big thing. There was darkness when we ate chicken. The men did not like it. Those of the world [i.e., those who had not joined the church] began singing songs about us saying 'the people of Ford eat things that smell.' We were blamed for it but because women in Maragoli had already eaten and nothing had happened to them it was argued that God had confirmed the eating of *engoko*."[20] Maria Maraga was not the first to break the taboo against eating chicken; in fact, it was her sister Rabeka Amigidzi. Maraga led the women in Tiriki to break the taboo. The archives never give the reasons for the taboo, but they do state that breaking it became a mark for the women to become Christians. For Maraga and other women it was viewed as a protest against an age-old custom, which was a symbol of their subordination.

An Analysis of Quaker Women's Agency

The chicken was an especially important bird for the Luyia, among whom the first Quaker missionaries settled. The Luyia include some seventeen dialects or sub-ethnic groups in Western Kenya. The Quaker strongholds were in six of these groups. The chicken was used as part of the diet, as an honorable gift given to guests, and as an object for sacrifice in some rites of passage.[21] In this single creature lay the means to feed, to communicate feelings of honor toward respected guests, and to reach out to the spiritual world. As such, chicken had material, social, and religious significance in the communities where the early Quaker missionaries established work. The lack of chicken in any home meant much more than just a physical absence: it was symbolic of the inability of the members of that home to respond adequately to the physical, social, and spiritual realities of normal existence in the community. It is not surprising, therefore, that the acquisition and multiplication of chickens were important concerns in every home. Wealth creation began with possession of chickens and then proceeded to other animals, such as goats, sheep, and cattle. Thus chicken, in addition to being of material, social, and spiritual importance, also had economic significance.

Even though women played a central role in the rearing of this all-important fowl in their homes, it was taboo for them to eat it; they were told that if they did, they would be cursed to remain unmarried. If they did marry, they would supposedly have deformed children or no children at all.[22] The consequences of the curse were that they would be denied the chance of becoming mothers, something that accorded them status and value in society. As a result of this prohibition, men were effectively able to deny women the ability to enjoy the products of their labor. No such restrictions were applied to men.

The prohibition against chicken implied a defect in women from which men did not suffer, and so they were able to do what women could not do, without suffering the consequences. Because of this prohibition, men ensured that women saw marriage and childbearing as the only means by which society could accord them respect and value. And since men were the ones who initiated marriage contracts with women, it is easy to see how the prohibition myth allowed men in that society to determine and control the forces and means of production.

The way women were made producers of material, economic, social, and religious resources, but denied access to their control through a prohibition myth designed by men, is what is referred to here as a chicken ideology. The ideology was the bedrock on which was based the philosophy and defense of sexual inequality between men and women in all aspects of society. When Maria Maraga led the women to break with the taboo, there were mixed feelings about it. The shock with which the people received the news was an indication that the taboo was about more than food. Maraga and her friends were reacting not only against the diet but also against the thinking on which inequality was based.

According to Festo Lisamadi, the women who broke with the taboo were ridiculed through songs of shame that served as a warning to those who would dare do the same.[23] Some of the girls who followed Maraga suffered physical harm from their families. This was the case for Marita wa Ayima, a sister to the Headman Kisala.[24] Her brother felt she had brought shame to both their family and his administration, since as a headman he was a custodian of his people's traditions. If his own sister was going against them, then his authority was undermined. Although these girls suffered both physical and psychological torture, they married some of the early converts who supported the move but also wanted to marry women who had been converted like them. In the book *Good to Eat*, Marvin Harris notes, "If food ways are largely emanations of ignorant, religious, or symbolic thoughts, then it is what people think that needs to be changed. If, on the other hand, what seem like harmful religious or symbolic thoughts are actually themselves embodied in or constrained by practical circumstances surrounding the production and allocation of food resources, then it is these practical circumstances that need to be changed."[25]

In leading women to break with the taboo, Maraga was using her knowledge of the taboo and the thinking behind it to provide another way of being in the new community. Maraga was able to lead the women's protest because she was convinced of her independence. Married to a first convert and being one herself, she used the opportunity to be a leader influencing both men and women, especially those who married girls under her care.

As a first convert and a house help to the first missionaries, Maraga was engaged in mission work run by the missionary women of her time. This work had been influenced by the ideology of separate spheres that defined the notions of "space, work, gender, and power."[26] Through home visitations, sewing lessons, childcare, cookery, and prayer meetings, missionary wives disseminated this separate-spheres worldview. Maraga used her position to learn and to become crucial in teaching and preparing other women for leadership. Along with other women, she succeeded in starting women's weekday meetings that met on Thursdays or Fridays. In these meetings the women read the Bible together and discussed spiritual and pastoral concerns. These assemblies grew in numbers and strength so that by 1946 the women discussed how they would establish a separate Quaker meeting focusing on women. This was not realized until later, however, because the men were afraid of losing the women and the material and spiritual contributions they made to the meetings. Maraga died in 1956, but the seeds she planted for the women's meetings had begun to germinate and grow into what today are women's meetings that continue to grapple with issues of patriarchy in the church.

The story of Maraga as read from the archival sources is complex because it contains an implicit critique of missionary perceptions of the place and role of women. Missionary writings oscillate between two depictions of women: that of pity on the one hand, and of admiration on the other. What follows is a previously quoted pitiful description of women: "[She is] practically a slave, a beast of burden, reckoned as just so much 'Mali' (property)"; "Womanhood is reduced to servitude, doomed to drudgery as mere beasts of burden"; "The women [are] bulwarks of superstition"; "Womanhood in Africa is womanhood without God."[27] A second description expresses admiration: "Almost the whole tribal organisation is built about the women of the tribe. They are a chief source of wealth, but their influence in maintaining the tribal custom is very great. Women carry the heavy load, for she is the burden bearer for the tribe."[28]

While missionary writings oscillate between these two paradigms of pity and awe, missionary work among women was established mostly on the basis of pity. The story of Maraga and the women she mentored is a challenge to this depiction, since it brings to light women demonstrating resilience, independence, and power. Her agency shows that they understood patriarchy and were able to create an identity by appropriating power, rather than being usurped by it.

The narratives of pity and awe fail to honor the ways in which women knew and understood the realities of both African and missionary patriarchies. Maria Maraga and other Quaker women like her were neither helpless victims nor the bastions of either African or missionary customs. The cases of Maria Maraga and the girls she prepared for marriage offer other narratives: narratives of subversion, but also of leadership that was significant for the growth of the mission. The standard depictions misrepresent women's lives, which in modern times have yet to be interpreted and represented.

This essay was about searching for the voices of women in the archives, namely through the case of Maria Maraga, the first woman convert from her community. We have noted the difficulties the researcher experiences in locating archival material dealing with women. We have also shown how women are rendered invisible and therefore powerless because their lives have not been reported. But the case of Maria has shown a way in which women's lives refuse to be identified with such trajectories of invisibility and powerlessness.

Notes

1. Adrian Hastings, "Were Women a Special Case?," in *Women and Missions: Past and Present, Anthropological and Historical Perceptions*, ed. Fiona Bowie, Deborah Kirkwood, and Shirley Ardener (Providence, RI: Berg, 1993), 110. See also Elizabeth Isichei, *A History of Christianity in Africa from Antiquity to the Present* (London: SPCK, 1995), 87, 190.

2. David Henige, *Oral Historiography* (London: Longman, 1982), 48.

3. Jan Vansina, *Oral Tradition: A Study in Historical Method* (London: Routledge and Kegan Paul, 1965), 195.

4. Fiona Bowie, "Introduction: Reclaiming Women's Presence," in *Women and Missions: Past and Present, Anthropological and Historical Perceptions*, ed. Fiona Bowie, Deborah Kirkwood, and Shirley Ardener (Providence, RI: Berg, 1993), 1.

5. Cherryl Walker, "Women and Gender in Southern Africa to 1945: An Overview," in *Women and Gender in Southern Africa to 1945*, ed. Cherryl Walker (London: James Currey, 1990), 3.

6. Mercy Amba Oduyoye, "The Search for a Two-Winged Theology: Women's Participation in the Development of Theology in Africa," in *Talitha Qumi!* ed. Mercy Amba Oduyoye and Musimbi Kanyoro (Ibadan: Daystar Press, 1990), 22.

7. Letter from Arthur Chilson, February 3, 1921, Kenya National Archives (hereafter KNA), Nairobi.

8. Willis Ray Hotchkiss, *Sketches from the Dark Continent* (London: Headley Brothers, 1903), quotes from pp. 30, 113, 55, and 80, respectively.

9. Esther Mombo, "*Harahamisi* and *Jumaa*: The Development of the Women's Meetings in East Africa Yearly Meeting of Friends (Quakers)," in *Her-Stories: Hidden Histories of Women of Faith in Africa*, ed. Isabel Apawo Phiri, Devarakshanam Betty Govinden, and Sarojini Nadar (Pietermaritzburg, South Africa: Cluster, 2002), 59–83.

10. Alta Hoyt, *We Were Pioneers* (Wichita: privately published, 1971), 36.

11. "Historia Yu Mushere Musaanji FAM Yearly Meeting. Maria Maraga Lung'aho Mukhaana wu Khuranga Wa Magumba," November 19, 1956, Friends' Kaimosi Office, Kaimosi, Western Kenya.

12. Thomas Lung'aho Ganira, *Daudi Lung'aho, An African Missionary, a Biography* (Tiriki, Kenya: East Africa Yearly Meeting of Friends, 1970), 9.
13. Ibid.
14. Friends African Mission report, 1905, KNA.
15. Ganira, *Daudi Lung'aho*, 26.
16. Hoyt, *We Were Pioneers*, 5.
17. Alta Hoyt, personal report, 1911, KNA.
18. "Chilsons Describe New Work," *American Friend*, March 18, 1920, 273.
19. Letter from Isaac Shinadira to Mr. Conover, November 23, 1920, KNA.
20. Rasoah Mutua, oral interview with the author, February 27, 1996.
21. Joseph Daniel Otiende, *Habari ca Abaluyia* (Nairobi: Eagle Press, 1949), 28; Daniel M. Wako, *The Western Abaluyia and Their Proverbs* (Nairobi: Kenya Literature Bureau, 1985), 15–16.
22. Bridget O'Laughlin, "Mediation of Contradiction: Why Mbum Women Do Not Eat Chicken," in *Woman, Culture, and Society*, ed. Michelle Zimbalist Rosaldo and Louise Lamphere (Stanford, CA: Stanford University Press, 1974), 302; John Robson, ed., *Food, Ecology and Culture: Readings in the Anthropology of Dietary Practices* (London: Gordon and Breach, 1980), 97–117; Olivia Nassaka, "Women and Taboo," in *Groaning in Faith: African Women in the Household of God*, ed. Musimbi R. A. Kanyoro and Nyambura Njoroge (Nairobi: Acton, 1996), 164. Among the Baganda, Nassaka notes that "a woman who was still of childbearing age should not eat eggs and chicken. If a woman broke this taboo, she would be regarded as a thief and an indecent woman."
23. Festo Lisamadi, oral interview, December 14, 1967, St. Paul's United Theological College.
24. Henry Asava, *Liguula lie lihandika* (Kisumu, Kenya: Evangel Press, 1968), 7.
25. Marvin Harris, *Good to Eat: Riddles of Food and Culture* (London: Allen and Unwin, 1986), 236.
26. Henrietta L. Moore, *Space, Text, and Gender: An Anthropological Study of the Marakwet of Kenya* (Cambridge, UK: Cambridge University Press, 1986), 147–52.
27. Hotchkiss, *Sketches from the Dark Continent*, quotes from pp. 30, 113, 55, and 80, respectively.
28. American Friends Board of Foreign Mission, *Fifteen Years in East Africa* (Richmond, IN: AFBFM Press, 1917), 3.

Works Cited

American Friends Board of Foreign Mission. *Fifteen Years in East Africa*. Richmond, IN: AFBFM Press, 1917.
Asava, Henry. *Liguula lie lihandika*. Kisumu, Kenya: Evangel Press, 1968.
Bowie, Fiona. "Introduction: Reclaiming Women's Presence." In *Women and Missions: Past and Present, Anthropological and Historical Perceptions*, edited by Fiona Bowie, Deborah Kirkwood, and Shirley Ardener, 1–19. Providence, RI: Berg, 1993.
Bowie, Fiona, Deborah Kirkwood, and Shirley Ardener, eds. *Women and Missions: Past and Present, Anthropological and Historical Perceptions*. Providence, RI: Berg, 1993.
Ganira, Thomas Lung'aho. *Daudi Lung'aho, an African Missionary, a Biography*. Tiriki, Kenya: East Africa Yearly Meeting of Friends, 1970.
Harris, Marvin. *Good to Eat: Riddles of Food and Culture*. London: Allen and Unwin, 1986.
Hastings, Adrian. "Were Women a Special Case?" In *Women and Missions: Past and Present, Anthropological and Historical Perceptions*, edited by Fiona Bowie, Deborah Kirkwood, and Shirley Ardener, 109–25. Providence, RI: Berg, 1993.

Henige, David. *Oral Historiography*. London: Longman, 1982.

Hotchkiss, Willis Ray. *Sketches from the Dark Continent*. London: Headley Brothers, 1903.

Hoyt, Alta. *We Were Pioneers*. Wichita: privately published, 1971.

Isichei, Elizabeth. *A History of Christianity in Africa from Antiquity to the Present*. London: SPCK, 1995.

Mombo, Esther. "*Harahamisi* and *Jumaa*: The Development of the Women's Meetings in East Africa Yearly Meeting of Friends (Quakers)." In *Her-Stories: Hidden Histories of Women of Faith in Africa*, edited by Isabel Apawo Phiri, Devarakshanam Betty Govinden, and Sarojini Nadar, 59–83. Pietermaritzburg, South Africa: Cluster, 2002.

Moore, Henrietta L. *Space, Text, and Gender: An Anthropological Study of the Marakwet of Kenya*. Cambridge, UK: Cambridge University Press, 1986.

Nassaka, Olivia. "Women and Taboo." In *Groaning in Faith: African Women in the Household of God*, edited by Musimbi R. A. Kanyoro and Nyambura J. Njoroge, 163–67. Nairobi: Acton, 1996.

Oduyoye, Mercy Amba. "The Search for a Two-Winged Theology: Women's Participation in the Development of Theology in Africa." In *Talitha Qumi! Proceedings of the Convocation of African Women Theologians*, edited by Mercy Amba Oduyoye and Musimbi Kanyoro, 27–50. Ibadan: Daystar Press, 1990.

O'Laughlin, Bridget. "Mediation of Contradiction: Why Mbum Women Do Not Eat Chicken." In *Woman, Culture, and Society*, edited by Michelle Zimbalist Rosaldo and Louise Lamphere, 301–18. Stanford, CA: Stanford University Press, 1974.

Otiende, Joseph Daniel. *Habari za Abaluyia*. Nairobi: Eagle Press, 1949.

Robson, John R. K., ed. *Food, Ecology and Culture: Readings in the Anthropology of Dietary Practices*. London: Gordon and Breach, 1980.

Vansina, Jan. *Oral Tradition: A Study in Historical Method*. London: Routledge and Kegan Paul, 1965.

Wako, Daniel M. *The Western Abaluyia and Their Proverbs*. Nairobi: Kenya Literature Bureau, 1985.

Walker, Cherryl. "Women and Gender in Southern Africa to 1945: An Overview." In *Women and Gender in Southern Africa to 1945*, edited by Cherryl Walker, 1–32. London: James Currey, 1990.

EARLY COLONIAL CATHOLICISM

Chapter 4

IN SEARCH OF KIRISHITAN WOMEN MARTYRS' VOICES IN THE EARLY MODERN JESUIT MISSION LITERATURE IN JAPAN

Haruko Nawata Ward

During the first half of the seventeenth century, over four thousand Japanese Christians, known as Kirishitans, became martyrs in Japan.[1] Of these, the names and some details of about two hundred women have been identified.[2] As of 2017, the Catholic Church had canonized two women martyrs as saints and beatified 150 women and girls. This mass martyrdom of women is surprising for two reasons. First, the number far exceeded that of martyrdoms in any Reformation camps in Europe and elsewhere. Second, Japanese religious traditions did not have any notion of martyrdom, and hitherto state executions for one's religious convictions had not occurred. Why did women choose to become martyrs? Since the Japanese authorities destroyed almost all writings of these female martyrs and survivors, it is challenging to search for their own explanations.

One of the possible ways to hear women's voices is to explore extant texts of Kirishitan literature, which the Jesuit missionaries, Japanese Jesuits, and Kirishitan women collaborated to produce. Some hagiographic texts of Kirishitan literature, which I discuss in this essay, convey a communal and interreligious theology of martyrdom, which women also shared. This common theology also prepared women to voice their resistance against gender oppression.

Historical Development of the Jesuit Japan Mission, Kirishitan Literature, Persecution, and Women

Francis Xavier (1506–1552), a Jesuit missionary, introduced Christianity to Japan in 1549 and left for China in 1551. During his brief stay, he recognized the potential for evangelization by communicating Catholic concepts using Buddhist ones. Although his own experiments were famously disastrous, his Jesuit successors took seriously this intersection of Catholicism and Buddhism.³ Soon they discovered that there were at least twelve different schools of Buddhism, some of whose practices had become closely amalgamated with Shinto. As early as the 1560s, Portuguese missionaries such as Luís Fróis (1532–1597) studied Buddhist texts and practices with the help of Japanese converts, many of whom were former Buddhist monks. The Society of Jesus Japan Mission (hereafter Jesuit Mission) admitted hundreds of male converts into their ranks of catechists (*dōjucu* and *cambō*), brothers (*irmãos*), and, beginning in 1601, priests (*padres*).⁴ By its *Constitutions*, the Society of Jesus is a male clerical order without a female branch; in Japan, the Jesuits did not admit women converts as *dōjucu*, nor did they found a female branch. Still, many Kirishitan women worked alongside these Jesuits and lay leaders until the close of the "Christian century" in the 1650s.⁵ These male and female converts supplied religious knowledge for the production of Kirishitan literature.

Recognizing the success of Kirishitan literature, Visitor Alessandro Valignano (1539–1606) imported a movable-type printing press in 1590, and the Jesuit Press in Japan began publishing books in 1591.⁶ By the time of the Great Expulsion of missionaries from Japan in 1614, the press had published at least sixty titles of Kirishitanban (entitled Christian editions).⁷ One of the first publications was a translation of hagiographies, titled *Sanctos no gosagveo no vchi nvqigaqi* (Excerpts from the *Acts of the Saints*), which I examine further below.

The Jesuits and their lay assistants carried out these literary activities amid the constant threat of regional wars and persecutions. When Xavier arrived in 1549, Japan had been divided into sixty-six fiefdoms, each of which was ruled by daimyo or warrior lords. These lords waged wars to expand their territories and gain central ruling power as the Ashikaga Shogunate (1478–1573) was on its last legs. Strongmen Oda Nobunaga (1534–1582) and Toyotomi Hideyoshi (1536–1598) successively rose to positions of "unifiers." In this rapidly shifting political landscape, the Jesuits had to rely on patronage and the mercy of local lords as well as these unifiers. They also needed to work in the context of complex international geopolitics in the age of European expansion into Asia. From the European point of view, Jesuit missionaries went to Japan rightly under the Portuguese *padroado real* (royal patronage), based on the Treaty of Tordesillas (1492). But the Portuguese Crown never acquired the military power to colonize faraway Japan and only desired trading rights. The Jesuits did not receive full financial support from Portugal. The Japanese lords and unifiers regarded the Jesuit missionaries as negotiating middlemen for the profitable Portuguese trade. Under these conditions, the Jesuit Mission practiced a policy of cultural accommodation rather than aggressive proselytization. Kirishitan conversions steadily increased, especially where lords also converted to become Kirishitan; in other places, however, the Jesuit Mission met local persecution.

In 1587, Hideyoshi issued the *Edict of Expulsion of Padres*, the first nationwide ban on Christianity, but did not strictly enforce it and ignored the Jesuits who continued their quiet mission. Books continued to be useful for communicating Christian ideas, as evidenced in the case of Lady Hosokawa Tama Gracia (1563–1600), who though confined to her residence by her husband received baptism by her lady-in-waiting Kiyohara Ito Maria (n.d.) and exchanged letters with the Jesuits. She studied, taught, and composed Kirishitan literature and possibly contributed revisions to *Contemptus mundi*, a translation of the *Imitation of Christ*. By 1595, the Kirishitan population grew to about 240,000, just over 1.3 percent of the total population. In 1597, Hideyoshi ordered the execution of twenty-three Franciscans and three Jesuits in Nagasaki. This was the first public execution of missionaries and lay Kirishitans. In his last years, beginning in 1591, Hideyoshi rose to the highest ranks of both imperial court official and government minister. Between 1592 and 1598, he also invaded Korea and China, bringing back hundreds of Korean hostages. In a few years, many of these hostages joined the Jesuit Mission as brothers and *dōjucu*. Such Korean women leaders as Ōta Julia (n.d.) and Pak Marina (ca. 1572–1636) would later perish in exile, and Isabel of Unzen died as a martyr in 1630.

After the Spanish conquest of Manila around 1570, the mendicant orders (Franciscans, Dominicans, and Augustinians) in the Philippines under the Spanish *patronato real* (royal patronage) began to seek entry into Japan. The Spanish annexation of Portugal (1580–1640) weakened Portuguese influence in Asia. Challenging Pope Gregory XIII's bull in 1585, which allowed only the Jesuits under the Portuguese *padroado* to labor in Japan, the mendicants secured Pope Paul V's bull in 1608, which legitimated their work in Japan. Not waiting for this bull, Franciscans began their mission in 1593,

Dominicans in 1602, and Augustinians in 1603. The Jesuit Mission expressed their anxieties about the mendicants' open proselytization, which disregarded their cultural accommodation and persuasion model of mission. They were also critical of the mendicants' recruitment of local converts into their membership in the third order of men and women, without proper education.[8] These intra-Catholic conflicts among the orders—connected to different Iberian patronages, the arrival of the Dutch East India Company in 1600, and the final unification of Japan under Tokugawa Ieyasu (1543–1616; r. 1603–5)—shifted the Japanese government's attitude toward Kirishitans. Ieyasu obtained the title of shogun (generalissimo) in 1603 and established the Tokugawa government, which lasted until 1867.

While the Tokugawa shogunate was consolidating its hegemony until 1615, it made many policies not only in its governing structure but also in its dealings with religious affairs. In 1607 Ieyasu—who abdicated his shogunal seat to his son Hidetada in 1605 but still exercised his authority as *ōgosho* (retired shogun)—established the *jukan*, or shogunal advisory office of Confucian scholars, who issued documents for social, educational, and religious policies based on Confucian principles. Still the Kirishitan population grew, reaching 370,000 by 1612. The Jesuits attributed the conversion of six thousand men and women in the Kyoto area between 1600 and 1612 to Naitō Julia (ca. 1566–1627) and the Miyako no bicuni, working with other women catechists. Julia, a former Buddhist abbess, founded the Miyako no bicuni, a society of nuns modeled after the Jesuit active apostolate, around 1600 with the approval of Fathers Gnechi-Soldo Organtino (1533–1609) and Pedro Moréjon (1562–1639). These women catechists utilized Kirishitan books in their ministries and possibly contributed to the writings of textbooks dealing with interreligious dialogue, such as *Myōtei mondō*, which Brother Fabian Fucan (ca. 1565–1621) published in 1605. In 1612, the second Shogun Hidetada (1579–1632; r. 1605–23) reissued the ban on Christianity and ordered the arrest of foreign missionaries and Kirishitans. In the so-called Great Expulsion of 1614, most of the Jesuits, mendicants, and several Kirishitan leaders were deported from Japan. Naitō Julia and fourteen members of her Miyako no bicuni were exiled to Manila with Father Moréjon and seven other Jesuit priests, fifteen brothers, and fifteen *dōjucu*. During Hidetada's reign, a total of 353 men and 73 women perished in the "Great Martyrdoms" in Kyoto (1619), Nagasaki (1622), and Tokyo (1623) and in other smaller-scale executions.

The third Shogun Iemitsu (1604–1651; r. 1623–51) thoroughly systematized the institutions and methods of Kirishitan extermination. Simultaneously, he exercised a xenophobic isolation policy and terminated Iberian contacts, beginning with Spain in 1624 and Portugal in 1639. Strict travel bans prohibited Japanese from going in and out of Japan. In 1636, all mixed-blood descendants of unions between European men and Japanese women were deported. The government issued five edicts of *sakoku* (closing of the nation) between 1633 and 1639 and in 1641 constructed the artificial island of Deshima in Nagasaki to enclose the facilities of its only Western trading partner, the Dutch East India Company, and sealed off all other borders. In 1630, the government prohibited the importation of any Christian publications from the West. Between 1637 and 1638, oppressed peasants in the Amakusa-Shimabara region rose to protest heavy taxation and forced labor. These thirty-seven thousand peasants, mostly Kirishitan men, women, and children, gathered under the charismatic soldier Amakusa Shirō Tokisada Jeronimo (ca. 1622–1638) who, waving his banner decorated with Eucharistic images, laid siege to the Hara Castle in Shimabara.[9] After a fierce battle, the government army of one hundred thousand massacred them all. This open "Kirishitan" rebellion alarmed the authorities. Already in 1636, the office of Nagasaki *bugyō* (magistrate) was ordered to strictly punish any suspicious Kirishitans. The neighborhood watch system functioned to expose any crypto-Kirishitan activities. Beginning in 1619 and continuing until 1870, *kōsatsu* plaques, which promised monetary rewards to those who informed on hiding missionaries and Kirishitan priests and brothers, were placed in every town center. Between 1624 and 1637, 798 male names and 250 female names are recorded as martyrs in Jesuit reports. Throughout this period, the Jesuits reported that Kirishitans read Kirishitan literature at their assemblies and that individual Kirishitan women martyrs and survivors of torture, such as Blessed Takeda Inez (ca. 1573–1603), Majencia of Kibaru (d. 1614), Ōta Julia (n.d.), and Luzia de la Cruz (ca. 1580–1656), owned and read Kirishitan hagiography and aspired to imitate Christ and martyr saints.

Kirishitans spoke against the imposition of one state religion of the Toyotomi and Tokugawa, who created their own cult of founder deities and placed all traditional religions under government control. In 1640, the shogunate set up the office of religious inquisition (*shūmon aratame*), notorious for its brutal torture to induce apostasy. They employed Buddhist priests and monks to coax Kirishitans to denounce their faith and to reeducate the apostate (*korobi*) in Confucian principles. The authorities required every Japanese citizen to be a certified member of the precinct Buddhist temple, and one of the duties of the inquisition was to conduct annual *efumi* examination at these temples, where each person was to step on the sacred Kirishitan image to show that he or she was not a Kirishitan. The raids into the underground Kirishitan communities continued under the fourth Shogun Ietsuna (1620–1680; r. 1651–80), lasting through 1790. The raids of 1657–58 in the greater Ōmura region produced 330 martyrs, of whom two hundred were women. The ban of Christianity continued while the government changed to the Meiji imperial government in 1868. The government finally lifted the ban in 1870 after the mass arrests of resurfaced Kirishitans between 1865 and 1870. During the long years of suppression, the underground Kirishitans preserved some Kirishitan literature, including the stories of certain saints.

Did Women Speak?

The search for past women's voices stands in continuity with the recent efforts to correct assumptions that women cannot be main subjects of historical research because no adequate sources by and on women in premodern societies exist. Since the 1970s, US-based historians have made great strides in uncovering women's histories in late medieval and early modern Europe. Sensitized by the women's liberation movement, pioneers such as Joan Kelly-Gadol (1928–1982) and Gerda Lerner (1920–2013) pursued sociocultural, anthropological, and political questions for rewriting history to make it more gender-inclusive. Soon followed numerous rediscoveries and an explosion of publications in critical editions and translations of once-forgotten women's writings. Between the 1980s and early 2000s, such social historians as Natalie Zemon Davis and Merry Wiesner-Hanks explored various aspects of gender and class power relations in women's lives, thoughts, and religions. Wiesner-Hanks, who published *Women and Gender in Early Modern Europe* in 1993 and revised it twice (in 2000 and 2008), also published *Christianity and Sexuality in the Early Modern World* first in 2000 and revised it in 2010. In this later version, she began to underscore the shift of focus toward global women's history. Current trends in revisionist histories are turning their attention to these "other" women as subjects. A newer search for the voices of women in the early modern world, led by Allyson Poska and others, has produced some good results, especially in transatlantic connections. Histories of early modern religious women in Asia are being written; however, while encyclopedic works demonstrate sophisticated approaches in examining various historical sources, Elizabeth Lehfeldt's chapter in *Ashgate Research Companion to Women and Gender in*

Early Modern Europe (2013) is the only place where the geography stretches to Japan, tacked on in a footnote. Historians of Japanese Buddhist women have offered much insightful research, such as Barbara Ruch's *Engendering Faith: Women and Buddhism in Premodern Japan* (2002). In comparison, only a few studies on Kirishitan women have appeared.

The case of Kirishitan women affiliated with the Japanese Jesuit Mission blurs the assumed sharp boundaries between the missionary and the missionized, colonial and the colonized, foreign and indigenous, and official and local Christianities in early modern global Catholicism. Biases in Reformation-era religious histories also contributed to the tardiness of research. Previously, Protestant scholarship predominated in North American studies of the Reformation, which anachronistically viewed "Rome" as the central power of Catholicism, and the orders as a monolithic, reactionary, and oppositional force against the Protestant Reformation, with the Jesuits as the legates of the pope pushing for the conquest of the whole world. This false assumption began to be corrected when John O'Malley published *The First Jesuits* in 1993 and introduced the voices of the early Jesuits, often struggling within the vibrant Catholic Reform movement. Since then, while maintaining healthy postcolonial critical perspectives on the study of the Jesuit missionary movement, historians of various Jesuit missions have uncovered evidence of the local agents, such as converts, translators, "native" clergy, antagonist rulers, women, war hostages, and slaves, who participated in, criticized, and transformed Catholicism into a local religion. While the Council of Trent (1545–63) forbade the translation of the Bible into vernacular languages, these missions, including the one in Japan, kept translating literature, including stories of the saints, which contained numerous biblical passages. Kirishitan literature was one of the products of such efforts.

The Council of Trent also reinforced the enclosure of women religious under the supervision of a parochial male hierarchy. However, in the renewed Catholic world, women and the Jesuits circumvented many rules, as in the case of Naitō Julia and the Miyako no bicuni. After the Japanese officials arrested, publicly tortured, and expelled them, other women continued in their apostolic ministries. While there are very few records about these women, the Jesuits, facing their own imminent arrest, left brief but numerous accounts of their martyrdom. Sifting through these to find women's voices may reveal other problems with historiographical assumptions. While not all women who aspired for martyrdom attained it, those women who went underground still treasured the stories of women martyr saints.

Creating Kirishitan Stories of Virgin Martyr Saints

The Catholic Reform focused on saints in Catholic devotion, and streamlined various medieval hagiographic traditions to identify important early church martyr saints. Kirishitan translations of these stories also took place during this period. Several points need to be made clear about the process of these translations.

First, as noted above, the translations were done in teams consisting of missionaries and Kirishitans. The Jesuit Mission did not seek prestige for a single author. This does not mean that the chief translators' responsibility was unclear. Often the chief translators state their intentions in their prefaces and sign their names. They emphasize that the work was done in collaboration with their colleagues, who were of the same mind.[10] Similarly, Maria Tymoczko gives an illustration of a Chinese history of translation, in which "teams of translators have traditionally worked together, with each member of the team operating primarily within a single linguistic and cultural framework." Tymoczko goes on to describe that "the first stage of translation is performed by a person with primary knowledge of and even loyalties to the source language and culture, followed by a polishing stage undertaken by someone with clear loyalties to the receptor language and culture (for example, a native in the receiving language often with mutual or no knowledge of the source language), with the whole process under the eye of an ideological supervisor."[11] It is very possible that women helped in polishing female discourses in stories of the female saints in Japanese, which is a highly gendered and class-conscious language, with female speech distinct from male speech, in each gradation of social class.

The second point is that the translators consciously chose characters for a gender-inclusive audience. The Japanese writing system used three kinds of characters: logographic *kanji* of Chinese origin, phonetic *kana* in syllabic units, and a combination of both, *kanamajiri*. The Jesuits added Roman alphabets (*rōmaji*) for phonetic transliteration. The translators of Kirishitan stories rejected *kanbun*, which is written only in *kanji* and read only by male elites. They decisively chose *kanamajiri*, which was most accessible to women readers. They also used *rōmaji*, which literate women also read.

Third, these translators preserved the orality of the Japanese text. In Japanese literary history, reading "involved a pronounced level of orality, typically in sociable settings, along with the strongly visual component imposed by the writing system."[12] The Jesuits were quick to adopt this custom of reading out loud or reciting, which was especially suited to church gatherings.[13] Stories of the saints were sung at first by Jesuit brothers, who had been former Buddhist ballad singer-storytellers, and the audience gave their feedback.[14]

Finally, the translators freely adapted Buddhist concepts and terminologies, both of which were commonly used.[15] Many converts were former leaders and practitioners in Zen or Jōdo (Pure Land) Buddhism. Others had also observed a sort of syncretistic medieval Shinto-Buddhism-folk religious tradition. The team also chose vocabulary from emerging neo-Confucianism, which fit to express a sense of honor toward the hierarchy of the Christian God, saints, and sacred objects. At the same time, if there were no equivalent between existing religious terms, they retained words in transliterated Portuguese, Latin, and Spanish.[16] At other times, they produced neologisms.

These patterns made Kirishitan translations at points both like and unlike traditional European and Japanese literature. Recent translation studies offer diverse definitions of translation beyond the modern Western obsession with the "accuracy" of linguistic transfer from a source text to a target language. A. E. B. Coldiron's examination of English translations of French Renaissance devotional literature shows a creativity akin to Kirishitan translations. These English translators freely added or omitted texts according to their needs of gender and religious discourses and, as a result, their translations took "on an independent life."[17] Kirishitan translators, too, were not literalists but more like "transwriters," as Li Sher-Shiueh saw from a case in the Jesuit China mission.[18]

Kirishitan translations appeared not as a product of the simple transfer of imposed colonial agendas and went beyond bilateral cultural exchange or indigenization. Rebekah Clements's study of early modern translations in Japan shows that in the history of Chinese-Japanese translation practices, "linguistic hybridization" was a normal feature.[19] In this tradition, "dichotomies between 'word for word' and 'sense for sense' or 'faithful' versus 'unfaithful' were not used." Instead, "the translators of the Tokugawa period also unashamedly omitted, and in places embellished, their source texts."[20] Thus translation may also connote "representation, transfer or transmission, transculturation, rewriting, and refraction," which can be classified as "digests, commentaries, vernacularizations, and parodies." Further, "'translation' exists as part of a network of other rewritings and refractions of the subject text and it may often be difficult to distinguish from other kinds of rewriting."[21] Even though Clements does not discuss Kirishitan literature, all these features apply to Kirishitan translations. As Clements cites and modifies Indra Levy's theory, Kirishitan translations, too, spoke in a "tertiary language, one that is not entirely 'foreign' or 'domestic,' but that clearly meditates between the two," and "may have a transformative effect on the target culture."[22] In Kirishitan translations of stories of the virgin martyr saints, while there were many positive retentions from the Buddhist culture, voices against its gender oppression resound in hopes of religious and societal transformation.

In at least two of three existent collections of Kirishitan stories, four virgin martyr saints make repeat appearances and thus seem to have been most popular. The prototype stories of St. Anastasia, St. Catherine of Alexandria, and St. Eugenia have similar descriptions of brutal torture and cruel executions. All three women were very learned princesses. St. Marina, the only nonexecuted martyr, came from a humbler background. The stories of St. Eugenia and St. Marina share a similar plotline as both women cross-dressed to pass as males and were accused of raping women. It appears that the stories of St. Eugenia and St. Marina were used to convey shifting voices of Kirishitan women over time.

Yōfō Paulo's Translation of St. Eugenia

Two texts of St. Eugenia's story are extant. One is in *Sanctos no gosagveo no vchi nvqigaqi* (Excerpts from the *Acts of the Saints*; hereafter *Nvqigaqi*), published in 1591.[23] Another is found in *Vidas gloriosas de algũns Sanctos e Sanctas* (Glorious lives of some male and female saints), a manuscript collection within the so-called Barreto copy (hereafter *Vidas*), dating also from around 1591.[24] Both texts use *rōmaji*. Kunimichi Fukushima compares these two and finds only some slight variations.[25] *Nvqigaqi* is a little more detailed. For example, the chapter heading of St. Eugenia's story in *Nvqigaqi* is "The Acts and Martyrdom of Virgin Saint Eugenia and Her Servants Protho and Iacinto; Found in *The Lives of the Fathers*, which St. Jerome edited, and the first volume of St. Antonino's writings. December 25," showing the source texts and the feast day.[26] The title in *Vidas* simply says, "On St. Eugenia and Her Servants Protho and Iacinto."[27]

The major difference is that *Nvqigaqi* names its translators. Brother Yōfō Paulo (ca. 1508–1595) and his son, Brother Vicente Tōin (ca. 1540–1609), translated the entire collection, in which Yōfō Paulo signed his name for four chapters, including that on St. Eugenia, and Vicente Tōin signed his name on twenty-nine. This demonstrates that the Jesuit Press did not hesitate to publish the names of these Japanese Jesuit brothers as the chief translators-editors without any accompanying European missionaries' names. Details of Yōfō Paulo's Japanese full name and earlier life are not known, except that he was a medical doctor from Wakasa.[28] He received his baptism from Father Gaspar Vilela (1525–1572) in Kyoto in 1560. He lived with his family and ran a medical practice in Sakai during the 1560s. It is most likely that during this time Yōfō Paulo frequented the house of Hibiya Ryōkei Diogo (n.d.) in Sakai. Ryōkei Diogo, a wealthy merchant, was a major patron of the Jesuit mission. He offered his large estate for the use of Father Vilela, Father Fróis and Brother Luís de Almeida (1522–1583), also a surgeon. It was there these Jesuits began the communal translating projects of the saints' stories. Records indicate that they learned much about gender-specific Japanese language and culture especially from the Hibiya's devout daughter Monica (ca. 1549–ca. 1577). It is imaginable that Yōfō Paulo also participated in these conversations.[29] Soon Yōfō Paulo found a new vocation, left his medical practice to his son Vicente Tōin to become *dōjucu* (assistant) to Father Cosme de Torres (1510–70), moved to Shimabara, and began his itinerant preaching around Kyushu. In 1580 the Society admitted both Yōfō Paulo and Vicente Tōin as Jesuit brothers, and Yōfō Paulo taught at the newly founded Jesuit College of Funai.[30] While the college relocated several times, Yōfō Paulo remained in the Funai district until he joined the Nagasaki Miséricordia sometime between 1589 and 1592 and died there in 1595.

The Japanese Jesuit Mission catalog of 1593, which gives information on all the members' language abilities in Latin and Japanese, lists Yōfō Paulo as the first among twenty-eight "Japanese Scholastic Brothers who have not mastered Latin but know Japanese letters only."[31] This list has made some historians think that Yōfō Paulo did not know European languages. This assumption is problematic because the catalog does not state the standard for measuring language skills. Most of the non-Japanese priests and brothers get high marks for their knowledge of the Japanese language, especially if they can preach in it, and their ability in Latin is not even questioned. While four of twelve non-Japanese young theological students are said to have "good knowledge of Japanese language," only five out of thirty-five of their Japanese classmates also have "good knowledge of Japanese literature," and others "mediocre" or "no" knowledge. Some Japanese students were advancing in Latin. The catalog gives a reverential description of eighty-five-year-old Yōfō Paulo, who "has been distinguished in the Japanese literature" and "has given great service to the Society with his literature" during his long tenure. However, even though his literary ability in Japanese is undebatable, we cannot be too quick to dismiss his knowledge of Iberian languages as he worked closely for decades with Portuguese missionaries, who may have been able to speak Japanese fluently but still used Portuguese in their written communications. It is doubtful that Yōfō Paulo translated St. Eugenia's story from the original Latin of St. Jerome and St. Antonino, as the chapter title states, and perhaps not the standard Latin translation from the anonymous Greek original.[32] It is possible that he used versions in Portuguese or Spanish as his source texts, as the missionaries may have brought these with them.

His wide-ranging literary contributions make it impossible to argue that Yōfō Paulo only knew Japanese. In his chronicle of the activities of the Jesuit Mission in 1560 in *História de Japam*, Luís Fróis describes how Father Vilela and Brother Lourenço debated with Buddhists, how Japanese converts helped them in understanding Buddhism, and he inserts paragraphs introducing Yōfō Paulo and Vicente Fōin. Fróis says that Dr. Yofoquen [sic] is "a distinguished man of Japanese language," and names three works that Yōfō Paulo later helped produce: namely, *Arte ne Lingua Japão* (Grammar of Japanese language); *Vocabulario* (Portuguese-Japanese dictionary); and *Doctrina Christiam* (Catechism).[33] Fróis goes on to attest to the literary talents of Yōfō Paulo, who helped the Jesuit Mission in the translations of "many lives of saints and other works by our [European] authors." Fróis concludes that the Japanese always want to hear the "elegance, beauty, and delicacy" of his language. It is notable also that Yōfō Paulo and Vicente Fōin provided a glossary titled "Cotoba no yauarague" in the appendix of *Nvqigaqi*. This title is a neologism derived from the verb *yauarageru*, or "to soften," and means "the softening of hard words into those more palatable."

In his chapter on St. Eugenia, although the source text is no longer identifiable, Yōfō Paulo retains the Latin prototype storyline. Virgin martyr saint Eugenia was a daughter of the Roman governor Philippe of Alexandria, Egypt; and his wife, Claudia. The legend dates her death to circa 258 in Rome. But subtly, Yōfō Paulo makes the city of Alexandria into Kyoto by using the Japanese word *racuchū*, a special term for the Japanese capital.

The strongest aspect of Yōfō Paulo's contextualization concerns Eugenia's gender. The prototype story describes many challenges that St. Eugenia, as a young noblewoman in the Roman patriarchal society, overcame in order to achieve her vocational aspiration.[34] Yōfō Paulo underscores several aspects of Eugenia's struggle of being a woman religious leader in Japanese society by adding numerous commentaries. First, as in ancient Rome, early modern Japan did not encourage women to pursue academic achievement. Before her conversion to Christianity, Princess Eugenia displays an extraordinary intellectual capacity. Eugenia studies the "liberal arts," which Yōfō Paulo explains consist of rhetoric, logic, law, and philosophy, as well as Latin. Eugenia reads big books easily, understands what she reads quickly, never forgets what she learns, and masters a breadth of scholarship. Yōfō Paulo uses an expression, "wondrous wisdom" (*fuxigui no von chiye*), to emphasize the unusualness of Eugenia's education and says that she did this "despite having a woman's body" (*von nhotai nite maximaxedomo*).[35] Throughout the chapter, he inserts this term *nhotai*, literally "woman's body," to remind the Kirishitan readers of Eugenia's being born a woman. In giving details of Eugenia's desire and capacity for higher learning, Yōfō Paulo may have been echoing the sentiment of many women readers, some of whom, despite the Confucian restrictions on women pursuing higher learning, studied Portuguese, Spanish, and Latin so that they might understand theological phrases, which remained untranslated in *rōmaji* or were transliterated and scattered within the Kirishitan literature.

The second aspect of gender in this story is about women and marriage duties. Yōfō Paulo says that even before her conversion to Christianity, Eugenia deeply desired a life of *ixxŏ fubon* (perpetual sexual renunciation).[36] Pressed by a marriage proposal from a high Roman official Aqilino (i.e., Aquilinus), Eugenia laments over her "existence as a woman" (*vonna no mi*) and "woman's place in the social hierarchy" (*vonna no xidai*) and says, "Born as a woman, I cannot live with my father and mother for life, but I must spend the rest of my life only with my husband, sharing my inner thoughts only with him, and talking intimately only with him as it is the . . . rule; however, I don't know his mind, his likes, what he might impose on me, or what his behaviors are like. . . . Because I am a woman, I do not have any control of my body or soul."[37] In these words, again, Yōfō Paulo perhaps speaks for Kirishitan women readers, protesting against Japanese feudal custom, in which such politically arranged marriages were the norm and women's wishes were disregarded.

Eugenia's sexual renunciation is paired with the stories of her two eunuch servants, Protho and Jacinto. Since court eunuchs did not exist in Japan, Yōfō Paulo adds a paragraph of explanation that *eunucho* were born men but were made to lose their maleness to serve among the court ladies. In search of a rationale for refusing a marriage proposal, Eugenia examines an unidentified Pauline epistle, which she owns among her books.[38] When she walks by a Kirishitan assembly on her outing, she hears Psalm 96:5—"All the gods of the peoples are idols, but the Lord made the heavens"—being sung. Intrigued, Eugenia sends Protho and Jacinto to ask Kirishitans the meaning of this scripture and receives a satisfying answer that the words of Prophet David and the words of Apostle Paul testify to the one true God. Then she declares that she is no longer the master over Protho and Jacinto and that now they are her spiritual brothers. Eugenia discloses to them her secret plan to enter the monastery dressed as a man, and in a warrior-like tone she says, "Let us go to the Kirishitan temple and join the fellows."[39] She successfully persuades Protho and Jacinto, and they appear before Bishop Eleno (i.e., Helenus) during his visit to the monastery. The bishop had a dream that revealed the truth about Eugenia's gender and told him to accept her. Using male speech, Eugenia introduces herself as Eugenio and the bishop praises her "manly" (*vonoco gamaxiqi*) intention to serve Jesus Christ in *ixxŏ fubon*. The bishop baptizes the three "brothers" and they join the monastery.

Yōfō Paulo frames Eugenia's gender-crossing in the context of Japanese Buddhist restrictions on women. He identifies that this monastery is indeed a famous "sacred zone forbidden to women" (*nhonin qeccai*).[40] Kirishitan women were well familiar with such places as Mount Hiei.[41] In order to transcend such a barrier, Eugenia shaves her hair (*cami uo sori*) and literally turns into a man (*nantai ni fenjite*). By using this expression, Yōfō Paulo again is referring to the Buddhist doctrine of *fenjō nanxi* (a woman turning into a man), based on the Lotus Sutra, which says that because of their inherent sinful nature, women could not attain enlightenment unless they literally turned into men.[42] Although both women's prohibition from entering male-only monasteries and Eugenia's cross-dressing as a means of entering such a monastery are in the prototype story, by applying the current Buddhist terms of *nhonin qeccai* and *fenjō nanxi* Yōfō Paulo contextualizes this story to the Japanese situation, where women's aspiration to pursue religious vocations is severely curtailed.

Yōfō Paulo continues the story that Eugenia "passes totally as a man" (*nanxini nari sumaxi tamai*),[43] and enjoys rigorous study in the monastery. She masters all the scriptures in two years, speaks in wise words, and acquires a gift of healing. She displays an angelic life in penitential discipline. However, Eugenia meets two challenges relating to gender. The first comes when the abbot of the monastery nominates "Eugenio" to be his successor before his death, and every member of the monastery elects her. Having "scruples about her female body" (*nhotai naru coto uo fabacari*), she consults the scriptures.[44] Finding Jesus's words to his disciples in Matthew

20:25–26—which says, "You know that the rulers of the Gentiles lord it over them.... It will not be so among you; but whoever wishes to be great among you must be your servant"—she insists on serving at the lowest rank in menial tasks, thus avoiding becoming an abbot.

Monk Eugenio/a faces another challenge when Melanthia, a rich noble young widow who was healed by Eugenia from her illness, becomes infatuated with her (thinking that Eugenia is a man). Melanthia pretends to have fallen ill again, calls for Eugenio/a, and asks Eugenio/a to marry her. Furious, Eugenio/a reprimands her harshly. Melanthia yells out that this monk tried to rape her. The scandal spreads across Egypt, reaching governor Philippe, in fact Eugenia's father, who orders the arrest of all the monks of Eugenia's monastery. When Philippe summons Eugenia, accusing Christ for teaching the monks such immoral acts, she replies that her Lord Jesus Christ only teaches the way of sexual renunciation (*ixxŏ fubon*). Although Eugenia first wants to spare Melanthia, she eventually speaks up for the sake of the fellow monks. She says, "The time to remain silent has passed, now is the time to speak,"⁴⁵ to demonstrate that "the Lord ... gives the woman the power of her man [*votto*]," and "she rips open her clothing." The text says, "And what a wonder, for in an instance, such an apparently valiant, energetic and strong man turns into a woman."⁴⁶ Yōfō Paulo renders this dramatic scene of Eugenia revealing her gender in "immediately returning to her woman's body" (*tachimachi nhotai ni cayeru*) to prove Buddhist *fenjō nanxi* meaningless. Eugenia in her female body in the zone forbidden to females in the monastery (*nhonin qeccai*) attains this divine power.

With this revelation, Eugenia is restored to her former position as the governor's daughter, and her father Philippe, mother Claudia, two brothers, and the entire city of Kyoto become devout Kirishitans. Soon the emperor in Rome deposes Philippe, charging him with the destruction of the statues of idols, which Yōfō Paulo translates as statues of Buddha (*Fonzon*). The new governor assassinates Philippe and imprisons and then expels Eugenia and Claudia, who return to Rome.

In the second half of her story, Eugenia exercises leadership in an underground community of Kirishitan monastic women. Yōfō Paulo's focus is the strong resistance that Eugenia and her community of women take up against the Roman emperor, whom he casts also as a Japanese Buddhist dictator. Eugenia and Claudia help convert many women to the Kirishitan faith and the way of sexual renunciation. Eugenia's first disciple is Basilla of royal lineage, who receives a secret baptism from Pope Cornelio (i.e., Cornelius). Nightly, Eugenia and Basilla gather an assembly of devout women (*jennhonin tachi*). As the great persecution of Emperor Valeriano (Valerianus) begins, Eugenia exhorts Basilla and her community of virgins to get ready for their martyrdom. She prays to the Son of God, who chose the Virgin as his mother for the sake of humanity, that God may reward these virgins under her care with martyrdom. And she says, "Hear, oh brethren, this is the time to harvest the fruit of grapes to be made into *saqe*. For with a sword they will cut off a bunch of grapes from the vine, crush them under their feet, and serve the *saqe* at the feast of the emperor."[47] Eugenia's valiant exhortation again demonstrates her gender fluidity. In addressing her women as brothers, she takes up the persona of Christ, who prophesies about the day of judgment to his disciples using a parable in which the owner of the vineyard punishes its wicked tenants, who killed the owner's son to steal his inheritance (Matthew 21:33–44). Then Eugenia mimics Christ, who says that he is the true vine and that the disciples are the branches bearing good fruit (John 15:1–7). She speaks as mother of these women: "Birthed from my body, you have become ripe fruit of grapes. Be prepared for the time when they crush you under their feet for the sake of the Lord."[48]

Within a few days, the emperor issues the orders of execution, charging Eugenia for the crime of proselytizing people for a mysterious Buddha (*Fonzon*) from Egypt, and charging "that she rebels against the governmental laws, despises traditional rituals of the imperial household, humiliates the national Buddha [*Fonzon*], and takes vows of abandoning the way of the husband and the wife."[49] Yōfō Paulo's rendition of this imperial edict reflects the Japanese authorities' intolerance of Kirishitan virgins, who refused arranged marriages for the sake of keeping the family lineage and rejected Buddhist rituals. The example of Eugenia's community might have provided a model for Naitō Julia and the Miyako no bicuni, who also took vows of chastity and criticized Buddhists working with the Japanese government. Likewise, when the officials confront Basilla, who broke her engagement to Pompeio, she declares that her husband is Jesus Christ, who is the great emperor of all emperors. The officials behead Basilla with Protho and Jacinto.[50] They drag Eugenia to the temple of Diana, but when Eugenia prays to the Kirishitan God the temple falls down, killing the pagan worshipers. Then they try to sink Eugenia into the Tiber River with a stone attached to her neck, but she floats up and worships Jesus Christ. They throw her into a burning oven, but she extinguishes the flames.

The theology of mystical union of divinity and humanity in the body of a woman martyr is clearly manifest in Eugenia's last days.[51] During Eugenia's ten-day imprisonment in a dark dungeon, Jesus Christ appears before her and feeds her, saying "I am your deeply beloved spouse Jesus Christ. Please eat from my own hands."[52] Christ also assures her saying, "On the day on which I come down from heaven, you will go up there."[53] Accordingly, Eugenia is beheaded on Christmas because "on the same day that the Lord received the human body, the Lord also united his body to the body of this good person [*jennin*], and consummated their destiny as spouses."[54]

Eugenia's body becomes a gender-neutral symbol of good humanity rather than remaining that of a devout woman (*jennhonin*). The Incarnation of Christ in a human body and Eugenia's martyred body are one inseparable theological unit. Soon after her burial, Eugenia appears to her mother, Claudia, in a bright vision and consoles her by saying that the Lord Jesus Christ has added Eugenia to the ranks of the Blessed (*Beato*), and her father to that of the Patriarchs (*Patriarcha*), and that Claudia also will be taken up on Sunday. Yōfō Paulo's adaptation of the familiar Buddhist words *jennin* and *jennhonin* (literally "good man" and "good woman") for the Kirishitan devout man and woman, as well as for male and female saint, makes the notion of Christian mystical union of Christ and the faithful (communion of all saints) as one body easily imaginable by the Kirishitan readers. Realizing this body, which is both male and female, in chastity and martyrdom, Kirishitan women, like Eugenia and Basilla, are free to pursue their new religious vocation.

Thus Yōfō Paulo's story of virgin martyr St. Eugenia contains the Kirishitan community's theological views on gender, women's sanctity, and resistance. In the context of a governmentally imposed Confucianized-Buddhist society, many Kirishitan women emulated St. Eugenia and came out of their submission and desired martyrdom (witnessing) to such an ideal. But not all of these women attained martyrdom.

St. Marina

Kirishitan stories of St. Marina appear in two collections: *Vidas* (Barreto manuscript) circa 1591, and *Martyrio no cagami* (Mirror of Martyrdom; hereafter, *Cagami*). *Cagami* circulated among the underground churches and was confiscated by the government around 1800.[55] It comprises only three stories of female saints: Anastasia, Catherine, and Marina. The content of St. Marina's story in *Cagami* in the *kanamajiri* script is almost identical to that in *Vidas* in *rōmaji*. Neither version reveals the translators' identity, nor the source text. They strip particularities of the prototype story, such as the names of the place (Bithynia) and Marina's father's name (Eugenios), and keep a simple plot.⁵⁶

The chapter heading of *Vidas*, "A vida da pacientissima e gloriosa Virgem Sancta Marina" (Life of the most patient and glorious Virgin Saint Marina), is telling: it is the story of patient suffering and not martyrdom of a virgin.⁵⁷ In fact, Marina's entry into the Kirishitan temple monastery as a boy ("Marino") was not by her own volition. Her father, who became a *xutqe* (monk), leaves the very young Marina with his relatives; however, because the *jūji* (head of the temple) becomes sympathetic to the father's grieving, he allows him to raise his child at the temple without realizing that Marina is a girl. When she turns fourteen, her father cautions her not to reveal that she is female in order not to destroy the temple. Her father dies when she is seventeen. The temple community allows Marino to stay and work, driving an oxcart between the temple and the harbor town seven kilometers away. As it was a custom for the monks to spend the evenings at the house of Pandocio on the way, Marina would also stay there. But Pandocio's unmarried daughter accuses "Marino" of impregnating her when her parents discover that she is expecting a child.

At *jūji*'s examination, Marina does not admit the charge but remarks, "Indeed, Padre, I am a sinner [*zainin*]," says that she will do the penance for her sins, and asks for his prayers.⁵⁸ This is the only time that Marina speaks in the story. The enraged *jūji* imprisons her and expels her from the monastery. Marina remains as a beggar just outside the temple gate, does her penance, and raises the abandoned baby of the woman for five years. At other monks' intercession, saying "Jesus Christ does not abandon the bad [*aqunin*]," the *jūji* allows Marina and the "fatherless child" in the compound even though *jūji* calls Marina a "bad mirror [*cagami*], which is unheard of."⁵⁹ For penance, Marina obeys *jūji*'s order and serves the community doing dirty menial labor. Shortly afterward Marina becomes sick and dies.

At the *jūji*'s order to prepare her body for burial, the monks undress her to bathe the corpse, and they are astounded to find that she is a woman: "When they strip her naked, she turns out to be a woman [*nhonin*]."⁶⁰ The monks praise Marina, saying "Despite being a woman, . . . what a good mirror [*cagami*] and incomparable patience [she demonstrated] throughout her life."⁶¹ When the *jūji* realizes his mistakes, he laments greatly. They bury her corpse in the temple treasure house (*fōden*). At Marina's death, the woman who had falsely accused her becomes possessed by the devil (*tengu*) for seven days and reveals the man who impregnated her. Hearing this miracle (*quidocu*), monks from other temples and neighbors from all classes flock to the "saint's" temple with crosses, to sing psalms (*Psalmos*) and hymns (*ymnos*).⁶² Answering their *oratio* (prayers), St. Marina works many miracles.

Unlike St. Eugenia's bold and dramatic resistance to systemic oppression both by the state and the dominant religion, the Kirishitan stories of St. Marina emphasize her virtues of humility, obedience, and patience. They omit the prototype's descriptions of St. Marina's wealthy background or becoming the abbot of the community. In fact, Marina is depicted as a poor orphan, a laborer in harsh conditions, and a beggar without learning or the official status of a monk. The thorough use of Buddhist terms makes her story read as if it is a Buddhist *setsuwa* (novella). The text of *Cagami* replaces some transliterated Kirishitan words in the text of *Vidas* with *kanji*, making the appearance of the text more Japanese. For example, *tentacion* (temptation) becomes 天田サン, and *penitentia* (penance) becomes ヘニ天シヤ, with the character 天, which is a symbol of heaven. Marina's own words "I am a sinner" reflect the long history of women's struggle with the idea that women are inherently sinful in both Christian and Buddhist traditions.⁶³ The monks' remark that "Jesus Christ does not abandon the bad [*aqunin*]" alludes to Luke 6:35 ("[God] is kind to the ungrateful and the wicked"). Even so, it sounds closer to Shinran's famous teaching in *Tannishō* (3:1), "The good [*jennin*] achieve salvation; much less, the bad [*aqunin*]," which means that Amidah Buddha saves those who rely not on their own power but acknowledge their powerlessness and rely on Amidah Buddha. These subtle changes that *Cagami* made reflect shifting voices of hidden Kirishitans during the long years of suppression.

Conclusion

If St. Eugenia's story conveys voices of resistance of the community of active Kirishitan women who aspired to martyrdom, St. Marina's quiet disguise until her miserable death may reveal the voices of resignation and patience of women and men in the underground Kirishitan communities. In 1634 St. Ōmura no Marina, a namesake of literary St. Marina and a Dominican tertiary, attained her martyrdom, but no Japanese records retain her identity. Lady Ōmura Marina (d. 1639), another namesake of St. Marina and a daughter of famous Kirishitan daimyo Ōmura Sumitada Bartolomeu (1533–1587), was an active protector of the Jesuit mission in Ōmura even after her brother daimyo Ōmura Yoshiaki Sancho (1569–1616) apostatized in 1606. A legend tells of her later life that because of the rumor of Kirishitan assassination of her brother Sancho, she was forced to be enclosed in a Buddhist temple in Tone but lived as a secret Kirishitan for the rest of her days.[64] Ōmura family official records erased her memory. Numerous underground Kirishitans in these remote regions endured harsh living conditions, disguised as Buddhists before the authorities in order to participate in rituals, but prayed secret prayers for repentance, circulating Kirishitan stories of women martyrs and waited for their day of liberation.

Notes

1. The term Kirishitan (noun and adjective) is a Japanization of the Portuguese *cristão* (Christian).

2. Records on women can be identified in catalogs such as Juan Ruiz-de-Medina, *El martirologio del Japón* (Rome: Institutum Historicum Societatis Iesu, 1999); and *Petoro Kibe to hyaku hachijūshichi junkyōsha* (Tokyo: Catholic Bishops' Conference of Japan, 2007). See also Juan Ruiz-de-Medina, *The Catholic Church in Korea: Its Origins, 1566–1784*, trans. John Bridges (Rome: Institutum Historicum Societatis Iesu, 1991).

3. On Xavier's experiments equating God with Dainichi, see Georg Schurhammer, *Das kirchliche Sprachproblem in der japanischen Jesuitenmission des 16. und 17. Jahrhunderts* (Tokyo: Deutsche Gesellschaft für Natur- und Völkerkunde Ostasiens, 1928).

4. The Jesuit Mission catalog of 1584 lists twenty-six Japanese brothers, fifteen of whom "had been in the Society since the early times and taken the vows," and nearly one hundred seminarians and *dōjucu*. It also lists the birthplaces of twenty-nine missionary priests and thirty "European" brothers in various places in Portugal, Spain, Italy, India, and Macau. See Joseph Franz Schütte, ed., *Monumenta historica Japoniae: Textus catalogorum Japoniae aliaeque de personis domibusque S. J. in Japonia informationes et relationes, 1549–1654* (Rome: Institutum Historicum Societatis Iesu, 1975) (hereafter *MHJ*), 152–81. This raises a question about the Jesuits' own sense of national identity in the cosmopolitan Society.

5. See Haruko Nawata Ward, *Women Religious Leaders in Japan's Christian Century, 1549–1650* (Farnham, UK: Ashgate, 2009); and Haruko Nawata Ward, "Women Apostles in Early Modern Japan, 1549–1650," in *Devout Laywomen in the Early Modern World*, ed. Alison Weber (Abingdon, UK: Routledge, 2016), 312–30.

6. On Alexandro Valignano and his importation of the movable-type press in Japan, see William J. Farge, *The Japanese Translations of the Jesuit Mission Press, 1590–1614: "De imitatione Christi" and "Guía de pecadores"* (Lewiston, NY: Edwin Mellen Press, 2003). See also Josef Franz Schütte, *Valignano's Mission Principles for Japan*, trans. John J. Coyne (St. Louis: Institute of Jesuit Sources, 1980–85); M. Antoni J. Üçerler, "The Jesuit Enterprise in Sixteenth- and Seventeenth-Century Japan," in *The Cambridge Companion to the Jesuits*, ed. Thomas Worcester (Cambridge, UK: Cambridge University Press, 2008), 153–68; and also J. F. Moran, *The Japanese and the Jesuits: Alessandro Valignano in Sixteenth-Century Japan* (London: Routledge, 1993).

7. See E. M. Satow, *The Jesuit Mission Press in Japan, 1591–1610* (Tokyo, 1888); and J. Laures, *Kirishitan Bunko: A Manual of Books and Documents on the Early Christian Mission in Japan; With Special Reference to the Principal Libraries in Japan and More Particularly to the Collection at Sophia University, Tokyo; With an Appendix of Ancient Maps of the Far East, Especially Japan*, 3rd ed. (Tokyo: Sophia University, 1957); and also Masayuki

Toyoshima, ed., *Kirishitan to shuppan* (Tokyo: Yagi shoten, 2013).

8. On the Jesuits' criticism against the mendicants, see C. R. Boxer, *The Christian Century in Japan, 1549–1650* (Berkeley: University of California Press, 1951), 137–87.

9. See Toshio Toda, *Amakusa Shimabara no ran: Hosokawa han shiryō ni yoru* (Tokyo: Shinjinbutsu Ōraisha, 1988).

10. For example, see the preface by Pero Ramón, the chief translator of the team of like-minded colleagues, in *Fides no dŏxi* (Amakusa, 1592), reprinted in facsimile in Hiroshi Suzuki, ed., *Kirishitanban Hiidesu no dōshi* (Osaka: Seibundō, 1985), 3–5. *Fides no dŏxi* is a Kirishitan translation of *Sumario* [or *Quinta parte*] *de la introducción del símbolo de la fe* by Luis of Granada.

11. Maria Tymoczko, "Ideology and the Position of the Translator: In What Sense Is a Translator 'In Between'?," in *Critical Readings in Translation Studies*, ed. Mona Baker (New York: Routledge, 2010), 224. Tymoczko does not refer to her source.

12. Henry D. Smith II, "The History of the Book in Edo and Paris," in *Edo and Paris: Urban Life and the State in the Early Modern Era*, ed. James L. McClain, John M. Merriman, and Ugawa Kaoru (Ithaca, NY: Cornell University Press, 1994), 348–49.

13. Tymoczko also notes the orality of Chinese tradition: "In the early days of translation in China, there were often even more stages, with oral recitation or reading of the source text by a speaker of the source language conjoined with ad hoc oral translation of the text passage by passage by a bilingual. The material was then transcribed into written language by a third team member, and polished and finalized by yet a fourth, the latter two of whom might not know the source language at all" (Tymoczko, "Ideology and the Position of the Translator," 228n15).

14. On the Jesuit singer-storytellers and translation of stories of the saints, see Juan G. Ruiz-de-Medina, *Iezusu kaishi to Kirishitan fukyō* (Tokyo: Iwata shoin, 2003), 131–68; see also Haruko Nawata Ward, "Images of the Incarnation in the Jesuit Japan Mission's Kirishitanban Story of Virgin Martyr St. Catherine of Alexandria," in *Image and Incarnation: The Early Modern Doctrine of the Pictorial Image*, ed. Walter S. Melion and Lee Palmer Wandel (Boston: Brill, 2015), 489–509.

15. On the Buddhist terms in *Contemptus mundi*, see Satoru Obara, ed., *Kontemutsusu munji* (Tokyo: Kyōbunkan, 2002), 296.

16. On the European loan words, see Kunimichi Fukushima, *Kirishitan shiryō to kokugo kenkyū* (Tokyo: Kasama shoin, 1973), esp. 142.

17. A. E. B. Coldiron, "Translation's Challenge to Critical Categories: Verses from French in the Early English Renaissance," in *Critical Readings in Translation Studies*, ed. Mona Baker (New York: Routledge, 2010), 352. In these translations one finds "a vernacular cosmopolitanism," "co-presence of cultures," "hybridity," "profusion of strange creole like new languages," "improvisation," and "a process of transculturation at work" that represents a multicultural "Renaissance" world (354–55).

18. See Li Sher-Shiueh, "The Archeology of a Dream: The *Shengmengge*. Its Translation and Its Transformation," in *Christianity and Cultures: Japan and China in Comparison, 1543–1644*, ed. M. Antoni J. Üçerler (Rome: Institutum Historicum Societatis Iesu, 2009), 66–80, esp. 73.

19. Rebekah Clements, *A Cultural History of Translation in Early Modern Japan* (Cambridge, UK: Cambridge University Press, 2015), 14.

20. Ibid., 13.

21. Ibid.

22. Indra Levy, "Introduction: Modern Japan and the Trialectics of Translation," *Review of Japanese Culture and Society* 20, no. 3 (December 2008): 3, as cited in ibid., 15.

23. There are two surviving copies of *Sanctos no gosagveo no vchi nvqigaqi* in Biblioteca Nazionale Marciana, Venice; and Bodleian Library, Oxford University, Oxford. The facsimile of the Marciana copy is published as Toshiaki Koso, ed., *Sanctos no gosagveo no vchi nvqigaqi*, 2 vols. (Tokyo: Yūshodo, 2006) (hereafter *Nvqigaqi*).

24. This codex, popularly called the Barreto copy according to its amanuensis Emmanuel Barreto (1564–1620), is in the Apostolic Library in the Vatican, Rome (*Codices Reginenses Latini* 459; hereafter *Reg. Lat.* 459). The collection bears the Portuguese title *Vidas gloriosas*

de algũns Sanctos e Sanctas, but its contents are all in Japanese in *rōmaji*. See J. F. Schütte, "Christliche japanische Literatur, Bilder und Druckblätter in einem unbekannten vatikanischen Codex aus dem Jahre 1591," *Archivum Historicum Societatis Iesu* 9 (1940): 226–80.

25. Kunimichi Fukushima, *Zoku zoku Kirishitan shiryō to kokugo kenkyū: Seijinden shō* (Tokyo: Kasama shoin, 1995).

26. This title in Japanese is "Sancta Evgenia Virgen to vonajiqu sono goqenin naru Protho, mata Iacinto no gosagvio, narabini Martyrio no yodai. Core S. Hieronymo no asobasaretaru Vidas patrum to S. Antonino no caqitamo joguan ni arauaruru mono nari. Decemb. 25." See *Nvqigaqi*, 2:109–40.

27. The original title is a mixture of Portuguese and Japanese: "De Sancta Eugenia Virgin sono guoquenin Proto et Jacynto." Likewise, the collection in *Vidas* (Barreto copy) has a Portuguese title, *Vidas gloriosas de algũns Sanctos e Sanctas*, but the text is in Japanese. See *Reg. Lat.* 459, 245v–62v.

28. See *MHJ*, 1328–29.

29. See *Cartas que os padres e irmãos da Companhia de Jesus que andão nos reynos de Japão escreverão aos da mesma Companhia da India, e Europa, desdo anno de 1549 ate o de 1580* (Évora: Manoel de Lyra, 1597), fols. 177r and 206v; and Luís Fróis, *História de Japam*, 5 vols., ed. José Wicki (Lisbon: Biblioteca Nacional, 1981), 2:170. On Hibiya Monica and the story of St. Catherine of Alexandria, see Haruko Nawata Ward, "Women, Households, and the Transformation of Christianity into the Kirishitan Religion," in *Catholic Missionaries in Early Modern Asia: Patterns of Localization*, ed. Nadine Amsler, Andreea Badea, Bernard Heyberger, and Christian Windler (New York: Routledge, 2020), 174–89.

30. With Valignano's initiative, the *seminario* of Shimo began in Arima in 1580 with twenty-two students and that of Miyako opened in Azuchi in 1581 with eight students. The *collegio* was founded in Funai in 1580, relocated about seven times, and in 1598 moved to Nagasaki, where it remained until its destruction in 1614.

31. *MHJ*, 321. See the entire list signed by Alexandro Valignano, who never learned Japanese (306–25).

32. "Decembris XXV: Vita Sanctæ Eugeniæ Virginis ac Martynis," in Jacques Paul Migne, ed., *Patrologia Latina* (hereafter Migne, *PL*) 73:605–24. This was drawn from Migne's critical edition of Heribert Rosweyde, ed., *Vitae Patrum* (Antwerp: Officina Plantiniana, 1628).

33. Fróis, *História*, 5:172. Fróis wrote this chapter sometime between 1584, when he received the order to write his *Historia*, and 1586, when he finished part 1. The Jesuit Press published *Arte ne Lingua Japão* (Grammar of Japanese language) (Amakusa, 1594) in Latin; *Vocabulario* (Portuguese-Japanese dictionary) (Amakusa,1595) and *Doctrina Christiam* (Catechism) in *kanamajiri* (Kazusa, 1591) and *rōmaji* (Kazusa, 1592). Although none of these bears Yōfō Paulo's name, *Arte* and *Vocabulario* cite many of his examples. Yōfō Paulo is attributed also to the Latin works *Catechismus* (Lisbon, 1595), *Fides no dōxi* (Amakusa, 1592), and *Contemptus mundi* (Amakusa, 1596); and José Wicki notes Esope's *Fables* (Kazusa, 1593) in *História*, 172n21. Yōfō Paulo is reported to have composed his own works such as *Irmão Paolo no monogatari* (Stories of Irmão Paolo), *Kurobune monogatari* (Story of the black ship), and *Morte no monogatari* (Story of death), but none of these is extant.

34. The prototype is found in Migne, *PL* 73:605–24. An English translation of the Greek text of Symeon Metaphrastes's *Menologion* is available as "Life, Conduct and Passion of the Holy Martyr of Christ Saint Eugenia and Her Parents," in Symeon, *Christian Novels from the Menologion of Symeon Metaphrastes*, ed. Stratis Papaioannou (Cambridge, MA: Harvard University Press, 2017), 183–261; and Jacobus De Voragine, *The Golden Legend: Readings on the Saints*, trans. W. G. Ryan, 2 vols. (Princeton, NJ: Princeton University Press, 2012), 2:165–67. The chapter heading in *Golden Legend* is "Saints Protus and Hyacinthus," but the main character of the chapter is Eugenia.

35. *Nvqigaqi*, 2:110.

36. The glossary of *Nvqigaqi* gives "Virgem" for *ixxŏ fubon*.

37. Ibid., 2:111–12: "vonna no miua chichi faua tote mo soi toguezu, votto ni nomi xitagaite, cocoro uo nocosazu arauaxi, xitaximi catarai, ixxe no aida soi fatçuru mono nareba, nani yori daijino sadame naruni,

uare sono fitono cocoro uo xirazu, nanitaru cata ni catamuqi, nanitaru coto uo votoxitçuqe; mimochiua nanito vosamaruzo, suqimo qiraimo cocoroyezu, catagui uo xiranu tocoroye yuqite, vonna no xidai niua vagamimo cocoromo vaga mamani naru majiqereba, vaga tameni samatague canarazu vocoru bexi."

38. Ibid., 2:113.
39. Ibid., 2:114: "Yza morotomoni Christan no tera ye mairite, ichimi to naru bexi."
40. Ibid., 2:115.
41. On the female-restricted precincts in Japanese Buddhist temples and monasteries, see Susan Matisoff, "Barred from Paradise? Mount Kōya and the Karukaya Legend," in *Engendering Faith: Women and Buddhism in Premodern Japan*, ed. Barbara Ruch (Ann Arbor: University of Michigan Press, 2002), 463–500.
42. The twelfth chapter of the Lotus Sutra contains the doctrine of *fenjō nanxi* (or, in its modern spelling, *henjō nanshi*). See Kazuhiko Yoshida, "The Enlightenment of the Dragon King's Daughter in the Lotus Sutra," trans. Margret H. Childs, in *Engendering Faith*, ed. Barbara Ruch, 297–324.
43. *Nvqigaqi*, 2:120. *Vidas* keeps Eugenia as Eugenia, which makes the motivation of the bishop's admittance of a woman in the monastery even more miraculous.
44. Ibid., 2:123.
45. Ibid., 2:128: "mugon no jicocu mo sugui quereba, monoyū, beqitoqi qitaru."
46. Ibid., 2:129: "von yxŏ uo fiqisaqi tamai, nhotai nite maximasu coto uo arauasan to voboximexeba, fuxiguinaru cana imamadeua samo guiriŏ ni xite, caigai xiqu icanimo tçuyoqi nanxi no yosouoi uo von tachidocoro ni fiqicayerare, tachimachi nhotai ni cayer[u]."
47. Ibid., 2:136: "icani qiŏdaixu ima ua budŏ no mi uo torite, saqe ni nasu jicocu nari. Sonoyuyeua: budŏ no fusa ua catana vomotte qiri, axi vomotte fumi xiboru mono nari to iyedomo, sono saqe ua teiuŏ no goxŭgui no goza ni izzuru mononari. Chi uo nagasazu xite, cuni uo qiri toru tamexi naxi."
48. Ibid., 2:137: "Von mi tachi ua vaga tainai yori ide, sacaye tamŏ budŏ no mi nari. Vonaruji ye taixi tatematçurite, fumi tçubusaren tomo gocacugo canyŏ nari."
49. Ibid., 2:137: "côgui no gofatto uo somuite, daidai tonaye qitaru chôca no von matçurigoto uomo azaqeri, von ie no Fozon uo iyaximu, fŭfu no michi uo fanasu nari."
50. Fukunaga notes a unique Japanese expression, "agui uo fanasaxe tamŏ" (let go of her chin), a euphemism for women's beheading. See Fukushima, *Zoku zoku*, 224.
51. Within Caroline Walker Bynum's extensive research in European women's understanding of this mystical union, in the period between the eleventh and the sixteenth centuries, especially helpful is *Holy Feast and Holy Fast: The Religious Significance of Medieval Women* (Berkeley: University of California Press, 1987).
52. *Nvqigaqi*, 2:139: "vare ua core von mino tçuma fucaqu taixet ni vomouaruru Iesu Christo nari. Vaga te yori xocubut uo bucuxerareyo."
53. Ibid., 2:139: "vare ten yori cudaritaru fi jŏten uo togueraru bexi."
54. Ibid., 2:139: "Von aruji ninguen no tai uo vqe tamŏ von fi vomotte, von aruji mata cono jennin to vontai uo auaxe tamai, von tçuma no yen uo musubi come tamŏ."
55. See M. Anesaki, *Kirishitan shūmon no hakugai to senpuku* (Tokyo: Dōbunsha, 1930), 131–239. *Martyrio no cagami* was found among the materials known as *Yasokyō sōsho* (Christian writings), which were confiscated during the First Uragami Raid of the hidden Kirishitans by the Nagasaki magistrate between 1789 and 1800. These materials are thought to have been first written between 1596 and 1614. In 1896 Naojirō Murakami made copies of the *Yasokyō sōsho*. In 1930 Masaharu Anesaki published an edition of Murakami copies and titled it *Martyrio no shiori* (Guidebook for martyrdom) in three parts, with part 3 being *Martyrio no cagami* (Mirror of martyrdom). The original has since been lost. A critical edition of a photocopy of the 1896 copy, housed in Sophia University, has been published in Satoru Obara, ed., *Kirishitan no junkyō to senpuku* (Tokyo: Kyōbunkan, 2006), 106–10.
56. For prototypes, see Simenon Metaphrastes, ed., "Bios Eugenios kai Marias tēs Thygatros/ Vita Beati Eugenii et Mariæ Filiæ Ejus," in Jacques Paul Migne, ed., *Patrologia*

Graeca 115:347–56. A similar story of Mary/Marinos is found in Honorius Augustodunensis, "Dominica X post Pentecosten" (Migne, *PL* 172:1053–54). An English translation from another source is found in "Life of St. Mary/Marinos," trans. Nicholas Costas, in *The Holy Women of Byzantium, Ten Saints' Lives in English Translation*, ed. Alice-Mary Talbot (Washington, DC: Dumbarton Oaks, 1996), 1–12; and also see De Voragine, *Golden Legend*, 1:324–25.

57. See the text of *Vidas* in *Reg. Lat.* 459, 229–32. See also Ignatius of Loyola, "Letter to Isabel Roser, Paris, November 10, 1532," in *Saint Ignatius of Loyola: Letters to Women*, ed. Hugo Rahner, trans. Kathleen Pond and S. A. H. Weetman (New York: Herder and Herder, 1960), 264–67. Interestingly Ignatius of Loyola (founder of the Society of Jesus) uses St. Marina's story as an example of patience, making her an unnamed "young girl," who disguises herself as a man to join the Franciscan monastery in Paris, is accused of impregnating another girl, suffers insults, and dies; after her death, the monks discover that the "friar" was a woman. Ignatius thus advises Isabel Roser (?–after 1554), a benefactor and spiritual companion before the establishment of the Society, to heed lessons of St. Marina and be patient in her trials. Ignatius admitted Roser and two other women into the nascent Society in 1545, but realizing that the female presence distracted the male Jesuits, he petitioned the pope to dismiss the women from the Society in 1546. The Society's *Constitutions* of 1552 clearly defines that women would not be a part of the Society.

58. Ibid., 230v: "icani Padre, Vare Va Zajnin nari."

59. Ibid., 231: "IESU Xº aqunin uo sute tamauanu"; 231v "chichi naqui co"; "Jendai mimon no axiqui cagami."

60. Ibid., 232: "fadaca ni naxite mireba nhonin nari."

61. Ibid.: "satemo vonna no mito xite xōgai no caguiri yoqui cagami to firui naqui cannin cana."

62. Ibid., 232v. See Obara, *Kirishitan no junkyō*, 110, for the addition of *xomyō* (Kirishitan adaptation of a Buddhist term for praise chants), in the text of *Cagami* of the underground Kirishitans.

63. See Ward, *Women Religious Leaders*, 51–52.

64. On the activities of Lady Ōmura Marina, see ibid., 320, 338; on the legends of Ina, a daughter of Ōmura Sumitada Bartolomeu and widow of Tomonaga Sumimori with the death name of Jishōin, who was believed to be Lady Ōmura Marina, see Matsuda Kiichi, *Ōtomo Sumitada den* (Tokyo: Kyōbunkan, 1978), 422–27. The legend still is told about her burial place in Jishōji temple, which can be translated as self-evident, self-revelatory, or natural-witness temple.

Works Cited

Anesaki, M. *Kirishitan shūmon no hakugai to senpuku*. Tokyo: Dōbunsha, 1930.

Boxer, C. R. *The Christian Century in Japan, 1549–1650*. Berkeley: University of California Press, 1951.

Bynum, Caroline Walker. *Holy Feast and Holy Fast: The Religious Significance of Medieval Women*. Berkeley: University of California Press, 1987.

Cartas que os padres e irmãos da Companhia de Jesus que andão nos reynos de Japão escreverão aos da mesma Companhia da India, e Europa, desdo anno de 1549 ate o de 1580. Évora: Manoel de Lyra, 1597.

Clements, Rebekah. *A Cultural History of Translation in Early Modern Japan*. Cambridge, UK: Cambridge University Press, 2015.

Coldiron, A. E. B. "Translation's Challenge to Critical Categories: Verses from French in the Early English Renaissance." In *Critical Readings in Translation Studies*, edited by Mona Baker, 337–56. New York: Routledge, 2010.

De Voragine, Jacobus. *The Golden Legend: Readings on the Saints*. Translated by W. G. Ryan. 2 vols. Princeton, NJ: Princeton University Press, 2012.

Dominica X post Pentecosten. In J.-P Migne, ed. *Honorii Augustodunensis Opera Omnia.* Patrologiæ Latinæ, 172, 1049–54. Paris: J.-P Migne and his successors,1895.

Farge, William J. *The Japanese Translations of the Jesuit Mission Press, 1590–1614: "De imitatione Christi" and "Guía de pecadores."* Lewiston, NY: Edwin Mellen Press, 2003.

Fróis, Luís. *História de Japam.* 5 vols. Edited by José Wicki. Lisbon: Biblioteca Naciona, 1976–1984.

Fukushima, Kunimichi. *Kirishitan shiryō to kokugo kenkyū.* Tokyo: Kasama shoin, 1973.

———. *Zoku zoku Kirishitan shiryō to kokugo kenkyū: Seijinden shō.* Tokyo: Kasama shoin, 1995.

Ignatius of Loyola, "Letter to Isabel Roser, Paris, November 10, 1532." In *Saint Ignatius of Loyola: Letters to Women*, edited by Hugo Rahner, translated by Kathleen Pond and S. A. H. Weetman, 264–67. New York: Herder and Herder, 1960.

Koso, Toshiaki, ed. *Sanctos no gosagveo go vchi nvqigaqi.* 2 vols. Tokyo: Yūshodo, 2006.

Laures, J. *Kirishitan Bunko: A Manual of Books and Documents on the Early Christian Mission in Japan; With Special Reference to the Principal Libraries in Japan and More Particularly to the Collection at Sophia University, Tokyo; With an Appendix of Ancient Maps of the Far East, Especially Japan.* 3rd ed. Tokyo: Sophia University, 1957.

Levy, Indra. "Introduction: Modern Japan and the Trialectics of Translation." *Review of Japanese Culture and Society* 20, no. 3 (December 2008): 1–14.

Li, Sher-Shiueh. "The Archeology of a Dream: The Shengmengge. Its Translation and Its Transformation." In *Christianity and Cultures: Japan and China in Comparison, 1543–1644*, edited by M. Antoni J. Üçerler, 66–80. Rome:

Institutum Historicum Societatis Iesu, 2009.

"Life of St. Mary/Marinos." Translated by Nicholas Costas. In *The Holy Women of Byzantium, Ten Saints' Lives in English Translation*, edited by Alice-Mary Talbot, 1–12. Washington, DC: Dumbarton Oaks, 1996.

Matisoff, Susan. "Barred from Paradise? Mount Kōya and the Karukaya Legend." In *Engendering Faith: Women and Buddhism in Premodern Japan*, edited by Barbara Ruch, 463–500. Ann Arbor: University of Michigan Press, 2002.

Matsuda, Kiichi. *Ōtomo Sumitada den.* Tokyo: Kyōbunkan, 1978.

Moran, J. F. *The Japanese and the Jesuits: Alessandro Valignano in Sixteenth-Century Japan.* London: Routledge, 1993.

Obara, Satoru, ed. *Kirishitan no junkyō to senpuku.* Tokyo: Kyōbunkan, 2006.

———, ed. *Kontemutsusu munji.* Tokyo: Kyōbunkan, 2002.

Petoro Kibe to hyaku hachijūshichi junkyōsha. Tokyo: Catholic Bishops' Conference of Japan, 2007.

Ruiz-de-Medina, Juan. *The Catholic Church in Korea: Its Origins, 1566–1784.* Translated by John Bridges. Rome: Institutum Historicum Societatis Iesu, 1991.

———. *Iezusu kaishi to Kirishitan fukyō.* Tokyo: Iwata shoin, 2003.

———. *El martirologio del Japón.* Rome: Institutum Historicum Societatis Iesu, 1999.

Satow, E. M. *The Jesuit Mission Press in Japan, 1591–1610.* Tokyo, 1888.

Schurhammer, Georg. *Das kirchliche Sprachproblem in der japanischen Jesuitenmission des 16. und 17. Jahrhunderts.* Tokyo: Deutsche Gesellschaft für Natur- und Völkerkunde Ostasiens, 1928.

Schütte, Josef Franz. "Christliche japanische Literatur: Bilder und Druckblätter in einem unbekannten vatikanischen Codex aus dem Jahre 1591." *Archivum Historicum Societatis Iesu* 9 (1940): 226–80.

———. *Monumenta historica Japoniae: Textus catalogorum Japoniae aliaeque de personis domibusque S. J. in Japonia informationes et relationes, 1549–1654*. Rome: Institutum Historicum Societatis Iesu, 1975.

———. *Valignano's Mission Principles for Japan*. Translated by John J. Coyne. St. Louis: Institute of Jesuit Sources, 1980–85.

Smith, Henry D., II. "The History of the Book in Edo and Paris." In *Edo and Paris: Urban Life and the State in the Early Modern Era*, edited by James L. McClain, John M. Merriman, and Ugawa Kaoru, 332–52. Ithaca, NY: Cornell University Press, 1994.

Suzuki, Hiroshi, ed. *Kirishitanban Hiidesu no dōshi*. Osaka: Seibundō, 1985.

Symeon. *Christian Novels from the Menologion of Symeon Metaphrastes*. Edited and translated by Stratis Papaioannou. Cambridge, MA: Harvard University Press, 2017.

Toda, Toshio. *Amakusa Shimabara no ran: Hosokawa han shiryō ni yoru*. Tokyo: Shinjinbutsu Ōraisha, 1988.

Toyoshima, Masayuki, ed. *Kirishitan to shuppan*. Tokyo: Yagi shoten, 2013.

Tymoczko, Maria. "Ideology and the Position of the Translator: In What Sense Is a Translator 'In Between'?" In *Critical Readings in Translation Studies*, edited by Mona Baker, 213–28. London: Routledge, 2010.

Üçerler, M. Antoni J. "The Jesuit Enterprise in Sixteenth- and Seventeenth-Century Japan." In *The Cambridge Companion to the Jesuits*, edited by Thomas Worcester, 153–68. Cambridge, UK: Cambridge University Press, 2008.

Vita Beati Eugenii et Mariæ Filiæ Ejus. In J.-P Migne, ed. *Symeon Metaphrastes Opera Omnia*. Patrologiae Graeca, 115, 347–356. Paris: J.-P Migne, 1864.

Vita Sanctæ Eugeniæ Virginis ac Martynis. In Heribert Rosweyde and J.-P Migne, ed. *Vitæ Patrum, Sive, Historiæ Eremiticæ Libri Decem: Auctoribus Suis Et Nitori Pristino Restituti Ac Notationibus Illustrati. Novissime corrigente et recensente. Patrologiæ Latinæ*, 73, 605–24. Paris: Garnier Fratres, and J.-P Migne and his successors, 1879.

Ward, Haruko Nawata. "Images of the Incarnation in the Jesuit Japan Mission's Kirishitanban Story of Virgin Martyr St. Catherine of Alexandria." In *Image and Incarnation: The Early Modern Doctrine of the Pictorial Image*, edited by Walter S. Melion and Lee Palmer Wandel, 489–509. Boston: Brill, 2015.

———. "Women Apostles in Early Modern Japan, 1549–1650." In *Devout Laywomen in the Early Modern World*, edited by Alison Weber, 312–30. New York: Routledge, 2016.

———. "Women, Households, and the Transformation of Christianity into the Kirishitan Religion." In *Catholic Missionaries in Early Modern Asia: Patterns of Localization*, edited by Nadine Amsler, Andreea Badea, Bernard Heyberger, and Christian Windler, 174–89. New York: Routledge, 2020.

———. *Women Religious Leaders in Japan's Christian Century, 1549–1650*. Farnham, UK: Ashgate, 2009.

Yoshida, Kazuhiko. "The Enlightenment of the Dragon King's Daughter in the Lotus Sutra." Translated by Margret H. Childs. In *Engendering Faith: Women and Buddhism in Premodern Japan*, edited by Barbara Ruch, 297–324. Ann Arbor: University of Michigan Press, 2002.

Chapter 5

NATIVE CHRISTIANITY AND COMMUNAL JUSTICE IN COLONIAL MEXICO

An Ambivalent History

Yanna Yannakakis

Christian evangelization in Mesoamerica produced an ambivalent history: the imposition by Christian missionaries of a foreign worldview that attempted cultural erasure, and creative adaption and innovation on the part of native peoples.[1] Missionary friars were key players in the sixteenth-century Spanish wars of conquest waged against America's indigenous populations. In the case of colonial Mexico, they oversaw both the destruction of the painted books that contained the sacred histories of the region's ethnic polities, and the suppression and murder of the priestly class. Although the missionaries destroyed indigenous knowledge, they also sought to preserve elements of it by commissioning pictographic manuscripts or copies of older texts that reproduced Mesoamerican sacred calendars and cosmological glossaries. They reframed the indigenous vision of the sacred within the colonial codices through discourses of idolatry, superstition, and evil, assigning them value-laden titles such as "The book of the life that the Indians made in their antiquity, and the superstitions and evil rites that they had and maintained."[2]

Alongside the violence, destruction, and reframing of knowledge, missionary friars pursued a strategy of persuasion made possible by diverse processes of cultural and linguistic translation. This "moral dialogue" occurred in special schools that the friars established for the sons of the native nobility, the most famous of which was the Colegio de Santa Cruz Tlatelolco.[3] There, Franciscan friars, led by Fray Bernardino de Sahagún, and their native pupils and co-authors produced *The Florentine Codex*, a text written in Spanish and Nahuatl that attempted to catalog crucial aspects of indigenous history, moral philosophy, language, healing, and ritual for the purposes of more effective evangelization.[4] This cross-cultural dialogue between Christian missionaries and the native nobility was replicated across New Spain through the translation of Christian texts into latinized native language texts used for the purposes of pastoral education and evangelization.[5] In many cases, the translation of Christian ideas and discourses by native people and missionaries, and their incorporation into native ritual and communal life, produced new, indigenous Christianities that met the spiritual needs and expectations of native people.[6]

The violence, repression, translation, and education of the Christian missionary enterprise made their marks on native society and culture. One of the most potent mechanisms, however, for the interpellation of Christianity into the fabric of native life was the political engagement of Mesoamerica's native elite with Christianity and its institutions. Some embraced it through dramatic public baptism, signaling a pact with the new conquerors defined by the acceptance of Spanish rule and the Catholic faith in exchange for native semi-sovereignty. Others openly defied the friars' spiritual tutelage and suffered violent repression and bloody extirpation campaigns. Many others occupied a space in between assimilation and resistance by participating in public Christianity and semi-clandestine native rituals and practices without contradiction.[7]

This essay explores how native lords, officials, and community leaders engaged with the violence and "moral dialogue" of the Spanish colonial mission enterprise to build new political and legal institutions in their semi-sovereign polities. The varied responses of native people to Christian evangelization created social and political tensions in native communities that gave rise to open conflict. Although the rhythm of the Christian ritual calendar and the care of Christian saints came to undergird communal life in native towns across Mesoamerica, native practices that did not conform to Christian norms continued to inform social life. As was true for Christians, the sacred could not be hived off from the everyday; it was immanent in the world and permeated the most quotidian activities. The heterodoxy of everyday life produced a constant undercurrent of tension between native villagers and Christian authorities, whether Spanish or native.

As parish priests and their native Christian allies policed the behavior of fellow villagers or squared off with rivals who were native ritual specialists, colonial courts figured centrally as a stage for native political conflicts.

Discourses about Christian morality, justice, and the law that were forged in the crucible of the "moral dialogue" provided the script. Two cases from different regions of colonial Mexico and different moments of Mexico's long three-hundred-year colonial history demonstrate how native people deployed Christian norms in colonial courts to discipline and neutralize political rivals. The distinct circumstances of the two cases show how Christianity and native institutions shaped one another, especially in the practice of communal justice. The first case, well known in the historical literature, provides an entry point for an analysis of how native people utilized the Spanish legal system and Christian institutions to pursue their own political ends. The second case, drawn from a collaborative historical-linguistic research project, provides a fine-grained picture of how native-missionary translation and "moral dialogue" formed the bedrock of colonial native justice and fanned the flames of native political rivalries.

The Case against Don Carlos Chichimecateuctli in New Spain's Inquisition

Native engagement with Christianity had political implications for the early postconquest period. Spanish authorities favored native Christian allies who they assumed would be loyal to them as governors of native polities. The postconquest system of native-Spanish alliances was facilitated by the cellular structure of the Mexica (Aztec) empire, of which the *altepetl* (the term for the native polities of central Mexico in Nahuatl, the language of central Mexico) served as the primary building block.[8] Tetzcoco was one of the most powerful native polities in the Basin of Mexico, having formed part of the core of the Mexica Triple Alliance. In a climactic moment of the conquest during the battle for the Aztec capital of Tenochtitlan, a faction of the Tetzcocan nobility led by the (in)famous Indian conquistador Ixtlilxochitl turned coat and allied with Hernán Cortés. As such, following the conquest, the Tetzcocans were viewed with favor by the new Spanish overlords.[9]

A crucial mechanism of the alliances between Spanish conquerors and the native rulers of central Mexico's *altepeme* (plural of altepetl)—and the communities of other regions of New Spain, such as Yucatan and Oaxaca—was the incorporation of the Catholic mission and missionary priests into the structure of native political authority.[10] As such, Christian laws and social norms exerted considerable influence on the practice of everyday life. Native marriage became a flashpoint as missionary priests and their native allies attempted to impose a colonial social order and new concepts of sexuality.[11]

To the chagrin of missionaries and colonial officials, polygyny—a practice long reserved for the pre-Hispanic indigenous elite that facilitated native political alliances and the dominance of larger *altepeme* (native polities) over smaller ones—proved especially durable. Missionary friars and their diocesan counterparts associated it with idolatry and the practices of old, worked hard to stamp it out, and used spiritual and temporal means to do so. In their view, polygyny counted as concubinage, which contravened the divine law of the Ten Commandments and posed a danger to the salvation of the native population. Concubinage was also a crime under Spanish civil law, much of which applied to the American colonies.[12] There was another, temporal imperative to ending native polygyny. In the colonial context, the Christian model of the nuclear family provided the unit for tribute payment and tax collection: the household. The maintenance of colonial social and economic order depended on it. The spiritual war against polygyny eventually destabilized the political alliances that undergirded indigenous rule, disrupted patterns of inheritance, and undermined the position of elite women in native society.[13]

The struggle to control native sexuality provides a rich entry point into the ways Christianity shaped the postconquest native social and political order. The 1539 trial and execution of don Carlos Chichimecateuctli, indigenous lord of Tetzcoco, by the Inquisition for idolatry provides one of the most notorious examples of the violence engendered by the imposition of Christian marriage and marks a turning point in the consolidation of Spanish control in central Mexico.[14]

Tetzcocan politics were notoriously factional, which helps to explain why the Tetzcocan nobility splintered during the crucible of the Spanish conquest.[15] The factionalism persisted into the early colonial period as upstart native lords curried favor, and Spanish authorities approved the succession of certain Tetzcocan lords over others. Don Carlos Chichimecateuctli was the son of Nezahualpilli, a revered pre-Hispanic lord of Tetzcoco, and brother of don Pedro Tetlahuehuetzquititzin, a postconquest lord (*tlatoani*) of Tetzcoco. When don Pedro died, don Carlos made a bid to succeed him through the pre-Hispanic practice of taking don Pedro's primary wife as one of his own. He needed to do this to boost the legitimacy of his claim to the Tetzcocan lordship. Though he was the son and brother of a lord, his mother was not a Mexica noblewoman but rather one of Nezahualpilli's lesser wives. As such, don Carlos hovered at the margins of the Tetzcocan nobility, and his efforts to claim the lordship of Tetzcoco drew the ire of powerful figures.[16]

Francisco Maldonado was one of these powerful men, and the one responsible for denouncing don Carlos to the Inquisition as a "heretical dogmatizer." Maldonado was emblematic of a new cadre of native Christians who enjoyed social and political mobility due to their close contacts with missionary friars. Maldonado was himself a native nobleman from the central Mexican altepetl of Chiconautla. As a young man, he attended the Franciscan-run Colegio de Santa Cruz Tlatelolco. He returned to his home altepetl to serve in the capacity of lay catechist, a common path for noble youth who attended the missionary schools. Maldonado claimed that during a visit don Carlos paid to Chiconautla, he heard him publicly denounce Christianity.[17]

Bishop Juan de Zumárraga—a Franciscan friar, the first bishop of New Spain, and an officer of the Inquisition—oversaw the case against don Carlos.[18] In the trial records, the political stakes of the case come to the fore. Don Carlos's sister, sister-in-law, and wife, who had publicly allied themselves with Christianity, testified against him—not for the crime of heretical dogmatism but rather for concubinage, to which don Carlos freely admitted. His brothers, who occupied high offices in the *cabildo* (Spanish-style municipal council) of Tetzcoco and counted among the high-ranking nobility, did not defend don Carlos in their testimonies, or even mention him, but rather attested to the measures they had taken to combat idolatry in the region. The explicitly damning testimony came from Chiconautla where, due to the custom of bilateral inheritance, don Carlos was a potential claimant to local lordship.[19]

The trial and execution of don Carlos Chichimecateuctli must be interpreted through the layered complexities of colonial politics. His pretensions to the lordship of Tetzcoco despite his marginal position within Tetzcoco's nobility, and the alienation of his female Christian kin, made him vulnerable to the charges of political rivals both within Tetzcoco and beyond.[20] Mexico's indigenous nobility quickly learned that charges of idolatry could be wielded against political opponents. Concubinage, though not idolatry by definition, was certainly associated with the pagan practices of the pre-Hispanic past. Finally, Francisco Maldonado, the native Christian who denounced don Carlos, was an ally of the Franciscans and Spanish officials of central Mexico. Notably, after don Carlos's execution, the Inquisition confiscated and sold part of don Carlos's noble estate to a Spaniard.[21]

The spectacle of don Carlos's trial and execution did not go unnoticed by the king of Spain and the Council of the Indies who judged as too harsh Zumárraga's zealous prosecution of the case and that of other native nobles suspected of backsliding. They stripped Zumárraga of his inquisitorial powers and removed New Spain's indigenous population from the jurisdiction of the Inquisition in 1571 on the grounds that they were Christian neophytes who were still learning about the faith and therefore prone to mistakes. Native idolatry henceforth fell under civil jurisdiction and was treated as a crime.[22]

From the Inquisition to the Native Tribunal

Early colonial public battles over pre-Hispanic practices, including idolatry and polygyny, diminished over time in their frequency and intensity in areas of high contact between Spanish clergy and native communities like central Mexico. Although these practices may have continued clandestinely in some communities, the indigenous rulers who mediated between Spanish authority and their indigenous communities understood the political and economic benefits of aligning themselves with Christianity. Spanish officials increasingly entrusted indigenous authorities with the task of policing their own communities and ensuring their compliance with Christian norms.

During the sixteenth century, the Spanish Crown granted semiautonomous jurisdiction to the native nobility of New Spain. Indirect rule by native lords made sense on a number of levels; Spain could not support a bureaucracy large enough to rule Mesoamerica's vast conglomeration of native polities, and native lords had the added benefit of enjoying political legitimacy. The Spanish Crown allowed native lords to rule their communities according to local laws and customs, provided they did not contravene Christianity. In addition to recognizing the semi-sovereignty of native lords, the Crown installed *cabildos* (town councils) in native communities. The cabildo was staffed by native nobility and lesser nobility; it became a vehicle for social mobility and an arena for political rivalry as the balance of power shifted from native lordship to the jurisdiction of the native cabildo, though in many cases the native hereditary nobility continued to exercise considerable influence and power as a shadow government.[23] The cabildo oversaw civil administration, including the collection of taxes and tribute, the orderly transfer of inherited property, and the organization of native labor.[24] Crucially, the cabildo was also designed to maintain social order through the exercise of first-instance civil and criminal jurisdiction. In short, it was a native tribunal.[25]

As was true of Spanish imperial authority more broadly, the civil authority of the native cabildo was reinforced by the parallel and overlapping authority of the ecclesiastical jurisdiction in native communities. Parish priests acted as ecclesiastical judges and punished villagers who did not comply with Christian norms. But not all native communities had parish priests; indeed, the scarcity of such figures increased with distance from central Mexico. In the absence of parish priests, social discipline was reinforced by a parallel body of native church officials, including lay catechists, choirmasters, sacristans, and priests' assistants who served as the eyes and ears of the Catholic Church. Drunkenness and failure to attend mass were punished by public lashings ordered and administered by native municipal and church officials. In this way, Christian discipline in native communities became the purview of native authorities.[26]

The Case against Juan Ramos in the Native Tribunal of San Juan Yatzona, Oaxaca

By the first decades of the seventeenth century in much of New Spain, especially central Mexico, native authority and Christianity were inextricably intertwined. The constant engagement with and re-elaboration of Christianity by native peoples through contact and conflict with missionary priests and colonial officials, and through the practices of their daily lives—self-governance, the administration of local justice, agriculture, death, the transference of property, collective labor, and the renewal of household and communal bonds—wove Christianity into the fabric of indigenous identity. The agonistic battles over pre-Hispanic ritual and sociocultural norms had largely faded into the past.

This did not mean, however, that Christianity had fully displaced an indigenous sociocultural order. Not all native people were willing to comply with the rituals of mass and confession, and the social conventions of monogamy and Christian marriage. Outside of central Mexico, in geographically peripheral regions characterized by large indigenous populations and few Spanish civil or religious authorities, missionary priests and native communities continued to struggle over the respective roles of Christianity and native ritual, and the relative authority of native Christians and native ritual specialists. The diocese of Oaxaca, in southern New Spain, was one of these peripheral regions. In contrast with the larger native polities of central Mexico, smaller, midsize polities characterized by great linguistic diversity occupied a rugged landscape. Whereas the conversion of a few highly visible nobles in central Mexico facilitated the legitimation of colonial rule, Oaxaca's decentralized sociopolitical structure posed challenges to the understaffed Dominican order, which struggled to attract resources and manpower.[27]

The Dominican order, known for its stern didacticism and orthodoxy, waged an on-and-off battle against what they called idolatry in Oaxaca's native communities through the seventeenth and early eighteenth centuries. Their strategies were diverse, ranging broadly from coercion to persuasion.[28] As was true of the early postconquest period in central Mexico, the key to the success of the missionary enterprise was to build alliances with native authorities who would serve as a vanguard for the process of extirpation.

The strategy of persuasion, which entailed cross-cultural communication, was based on a model tested in central Mexico and other regions of the world where missionary orders sought to convert native populations to Christianity. Missionaries in cooperation with native elites familiar with the ceremonial high registers of their native languages produced bilingual dictionaries, grammars, and confessional manuals intended to help parish priests with their pastoral duties. They also produced bilingual catechisms to be used by missionary priests and native lay catechists for the purpose of educating the indigenous population in the basics of the faith. Other bilingual and native language genres that grew out of the collaborative translation work of missionary friars and native elites included confessional manuals, sermons, and exempla, all of which were intended to teach and reinforce Christian values and behaviors.[29]

In their bilingual texts, missionaries engaged with indigenous ritual practice with great ambivalence. On the one hand, they had to acknowledge its hegemonic power and the ways in which it undergirded and invoked native authority. On the other, they had to combat it in order to ensure the uncontested dominance of Christianity. They tried to achieve this by using indigenous practices as analogies for Christian norms and practices, while at the same time relegating indigenous practices to a pre-Hispanic past. At other times, they explicitly identified indigenous practice with idolatry.[30]

In Oaxaca's northern sierra, according to church authorities, the indigenous population was especially reluctant to give up the ways of their ancestors. Part of the problem, the friars and secular hierarchy insisted, had to do with the region's rugged mountainous geography, which impeded the expansion of the Dominican mission into the region and provided a disincentive to Spanish settlement. Until 1700, less than 10 percent of the district's native communities had a resident priest.³¹ Linguistic diversity also posed a challenge; there were five languages spoken in the region. The relative absence of Spanish settlers meant that a small handful of Spanish officials and missionary priests had to rely heavily on native authorities to uphold Christian norms and colonial rule. The dearth of colonial officials also provided a space for native autonomy and the persistence of native ritual.³²

Dominican and secular officials responded to the persistence of "idolatry" in Oaxaca's northern sierra with sporadic extirpation efforts, which entailed the active support of native Christians who served as lay catechists and priest's assistants. After 1660, these efforts escalated into a wholesale campaign, culminating in the Cajonos Rebellion of 1700 in which native people in the Cajonos region of Villa Alta rose up violently against Dominican friars, Spanish officials, and their native allies. Repression followed in the wake of the rebellion. Thirty-four indigenous leaders were tried and convicted for the murder of the priest's assistants of the native town of San Francisco Cajonos, and for instigating the rebellion. Fifteen of them were executed. Parish inspections ensued, during which native villagers turned over their ritual objects and texts to Spanish authorities, denounced their ritual specialists, and led church and civil officials to their sacred sites.³³

During the cycle of extirpation in the northern Oaxacan district of Villa Alta that endured from 1660 to 1700, the conflict between Christian marriage and polygyny emerged as a flashpoint, as it did in the case of don Carlos Chichimecateuctli. This time the primary actors were not inquisitors or central Mexican native lords but rather Dominican missionaries, native municipal authorities acting as judges of first instance, and the villagers of a remote mountain district. A small cache of criminal records written in the native languages of the region provide a fine-grained picture of how native-Christian engagement and struggle—and the cultural and linguistic translation that it entailed—shaped native communal justice. In the space that remains, I will focus on a criminal case of concubinage to explore how native authorities used Christian norms and discourses to punish their rivals and discredit the ways of the past. Through their deployment of Christian morality as a mode of social discipline and criminal justice, they helped to weave Christian norms into the fabric of local society and into their authoritative discourse.³⁴ The case has many resonances with the Inquisition case against don Carlos Chichimecateuctli over a century earlier, but it also provides subtler evidence of change over time and regional difference.

In 1661 the native judges of the Indian town of San Juan Yatzona wrote a record in Nexitzo Zapotec, the local language, detailing the crimes of Juan Ramos, a member of the community, who according to them had committed the crime of concubinage.[35] Unlike don Carlos Chichimecateuctli, Juan Ramos was not a great lord from a long-standing indigenous noble lineage but rather a *principal*, one of a select group of village notables, or lesser nobility, who rotated in and out of municipal office-holding. At the time of the Spanish conquest, the Zapotec region of the Sierra Norte had only been settled one hundred years prior by migrants from the Valley of Oaxaca. Sierra Zapotec communities were formed by clans and extended families, some of which were more powerful than others.[36] By comparison with the indigenous nobility of central Mexico, the Valley of Oaxaca, and the Oaxacan Mixteca, northern sierra Zapotec nobles were relatively poor in land and dependents, and the social distance between nobles and commoners was short.[37] Those of highest status memorialized their lineages in pictorial genealogies painted on cloth to support claims to land and noble privileges. As in other regions of New Spain, Spanish officials referred to these men as *caciques* and *principales*, denoting higher and lesser noble status respectively.[38] *Principales* from different lineages often competed with one another to control the native municipal government and the interests of their extended kin group.[39]

After the standard opening of the criminal case against Juan Ramos in which the native judges recorded the date and identified themselves as the officials of the community gathered in the "court of the king," the judges recounted in explicit detail Ramos's sexual relations with multiple women, who were cited by name, or identified as the wife of a community member. It is notable that the sexual crimes cited encompassed a wide range of relationships, which in Christian terms included fornication and adultery. All these acts were prosecuted under the rubric of concubinage, under whose umbrella New Spain's missionaries included all "temporary and permanent unions not legitimated by the sacrament of marriage."[40]

The criminal record provided much detail about Ramos's sexual encounters, including information about where, how, and how many times Ramos and his partners were caught, which served to dramatize the behavior and scandalize a Christian reader, like a court interpreter or Spanish judge. The women who allegedly had sexual relations with Juan Ramos took an active role in the narrative; none of them was portrayed as a passive victim. In one instance, a woman left her husband for Ramos for one month. In another instance, a woman who alleged that Ramos raped her took her case against him to the Spanish magistrate. Notably, women also played a key role as witnesses in the case of don Carlos Chichimecateuctli.

Each sexual encounter was listed numerically (the first episode, second episode, etc.), such that they added up to a full picture of the crimes/sins of Juan Ramos. After the list of sexual acts, the authorities summarized the case by arguing that Juan Ramos was not a good Christian, that he lived like the Zapotecs of old, and that he did not conform to the expectations of the Indian republic, including Catholic education, hard work, and service to the church. Instead, he drank and fornicated. Through this narrative, the document's authors built a case that Juan Ramos did not conform to Christian norms of sexual behavior and, implicitly, a case that highlighted their good governance and Christian morality.

The native judges concluded the document by forbidding Ramos to ever hold office, enter the municipal hall, or claim status as a village notable; essentially, they demoted him to commoner status. They ordered that if he did not conform to the sentence, he should be whipped fifty times, jailed for one month, and charged a twenty-peso fine. He should also be mounted on a horse, whipped on every corner of the village, and exiled for three months. They also ordered that if any other village notable were to unite with him or help him to attain village office, they, too, would be considered a commoner. Finally, they ordered that the document be taken to the Spanish magistrate so that he could be aware of Juan Ramos's crimes. The sentence in the case of Juan Ramos is emblematic of the political factionalism in San Juan Yatzona and other Indian towns of the district of Villa Alta during this period, as competing groups of *principales* attempted to dominate village government. Often, the groups conflicted over the place of Christianity in village life and the relationship of the cabildo with Spanish church and civil officials. It is clear that the cabildo did not want Juan Ramos to exercise political power in the village.

The punishment concocted by the cabildo of San Juan Yatzona reveals a gap between the law in theory and in practice. According to the laws of the Indies, in some regions of the Americas civil and ecclesiastical authorities punished Indians severely for the crime of concubinage, a practice with which the Crown disagreed. In a 1536 decree, the king mandated that Indian men should not be punished harshly by civil or ecclesiastical authorities for concubinage and that if Indians had been fined for the crime, restitution of such fines should be made.[41] In the case of Indian women, it mandated against sending them to *casas de recogimiento* (the homes of Spaniards who would police their sexuality) or remanding them to the personal service of

Spanish officials or religious officials. This decree reflects the special status held by Indians in the Spanish legal system; they were accorded a degree of leniency due to their status as newcomers to the Christian faith and the practice of Christian monogamy. This same logic informed the Crown's decision to remove Indians from the jurisdiction of the Inquisition in 1571. The case against Juan Ramos makes clear that the native authorities of San Juan Yatzona took it on themselves to ignore such calls for leniency and prescribe instead harsh punishment.[42]

The case against Juan Ramos served many purposes. One was to make a case that Juan Ramos was a criminal by detailing his sexual behavior. Another was for the cabildo to present themselves as good Christians and colonial officials. The cabildo achieved this through linguistic and rhetorical strategies and through oppositions. The most important opposition addressed the political climate of the region at the time: the extirpation of idolatry. This is clear in the framing of Juan Ramos's behavior as belonging to the time of Zapotec antiquity, and not the time of the Christian doctrine.

Christian notions of proper sexual comportment—monogamy through the sacrament of marriage—structured the case against Juan Ramos in a dialogic way; the narrative that unfolded evaluated Juan Ramos's actions against the Christian ideal, thereby illuminating his sinfulness and criminality. The notion of "old law" worked alongside Christianity to structure the document temporally: the authors of the case located Juan Ramos's promiscuous conduct in the "old law," the time before Christianity, and categorized his behavior as morally reprehensible and anti-Christian, thereby positioning its authors—the municipal council acting as first-instance judges—as upholders of Christian law. In the opening passage of the document, the municipal officers stated, "We the judges say that he is not a Christian, that he does not know the holy Doctrine, he is like a man of olden times [*benne golaza*], he lives in the law of olden times [*leo golaza*]."[43] In this excerpt, the authors of the document use the Zapotec term *benne golaza* (literally "man formerly") and a modified Spanish loanword for law (*ley*)—*leo*—to create the construction *leo golaza* (literally "law formerly"), which expresses the idea of someone living according to an older regime. In a later passage in the case, the authors referred again to "the old law," but this time through the voice of Marta de la Cruz, whom Juan Ramos allegedly raped: "Marta de la Cruz said, 'Why did you take me by force, there is no God, there is no king, you are still in the time of the old law, you live according to the old word [*sic*; a metaphor for regime or law]."[44] The use of "still" emphasized temporality and conflict: it suggested that Juan Ramos's actions took place within—and were symptomatic of—a transitional period between the old law—that which belonged to the time before Christianity (the Christian idea of "gentility")—and the new regime. Through Marta de la Cruz, the cabildo of Yatzona criminalized the normative order—the "old word"— of the pre-Christian past. Throughout the criminal record, the idea of the Zapotec past was expressed by the term *golaza*, written as *colaça* or *colaaza* in Valley Zapotec, which Dominican missionaries translated as "formerly" or "of old."[45]

The idea of native antiquity played a central role in the bilingual texts that Dominican missionaries and their native elite allies produced for pastoral education, confession, sermons, and other activities. Dominican missionaries made frequent use of the term *golaza*/*coláça* in order to put Christian doctrine and the "old law" into moral dialogue. In some instances, they used *colaça* in constructions that took on positive or neutral meaning, but in others, the notion of "formerly" took on a negative connotation, associated with idolatry. For example, in Pedro de Feria's translation and explanation of the "Our Father" in his bilingual catechism *Doctrina christiana en lengua castellana y çapoteca* (1567), the first Zapotec-language catechism produced in the Valley of Oaxaca, he used *colaça* twice, first to translate the positive idea of "Old Christians" (*cristianos colaça*) and second to convey the negative idea of the practices of an idolatrous pre-Christian past: "When you need something, do not go to ask your idols of wood and stone, nor confide in your dead (as you did formerly [*colaça*]), rather only to God should you tell of your needs."[46]

In a section of Feria's catechism devoted to idolatry and its punishment, he used a construction with *colaça* to index "ancestors" (*antepasados* in Spanish) with a negative connotation: "Chela tichacani coxiguie bezeloo beni cotij colaça" (And that teaching with which the devil tricked the ancestors).[47] Here, Feria took aim at the ancestors, who were central figures in Zapotec cosmology, mythical founders of their communities, and local deities. The ancestors played a central role in the ritual practices of Zapotec communities in the pre-Hispanic and colonial periods. Ritual specialists provided a vital link between the community and its ancestors, regulating both ritual life and social and moral order.[48] By reducing the regime of the ancestors to the devil's trickery, Feria worked to undercut the central place that the ancestors continued to maintain in communal ritual life, despite missionary efforts at evangelization.

Feria's translations shaped later missionary texts, which is evident in the continued association of the pre-Christian past with idolatry. For example, in his first exempla in his 1666 *Miscelaneo espiritual*, Dominican friar Cristóbal de Agüero used *colaaza* to refer to a depraved time before Christianity. In Francisco Pacheco de Silva's 1687 bilingual catechism, he used *golaza* to modify the term "idols," as in the "idols of former times."⁴⁹

Through missionary translation, the sacred practices associated with the past and the regime of the ancestors were deemed "idolatrous." The negative meaning of *golaza* in the case against Juan Ramos drew strongly from missionary discourse regarding idolatry and the pre-Christian past. When the native judges of San Juan Yatzona accused Juan Ramos of living in the "old law," the term that they used—*leo golaza*—marked not merely a distinction between old law and new but, more pointedly, between the law of the ancestors, cast as idolatry, and the Christian present. The practice of polygyny—glossed as "concubinage"—belonged to the old law.

The expression "old law" connected the local context of Villa Alta, Oaxaca, to a deep history of Iberian political-religious conflict. The "old law" associated Juan Ramos's behavior with that of an especially maligned and criminalized social group in the Iberian legal tradition: *conversos* (Jews who had converted to Christianity after the forced expulsion and conversions of the 1490s). *Conversos* and *moriscos* (Muslims who remained in Iberia and converted to Christianity following the Christian reconquest) often referred to their respective faiths—either Judaism or Islam—as the "old law" (*ley antigua* in Spanish).⁵⁰ Like the conversos and moriscos of the Iberian Peninsula, Mexico's indigenous peoples found themselves caught between an evangelizing church and their own traditions of authority and morality. Indeed, during the sixteenth and seventeenth centuries Spanish ecclesiastical officials made comparisons between the Jews and indigenous peoples of the Americas in an effort to determine how to categorize and treat native converts. Some officials argued that Indians and Jews were profoundly dissimilar as converts since Indians did not live according to a religion or law, as did the Jews; rather, they had lived according to natural law, which made it easier for them to embrace Christianity. Others firmly equated Indians with Jews, arguing that like the Jews, Indians were idolaters who held on to their old law while pretending to accept Christianity.⁵¹

Don Isidro de Sariñana y Cuenca, bishop of Oaxaca from 1683 to 1696, and Diego Jaimes Ricardo Villavicencio, a secular priest and zealous extirpator who worked in Tlaxcala and Oaxaca, viewed indigenous people through the lens of the backsliding converso. Sariñana was a prime mover of the extirpation of idolatry in late seventeenth-century Oaxaca. Villavicencio, an acolyte of Sariñana, published in 1692 an extirpation manual, *Luz y methodo de confesar idolatras, y destierro de idolatrias, debajo del tratado siguiente: Tratado de avisos y puntos importantes, de la abominable seta* [sic; secta] *de la idolatria*, in which he made frequent and disparaging parallels between the native population and Jews.[52] It is possible that the construction *leo golaza* was inspired by the ideas and rhetoric circulated by Sariñana, Villavicencio, and like-minded theologians.

As the movement of concepts and ideas across Spanish and Indian civil and ecclesiastical jurisdictions makes clear, translation was not a linear process that originated in one language and moved to another. Rather, it was a constant movement back and forth across institutional contexts and the geographic spaces of the Spanish empire. The opposition between the old law and the new expressed the position of Spanish law in relation to an indigenous normative order that it sought to eradicate. It also served to express intracommunal political conflict between native officials who signaled their Christian identities throughout the criminal record they authored and their rivals who they persecuted in the name of the law of God and king.

Conclusion

Christianity undergirded Spanish colonialism in the Americas in myriad ways: the formation of nuclear families within indigenous communities, the valorization of a new moral order, and the introduction of new rhythms of everyday life at the individual and community level. At the same time, the transformations that Christian missionaries hoped to achieve were often partial and ambivalent. Native people continued to practice native rituals and engage in social relations that contradicted Christian norms while incorporating Christianity into their individual and communal identities. Christianity also formed the bedrock of political alliances between Spanish ecclesiastical and civil officials and native lords and rulers. This dynamic situation shaped colonial institutions as much as it did indigenous society.

Just as important, native people played on the ambivalence of the Christian missionary enterprise in New Spain by deploying Christian symbols and discourses for their own ends in a variety of settings, including colonial courts. Native marriage became a flashpoint of Spanish-indigenous and inter-indigenous conflict from the colonial core of central Mexico to the rugged mountains of Oaxaca. Native élites deployed charges of idolatry and concubinage against their rivals to remove them from office or dispossess them of their status and property. This strategy had spectacularly violent consequences in the case of don Carlos Chichimecateuctli and contributed to the end of the Inquisition's jurisdiction over native people.

Whereas an institution external to the *altepetl* of Tetzcoco tried don Carlos, Juan Ramos was tried for concubinage by a tribunal made up of judges from his own community, who through the subtlety of translation linked his sexuality to idolatry. This was no small matter given the broader context of an extirpation campaign. In both cases, native authorities and witnesses leveled charges of concubinage against native rivals instrumentally, as expressions of political conflict. At the same time, the devaluation and criminalization of those who lived like the ancestors demonized and criminalized the native past and non-Christian elements of native authority. Whether native villagers positioned themselves with or against Christian authorities and their native allies, this subtle process of translation infiltrated the exercise of local authority, communal justice, the practice of everyday life, and the native language itself.

The ambivalent interaction of the Christian missionary enterprise and native communal justice continues to reverberate in the mountainous district of Villa Alta, Oaxaca, and throughout Mexico. On August 1, 2002, Pope John Paul II beatified Juan Bautista and Jacinto de los Angeles, two Zapotec men from Oaxaca's northern sierra who died during the 1700 Cajonos Rebellion. The men were native Christians and priest's assistants (*fiscales*) from San Francisco Cajonos. According to Spanish criminal records, they had informed Dominican friars that their fellow villagers were engaging in clandestine native rituals. Witnesses claimed that the two men were killed by order of the native officials of San Francisco Cajonos. The beatification ceremony took place alongside the canonization ceremony of Juan Diego, the indigenous farmer who in 1531, according to various accounts, encountered the Virgin of Guadalupe, Mexico's patron saint. The event, in which purportedly indigenous music, dance, and ritual were performed, was attended by tens of thousands of people. But the reaction was one of ambivalence: many Mexicans, some of whom were indigenous, were proud; others, who viewed the indigenous "martyrs" as traitors, were outraged. For its part, the Catholic Church took the opportunity to tout the canonization of its first indigenous American saint and the beatification of two Zapotec Christians who may well be on the road to sainthood.[53]

Notes

1. In her groundbreaking study of Spanish conquest and Christian evangelization in Yucatan, Inga Clendinnen applies the concept of ambivalence as an alternative to Robert Ricard's "spiritual conquest." Inga Clendinnen, *Ambivalent Conquests: Maya and Spaniard in Yucatan, 1517–1570* (Cambridge, UK: Cambridge University Press, 1987); see also Robert Ricard, *The Spiritual Conquest of Mexico: An Essay on the Apostolate and the Evangelizing Methods of the Mendicant Orders in New Spain, 1523–1572* (Berkeley: University of California Press, 1974).

2. The title in the original Spanish: *Libro de la vida que los indios antiguamente hacían, y supersticiones y malos ritos que tenían y guardaban*. Ferdinand Anders and Maarten Jansen et al. (with contributions by Jessica Davilar and Anuschka Van't Hooft), *Libro de la vida: Códice Magliabechiano: Texto explicativo del llamado Códice Magliabechiano* (Mexico City: Fondo de Cultura Económica, 1996).

3. Louise Burkhart, *The Slippery Earth: Nahua-Christian Moral Dialogue in Sixteenth-Century Mexico* (Tucson: University of Arizona Press, 1989).

4. Bernardino de Sahagún, *Florentine Codex: General History of the Things of New Spain*, trans. Arthur J. O. Anderson and Charles E. Dibble, vol. 12 (Santa Fe, NM: School of American Research and University of Utah, 1975).

5. William F. Hanks, *Converting Words: Maya in the Age of the Cross* (Berkeley: University of California Press, 2010); Nancy Farriss, with Juana Vásquez Vásquez, *Libana: El discurso ceremonial mesoamericano y el sermón cristiano* (Mexico City: Artes de México, 2014); Nancy Farriss, *Tongues of Fire: Language and Evangelization in Colonial Mexico* (New York and London: Oxford University Press, 2018); Martina Schrader-Kniffki and Yanna Yannakakis, "Sins and Crimes: Zapotec-Spanish Translation in Catholic Evangelization and Colonial Law (Oaxaca, New Spain)," in *Missionary Linguistics V / Lingüística Misionera V: Translation Theories and Practices*, ed. Otto Zwartjes, Klaus Zimmerman, and Martina Schrader-Kniffki (Amsterdam: John Benjamins, 2014), 161–99; Yanna Yannakakis and Martina Schrader-Kniffki, "Between the 'Old Law' and the New: Christian Translation, Indian Jurisdiction, and Criminal Justice in Colonial Oaxaca," *Hispanic American Historical Review* 96, no. 3 (2016): 517–48; Yanna Yannakakis and Martina Schrader-Kniffki, "Contra Juan Ramos por el delito de concubinato: traducción Cristiana y jurisdicción indígena en Oaxaca, siglo XVII," in *Los indios ante la justicia local: Intérpretes, funcionarios y litigantes en Nueva España y Guatemala (siglos XVI–XVIII)*, ed. Yanna Yannakakis, Martina Schrader-Kniffki, and Luis Alberto Arrioja Díaz Viruell (Zamora, Mexico: Colegio de Michoacán, 2019), 31–52.

6. Mark Z. Christensen, *Nahua and Maya Catholicisms: Texts and Religion in Colonial Central Mexico and Yucatan* (Stanford, CA: Stanford University Press, 2013); Mark Z. Christensen, *Translated Christianities: Nahuatl and Maya Religious Texts* (University Park: Pennsylvania State University Press, 2014); David Tavárez, *Words and Worlds Turned Around: Indigenous Christianities in Colonial Latin America* (Boulder: University Press of Colorado, 2017).

7. J. Jorge Klor de Alva, "Spiritual Conflict and Accommodation in New Spain: Toward a Typology of Aztec Responses to Christianity," in *The Inca and Aztec States, 1400–1800: Anthropology and History*, ed. George A. Collier, Renato Rosaldo, and John D. Wirth (London: Academic Press, 1982), 345–66.

8. James Lockhart, *The Nahuas after the Conquest: A Social and Cultural History of the Indians of Central Mexico, Sixteenth through Eighteenth Centuries* (Stanford, CA: Stanford University Press, 1992).

9. Amber Brian, Bradley Benton, and Pablo Garcia Loaeza, eds., *The Native Conquistador: Alva Ixtlilxochitl's Account of the Conquest of New Spain* (University Park: Pennsylvania State University Press, 2015), 37–52.

10. Nancy Farriss, *Maya Society under Colonial Rule: The Collective Enterprise of*

Survival (Princeton, NJ: Princeton University Press, 1984); William Taylor, *Magistrates of the Sacred: Priests and Parishioners in Eighteenth-Century Mexico* (Stanford, CA: Stanford University Press, 1996); María de los Angeles Romero Frizzi, *El sol y la cruz: Los pueblos indios de Oaxaca colonial* (Mexico City: Instituto Nacional de Antropología e Historia, 1996).

11. Susan Kellogg, *Law and the Transformation of Aztec Culture, 1500–1700* (Norman: University of Oklahoma Press, 1995); Susan Kellogg, *Weaving the Past: A History of Latin America's Indigenous Women from the Pre-Hispanic Period to the Present* (Oxford, UK: Oxford University Press, 2005); Susan Schroeder, Stephanie Wood, and Robert Haskett, eds., *Indian Women of Early Mexico* (Norman: University of Oklahoma Press, 1997); Steve J. Stern, *The Secret History of Gender: Women, Men, and Power in Late Colonial Mexico* (Chapel Hill: University of North Carolina Press, 1997); Pete Sigal, *The Flower and the Scorpion: Sexuality and Ritual in Early Nahua Culture* (Durham and London: Duke University Press, 2011); Pete Sigal, *From Moon Goddesses to Virgins: The Colonization of Yucatecan Maya Sexual Desire* (Austin: University of Texas Press, 2000); Kevin Terraciano, "Crime and Culture in Colonial Mexico: The Case of the Mixtec Murder Note," *Ethnohistory* 45, no. 4 (Autumn 1998): 709–45; John F. Chuchiak IV, "The Sins of the Fathers: Franciscan Friars, Parish Priests, and the Sexual Conquest of the Yucatec Maya, 1545–1808," *Ethnohistory* 54, no. 1 (Winter 2007): 70–127; Lisa Sousa, *The Woman Who Turned into a Jaguar, and Other Narratives of Native Women in Archives of Colonial Mexico* (Stanford, CA: Stanford University Press, 2017).

12. On the sins and crimes of lust (*lujuria*), including concubinage, and how missionary friars applied them to indigenous practices of polygyny, especially among the Nahua, see Danièle Dehouve, *Relatos de pecados en la evangelizacion de los indios de Mexico* (Mexico City: CIESAS, 2010), 96–101.

13. Ross Hassig, *Polygamy and the Rise and Demise of the Aztec Empire* (Albuquerque: University of New Mexico Press, 2016).

14. Luis Obregón González, *Proceso inquisitorial del cacique de Tetzcoco* (Mexico City: Eusebio Gómez de la Puente, 2010); Serge Gruzinski, *Man-Gods in the Mexican Highlands: Indian Power and Colonial Society, 1520–1800*, trans. Eileen Corrigan (Stanford, CA: Stanford University Press, 1989); Patricia Lopes Don, "The 1539 Inquisition Trial of Don Carlos of Texcoco in Early Colonial Mexico," *Hispanic American Historical Review* 88, no. 4 (November 2008): 573–606.

15. Camilla Townsend, "Polygyny and the Divided Altepetl: The Tetzocan Key to Pre-conquest Nahua Politics," in *Texcoco: Prehispanic and Colonial Perspectives*, ed. Jongsoo Lee and Galen Brokaw (Boulder: University Press of Colorado, 2014), 93–116.

16. Bradley Benton, *The Lords of Tetzcoco: The Transformation of Indigenous Rule in Postconquest Central Mexico* (Cambridge, UK: Cambridge University Press, 2017), 39–45.

17. David Tavárez, *The Invisible War: Indigenous Devotions, Discipline, and Dissent in Colonial Mexico* (Stanford, CA: Stanford University Press, 2011) 43–44.

18. Richard E. Greenleaf, *Zumárraga and the Mexican Inquisition, 1536–1543* (Washington, DC: Academy of American Franciscan History, 1961).

19. Benton, *Lords of Tetzcoco*, 39–45.
20. Ibid.

21. Charles Gibson, *The Aztecs under Spanish Rule: A History of the Indians of the Valley of Mexico, 1519–1810* (Stanford, CA: Stanford University Press, 1964); Susan Schroeder, "The Oztoticpac Lands Map: A Reexamination," in *Land and Politics in the Valley of Mexico: A Two-Thousand-Year Perspective*, ed. H. R. Harvey, 163–86 (Albuquerque: University of New Mexico Press, 1991).

22. Richard E. Greenleaf, "The Inquisition and the Indians of New Spain: A Study in Jurisdictional Confusion," *Americas* 22, no. 2 (July 1966): 181–96.

23. Margarita Menegus Bornemann, *Del senorio indigena a la republica de indios: El caso de Toluca, 1500–1600* (Mexico City: CONACULTA, 1994); Sergio Quezada, *Pueblos y caciques yucatecos, 1550–1580* (Mexico City: El Colegio de Mexico, 1993); Sergio Quezada, *Maya Lords and Lordship: The*

Formation of Colonial Society in Yucatán, 1350–1600, trans. Terry Rugeley (Norman: University of Oklahoma Press, 2014); Andrea Martínez Baracs, *Un gobierno de indios: Tlaxcala, 1519–1750* (Mexico City: Fondo de Cultura Económica, 2008).

24. Robert Stephen Haskett, *Indigenous Rulers: An Ethnohistory of Town Government in Colonial Cuernavaca* (Albuquerque: University of New Mexico Press, 1991).

25. Yannakakis and Schrader-Kniffki, "Between the 'Old Law' and the New."

26. Taylor, *Magistrates of the Sacred*.

27. John K. Chance, *Conquest of the Sierra: Spaniards and Indians in Colonial Oaxaca* (Norman: University of Oklahoma Press, 1989); Kevin Terraciano, *The Mixtecs of Colonial Oaxaca: Ñudzahui History, Sixteenth through Eighteenth Centuries* (Stanford, CA: Stanford University Press, 2001).

28. Tavárez, *The Invisible War*.

29. Farriss, *Libana*.

30. Ibid.; Schrader-Kniffki and Yannakakis, "Sins and Crimes"; Yannakakis and Schrader-Kniffki, "Between the 'Old Law' and the New."

31. Chance, *Conquest of the Sierra*, 59.

32. Yanna Yannakakis, *The Art of Being In-Between: Native Intermediaries, Indian Identity, and Local Rule in Colonial Oaxaca* (Durham, NC: Duke University Press, 2008).

33. José Alcina Franch, *Calendario y religión entre los zapotecos* (Mexico City: UNAM, 1993); Yannakakis, *Art of Being In-Between*; Rosalba Piazza, *La conciencia oscura de los naturales: Procesos de idolatría en la diócesis de Oaxaca (Nueva España), siglos XVI–XVIII* (Mexico City: UNAM, 2013); Tavárez, *Invisible War*.

34. The analysis of this case is drawn from my ongoing collaborative research project with Martina Schrader-Kniffki. An expanded version can be found in Yannakakis and Schrader-Kniffki, "Between the 'Old Law' and the New."

35. "Auto de Juan Ramos," 1661, submitted as evidence in "Contra don Pablo de Vargas por peculado y robo de la caja común," 1687, Archivo Histórico Judicial de Oaxaca, Villa Alta Criminal (hereafter AHJO Villa Alta Criminal), leg. 4, exp. 5, fols. 8v–9v.

36. Michel Oudijk, *Historiography of the Bènizàa: The Postclassic and Early Colonial Periods (1000–1600 A.D.)* (Leiden: University of Leiden, 2000).

37. Chance, *Conquest of the Sierra*.

38. See Michel Oudijk's analysis of the Lienzos of Tiltepec and Tabáa in Oudijk, *Historiography of the Bènizàa*.

39. Chance, *Conquest of the Sierra*; Yannakakis, *Art of Being In-Between*.

40. Dehouve, *Relatos de pecados*, 96.

41. Carlos II, *Recopilación de leyes de los reinos de las Indias* (Madrid: Julián Paredes, 1681), fol. 296.

42. They were not alone in ignoring calls for leniency. In other cases from Oaxaca adjudicated by native cabildos and Spanish magistrates, punishment for concubinage and adultery was harsh. For cases from Villa Alta roughly contemporaneous with that of Juan Ramos, see San Francisco and Santo Domingo Cajonos, "Contra Jacinto Gabriel for homicidio y adulterio," leg. 1, exp. 9 (1659), AHJO Villa Alta Criminal; "Contra Tomás Gonzalo por estar amancebado publicamente con su madrastra," leg. 1, exp. 6.1 (1667), AHJO Villa Alta Criminal. In his study of Indian parishes in eighteenth-century Mexico, *Magistrates of the Sacred*, Taylor argues that punishment of concubinage and adultery at the hands of Indian officials, parish priests, and Spanish magistrates was often harsh.

43. "Auto de Juan Ramos," 1661, fol. 8v., AHJO Villa Alta Criminal. The Zapotec original reads as follows: "Rinaao netto Justicia aca naccae christiano ava nezenie santa doctrina cattizo benne golazannaae cattizi leo golaza"

44. "Auto de Juan Ramos," 1661, fol. 9, AHJO Villa Alta Criminal. The Zapotec original reads as follows: "Gonna marta de la cruz bixa niha quie goxeno neta iela gotilla acca yoho Dios acca yoho Rey nna yleoo golaza nacca naa racca no gonano golalazi titzanij."

45. The missionary texts that we analyze hew to Juan de Córdova's translation of *antiguamente* ("formerly") as *coláça* (here, written in Valley Zapotec orthography). Juan de Córdova, *Vocabulario en lengua çapoteca* (Mexico City: Por Pedro Ocharte y Antonio

Ricardo, 1578), fol. 30r; *antiguamente = coláça, cochij, colàala, huayée*.

46. Pedro de Feria, *Doctrina Christiana en lengua Castellana y Çapoteca compuesta por el muy reuerendo padre fray, prouincial de la Orden de Sancto Domingo, en la prouincia de Sanctiago de la nueua Hespaña* (Mexico City: Casa de Pedro Ocharte, 1567), fols. 49r, 112r.

47. Farriss translates *beni cotij colaça*, the construction that Feria translates as *antepasados*, as *la gente asentada hace mucho tiempo*. See Farriss, *Libana*, 141. Another possibility is that *beni cotij* means *los muertos* (the dead), and the full construction would therefore mean *hombre muerto anciano* (a dead elder), a translation for *antepasados* (ancestors).

48. Franch, *Calendario y religión entre los zapotecos*, 114; Tavárez, *Invisible War*, 200–207, 222–23; Farriss, *Libana*, 59.

49. Francisco Pacheco de Silva, *Doctrina cristiana, traducida de la lengua castellana en lengua zapoteca nexitza. Con otras adiciones útiles y necesarias para la educacion católica y excitacion á la devocion cristiana* (1687; repr., Oaxaca, Mexico: Tip. de L. San-German, á cargo de Juan Mariscal), fol. 151.

50. Stuart B. Schwartz, *All Can Be Saved: Religious Tolerance and Salvation in the Iberian Atlantic World* (New Haven, CT: Yale University Press, 2014), 51–56.

51. María Elena Martínez, *Genealogical Fictions: Limpieza de Sangre, Religion, and Gender in Colonial Mexico* (Stanford, CA: Stanford University Press, 2008), 204.

52. Ibid., 208–11; Tavárez, *Invisible War*, 179–91.

53. Yannakakis, *Art of Being In-Between*; Rosalba Piazza, "Los 'mártires' de San Francisco cajonos: Preguntas y respuestas ante los documentos de archivo," *Historia Mexicana* 58, no. 2 (2008): 657–752. A recording of the beatification ceremony can be accessed on YouTube; see https://www.youtube.com/watch?v=AsopwmSWhvA.

Works Cited

Anders, Ferdinand, and Maarten Jansen et al. (with contributions by Jessica Davilar and Anuschka Van't Hooft). *Libro de la vida: Códice Magliabechiano: Texto explicativo del llamado Códice Magliabechiano*. Mexico City: Fondo de Cultura Económica, 1996.

Baracs, Andrea Martínez. *Un gobierno de indios: Tlaxcala, 1519-1750*. Mexico City: Fondo de Cultura Económica, 2008.

Benton, Bradley. *The Lords of Tetzcoco: The Transformation of Indigenous Rule in Postconquest Central Mexico*. Cambridge, UK: Cambridge University Press, 2017.

Bornemann, Margarita Menegus. *Del senorio indigena a la republica de indios: El caso de Toluca, 1500-1600*. Mexico City: CONACULTA, 1994.

Brian, Amber, Bradley Benton, and Pablo Garcia Loaeza, eds. *The Native Conquistador: Alva Ixtlilxochitl's Account of the Conquest of New Spain*. University Park: Pennsylvania State University Press, 2015.

Burkhart, Louise. *The Slippery Earth: Nahua-Christian Moral Dialogue in Sixteenth-Century Mexico*. Tucson: University of Arizona Press, 1989.

Carlos II. *Recopilación de leyes de los reinos de las Indias*. Madrid: Julián de Paredes, 1681.

Chance, John K. *Conquest of the Sierra: Spaniards and Indians in Colonial Oaxaca*. Norman: University of Oklahoma Press, 1989.

Christensen, Mark Z. *Nahua and Maya Catholicisms: Texts and Religion in Colonial Central Mexico and Yucatan*. Stanford, CA: Stanford University Press, 2013.

———. *Translated Christianities: Nahuatl and Maya Religious Texts*. University Park: Pennsylvania State University Press, 2014.

Chuchiak, John F., IV. "The Sins of the Fathers: Franciscan Friars, Parish

Priests, and the Sexual Conquest of the Yucatec Maya, 1545–1808." *Ethnohistory* 54, no. 1 (Winter 2007): 70–127.

Clendinnen, Inga. *Ambivalent Conquests: Maya and Spaniard in Yucatan, 1517–1570*. Cambridge, UK: Cambridge University Press, 1987.

Córdova, Juan de. *Vocabulario en lengua çapoteca*. Mexico City: Por Pedro Ocharte y Antonio Ricardo, 1578.

Dehouve, Danièle. *Relatos de pecados en la evangelizacion de los indios de Mexico*. Mexico City: CIESAS, 2010.

Farriss, Nancy. *Maya Society under Colonial Rule: The Collective Enterprise of Survival*. Princeton, NJ: Princeton University Press, 1984.

———. *Tongues of Fire: Language and Evangelization in Colonial Mexico*. New York: Oxford University Press, 2018.

Farriss, Nancy, with Juana Vásquez Vásquez. *Libana: El discurso ceremonial mesoamericano y el sermón cristiano*. Mexico City: Artes de México, 2014.

Feria, Pedro de. *Doctrina christiana en lengua castellana y çapoteca compuesta por el muy reuerendo padre fray, prouincial de la Orden de Sancto Domingo, en la prouincia de Sanctiago de la nueua Hespaña*. Mexico City: Casa de Pedro Ocharte, 1567.

Franch, José Alcina. *Calendario y religión entre los zapotecos*. Mexico City: UNAM, 1993.

Frizzi, María de los Angeles Romero. *El sol y la cruz: Los pueblos indios de Oaxaca colonial*. Mexico City: Instituto Nacional de Antropología e Historia, 1996.

Gibson, Charles. *The Aztecs under Spanish Rule: A History of the Indians of the Valley of Mexico, 1519–1810*. Stanford, CA: Stanford University Press, 1964.

González, Luis Obregón. *Proceso inquisitorial del cacique de Tetzcoco*. Mexico City: Eusebio Gómez de la Puente, 2010.

Greenleaf, Richard E. "The Inquisition and the Indians of New Spain: A Study in Jurisdictional Confusion." *Americas* 22, no. 2 (July 1966): 181–96.

———. *Zumárraga and the Mexican Inquisition, 1536–1543*. Washington, DC: Academy of American Franciscan History, 1961.

Gruzinski, Serge. *Man-Gods in the Mexican Highlands: Indian Power and Colonial Society, 1520–1800*. Translated by Eileen Corrigan. Stanford, CA: Stanford University Press, 1989.

Hanks, William F. *Converting Words: Maya in the Age of the Cross*. Berkeley: University of California Press, 2010.

Haskett, Robert Stephen. *Indigenous Rulers: An Ethnohistory of Town Government in Colonial Cuernavaca*. Albuquerque: University of New Mexico Press, 1991.

Hassig, Ross. *Polygamy and the Rise and Demise of the Aztec Empire*. Albuquerque: University of New Mexico Press, 2016.

Kellogg, Susan. *Law and the Transformation of Aztec Culture, 1500–1700*. Norman: University of Oklahoma Press, 1995.

———. *Weaving the Past: A History of Latin America's Indigenous Women from the Pre-Hispanic Period to the Present*. Oxford, UK: Oxford University Press, 2005.

Klor de Alva, J. Jorge. "Spiritual Conflict and Accommodation in New Spain: Toward a Typology of Aztec Responses to Christianity." In *The Inca and Aztec States, 1400–1800: Anthropology and History*, edited by George A. Collier, Renato Rosaldo, and John D. Wirth, 345–66. London: Academic Press, 1982.

Lockhart, James. *The Nahuas after the Conquest: A Social and Cultural History of the Indians of Central Mexico, Sixteenth through Eighteenth Centuries*. Stanford, CA: Stanford University Press, 1992.

Lopes Don, Patricia. "The 1539 Inquisition Trial of Don Carlos of Texcoco in Early Colonial Mexico." *Hispanic American Historical Review* 88, no. 4 (November 2008): 573–606.

Martínez, María Elena. *Genealogical Fictions: Limpieza de Sangre, Religion, and Gender in Colonial Mexico*. Stanford, CA: Stanford University Press, 2008.

Oudijk, Michel. *Historiography of the Bènizàa: The Postclassic and Early Colonial Periods (1000–1600 A.D.)*. Leiden: University of Leiden, 2000.

Piazza, Rosalba. *La conciencia oscura de los naturales: Procesos de idolatría en la diócesis de Oaxaca (Nueva España), siglos XVI–XVIII*. Mexico City: UNAM, 2013.

———. "Los 'mártires' de San Francisco cajonos: Preguntas y respuestas ante los documentos de archivo." *Historia Mexicana* 58, no. 2 (2008) 657–752.

Quezada, Sergio. *Maya Lords and Lordship: The Formation of Colonial Society in Yucatán, 1350–1600*. Translated by Terry Rugeley. Norman: University of Oklahoma Press, 2014.

———. *Pueblos y caciques yucatecos, 1550–1580*. Mexico City: El Colegio de Mexico, 1993.

Ricard, Robert. *The Spiritual Conquest of Mexico: An Essay on the Apostolate and the Evangelizing Methods of the Mendicant Orders in New Spain, 1523–1572*. Berkeley: University of California Press, 1974.

Sahagún, Bernardino de. *Florentine Codex: General History of the Things of New Spain*. Translated by Arthur J. O. Anderson and Charles E. Dibble. Vol. 12. Santa Fe, NM: School of American Research and University of Utah, 1975.

Schrader-Kniffki, Martina, and Yanna Yannakakis. "Sins and Crimes: Zapotec-Spanish Translation in Catholic Evangelization and Colonial Law (Oaxaca, New Spain)." In *Missionary Linguistics V / Lingüística Misionera V: Translation Theories and Practices*, edited by Otto Zwartjes, Klaus Zimmerman, and Martina Schrader-Kniffki, 161–99. Amsterdam: John Benjamins, 2014.

Schroeder, Susan. "The Oztoticpac Lands Map: A Reexamination." In *Land and Politics in the Valley of Mexico: A Two-Thousand-Year Perspective*, edited by H. R. Harvey, 163–86. Albuquerque: University of New Mexico Press, 1991.

Schroeder, Susan, Stephanie Wood, and Robert Haskett, eds. *Indian Women of Early Mexico*. Norman: University of Oklahoma Press, 1997.

Schwartz, Stuart B. *All Can Be Saved: Religious Tolerance and Salvation in the Iberian Atlantic World*. New Haven, CT: Yale University Press, 2014.

Sigal, Pete. *The Flower and the Scorpion: Sexuality and Ritual in Early Nahua Culture*. Durham, NC: Duke University Press, 2011.

———. *From Moon Goddesses to Virgins: The Colonization of Yucatecan Maya Sexual Desire*. Austin: University of Texas Press, 2000.

Silva, Francisco Pacheco de. *Doctrina cristiana, traducida de la lengua castellana en lengua zapoteca nexitza: Con otras adiciones útiles y necesarias para la educacion católica y excitacion á la devocion Cristiana*. 1687. Reprint, Oaxaca, Mexico: Tip. de L. San-German, á cargo de Juan Mariscal.

Sousa, Lisa. *The Woman Who Turned into a Jaguar, and Other Narratives of Native Women in Archives of Colonial Mexico*. Stanford, CA: Stanford University Press, 2017.

Stern, Steve J. *The Secret History of Gender: Women, Men, and Power in Late Colonial Mexico*. Chapel Hill: University of North Carolina Press, 1997.

Tavárez, David. *The Invisible War: Indigenous Devotions, Discipline, and Dissent in Colonial Mexico*. Stanford, CA: Stanford University Press, 2011.

———. *Words and Worlds Turned Around: Indigenous Christianities in Colonial Latin America*. Boulder: University Press of Colorado, 2017.

Taylor, William. *Magistrates of the Sacred: Priests and Parishioners in Eighteenth-Century Mexico*. Stanford, CA: Stanford University Press, 1996.

Terraciano, Kevin. "Crime and Culture in Colonial Mexico: The Case of the Mixtec Murder Note." *Ethnohistory* 45, no. 4 (Autumn 1998): 709–45.

———. *The Mixtecs of Colonial Oaxaca: Ñudzahui History, Sixteenth through Eighteenth Centuries*. Stanford, CA: Stanford University Press, 2001.

Townsend, Camilla. "Polygyny and the Divided Altepetl: The Tetzocan Key to Pre-conquest Nahua Politics." In *Texcoco: Prehispanic and Colonial Perspectives*, edited by Jongsoo Lee and Galen Brokaw, 93–116. Boulder: University Press of Colorado, 2014.

Yannakakis, Yanna. *The Art of Being In-Between: Native Intermediaries, Indian Identity, and Local Rule in Colonial Oaxaca*. Durham, NC: Duke University Press, 2008.

Yannakakis, Yanna, and Martina Schrader-Kniffki. "Between the 'Old Law' and the New: Christian Translation, Indian Jurisdiction, and Criminal Justice in Colonial Oaxaca." *Hispanic American Historical Review* 96, no. 3 (2016): 517–48.

———. "Contra Juan Ramos por el delito de concubinato: Traducción Cristiana y jurisdicción indígena en Oaxaca, siglo XVII." In *Los indios ante la justicia local: Intérpretes, funcionarios y litigantes en Nueva España y Guatemala (siglos XVI–XVIII)*, edited by Yanna Yannakakis, Martina Schrader-Kniffki, and Luis Alberto Arrioja Díaz Viruell, 131–52. Zamora, Mexico: Colegio de Michoacán, 2019.

Chapter 6

OCAÑA'S MONDRAGÓN IN THE "EIGHTH WONDER OF THE WORLD"

Kenneth Mills

Diego de Ocaña was a Spanish friar of the Order of St. Jerome—a Hieronymite—who traveled through much of the southernmost Spanish viceroyalty in the Americas, Peru, between 1599 and 1606. He was an alms collector who became a painter of religious images and an orchestrator and corrector of devotion on behalf of Our Lady of Guadalupe de Extremadura (in what is today western Spain). If, like most novices in his day, he took his vows in the Hieronymite house at Guadalupe in Extremadura at the age of eighteen years, then Ocaña was about twenty-nine when he departed for the Indies. Most of what we can learn about him and his experiences en route derive from an untitled, illustrated, mostly holograph manuscript of 319 (double-sided, at points erratically numbered) folio pages that he left with trusted acquaintances upon his death in Mexico City in 1608.[1]

Diego de Ocaña was a readerly writer—a writer who drew on diverse readings as he accounted for himself, especially before other readers, whether Hieronymite or otherwise. This will seem the most obvious of observations—for what religious and aspirant chronicler did *not* read?—until one explores what Ocaña makes of his reading; how pivotal his mode of taking inspiration from a received fragment—whether textual, oral, or visual—and exploring how its shape and suggestions might offer at least initial form to his tellings. I explore Ocaña's capacity for "reading," then, in several senses. I find him sensing and ferreting out of what mattered to people in the places he visited, then intuiting ways of narrating these observational discoveries in ways plausible and complementary to his nearly continuous combings and pluckings from the words and images in published works, circulating manuscripts, and local talk.

Diego de Ocaña represents himself in words and drawings as the chronicler of his own journey, a participant-teller. And yet the reality he portrays is, as Mikhail Bakhtin has observed in broader contexts, "one of many possible realities."[2] As a result, the journey of which Diego de Ocaña tells is one that begs us, time and again, *not* to proceed as if the borders separating fabrication from truth-telling, fiction from nonfiction, are fixed, as if "laid up in heaven."[3]

Who did Diego de Ocaña imagine to be his principal readers? His manuscript suggests that his primary intended audience were Hieronymite superiors and brethren in Guadalupe de Extremadura, but also the king, his royal councilors of the Indies, and other literate parties—especially churchmen, who were encouraged to report on all things significant and notable in the contemporary Spanish world. His extant manuscript has no title, nor the dedicatory epistle or prefatory remarks that his contemporaries customarily employed to nod to their intentions. Yet Ocaña's persistent merging of purposeful reportage with accounts of adventurous and otherwise entertaining excursions, along with other internal evidence (for example, some chapter titles and transitional segments), suggest the ambition to publish his account for this wider readership.[4]

The readers for whom Diego de Ocaña most yearned were those with whom he shared reference points across an array of literary traditions: readers who would expect the contemporary forms and styles he favored and with which he repeatedly played. They would appreciate Ocaña's allusions and respect the wisdoms they conveyed, share in his discomfort as much as his feelings of triumph, and thus in many ways be able to partake of the world the Hieronymite both experienced and needed to imagine.

Literary scholars and art historians have proffered a number of ways to describe how tellers or artists receive, draw on, and rework the forms of past traditions that they share—or partially share—with an intended audience in a present. Erich Auerbach posited that such "omnitemporalness," the embedding of special scenes and dramas from the authorized past in later, everyday presents, to be a determined Christian narrative inclination, especially in medieval and early modern Spain.[5] In the realm of works of art, Alexander Nagel and Christopher Wood have proposed a state of being that amounts to something similar, a "plural temporality."[6] A related way of understanding how an early modern participant-teller such as Diego de

Ocaña employs shared tools and forms as he reworks revered classical and early Christian stories has been characterized as "literary paraphrase" by Scott Fitzgerald Johnson.[7]

While bits of information, narrative patterns, and guiding metaphors of revered texts from the past condition expectations, once lifted and twisted into place their role in an author's illumination of a new present is rarely a constraining one. Idiosyncrasies abound, and significant changes to earlier scripts, the adaptations, are not only permitted but positively expected. Intended readers of the narrative re-creations may not consciously recognize an original source any more than an author will be closely aware, cite it directly, or adhere to it faithfully. And yet, the principal characteristics of the source have been sufficiently internalized by a cross-temporal community of readers such that, when performed effectively, an audience will expect and feel persuaded by the author's moves, the appropriations and analogies in play, and by what I shall call the re-created story's moral force and energy. As in not a few artistic creations of the day, allusions buttress illusion, and deceptions the unfolding of "truth."[8] The familiar story shapes create kinds of comfort by communicating moods and textures, and by playing on cultural codes, visions, and ends that the author shares—however imperfectly—with readers, real and imagined. As such, the relationship of a renewed telling to its inspiration has a particularly supple power, a power driven not by strict accuracy but rather by "elasticity" within a broader consistency.[9]

One striking aspect within Diego de Ocaña's account of his journey is his representation of Christianizing people of indigenous and mixed descent, among the "new kinds of people" who make up the principal subject of this volume.[10] Before concentrating on a particularly illuminating example of this variety, a few key elements of context are necessary. Below, I will provide introductions, first, to Ocaña's officially sanctioned purpose in the Americas; second, to the manuscript in which he recorded the account of his journey; and third and finally, to what we can know about the narrative opportunities that the composition and the expectations of his audience provided, shaping the reality Ocaña envisioned in words and illustrations. I then turn to my case in point.

Ocaña's Official Purpose in Spanish America

As an agent—a *demandador*—of a storied advocation of the Virgin Mary, dispatched to the Indies with a more experienced partner (Martín de

Posada, who would die early in the journey) on the authority of his Hieronymite superiors at Guadalupe and of a young King Philip III, Diego de Ocaña had a defined brief and sense of mission. He was, first and foremost, to gather alms and bequests (*demandas, limosnas*), acting as a pious fund raiser. But he was simultaneously to serve as a messenger and promoter, seeking to spark and nourish devotion, working as needed—and everywhere along his itinerary—on behalf both of his Hieronymite house and of its guardianship of its miraculous sculpted image of the Virgin Mary.

But Diego de Ocaña is different from contemporary alms collectors in several ways, not least in his expansive and unusually articulate embrace of his role as a participant-teller. To be sure, his authority would be constructed through the provision of empirical and experiential information, and in this sense and others, Ocaña carried on established traditions and practices. We know from his own pen and ink that he intended his alms collections in the Indies to do just as his predecessors had done across the Iberian Peninsula since the early fourteenth century. These collections served the pilgrims who flocked to the shrine in Extremadura to give thanks to the miraculous image for favors received and to pray for miracles, and to maintain a Hieronymite house befitting the guardians of this advocation of the Mother of God.[11]

Adapting well-worn methods honed by scores of these alms-gathering predecessors from Guadalupe, his responsibilities in the Americas typically began with his homing in on urban centers. A survey of each local scene ensued, consisting of encouragement and keen information-gathering to which I shall return, followed by his search for and coaxing of likely sources of funding, and then an elaboration on whatever orchestrational acts he judged appropriate for the founding of a new sacred foundation (or the correction of an errant one) in the name of Our Lady. He espied and cultivated his likely patrons and donors amid the wealthy and pious. He recruited locally influential stewards and members for lay religious associations, the best of whom were meant to become his local deputies and continuing watchpersons; these individuals were to oversee alms-collection regimes meant to endure long after his departure. Diego de Ocaña occasionally delivered sermons himself but also secured the services of skilled local preachers, briefing each of them as needed on the miraculous history of the Guadalupan Mary. In the key urban settings of Lima, Potosí, Chuquisaca (today's Sucre), Cusco, and Ica, his orchestrations culminated in elaborate periods of sacred festivity and strategic processions of welcome for "true likenesses," re-creations of the sculpted original that Ocaña himself painted, saw enshrined, and then carefully chronicled.[12] His was a multimedia onslaught whenever it could be. In both Potosí and Chuquisaca, the directed sermons and festivities were bolstered by a three-act play portraying the miraculous history of the Virgin of Guadalupe, a work that Ocaña himself composed.[13]

The Manuscript

It is impossible to determine with certainty just when and how Diego de Ocaña composed his manuscript of many parts and shifting styles. Suffice it to say here that signals within the work itself, corroborating evidence, and contemporary practice suggest that it came together by Ocaña's hand, gradually, between 1599 and his death in 1608, and especially through a series of compositional bursts of remembering and marshaling of segments. Beginning from notes, narrative fragments from which he would elaborate, and sketches and watercolors made along the way and completed after the fact, the Hieronymite appears to have composed and compiled his manuscript's key segments, ultimately producing a fair copy written mostly by his own hand, during two longer sojourns and convalescences in Lima, in Potosí, and finally in Mexico City, to which he traveled in early 1606 and where he would die in 1608.

A number of Ocaña's contemporaries produced well-thumbed accounts of the Indies in which they self-consciously addressed readers in what the Jesuit José de Acosta called his "diverse voices," and in which they broke with and fused ill-fitting genre categories.[14] Even so, the nature and character of Ocaña's manuscript assemblage takes the practice to new heights. In the most basic terms, Ocaña slips inconsistently between at least three sometimes overlapping modes of telling: the notably dutiful report of an alms gatherer and orchestrator of devotion; a lively, mobile reflection on certain, variously memorable moments and places along his journey; and a reckoning with all manner of human, natural, and marvelous phenomena. Along the way, the author gives priority to a variety of adventures, both sacred and otherwise. He is not above inserting his narrated self and the Guadalupan Mary into moments, spaces, and happenings they did not exactly attend as told, or adapting observations penned by writerly predecessors or contemporaries he does not cite, with those of Pedro de Cieza de León (who had trod many of his paths a half century before) and Reginaldo de Lizárraga (with whom he notably overlapped in Lima) being among the more prominent. He evinces keen interest in local gossip, reigning opinions, and pious hearsay, and he is attentive to the emotional and physical effects of his surroundings on his body and mission, and to how the natural world and built environments affect another of his near-continuous narrative threads—an intensely personal and sometimes spiritual accounting.[15] The work also contains thirty-one illustrations in watercolors and ink, the three-act play, and a brace of litanies and hymns he composed in praise of the Guadalupan Mary's miraculous history. In short, Diego de Ocaña creates a range of materials that inform my particular focus in this essay, his inveterate shapeshifting as a readerly participant-teller. As often in the thrall of narrative need as in the service of imparting empirical information, Ocaña proves adept in the art of simultaneously sating and surprising his cherished audience by combining and adapting the frames, incidents, and tones of "familiar tales." He does so in such a way as to give his tellings what (in another context, that of Aleppo) Alexander and Patrick Russell once described as "an air of novelty even to persons who at first imagine they are listening to tales with which they are acquainted."[16] The Hieronymite Ocaña is another such teller, conveying what mattered to him about a set of American realities he is effectively forging for and with his readers' expectations. Again and again, for teller as much as reader, several approaches to "what happened" converge, mingle, but rarely meet.

Narrative Opportunities

As I have been emphasizing, across his manuscript's whole, Ocaña makes the most of a series of narrative opportunities. I contend that these interpolated tellings, while often curious departures from the apparent main trunk of his account, are not simply entertaining digressions. They figure, rather, amid the features that prove most vital to an unravelling of what may matter most about the Hieronymite's manuscript. Ocaña's affinity for episodic narrative fuels his depictions of reality in the Indies, circa 1600, a reality that intrigues and vexes him, and from which he can rarely escape for long.

Significantly, while Ocaña recounts most of these episodes as experiences that actually happened, he does not disguise that he is engaged in a protracted act of remembering. The people, surroundings, and encounters he plucks out and renders from his journey-as-remembered are the ones deemed worthy of recollection, the ones that have stuck around for him, seeming particularly powerful in some way. In cases such as the one I explore below, evidence suggesting Ocaña's acts of distillation and adaptation is omnipresent. The relationship between, on the one hand, *actual* incidents, people, and places that Ocaña personally knew or of which he learned (and I can confirm by complementary archival research), and, on the other, his illuminations of memory, desire, fear, and anxiety, is at the core of my inquiry.

Taken as a whole, Diego de Ocaña's episodic recollections can be said to possess four, sometimes coexisting, qualities. First and most basically—and featuring the employ of various truth-telling expressions favored by his contemporaries—Ocaña presents himself as having been on the scene, one capable of furnishing eyewitness accounts and details. Whether he was physically present in all the places, much less active in all the ways he describes on the occasions he claims, remains an open, and ultimately not the most productive, question. A second quality in the episodes is the ways in which the situations, angles of telling, and emplotments Ocaña relates have been shaped by what he draws from others. Ocaña's eye and ear for popular information and explanation, like his other kinds of readerly borrowing and shaping, have their own particularities but are entirely in keeping with the methods employed by a line of chroniclers of things of the New World stretching from Pietro Martire d'Anghiera through the aforementioned Pedro de Cieza de León to those of his own time.[17]

Frequently convergent with these first two qualities within his narrated episodes is, third, a more markedly imaginative aspect. Many of Ocaña's tellings, while clearly based on real people, events, and places, are simultaneously driven by invention, by embellishments of various kinds, by convenient shifts of timing, and by a series of related moves in which Ocaña elaborates considerably on situations and incidents. Also convergent is a fourth narrative quality, and one to which I have been building: his episodes' relationship to preponderant literary models and exempla. I delve more deeply here. More often than not, the directions that Ocaña's episodic narrations take, as well as their style of rendering, betray the influence of literary forms and traditions with which the Hieronymite and his readers were deeply familiar. These traditions frequently contribute frame tales that lend shape (and often more) to what Diego de Ocaña narrated as having occurred to or around him. The inspiring frames, like other aspects of the older stories' integration, while often entertaining, is far from only playful: these are needful readerly fusions. For the frame tales provide Ocaña with a means to navigate a heady mix of fascination, discomfort, and perplexity that America summons in him (as it did in other social chroniclers) and then to generate the meanings and truths he hopes readers will derive from his rememberings and tellings.[18] His effort itself becomes revealing, creating fissures he cannot seal, difficulties he tries but cannot write smoothly through. As I hope to demonstrate, the Hieronymite's depictions of his most troubling and complex subjects often reveal far more than he could have intended.

While the narrative forms from which Ocaña drew will seem extensive, it is important to recognize them within the diverse inspirations of the imperial Spanish world, the reflections of an era of expansion and overstretch and their many aftermaths. They include, most prominently, classical histories, passages from scripture, patristic and theological writings, apostolic acts and pilgrim's journeys through the Holy Land and other sacred landscapes, saints' lives and miracle narratives, as well as the popular chivalric, earliest picaresque, pastoral, and dramatic works, and the different chronicling traditions from before and after Columbus's accidental landfall in the Americas.

How and why did drawing on such resources work? In short, audience's expectations were met, if not exceeded, and their levels of comfort and curiosity were increased. Powerful classical and biblical exempla had long been adapted and restaged according to the subjective needs and expectations of tellers in new presents.[19] Thus, what a reader in our day might call Ocaña's authoritative stance would only have been enhanced by this kind of time- and source-play. Ocaña's employ of shared and even beloved narrative frames, "classic" incidents, and telling details and characters, would trigger in his readers not only a warm trust but also a sense "of time [and space] folding over on itself . . . [a] doubling of the fabric of experience," a rendering that made things just right.[20] Experiences in the far-off Indies, even when couched as bizarre or extravagant, worked best when they spoke to readers in narrative forms honed and familiar. Ocaña's tellings needed to be "emanations of past time" and of known spaces, ones that engaged with a broad spectrum of texts and brought knowing smiles with their diverting wisdoms.[21]

The Case Study

I turn now to an example in which Diego de Ocaña makes narrative sense of a person and through him evokes a particularly prominent American place and its workings, doing so by means of precisely the kind of needful readerly fusion I have introduced. In this case, Ocaña relates what he purports to have been an experience in the silver-mining center of Potosí in 1600 in the shape of an encounter rendered most famously by Herodotus sometime before 425 BCE. The frame story is not cited (or even followed closely), nor is it alone as inspiration;[22] its employ, fired by Ocaña's fascination with a particularly complex person and place, is entirely implicit, shared between the teller and his audience. The narrative outcome would have entertained its contemporary readers, but it was also intended to inform them of Potosí—perhaps as enchanting and terrifying an "elsewhere" as existed in the burgeoning late sixteenth- and early seventeenth-century Spanish imagination.[23]

Potosí

At the dawn of the seventeenth century, the silver-mining center of Potosí (the *villa imperial de Potosí*, in what is today highland Bolivia) was a place of undeniable opportunity, ostentatious wealth, and crushing misery. 120,000 and perhaps as many as 160,000 inhabitants resided there, most of whom were indigenous mineworkers and their soon-to-be widows and families.[24] Within a few years of the "discovery" in 1545 of vast silver reserves beneath what would become known as the *cerro rico* (the rich mountain), silver extraction and refinement, the complementary market in goods and necessities for so many people, had reached what for contemporaries were scarcely imaginable proportions. Cieza described the "more than three million ducats" dispatched to Spain as the king's "royal fifth" of reported silver profits between 1548 and 1551 as but a portion of all that was extracted (an insinuation to which I will return), and far greater than anything the Spanish had ever encountered.[25] In 1550, Cieza's contemporary, the Dominican friar Domingo de Santo Tomás, characterized Potosí as "a mouth of hell" that devoured all who ventured near. Peru had been notoriously wracked by decades of disorder, rebellions, and bitter civil wars between Spanish rivals. Thus the recent discovery of silver and the ensuing greed and coerced labor in and about these mines, Santo Tomás assured his monarch and Council of the Indies, were putting the finishing touches to the complete perdition of these lands.[26] The descriptions of working conditions in Potosí's mines accumulated over the course of the sixteenth century. Those penned by the Jesuit José de Acosta in the 1570s and 1580s (and published in 1590) had additional influence on what the readerly Ocaña would seek, see, and present. Acosta wrote of mining tunnels and galleries designed hastily and in order only to extract ore more quickly and cheaply, of a subterranean darkness alleviated only by the light of candles, of the incessant blows of hammers on rock, of rickety ladders between makeshift wooden platforms, and of the ladders up and down that men climbed and climbed, extending "often more than 150 *estados* [235 meters], which is so terrible a thing," wrote Acosta, "that even the thought of which makes one tremble."[27]

In thinking over all that moved, lived, and died within and around Potosí's signature conical mountain the Hieronymite Diego de Ocaña strode a few narrative pathways. He played, for instance, on the fearsome descriptions penned by his religious predecessors, Santo Tomás and Acosta, while adding something of his own. He termed the *cerro rico* nothing less than "the eighth wonder of the world, and the greatest of them all." Potosí was terrifically enticing. There was so much to see and ponder, and deeper into his description of the place the Hieronymite glimpsed the terrifyingly magnificent Providence that Cieza had contemplated a half century before. "Strong" and "profitable" God-given winds allowed navigation of the seas, Cieza marveled, and it was wind that fired the thousands of "so ingenious" small furnaces of stone and clay (*guayras*) with which indigenous operators smelted oxidized silver ore on the ridges and hills above Potosí, all of which led to "wealth never before seen or heard of."[28] The medieval notion of a *machina mundi*, an intricate machine of the world or universe operating beneath an Almighty God's gaze, was pressed into service in descriptions of the Indies by the likes of Acosta; and so it was for Luis Capoche in 1585, and for Ocaña in his wake, to characterize complex Potosí "a machine, miraculously sustained by God" himself.[29]

With the exception of a foray to Porco in the boom city's environs, Diego de Ocaña resided in Potosí for more than fifteen months, between July 1600 and November 1601. Over the course of his stay, Ocaña would attempt to see things for himself, an effort to which he repeatedly draws his readers' attention. He claims to have spent some eight days on the *cerro rico*, entering the mines of this principal mountain and passing among the mine owners, the indigenous mineworkers, and other functionaries. The Hieronymite's insistence on his firsthand knowledge of several features, including the names of certain adits—an adit being a horizontal tunnel (or *socavón*) for mining—and work regimes, is striking, but it also follows contemporary convention for setting the scene by establishing eyewitness authority. Notably for our purposes the eyewitnessing does not appear without Ocaña's simultaneously common admission of dependence on information gleaned from dependable others.

Within and beneath the reddish conical presence of the *cerro*, at such an altitude and in such conditions, what struck Ocaña most were people. People seemed to be everywhere, cogs in the wondrous, terrible machine. Potosí's people intrigued the Hieronymite in several ways, often going beyond his writerly predecessors' eye-catching but ultimately vague marvelings at human numbers and the diversity and provenances of workers and market goods.[30] Ocaña is fascinated by how a good number of local people did not turn out to be who or quite what he expected. I characterize his reactions to the surprise of certain local characters as narrative refuges, spaces in which he tells stories, sets scenes, and describes incidents in order to work through, to reckon, and to cope with what seems to be before him. These narrations become my principal quarry.

Ocaña approaches the opportunity to describe certain kinds of people in Potosí, as elsewhere, as puzzles to start, if not to solve. To be sure, from his impressions and knowledge of these people, he fashions narratives through which he seeks to convey a set of broader intentions and meanings. But what may ultimately be more significant is all that Ocaña "lets slip" through these exemplifications.[31] For, in concert with their tremendous allure, and as I have hinted, the people puzzles prove quite impossible to contain much less satisfactorily finish. In their thrall, Ocaña shows not only a reality he means to control and convey through his acts of imaginative telling but also his own ultimate perplexity before the very New World persons, settings, and predicaments about which he writes.

Pedro de Mondragón

"There are very rich Indians in Potosí," explains Diego de Ocaña, "and in particular one named Mondragón."[32] The abrupt opening of this narrative episode conveys the germ of the Hieronymite's performance of surprise, his racialized sense of a paradox worth marveling over. Observers of Potosí who preceded him, notably including Cieza, had remarked on how all manner of people, including indigenous inhabitants, were gaining wealth and status at what seemed to them a dizzying pace. Even if Ocaña would thus have been primed by his reading to seek such persons, and thus should not actually have been surprised to find "very rich Indians" like this "Mondragón," he wagers that many of his readers will be. What they have been conditioned to expect about indigenous people, about Potosí and the Indies more generally, is not what he has found.

A local officeholder, a mine owner, an enterprising silver merchant, and the principal engine behind the foundation of Potosí's first "bank," Pedro de Mondragón would have been between fifty-five and sixty years of age as the Hieronymite arrived in the *villa imperial* in 1600.[33] Relatively plentiful contemporary documentation reveals a rounded figure, "fraught with [a] background" of which the Hieronymite was either partly aware or chose selectively to avoid.[34] All that combined, in the first instance, to make Mondragón irresistible to Ocaña the itinerant alms collector as a potential donor, and to Ocaña the participant-teller as a seemingly ideal protagonist, would render him problematic in the end. Mondragón had been raised in privilege, the acknowledged son of a well-rewarded conquistador and a noble indigenous mother, to both of whom I shall return. Suffice it to say for the moment that from his father, a loyal first citizen of Spanish Cusco and lucrative trader in coca leaves between Cusco and Potosí, Pedro inherited a fortune. His family wealth and position aside, Pedro de Mondragón had grown even more affluent and influential through his own mining and other initiatives. Ocaña grew transfixed by the way Pedro de Mondragón, quite literally, went about making his own money and way.

"The business in which he engages," Ocaña explains, "is the buying of *piñas* [compact fist-sized ingots of silver amalgam shaped like "pine cones" by their molds] and the making of bars and minted coins."[35] Mondragón was indeed a "silver broker or *arbitrageur*," one who, like others of his entrepreneurial ilk, had made himself wealthy as an integral middleman: a link between the many owners of mines and refineries, on the one hand, and the precious supply of mercury, as well as the royal mint and its array of subcontracted cutting houses where currency was manufactured, on the other.[36] In this American place, which between 1575 and 1640 produced nearly 50 percent of the silver that was fast transforming a globalizing world, the wealth soon commanded by *mercaderes de plata* such as Pedro de Mondragón was vital.[37]

With their accumulated reserves of the royal mercury required by the mill owners to whom they extended credit, the silver brokers held what Kris Lane has characterized as "a privileged, almost monopoly post."[38] Providing mercury on credit to these others, they became flush with money and critical to the inner workings of Potosí at its extractive height. They gathered ore, *piñas*, and bars from the refineries, and from mine owners large and small, making more and more raw silver effectively theirs, repayments for the loans and advances they had extended. While most everyone was suspected of siphoning undeclared profits in Potosí, concerns about insufficient supervision that focused in upon indigenous pilfering of silver became especially rampant, reflected and doubtless bolstered by Cieza's claim in 1549 that it was widely believed that Indians "made off with great treasures to their home territories."[39] "This was the reason Indians came to Potosí from throughout the land, to take advantage," continued Cieza, conveniently sidestepping just how many native Andeans were (and would long continue to be) forced to come and, in many cases, to die.[40] Regulations intended to rein in corruption and monopolistic maneuvering had been set down by Viceroy Francisco de Toledo three decades before Ocaña's arrival, but oversight remained spotty when not grown entirely lax. Rumors, suspicion, and resentments abounded. And for those canny enough to learn the guidelines, scrupulously meet the basic requirements, but then exploit the thirst for credit from any who could afford to extend it—for those prepared to tread the fine line between compliance and malfeasance at various stages of the process—there was vast opportunity for self-enrichment.

The brokers "had become accustomed to using the mint as a cash machine or, more properly, as a private money factory."[41] Once the raw silver they had accumulated was assayed, and they had paid their due for this service along with the royal tax of one-fifth of the metal's value, the silver brokers were free to deliver their silver to the mint in which their own money would be made. It was also the case that it was all their money that allowed the likes of Mondragón to stoke their pride by currying favor with the Crown in several ways, not least through direct loans to the Royal Treasury that would allow the annual silver shipments to sail.

It is thus not surprising that, as Diego de Ocaña arrived in Potosí and began to ask around, the figure of Pedro de Mondragón leapt to his attention. Here might be a crucial fount of alms, and perhaps also an influential recruit, one whose social position, and potential for devotional and generous exemplarity, might sway others toward the Guadalupan Mary in this multi-ethnic swirl of a setting.

My approach to Pedro de Mondragón, like my discussion of Ocaña's experience and representation of him, is informed by an unusually abundant vein of documentation: the last will of Juan de Mondragón, who died in 1587, and who named his son Pedro as heir; the extensive witness testimonies in the *informaciones* gathered in 1603 as record of the many merits and services rendered to their fellow citizens and the Spanish Crown by Juan de Mondragón and Pedro de Mondragón; a letter from the Audiencia (regional high court) of La Plata to the king of Spain in 1603; and contemporary documentation pertaining to Mondragón's presence and activity on Potosí's municipal council.⁴² Having imbibed something of the contemporary suspicions around indigenous enrichment in the *villa imperial*, we do well to drink in the complicating, rounder picture of how Mondragón's erstwhile peers chose to represent the silver broker and his activities. For instance, the *audiencia*'s letter reads resoundingly positive, drawing royal attention to one after another of Mondragón's distinctions and services rendered.

Mondragón had served as *regidor* (city councilman) on Potosí's municipal council (*cabildo*), and as chief magistrate (*alcalde ordinario*).⁴³ Like many a local notable in his day, Pedro de Mondragón had both been rewarded by and purchased his office on the *cabildo*, making his money talk to the tune of 20,000 pesos for this position; even more impressively, Mondragón held in the *cajas reales* of Potosí the title of "master of weights and measures," a lifetime appointment.⁴⁴ A community officeholder with judicial authority and considerable financial interests, this silver broker lived as he dealt, which is to say that he was in the public eye, engaged, and thus turning up in various kinds of documentation from his time and place.⁴⁵

Being Mestizo

It matters that the person Diego de Ocaña identified as "Indian" was mestizo, his parents' respective Spanish and indigenous ethnicities openly noted in contemporary documentation, including the letter from the judges of the *audiencia*. Here is a colonial-era Andean case of "situational" ethnicity—a case in which a person either slips or is caught in the noose of one or another of the terms bestowed on him or her according to the view or needs of another. The fact that historical interpreters and ethnographers have tended to employ terms such as mestizo as if they are reliable ethnic markers only underscores how much such descriptors have long posed "a challenge to categorization itself."⁴⁶ It suited the purpose of the *audiencia* and many contemporaries in the southern and central Andes to present Pedro de Mondragón not as an "Indian" as Ocaña did but rather as one whose mestizo-ness connoted positive distinction (as opposed to inclining the other way, as could occur and, in time, became more common). In the case of Pedro de Mondragón (as in others), parents mattered.

Pedro de Mondragón was, arguably, one of the many and the ever increasing, a mestizo—a "new kind of people," "a protean individual."⁴⁷ He was a striver, a "social climber" to be sure, but, ultimately, if it suited the purposes of the ones describing him, Pedro de Mondragón's ways of being, his accomplishments, his utility to others, might be celebrated, alongside several contemporary mestizo lives and lineages.

His Spanish father was a native of Eskoriatza in the Léniz Valley in the Basque province of Guipúzcoa. Having traveled to Peru in search of his fortune, like many of his generation Juan de Mondragón found his dreams delayed as he was drawn into the king's forces in the region's bitter civil wars. Well rewarded, he settled in the newly pacified former Inkaic capital of Cusco, where his future in business made him wealthy. Juan de Mondragón became a "coca lord," engaged in the extremely lucrative transport of coca leaves between Cusco and Potosí.[48] In Cusco he kept a magnificent home, where his son Pedro was raised, and from which, in time, father and son traveled and worked together.[49]

Several witnesses claimed that when Juan de Mondragón met one "Doña Francisca"—the indigenous noblewoman who would become Pedro's mother—in Cusco, both parties were "single" and remained so, and that only later did Francisca "marry a[nother] Spaniard."[50] No appreciable stigma appears to be attached by the notary to this or other witnesses' description of the couple's postconquest union. The judges of the *audiencia* of La Plata, too, describe Mondragón's mother in carefully positive terms, as an "*india palla*, [one of the women] who, among the Indians, are taken to be nobility."[51] Several Spanish witnesses added *ñusta* to Francisca's designation as *palla*, loaned from the Quechua *ñusta* to indicate an Inka princess or, perhaps even more cross-culturally and poetically, maiden.[52]

Not much is known about Pedro de Mondragón's upbringing in his father's sumptuous home or about contact with his mother, but all who knew them emphasized that Pedro was openly acknowledged as his father's son and heir—this detail a silent signal that such acknowledgment, not to mention vast inheritances, might be withheld in the cases of other mestizos born out of wedlock.

As for Mondragón's mother, Doña Francisca of Cusco, and Ocaña's description of her as a *palla rica* at the turn of the seventeenth century, it is worth lingering here, too. In order to think further about how the ways in which the Hieronymite's views not only of the noblewomen of Inka descent but also of the independent, resourceful, and sometimes wealthy indigenous women in Potosí (and other places) who were also sometimes known as *pallas* may relate to his representation of Pedro de Mondragón.

Diego de Ocaña's sense of indigenous women is multidirectional and, if one is not careful, can appear riven with contradictions.[53] The *pallas* had been "queens" in Inka times and were more broadly "a female nobility," he explains, repeating common knowledge in his day.[54] And yet, as I have hinted, there was clearly significant slippage when it came to contemporaries identifying such people and their descendants in practice.

For Ocaña, *palla* also signaled a contemporary sense of indigenous social and moral declension, what some others would find reason to lament as symptomatic of a far broader devastation. A *palla* might well be putting on airs, canny but not particularly wealthy, more enterprising than deserving—the female version of *pícaro*, a *pícara*—which is to say rogue or rascal, whose mix of pluck, pretense, and precarity had begun to infuse contemporary imaginations in the peninsular Spanish kingdoms and broader Spanish world and would have resounded with Ocaña and his readers. Yet he was not alone among peninsular commentators in having found the women he is calling *pallas*—sometimes categorized as "the women of Cusco" or of the broader highlands[55]—to be more attractive than those of other indigenous women. Cieza's characterizations would have prepared Ocaña the reader not only to expect "the most beautiful indigenous women of Cusco, and in all the land, in this place [of Potosí]" but also to connect them and their purported behavior to the increasing number of "free Indians, who can serve whomever they wish," maybe even themselves.[56] In this instance, it becomes clear that, much as he and his contemporaries would shower admiration on the Inkas (especially past, but also present) at the expense of native Andeans, in general Ocaña means to contrast *pallas* with the commoners who lived in what struck him as filth and squalor in the *rancherías* at the foot of the *cerro rico*.[57]

All that is disconcerting and reprehensible about the women of the *rancherías* flows from his sense of their proximity to the earth: they live in squat houses that seem, Ocaña writes, "like pigsties . . . without beds, [and] they sleep on the ground, with little more than an animal skin beneath them."[58] They go barefoot, again on the soil. Their dark hair hangs long and loose, Ocaña continues, framing faces in which the filth from not bathing, for him, is compounded by the effect of a kind of "makeup" he claims the women are in the custom of smearing on. How different from the visages of the *pallas*, he implies. Some in the *rancherías* so thoroughly cover their faces with a "colored earth" of "reddish ochre" that "it seems as if they have donned red masks," he writes, while others—who favor "a color [that is] a little more yellow"—apply it only to their cheeks and noses, which reminds the Hieronymite of so many "demons."[59]

Ocaña's Portrayal of Mondragón

His parents set in our mental tow, I return now to Pedro de Mondragón and Ocaña's portrayal of him. We cannot be sure about precisely when Diego de Ocaña resolved to visit the silver broker, nor even if the visit occurred. Further, if it did happen, we cannot be certain about just what kind of a visit it was. I shall suggest that most everything—how Mondragón would be rendered, what aspects of his being and ways would seem most significant—depended on how a quite possibly very different or nonexistent visit would be re-created in the Hieronymite's imagination.

"One day," Ocaña writes, signaling his shift of narrative register, "I went to this Indian's house." Indeed, "one might come [all the way] from Spain just to see him and his home," he entices further.[60] "I found him eating on the ground, off a low table," Ocaña claims, lapsing into a racializing set of measurements related to his descriptions of indigenous women in the *rancherías*. He plays on more favored tropes, most obviously to degrade his subject, but just as importantly to set up the "surprise" that is coming, the simultaneity of such purported barbarity with the purported contradiction of this man's evident wealth, perspicacity, and power. Because "the Indians ordinarily eat on the ground, without so much as a table or chair, always squatting on their heels," it only followed that Mondragón who, while noted to be "Hispanicized in his dress," would prefer "a table, but very low," Ocaña explains, "like a little bench."[61] If his table only rises so high, so, too, is it with his Spanish fashions. Just as what lies below the low table is the soil floor on which the "Indian" is said to be content to squat down and eat, Mondragón's body, a purportedly indigenous body, pulses beneath Spanish finery. Mondragón is sketched quickly and crudely: his capacity for the cultural transformation in which he is so clearly engaged is judged to fall short, and laughably so. The person is subject to ridicule, measured, for the moment at least, entirely in the realms of exterior surroundings, trappings, and ill-fitting things. The subject is strategically seen from the ground up, and from the outside in.

If Diego de Ocaña fastens first on the insufficiency of his host's table and chair, as on the way his lace and hose seem upon him, it is not long before it is also Mondragón's behavior that is found wanting. "He keeps all of what he owns in his home," Ocaña observes, "right there for all to see. He has a room filled with silver, in one part the bars, in another the *piñas*, and in still another part, in earthenware jugs, the *reales* [minted coins]."[62] Because "it delighted me to see so much silver altogether in one place," writes Ocaña, "I asked him how much was there before me, to which he responded, 'There are 300,000 *pesos de plata ensayada*.'"[63] The figure, 300,000 pesos in hard silver, present in the broker's home, was so large that it would have been scarcely fathomable to the Hieronymite's early seventeenth-century Spanish readers. As for Mondragón keeping such a valuable heap right beneath his gaze, the practice was not bizarre in the local context, nor as miserly as the Hieronymite pretended. It was in fact entirely typical of those who made money in Mondragón's time and place to keep a small fortune close to their person at any one time.[64]

That his depiction of the unseemly hoard follows Ocaña's denigration of the purported furniture and dining practices of this "rich Indian" only raises the stakes. The way he is drawing attention to Mondragón is performed, in large part, for rhetorical effect and narratively to set up what comes next. However, contemporary evidence collected from knowledgeable witnesses just a few years after Ocaña's time in Potosí joins the praise that the pragmatic judges of the *audiencia* had showered on Mondragón, presenting a very different picture, and one that even touched on the silver broker's domestic life.

We are introduced to a "very rich man, who owned mines and mills and a [great] adit on *cerro rico*," Alonso Quiñones testified on November 8, 1603. Quiñones, like most other witnesses, did not fail to list the impressive string of local offices Mondragón had held in Potosí, in each of which "he made a good account of himself, including his present office as His Majesty's Treasurer." But most interesting for our present line of inquiry is a detail the witnesses included about Pedro de Mondragón's household, the very home to which Ocaña claims to have paid a visit. Quiñones suggests that Mondragón did indeed live in Potosí—not on earthen floors and at low tables, but in the manner to which he had become accustomed while growing up in the luxurious home of his father, Juan, in Cusco. There was no notable person's home that was finer, asserted one witness, nor one better served.[65]

The Frame Story of Croesus of Lydia

The Hieronymite's portrayal of an unseemly Pedro de Mondragón, showing off his domestic stockpile of silver in rich Potosí, is calculated for deepest resonance—a resonance that embraces but also goes well beyond contemporary Spanish assumptions about how an "Indian" of newly acquired, great wealth might live. To achieve the effect he desired, Diego de Ocaña counted on more than his Spanish readers' prejudices and anxieties. He needed their familiarity with the perils of the earthly luxury, as epitomized (and later Christianized) in the ancient story of a visit that wise Solon of Athens is said to have made to the palace of Croesus, the wealthy king of Lydia in the sixth century BCE.[66] Thought to have been penned before 425 BCE, Herodotus's certainly fictive rendering of a visit paid to King Croesus's palace at Sardis by Solon fuels Ocaña's imagination as much as his readers' expectations about how the Hieronymite's visit to one such as Mondragón in Potosí ought to unfold.[67]

Herodotus's Croesus is fresh from a string of conquests and "at the very height of his wealth"[68] as Solon, a noted statesman and poet from Athens, arrives at his palace in Sardis (today Sart, in western Turkey). Not content simply to exude magnificence before his visitor, Croesus has Solon "tour through the treasuries," granting him an opportunity to stagger in awe before the "great riches."[69]

Imagining himself the happiest and most prosperous of men, the self-absorbed but naggingly insecure Croesus praises Solon's reputation for wisdom before asking the visitor to confirm the king's sense of self. Solon offers no such comfort to power. Contending that "human life [and thus happiness or dejection] is pure chance" in any event, Solon presents a barrage of details drawn from the lives of phenomenally happy persons: those whose worldly riches and power were modest, and whose incapacity to gratify their passions contrasted sharply with the abundance all about the Lydian king. Croesus is left pitiable. He fishes, in increasing despair, for a second- or even a strong third-place finish amid the happiest of men in Solon's view. In assessing what ultimately mattered in each example's case, Solon serves as Herodotus's mouthpiece for (what can fairly be described as swathes of ancient Greek) wisdom. What matters to any person's happiness is his virtue, not the earthly parading of virtue through riches and otherwise ostentatious display but the kind of virtue acknowledged by all kinds of others, the sort of good health and fortune that can fill a human life with blessings, the wonders that follow from such a life, and especially the sublime contentedness that infuses such a person at the point of death.[70]

Croesus, vexed by his visitor's failure to be impressed by his wealth—but still resisting Solon's teachings about the fickleness of earthly fortune and how true happiness can be judged only at death—meets his comeuppance in the form of a string of misfortunes. Croesus eventually finds himself defeated by the Persian armies commanded by Cyrus the Great. Shackled in irons, distraught on the pyre where he and his family are to be burned alive before the victorious Cyrus, Croesus is finally capable of reflecting on Solon's words. Croesus's repeated cries of Solon's name, as his conqueror's flames lick at his body, cause Cyrus to wonder about some last-minute signal from the gods, and kindle in him a curiosity about this Athenian named Solon and his message.

When Cyrus's order that the consuming fire be extinguished looks to have been given too late, only the already-sizzling Croesus's own invocation of his beloved Apollo—who wastes no time in interceding with Zeus—brings the great shower of rain that saves Croesus's life. The story concludes, in Herodotus's telling, with Croesus spared, utterly changed, made a generous and becoming adviser in the court of his conqueror and likewise openly transformed Cyrus the Great.[71]

Croesus and Mondragón

The story of Croesus and Solon resided deeply within how both Diego de Ocaña and his intended readers perceived the world to work. While the Hieronymite neither cites nor perhaps even directly consults the classical exemplum with which he has begun to play in describing Pedro de Mondragón, the classical story creates a frame. And it offers a means and a direction to experience, contributing certain features, turns, and traits. It is from these that Ocaña's rendering can most effectively grow. It is part of the power of any re-creation of the story of Croesus and Solon that it works on many levels, even the most superficial—such as when a reader fathoms only that a fatal flaw afflicts, and corresponding ills befall, anyone dubbed as "rich as Croesus." And yet the more Ocaña's reader knows, the more ingenious the Hieronymite's framing and rendering of Pedro de Mondragón of Potosí becomes.

It was during Croesus's reign that the first gold and silver coins were minted in Asia Minor.[72] So he, too, had been a moneymaker, literally fabricating some of the treasure on which he sat at Sardis. More significantly for Ocaña, Croesus was an open and exemplary benefactor of the gods and pious causes, his fabulous donations to the cult of the Pythian Apollo at Delphi and other sanctuaries complementing his support of the great temples to Artemis at Ephesus and Sardis.[73] Moreover, his giving inspired a far wider and humbler set of dedicants.[74] Here, then, was a most evocative ancient protagonist, known to have worked to the collective spiritual good, mobilizing his considerable power and wealth as piety, and lavishing gifts on the gods.

Almost two thousand years later, the Lydian king became the primary inspiration for Ocaña's narrated re-creation of Mondragón the "rich Indian," maker of money and dispatcher of silver to Spain from Potosí. To fashion his Mondragón, Ocaña draws into a rendering of his experiences in Potosí the intellectual and moral directions and energies that had long coursed through the ancient story of Croesus. These are properties with which Ocaña feels free to play, reconfiguring matters for his own purposes and for those of his early modern Spanish readers. At the moment of composition, Ocaña is remembering, which is to say he is reencountering, Pedro de Mondragón and the machine of Potosí in search of meaning, in search of what they have meant to his journey to and through the Indies. Ocaña's literary enterprise amounts to making what John Lyons has called "common cause" with his intended audience, presenting "the world the way it is"—in this case, a reality of Potosí that is shaped by recognized figures, examples, and uncannily useful elements drawn from a frame story, here that of Solon's visit to Croesus.[75]

And yet, frame and reshape as he might, any hope that Diego de Ocaña might have entertained about ultimately containing his subject, let alone demeaning his nature, fast ran into challenges, as the sources and means and sheer magnitude of the silver man's wealth emerged. Pedro de Mondragón is "one of the [Crown's] most useful vassals," the judges of the Audiencia of La Plata contended only a few years later, in 1603, underscoring what witnesses in the *informaciones* concerning Juan and Pedro de Mondragón had established more precisely.[76] The prevailing vision of what made for his "utility" began with his apparently unblemished record of fiscal rectitude at a time when the only thing more rampant than the actual pilfering of the king's share of silver extracted from the *cerro rico* was suspicion of it. And yet, as much as his regular fulfillment of the "royal fifth" from any profits gained from "his mines and ore" was stressed,[77] reported rectitude was the least one might expect from an upstanding silver-mine owner and merchant. Witnesses stressed that Pedro de Mondragón also be credited not only as an invaluable investor in mines and mills but also as the mining innovator that he was, not least because of a large adit he had cut into the *cerro rico* in order to reach bodies of ore in vein systems far below the ground, and into which Mondragón had reportedly invested and was still sinking large amounts of money and effort. A typical adit "cost as much as the construction of a sizeable church."[78] And because not all adits were nearly as well aimed and designed, and thus as successful, as Mondragón's, it is little wonder his investments were lauded by contemporary observers as vital contributions.[79]

Even so, if contemporaries drew their attention most especially to one of Pedro de Mondragón's contributions, it was his periodic bankrolling of the Crown's shipments of silver, something that had come to Ocaña's attention two years earlier: "On many occasions [Mondragón] has loaned [literally "extended by his very long hand"] a great quantity of pesos" to ensure that "the shipment of silver would be dispatched to Your Majesty each year." The *oidores* of the Audiencia of La Plata emphasize the free volition of their man and his loans, in exemplary service to the king, echoing the witnesses' references to his "very great generosity": their message is that Pedro de Mondragón does this all the time and he does not have to be asked. He acts "without any concern for his self-interest."[80]

Through his subterranean investments, his accumulating fortune and, above all, his command of cash advances for mine owners and loans to the Crown, Pedro de Mondragón came to enjoy respect and a widening sphere of influence. The mestizo silver broker's "money factory" grew, bringing royal notice. On February 8, 1609, a rare kind of royal decree, one bearing King Philip III's own signature, was sent directly to "Pedro de Mondragón, resident of Potosí," in gratitude for his services and particularly for the latest loan, extended the year before, for 60,000 *ducados*.[81]

In his own way, Diego de Ocaña gradually absorbed and narrated the revelation of Pedro de Mondragón in remembering his purported encounter with him in 1600–1601, with the apparent contradictions to the Hieronymite's initial impressions only making this human subject and his setting more astonishing, unsettling, and worthy of attention. The friar's quick mockery of the man's low table and piles of silver recedes without disappearing as the perfection of Mondragón's local know-how and economic positioning becomes more apparent to the very same reporter. Indeed, Ocaña is our guide as an alternative interpretation of the tripartite organization of silver inside Mondragón's great room intrudes on his own mind. The remembered home is transformed, signifying not the temptation of vanity or unseemly extravagance but a masterly middleman's genius of scale. It was the process of extraction, transformation, and dispatch that Mondragón had come to command from his home that required partition, serving the process by which he had effectively privatized the transmutation of raw silver and *piñas* (one) into bars (two), and then into coins (three), all beneath his own roof and gaze.

The same Hieronymite who had brought the "rich Indian" to earth now marvels over how, at each stage of the process, Mondragón soars and "earns a certain percentage, in such a way that [his profits] only continue to grow." Holding the extracted silver close might seem small-time at first, but it proves to be key to making big profits. "Because he keeps what he has in-house, and does not involve himself in other dealings that might risk his livelihood," the man thrives, Ocaña explains, making himself more and more indispensable.[82] The local mine owners know when and how to go to him with their silver and to repay their debts, while the assayers at the *casa de moneda* (royal mint) and their subcontracted coin cutters all await their role in the making of his money. All the while it is the royal treasury, arguably the king himself, who ends up most hung on the hook fashioned by Pedro de Mondragón and others of his ilk.

Ocaña reveals the contours of an ultimately righteous and admirable one who got away, of one who at the very least defied the extent of his wishes, of a Mondragón who might have been. After noting the silver merchant's wealth and acumen, Ocaña mentions that Pedro de Mondragón has been giving alms, but not in a public manner that might render his pious donations exemplary and influence others to do the same within their means. "He is a man who elects to give his many alms in secret, not in public," Ocaña confesses, "and thus it is [commonly] believed that he does not do it."[83]

Conclusion

The episode featuring Pedro de Mondragón is ultimately but a part of what Diego de Ocaña reveals about Potosí, circa 1600. That it offers one of Ocaña's most telling points of entry derives both from what he does and does not choose to face. In the person of Mondragón Ocaña finds what he most desires and what he most fears. And thus it is that Ocaña's Mondragón is offered up to readers both in a story he is able to tell and in others that he is not.

The tale of Croesus, tacking across narrative time—its original details bent and twisted, its original lessons diverted and adapted—was meant to provide the kind of buttress people yearn for when disorder threatens and thus to lend readers succor. Diego de Ocaña employs the story's power as a sense-making device for Spanish Catholic Christians (and an array of Christianizing persons) before the increasingly vast and baffling social landscape not only of teeming Potosí but also of the early modern Spanish world.

Social order demanded containment in the aspirant ruling mindset, and in the face of this, Mondragón represented radical overspill. Dynamic embodiments such as him—whether indigenous, African or, like Mondragón, of mixed race—were proving as ubiquitous and insuppressible as they were difficult for Spanish commentators to countenance. These observers sensed something profoundly significant occurring in and through such individuals. But the acts of distilling and of subjecting to ridicule their worrisomely complex protagonisms, and the transforming realities of their times and places, much less accepting or encouraging them openly, were quite other matters. The emerging truths were as hard to live with as they were to suppress, "difficult middles" that discomfited prevailing prejudices and the mythohistories that conferred and maintained Spanish political, economic, and spiritual dominance.[84] Just as earlier authors had evoked frame stories honed in the late antique Mediterranean basin and in medieval Europe in an attempt to contain such people within narratives that saw good triumph over evil, preachers thwarting demons and sorcerers, and conversions driven by miracle, Ocaña, at the turn of the seventeenth century, fashions an ingenious but ultimately ill-fitting mold on the bursting intelligence and entrepreneurial verve of Pedro de Mondragón.[85]

When Pedro de Mondragón is narratively spun by Ocaña as a Christian and Hispanicizing indigenous person who does not live and give as he might, he represents a form of social and spiritual disorder. A potent example of intercultural transformation, an evident conqueror of his mid-colonial domain, this mestizo-called-Indian Pedro de Mondragón who might have been the Hieronymite's exemplary patron and alms giver represents the kind of trouble from which he cannot quite look away. The more Mondragón is desired, the more he thwarts in response, and the more Diego de Ocaña's remarkable portrayal unfolds, the more he ends up a portal through which we may see far more than its narrator intended.

Notes

Quotation in the title from Diego de Ocaña, "Relación del viaje de fray Diego de Ocaña por el Nuevo Mundo (1599–1605)," Biblioteca de la Universidad de Oviedo, Spain, M.215, fol. 168v, from his description of the *cerro rico*, the "rich mountain" of Potosí, in what is today Bolivia, as "the eighth wonder of the world, and the greatest of them all." Thanks to Arun Jones for his insights and skillful editing, and also to Scott Sessions, Clifton Crais, William B. Taylor, and Dana Leibsohn, Kris Lane for timely, attentive nudges along this essay's way.

1. The manuscript, called the "Relación del viaje de fray Diego de Ocaña por el Nuevo Mundo (1599–1605)" (hereafter "Relación"), resides in the Biblioteca de la Universidad de Oviedo in Spain, designated M.215. See also the modern scholarly edition (which, for the ease of readers, I will cite along with the original), Diego de Ocaña, *Viaje por el nuevo mundo: De Guadalupe a Potosí, 1599–1605*, ed. Blanca López de Mariscal and

Abraham Madroñal Durán, with the collaboration of Alejandra Soria (Madrid: Editorial Iberoamericana; Frankfurt: Vervuert; Mexico: Bonilla Artigas Editores; Monterrey: Instituto Tecnológico de Estudios Superiores de Monterrey, 2010) (hereafter *Viaje*).

2. Mikhail Bakhtin, *The Dialogic Imagination: Four Essays*, ed. Michael Holquist, trans. Caryl Emerson and Michael Holquist (Austin: University of Texas Press, 1981), 37. Hayden White has been criticized as much as he has been admired for his work along these lines, particularly his identification, nearly a half century ago, of the entwinement of poetics (and thus fiction-making) with historiography. See his *Metahistory: The Historical Imagination in Nineteenth-Century Europe* (Baltimore: Johns Hopkins University Press, 1973), esp. 82–85.

3. Bakhtin, *Dialogic Imagination*, 33.

4. The manuscript in fact long remained unpublished and partly miscataloged. In the final third of the twentieth century, the first of two modern editions appeared, prepared by the former Franciscan friar Arturo Álvarez Álvarez: Diego de Ocaña, *Un viaje fascinante por la América Hispana del siglo XVI* (Madrid: Studium, 1969), which was followed, with various abridgments and omissions, by *A través de la América del Sur* (Madrid: Historia 16, 1987). Two more serviceable editions have followed, that of López de Mariscal and Madroñal Durán in 2010 and of Beatriz Carolina Peña in 2013. For a characterization and review of these editions, see Kenneth Mills, "On the Presentation of Diego de Ocaña, O. S. H. (ca. 1570–1608)," *Colonial Latin American Review* 25, no. 4 (2016): 559–67; also Kenneth Mills, "Diego de Ocaña (ca. 1570–1608)," in *Guide to Documentary Sources for Andean Studies, 1530–1900*, ed. Joanne Pillsbury (Norman: University of Oklahoma Press; Washington, DC: Center for Advanced Study in the Visual Arts, National Gallery of Art, 2008), 3:457–64.

5. Erich Auerbach, *Mimesis: The Representation of Reality in Western Literature*, trans. Willard R. Trask (1946; repr., Princeton, NJ: Princeton University Press, 1953), 161–62.

6. Alexander Nagel and Christopher S. Wood, *Anachronic Renaissance* (New York: Zone Books, 2010), 7–19, esp. 16. For me, the idea takes forward what George Kubler suggested nearly a half century before about the diffusion and regeneration of older artistic forms in new, transoceanic contexts: see Kubler, *The Shape of Time: Remarks on the History of Things* (New Haven, CT: Yale University Press, 1962), esp. 17–24; and my elaborations in Kenneth Mills, "Religion in the Atlantic World," in *The Oxford Handbook of the Atlantic World, 1450–1850*, ed. Nicholas Canny and Philip Morgan (Oxford, UK: Oxford University Press, 2011), 433–48, esp. 433–34.

7. Scott F. Johnson, "*The Life and Miracles of Thekla*": *A Literary Study* (Washington, DC: Center for Hellenic Studies; Cambridge, MA: Harvard University Press, 2006), 6–10; see also Scott F. Johnson, "Late Antique Narrative Fiction: Apocryphal Acta and the Greek Novel in the Fifth-Century *Life and Miracles of Thekla*," in *Greek Literature in Late Antiquity: Dynamism, Didacticism, Classicism*, ed. Scott F. Johnson (Aldershot, UK: Ashgate, 2006), 189–207, esp. 204.

8. Felipe Pereda, *Crime and Illusion: The Art of Truth in the Spanish Golden Age*, trans. Consuelo López-Morillas (Turnhout, Belgium: Brepols, 2018).

9. Johnson, "*Life and Miracles of Thekla*," 6–10; on this writer-to-reader "elasticity," see also Averil Cameron, *Christianity and the Rhetoric of Empire: The Development of Christian Discourse* (Berkeley: University of California Press, 1991), esp. chap. 3.

10. Stuart B. Schwartz and Frank Salomon, "New Peoples and New Kinds of People: Adaptation, Readjustment, and Ethnogenesis in South American Indigenous Societies (Colonial Era)," in *Cambridge History of Native Peoples of the Americas*, vol. 3, *South America*, pt. 2, ed. Frank Salomon and Stuart B. Schwartz (Cambridge, UK: Cambridge University Press, 1999), 443–94.

11. See Françoise Crémoux, *Pèlerinages et miracles à Guadalupe au XVIe siècle* (Madrid: Casa de Velázquez, 2001).

12. Notably and insightfully attentive to Ocaña's interest in, and promotion of, baroque and particularly sacred festivity is Francisco Javier Campos y Fernández de

Sevilla's "El monje jerónimo fray Diego de Ocaña y la crónica de su viaje por el Virreinato del Perú (1699–1606)," in *Fray Diego de Ocaña y la Virgen de Guadalupe*, ed. Francisco Javier Campos y Fernández de Sevilla and Erman Guzmán Reyes (Lima: Gráfica DLC EIRL; Arzobispado de Lima, 2014), 9–124.

13. See Kenneth Mills, "Diego de Ocaña's Hagiography of New and Renewed Devotion in Colonial Peru," in *Colonial Saints: Discovering the Holy in the Americas*, ed. Allan Greer and Jodi Bilinkoff (New York: Routledge, 2003), 51–76.

14. José de Acosta, *Historia natural y moral de las Indias* (Seville: Casa de Juan de León, 1590), dedicatory epistle, 12, 10.

15. See Kenneth Mills, "Mission and Narrative in the Early Modern Spanish World: Diego de Ocaña's Desert in Passing," in *Faithful Narratives: Historians, Religion, and the Challenge of Objectivity*, ed. Andrea Sterk and Nina Caputo (Ithaca, NY: Cornell University Press, 2014), 115–31; and Kenneth Mills, "Una sacra aventura en tierras que se volvían santas: Diego de Ocaña, O.S.H., 1599–1608," *Allpanchis* 46, nos. 83–84 (2019): 69–113.

16. From the characterization of the special aptitude of Aleppine storytellers by Alexander Russell and Patrick Russell in *The Natural History of Aleppo*, vol. 1 (London: G. G. and J. Robinson, 1794), 148–49, cited in Paulo Lemos Horta's remarkable *Marvellous Thieves: Secret Authors of the Arabian Nights* (Cambridge, MA: Harvard University Press, 2017), 33–34.

17. In the case of Martire's methods and position as an early interpreter of the Indies, I am indebted to the thoughts and emerging writing of Sarah L. Reeser in "The Whole Hand of the Giant: Geography, Vision, and Materiality in the Late Medieval and Early Modern Atlantic World," (PhD diss., 2020, University of Toronto). See also Mary Beagon, "Peter Martyr's Use of Pliny," *International Journal of the Classical Tradition* 21, no. 3 (2014): 223–44. On Cieza, see especially Luis Millones Figueroa, *Pedro de Cieza de León y su Crónica del Perú: La entrada de los Incas en la historia universal* (Lima: IFEA and Pontificia Universidad Católica del Perú,

2001), and *Pedro de Cieza de León: 500 años de historia* (Llerena: Sociedad Extremeña de Historia, 2018). My larger point challenges the persistently simplistic binaries that would separate the authority of contemporary eyewitnesses in the Indies not only from "distant" commentators in Europe but also from the kinds of information a person *in* the Indies does not so much see for himself as derive and consider from the pens, eyes, ears, and voices of a vast array of others, most but not all of them predecessors.

18. See Homi Bhabha on seemingly unstable, hybridic zones—a "Third Space"—in which apparent opposites mix, and where not a few authors have been forced to confront difference and generate "enunciations" of reality: "How Newness Enters the World: Postmodern Space, Postcolonial Times and the Trials of Cultural Translation," in *The Location of Culture* (London: Routledge, 1994), 212–35, esp. 225.

19. Auerbach, *Mimesis*, esp. chap. 7.

20. Nagel and Wood, *Anachronic Renaissance*, 9.

21. Kubler, *Shape of Time*, 19.

22. Ocaña also engages his and readers' familiarity with complementary passages from the Gospels of Matthew and John in the depiction that follows, but space does not permit exploration of these important, additional layers to his telling.

23. Cervantes's Don Quixote hankers after "a world elsewhere," a protagonistic trope employed also by countless contemporary participant-tellers in extra-European worlds. See Miguel de Cervantes Saavedra, *Don Quixote de la Mancha*, ed. Francisco Rico, with Joaquín Forradellas, 2 vols. (1605 and 1615; repr., Barcelona: Instituto Cervantes, 1998), pt. 3, chap. 3, p. 135.

24. The commonly accepted figures tell of at least 100,000 to 120,000 people, and probably tens of thousands more. See Peter Bakewell, *Silver and Entrepreneurship in Seventeenth-Century Potosí: The Life and Times of Antonio López de Quiroga* (1988; repr., Dallas: Southern Methodist University Press, 1995), 22–23, 190–91nn43, 45, 46, and also *Miners of the Red Mountain: Indian Labor*

in Potosí, 1545–1650 (Albuquerque: University of New Mexico Press, 1984), 111–12n69.

25. Pedro de Cieza de León, whose first observations about all manner of things in Peru were absorbed comprehensively by Ocaña and other readerly contemporaries, visited Potosí in 1549, just as its population and production exploded under the eye of magistrate Polo de Ondegardo, from whom the soldier-chronicler gained his many numbers: *Parte primera de la Chronica del Peru* (Antwerp: Juan Bellero a la enseña del Salmón, 1554), cap. 109, fols. 260v–61r, esp. fol. 261r.

26. José María Vargas, *Fr. Domingo de Santo Tomás, defensor y apóstol de los indios del Perú: Su vida y sus escritos* (Quito: Editorial Santo Domingo, 1937), 1–32, esp. 15–16.

27. José de Acosta, *Historia natural y moral de las Indias*, ed. Edmundo O'Gorman (1940; repr., Mexico City: Fondo de Cultura Económica, 1962), book 4, chap. 8, p. 156.

28. Cieza de León, *Parte primera*, cap. 109, fols. 261v–262r and 259v; see also Kris Lane, *Potosí: The Silver City That Changed the World* (Berkeley: University of California Press, 2019), 48–50.

29. "Relación," fol. 170r; *Viaje*, 257. See Acosta, *Historia natural y moral* (1590), dedicatory epistle, 7. For Luis Capoche, see Audiencia de Charcas 134, 1585, Archivo General de Indias, Seville (hereafter AGI); and Luis Capoche, *Relación general del asiento y Villa Imperial de Potosí y de las cosas mas importantes a su gobierno, dirigida al Excmo. Sr. don Hernando de Torres y Portugal, conde del Villar y virrey del Perú*, ed. Lewis Hanke (1585; repr., Madrid: Ediciones Atlas, 1959).

30. For instance, see Cieza, *Parte primera*, cap. 109, fols. 260v and 262v–263r.

31. The phrase, from Rolena Adorno, long exemplifies her critical practice; see, for example, *Guaman Poma y su crónica ilustrada del Perú colonial* (Copenhagen: Museum Tusculanem Press, 2001), 36, and in the approach, co-authored with Patrick Pautz, *Álvar Núñez Cabeza de Vaca: His Account, His Life, and the Expedition of Panfilo de Narvaez*, 3 vols. (Lincoln: University of Nebraska Press, 1999), 1:106.

32. "Relación," fol. 180r; *Viaje*, 270. The original reads as follows: "Hay en Potosí indios muy ricos, en particular uno que se llama Mondragón."

33. Charcas 82, no. 7, Antonio Quiñones testimony on November 8, 1603, fol. 18r, AGI.

34. Auerbach discusses the significance of this deepening, complicating quality in biblical characters in contrast to the Homeric heroes who, in the "Western" tradition, came before. See *Mimesis*, 12.

35. "Relación," fols. 180r–v; *Viaje*, 271.

36. Kris E. Lane, "From Corrupt to Criminal: Reflections on the Great Potosí Mint Fraud of 1649," in *Corruption in the Iberian Empires: Greed, Custom, and Colonial Networks*, ed. Christoph Rosenmüller (Albuquerque: University of New Mexico Press, 2017), 33–61, esp. 43, 49. For more on and around this theme, see a prominent thread in Lane's *Potosí*.

37. John J. TePaske, *A New World of Gold and Silver*, ed. Kendall W. Brown (Leiden: Brill, 2010), 144.

38. Lane, "From Corrupt to Criminal," 49; Bakewell, *Silver and Entrepreneurship*, 37.

39. Cieza, *Parte primera*, cap. 109, fols. 261r and 262r.

40. Ibid., cap. 109, fol. 262r.

41. Lane, "From Corrupt to Criminal," 49.

42. Contratación 244, no. 26 (1595, 1607), AGI; Audiencia de Charcas 82, no. 7 (1603), AGI; Libro de Acuerdos, Audiencia de Charcas, tomo 13, fol. 26r, Archivo y Biblioteca Nacional de Bolivia (hereafter ABNB); Audiencia de La Plata to the King, La Plata, December 26, 1603, ABNB; Cabildo de Potosí, Libro de Acuerdos, tomo 9, fol. 162v, Cabildo de Potosí, February 17, 1601, ABNB; Cabildo de Potosí, Libro de Acuerdos, tomo 14, fol. 1r, Cabildo de Potosí, July 1, 1614, ABNB; Audiencia de Charcas 415, Leg. 2, February 8, 1609, fol. 216v, AGI.

43. Cabildo de Potosí, Libro de Acuerdos, tomo 9, fol. 162v, ABNB; Cabildo de Potosí, February 17, 1601, ABNB; Cabildo de Potosí, Libro de Acuerdos, tomo 14, fol. 1r, ABNB; Cabildo de Potosí, July 1, 1614, ABNB; Witness Alonso Quiñones of Potosí on November 8, 1603, Audiencia de Charcas 82, no. 7, fol. 21r, AGI.

44. Libros de Acuerdos, Audiencia de Charcas, tomo 13, Audiencia de La Plata to the King, La Plata, December 26, 1603, fol. 26v, ABNB; confirmed at Audiencia de Charcas 82, no. 7, fol. 21r, AGI. Ocaña gets Mondragón's most prestigious office exactly right, as a *"fiel ejecutor perpetuo"*: "Relación," fol. 180r; *Viaje*, 270.

45. Jane E. Mangan, *Trading Roles: Gender, Ethnicity, and the Urban Economy in Colonial Potosí* (Durham, NC: Duke University Press, 2005), 226–27.

46. Joanne Rappaport, *The Disappearing Mestizo: Configuring Difference in the Colonial New Kingdom of Granada* (Durham, NC: Duke University Press, 2014), 13.

47. Schwartz and Salomon, "New Peoples and New Kinds of People," 494, 487; Rappaport, *Disappearing Mestizo*.

48. Charcas 82, 1603, no. 7, fol. 19r, AGI.

49. Captain Amerossio Fernández Azceytuno, who claimed to have known both father and son for about thirty-five years, testified in Potosí on November 13, 1603: Charcas 82, no. 7, fols. 24r–24v, AGI.

50. Charcas 82, no. 7, fol. 16r, 19v, AGI.

51. Libros de Acuerdos, Audiencia de Charcas, tomo 13, Audiencia de La Plata to the King, La Plata, December 26, 1603, fols. 26r and 26v, ABNB.

52. For instance, see Charcas 82, no. 7, fols. 12v–13r and 16r, AGI.

53. Arguing differently, and taking her lead particularly from Diego de Ocaña's watercolor and ink illustrations of indigenous women, and from his depiction of these figures alongside indigenous men, is Beatriz Carolina Peña, *Imágenes contra el olvido: El Perú colonial en las ilustraciones de fray Diego de Ocaña* (Lima: Fondo Editorial de la Pontificia Universidad Católica del Perú, 2011).

54. "Relación," fols. 332v and 333r; *Viaje*, 468, with the caption at the foot of fol. 333r.

55. For example, see Cieza, *Parte primera*, cap. 41, fols. 107r–v and cap. 19, fol. 49r; and Agustín de Zárate, *Historia del descubrimiento y conquista del Perú* (Antwerp: En casa de Martin Nucio, a las dos Cigueñas, 1555), fol. 13v.

56. Cieza, *Parte primera*, cap. 110, fol. 263r.

57. "Relación," fols. 174r–v; *Viaje*, 263–64.

58. "Relación," 174r; *Viaje*, 263.

59. Ibid.

60. "Relación," fol. 180r; *Viaje*, 270.

61. "Relación," fol. 180r; *Viaje*, 270–71.

62. "Relación," fol. 180r; *Viaje*, 271.

63. Ibid.

64. See the case of Antonio García Vásquez, recorded by Bartolomé Arzáns de Orsua y Vela (1676–1736). Arzáns de Orsua y Vela, *Relatos de la villa imperial de Potosí: Antología* (1626; repr., Potosí: Plural Editores, 2000), 124, 121.

65. Alonso Quiñones, Charcas 82, no. 7, fol. 21r, AGI.

66. Herodotus, *Histories* 1.29–45 and 1.85. Translations of this source are drawn from Herodotus, *The Landmark Herodotus: The Histories*, ed. Robert B. Strassler, trans. Andrea L. Purvis (New York: Pantheon Books, 2009).

67. Solon—wise man, legal thinker, and political reformer—very much existed, and a fragment of his writings have been recovered. But, even on the cold basis of chronology alone, it is highly unlikely that an actual interview between him and Croesus is anything but the product of Herodotus's imagination. Solon served as archon of Athens in 594–593 BCE and thus would have died before 560, just as Croesus became king of Lydia. See Molly Miller, "The Herodotean Croesus," *Klio* 41 (1963): 58–94; also Herodotus, *Histories* 1.29 1a.

68. Herodotus, *Histories* 1.29.

69. Ibid., 1.30.

70. Charles C. Chiasson, "The Herodotean Solon," *Greek, Roman, and Byzantine Studies* 27, no. 3 (1986): 249–62; Herodotus, *Histories* 1.32, 1.30–33.

71. Herodotus, *Histories* 1.29–45, 1.85–90.

72. Andrew Ramage and Paul Craddock, *King Croesus's Gold: Excavations at Sardis and the History of Gold Refining* (Cambridge, MA: Harvard University Press, 2000).

73. Herodotus, *Histories* 1.92, 1.50–51; Angela Heloiza Buxton, "Lydian Royal Dedications in Greek Sanctuaries" (PhD diss., University of California, Berkeley, 2002); H. W. Parke, "Croesus and Delphi," *Greek, Roman, and Byzantine Studies* 25, no. 3 (1984): 209–32; Gregory Crane, "The Prosperity of

Tyrants: Bacchylides, Herodotus, and the Contest for Legitimacy," *Arethusa* 29, no. 1 (1996): 57–85.

74. Crawford H. Greenewalt, Jr., "The Gods of Lydia," *The Archaeological Exploration of Sardis*, accessed May 13, 2020, http://sardisexpedition.org/en/essays/latw-greenewalt-gods-of-lydia, working from Michael Kerschner, "Lydische Weihungen in griechischen Heiligtümern," in *Stranieri e non cittadini nei santuari greci: Atti del convegno internazionale*, ed. Alessandro Naso (Florence: Felice Le Monnier, 2006), 253–91.

75. Though he is not discussing the rhetorical afterlives of Herodotus and Croesus per se, I cite what John D. Lyons expresses in *Exemplum: The Rhetoric of Example in Early Modern France and Italy* (Princeton, NJ: Princeton University Press, 1989), 4–5. My thanks to Scott Sessions for his encouragement of greater attention to Lyons and to the exemplary aspect within Ocaña's portrayals.

76. Libro de Acuerdos, Audiencia de Charcas, tomo 13, fol. 26r, Audiencia de La Plata to the King, La Plata, December 26, 1603, ABNB.

77. See the apparently meticulous, year-by-year accounting between 1579 and 1603, Charcas 82, no. 7, fols. 33v–42r, AGI.

78. Kris Lane, "Potosí Mines," in *Oxford Research Encyclopedia of Latin American History*, ed. William Beezley (Oxford, UK: Oxford University Press, 2015). http://latinamericanhistory.oxfordre.com/view/10.1093/acrefore/9780199366439.001.0001/acrefore-9780199366439-e-2.

79. Meneses at Charcas 82, no. 7, fol. 31r, AGI; see also fols. 14r, 15v, 19v, 21r, AGI.

80. Libros de Acuerdos, Audiencia de Charcas, tomo 13, Audiencia de La Plata to the King, La Plata, December 26, 1603, ABNB; Charcas 82, no. 7, fol. 28v, AGI.

81. Charcas 415 Legajo 2, fol. 216v, AGI; Alberto Crespo Rojas, *La guerra entre vicuñas y vascongados (Potosí, 1622–1625)* (Lima: Tipografía Peruana, 1956), 29; Paulina Numhauser, "Un asunto banal: Las luchas de vicuñas y vascongados en Potosí (siglo XVII)," *Illes i Imperis* 14 (2011): 132n67.

82. "Relación," fol. 180v; *Viaje*, 271.

83. "Relación," fol. 180v; *Viaje*, 271. Ocaña adapts a portion of Jesus's Sermon on the Mount, teaching that God sees and will ultimately reward giving done in secret: Matt 6:4.

84. Jeffrey Jerome Cohen, *Hybridity, Identity, and Monstrosity in Medieval Britain: On Difficult Middles* (New York: Palgrave Macmillan, 2006).

85. Cieza, *Parte primera*, caps. 117 and 118, fols. 273v–80r.

Works Cited

Acosta, José de. *Historia natural y moral de las Indias*. Seville: Casa de Juan de León, 1590.

———. *Historia natural y moral de las Indias*. Edited by Edmundo O'Gorman. 1940. Reprint, Mexico City: Fondo de Cultura Económica, 1962.

Adorno, Rolena. *Guaman Poma y su crónica ilustrada del Perú colonial*. Copenhagen: Museum Tusculanem Press, 2001.

Adorno, Rolena, and Patrick Pautz. *Álvar Núñez Cabeza de Vaca: His Account, His Life, and the Expedition of Pánfilo de Narváez*. 3 vols. Lincoln: University of Nebraska Press, 1999.

Auerbach, Erich. *Mimesis: The Representation of Reality in Western Literature*. Translated by Willard R. Trask. 1946. Reprint, Princeton, NJ: Princeton University Press, 1953.

Bakewell, Peter. *Miners of the Red Mountain: Indian Labor in Potosí*. Albuquerque: University of New Mexico Press, 1984.

———. *Silver and Entrepreneurship in Seventeenth-Century Potosí: The Life and Times of Antonio López de Quiroga*. 1988. Reprint, Dallas: Southern Methodist University Press, 1995.

Bakhtin, Mikhail. *The Dialogic Imagination: Four Essays*. Edited by Michael Holquist. Translated by Caryl

Emerson and Michael Holquist. Austin: University of Texas Press, 1981.

Beagon, Mary. "Peter Martyr's Use of Pliny." *International Journal of the Classical Tradition* 21, no. 3 (2014): 223–44.

Bhabha, Homi. "How Newness Enters the World: Postmodern Space, Postcolonial Times and the Trials of Cultural Translation." In *The Location of Culture*, 212–35. London: Routledge, 1994.

Buxton, Angela Heloiza. "Lydian Royal Dedications in Greek Sanctuaries." University of California, Berkeley, 2002.

Cameron, Averil. *Christianity and the Rhetoric of Empire: The Development of Christian Discourse*. Berkeley: University of California Press, 1991.

Campos y Fernández de Sevilla, Francisco Javier. "El monje jerónimo fray Diego de Ocaña y la crónica de su viaje por el Virreinato del Perú (1699–1606)." In *Fray Diego de Ocaña y la Virgen de Guadalupe en el virreinato del Perú: El lienzo de la Santa Iglesia Catedral de Lima*, edited by Francisco Javier Campos y Fernández de Sevilla and Erman Guzmán Reyes, 9–124. Lima: Gráfica DLC EIRL; Arzobispado de Lima, 2014.

Capoche, Luis. *Relación general del asiento y Villa Imperial de Potosí y de las cosas mas importantes a su gobierno, dirigida al Excmo. Sr. don Hernando de Torres y Portugal, conde del Villar y virrey del Perú*. 1585. Reprint, Madrid: Ediciones Atlas, 1959.

Cervantes Saavedra, Miguel de. *Don Quixote de la Mancha*. Edited by Francisco Rico, with Joaquín Forradellas. 2 vols. 1605 and 1615. Reprint, Barcelona: Instituto Cervantes, 1998.

Chiasson, Charles C. "The Herodotean Solon." *Greek, Roman, and Byzantine Studies* 27, no. 3 (1986): 249–62.

Cieza de León, Pedro de. *Parte primera de la chronica del Peru*. Antwerp: Juan Bellero a la enseña del Salmón, 1554.

Cohen, Jeffrey Jerome. *Hybridity, Identity, and Monstrosity in Medieval Britain: On Difficult Middles*. New York: Palgrave Macmillan, 2006.

Crane, Gregory. "The Prosperity of Tyrants: Bacchylides, Herodotus, and the Contest for Legitimacy." *Arethusa* 29, no. 1 (1996): 57–85.

Crémoux, Françoise. *Pèlerinages et miracles à Guadalupe au XVIe siècle*. Madrid: Casa de Velázquez, 2001.

Crespo Rojas, Alberto. *La guerra entre vicuñas y vascongados (Potosí, 1622–1625)*. Lima: Tipografía Peruana, 1956.

Figueroa, Luis Millones. *Pedro de Cieza de León: 500 años de historia*. Llerena: Sociedad Extremeña de Historia, 2018.

———. *Pedro de Cieza de León y su crónica del Perú: La entrada de los incas en la historia universal*. Lima: IFEA and Pontificia Universidad Católica del Perú, 2001.

Herodotus. *The Landmark Herodotus: The Histories*. Edited by Robert B. Strassler. Translated by Andrea L. Purvis. New York: Pantheon Books, 2009.

Horta, Paolo Lemos. *Marvellous Thieves: Secret Authors of the Arabian Nights*. Cambridge, MA: Harvard University Press, 2017.

Johnson, Scott F. "Late Antique Narrative Fiction: Apocryphal Acta and the Greek Novel in the Fifth-Century *Life and Miracles of Thekla*." In *Greek Literature in Late Antiquity: Dynamism, Didacticism, Classicism*, edited by Scott F. Johnson, 189–207. Aldershot, UK: Ashgate, 2006.

———. *"The Life and Miracles of Thekla": A Literary Study*. Washington, DC: Center for Hellenic Studies; Cambridge, MA: Harvard University Press, 2006.

Kerschner, Michael. "Lydische Weihungen in griechischen Heiligtümern." In *Stranieri e non cittadini nei santuari greci: Atti del convegno internazionale*, edited by Alessandro Naso, 253–91. Florence: Felice Le Monnier, 2006.

Kubler, George. *The Shape of Time: Remarks on the History of Things*. New Haven, CT: Yale University Press, 1962.

Lane, Kris E. "From Corrupt to Criminal: Reflections on the Great Potosí Mint Fraud of 1649." In *Corruption in the Iberian Empires: Greed, Custom, and Colonial Networks*, edited by Christoph Rosenmüller, 33–61. Albuquerque: University of New Mexico Press, 2017.

———. "Potosí Mines." In *Oxford Research Encyclopedia of Latin American History*, edited by William Beezley. Oxford, UK: Oxford University Press, 2015. http://latinamericanhistory.oxfordre.com/view/10.1093/acrefore/9780199366439.001.0001/acrefore-9780199366439-e-2.

———. *Potosí: The Silver City That Changed the World*. Berkeley: University of California Press, 2019.

Lyons, John D. *Exemplum: The Rhetoric of Example in Early Modern France and Italy*. Princeton, NJ: Princeton University Press, 1989.

Mangan, Jane E. *Trading Roles: Gender, Ethnicity, and the Urban Economy in Colonial Potosí*. Durham, NC: Duke University Press, 2005.

Miller, Molly. "The Herodotean Croesus." *Kilo* 41 (1963): 58–94.

Mills, Kenneth. "Diego de Ocaña." In *Guide to Documentary Sources for Andean Studies, 1530–1900*, edited by Joanne Pillsbury, 3:457–64. Norman: University of Oklahoma Press; Washington, DC: Center for Advanced Study in the Visual Arts, National Gallery of Art, 2008.

———. "Diego de Ocaña's Hagiography of New and Renewed Devotion in Colonial Peru." In *Colonial Saints: Discovering the Holy in the Americas*, edited by Allan Greer and Jodi Bilinkoff, 51–76. New York: Routledge, 2003.

———. "Mission and Narrative in the Early Modern Spanish World: Diego de Ocaña's Desert in Passing." In *Faithful Narratives: Historians, Religion, and the Challenge of Objectivity*, edited by Andrea Sterk and Nina Caputo, 115–31. Ithaca, NY: Cornell University Press, 2014.

———. "On the Presentation of Diego de Ocaña, O. S. H. (ca. 1570–1608)." *Colonial Latin American Review* 25, no. 4 (2016): 559–67.

———. "Religion in the Atlantic World." In *The Oxford Handbook of the Atlantic World*, edited by Nicholas Canny and Phillip Morgan, 433–48. Oxford, UK: Oxford University Press, 2011.

———. "Una sacra aventura en tierras que se volvían santas: Diego de Ocaña, O.S.H., 1599–1608." *Allpanchis* 46, nos. 83–84 (2019): 69–113.

Nagel, Alexander, and Christopher S. Wood. *Anachronic Renaissance*. New York: Zone Books, 2010.

Numhauser, Paulina. "Un asunto banal: Las luchas de vicuñas y vascongados en Potosí (siglo XVII)." *Illes i Imperis* 14 (2011): 113–38.

Ocaña, Diego de. *Memoria viva de una tierra de olvido: Relación del viaje al Nuevo Mundo de 1599 a 1607*. Edited by Beatriz Carolina Peña. Barcelona: Paso de Barc, 2013.

———. *A través de la América del Sur*. Edited by Arturo Álvarez. Madrid: Historia 16, 1987.

———. *Un viaje fascinante por la América Hispana del siglo XVI*. Edited by Arturo Álvarez. Madrid: Studium, 1969.

———. *Viaje por el nuevo mundo: De Guadalupe a Potosí, 1599–1605*. Edited by Blanca López de Mariscal and Abraham Madroñal Durán, with the collaboration of Alejandra Soria. Madrid: Editorial Iberoamericana; Frankfurt: Vervuert; Mexico: Bonilla Artigas Editores; Monterrey: Instituto Tecnológico de Estudios Superiores de Monterrey, 2010.

Orsua y Vela, Arzáns de. *Relatos de la villa imperial de Potosí: Antología*. 1626. Reprint, Potosí: Plural Editores, 2000.

Parke, H. W. "Croesus and Delphi." *Greek, Roman, and Byzantine Studies* 25, no. 3 (1984): 209–32.

Peña, Beatriz Carolina. *Imágenes contra el olvido: El Perú colonial en las ilustraciones de fray Diego de Ocaña.* Lima: Fondo Editorial de la Pontificia Universidad Católica del Perú, 2011.

Pereda, Felipe. *Crime and Illusion: The Art of Truth in the Spanish Golden Age.* Translated by Consuelo López-Morillas. Turnhout, Belgium: Brepols, 2018.

Ramage, Andrew, and Paul Craddock. *King Croesus's Gold: Excavations at Sardis and the History of Gold Refining.* Cambridge, MA: Harvard University Press, 2000.

Rappaport, Joanna. *The Disappearing Mestizo: Configuring Difference in the Colonial New Kingdom of Granada.* Durham, NC: Duke University Press, 2014.

Reeser, Sarah L. "The Whole Hand of the Giant: Geography, Vision, and Materiality in the Late Medieval and Early Modern Atlantic World." PhD diss., University of Toronto, forthcoming.

Schwartz, Stuart B., and Frank Salomon, "New Peoples and New Kinds of People: Adaptation, Readjustment, and Ethnogenesis in South American Indigenous Societies (Colonial Era)." In *Cambridge History of Native Peoples of the Americas*, vol. 3, *South America*, pt. 2, edited by Frank Salomon and Stuart B. Schwartz, 443–94. Cambridge, UK: Cambridge University Press, 1999.

TePaske, John J. *A New World of Gold and Silver.* Edited by Kendall W. Brown. Leiden: Brill, 2010.

Vargas, José Maria. *Fr. Domingo de Santo Tomás, defensor y apostól de los indios del Perú: Su vida y sus escritos.* Quito: Editorial Santo Domingo, 1937.

White, Hayden. *Metahistory: The Historical Imagination in Nineteenth-Century Europe.* Baltimore: Johns Hopkins University Press, 1973.

Zárate, Agustín de. *Historia del descubrimiento y conquista del Perú.* Antwerp: En casa de Martin Nucio, a las dos Cigueñas, 1555.

CHRISTIAN NATIONALISM

Chapter 7

THEY TALK. WE LISTEN?

Native American Christians in Speech and on Paper

Christopher Vecsey

The Question

Can Native American Christians speak? Of course they can, and they have always had that human capacity. However, when a contemporary historian such as myself attempts to fathom the consciousness and behavior of past American Indians engaged with Christian traditions, the looming question has been: Could they write?[1] In this essay I wish to affirm Native American Christians as speakers, writers, and exponents of native Christianity, whose testimonies and teaching are worth our heed.

As I have tried to narrate the religious history of Native Americans, primarily in what is now the United States and Canada—and especially their encounters with Christianity—I have faced an apparent problem.[2] Before the nineteenth century, few aboriginal Indians north of Mexico left any written records, beyond the pictographic, and as they responded to Christian evangelical overtures, and even as they have become Christians, most of their spoken words evaporated into air.

Of course, Europeans recorded native utterances: queries regarding Christian messages, arguments of resistance, syncretic postulations, conversions, devotions, and the like. Colonial and missionary archives are full of these records, and many of them are published, most famously *The Jesuit Relations of New France*, and more recently Moravian mission writings from the mid-Atlantic colonies.[3] The obvious difficulty with these and other eyewitness missionary accounts is hermeneutical: To what degree are the Indian quotations authentically their own? How much do they express Euro-American projections and misunderstandings, through the filters of prejudice and translation?

Over the past half century the ethnohistorical spirit has moved scholars like myself to comprehend American Indian agency, both individual and community-wide. Earlier studies of missions were content to focus on the missionaries themselves, usually in heroic poses but increasingly through critical lenses.[4] Like my cohort I have been unwilling to give the literate non-Indians the whole say. This has meant a task of weighing native words cited in the archives and publications, without ever being certain of their validity as accurate portrayals of Indian ideas.

American Indian Protestants

Recent studies of indigenous encounters with colonial-era Christianity in New England have emphasized native agency in adopting, resisting, and adapting to Christian overtures. No longer willing to rely on semi-fictional projections of "praying Indians" and "Indian converts" by missionaries such as John Eliot and Experience Mayhew, historians have located the "bicultural" biblical marginalia of Massachusetts speakers—and writers!—as they commented on scriptural passages, thus creating "an alternative 'text' in the margins."[5] Serving as cultural intermediaries, these literate Christian Indians of New England, such as the Nipmuck convert James Printer, helped translate the Bible into Indian tongues, even as they viewed books and literacy in "complex and conflicted ways."[6] Indian Christians became literate and began to pen, as well as speak, their thoughts about scripture, mores, theodicy, original sin, as well as race and survival, as they solidified their Indian Christian communities.[7] Yet they were "caught in the middle of two cultures" with ambivalent loyalties to both. They possessed "the power to write but . . . could no longer speak for their people."[8]

Literate Indian Christians in New England left their mark for historians to discover, as they "reconfigured Christian theology to meet their own political goals."[9] For the most part, however, the native Christians—even as they have come to life as actors on the pages of more recent tomes—continue to speak through the writings of the non-Indian missionaries. Other scholars have sought out the "tutor'd mind" of "Indian missionary-writers" who articulated their ambiguous places as native Christians.[10] Edward E. Andrews has examined the lives and writings of many American Indians in the British colonies who became Protestant evangelists among their own and neighboring peoples.[11] From copious evidence—letters, sermons, and songs from archival and secondary sources—it is clear that these ministers both challenged and harnessed colonial Christianity, making use of their networks of kinship as cultural mediators in order to create semi-independent congregations as legitimate heirs to multiethnic Christianity. They appropriated Christian spiritual power for Indian purposes, translated Christian ideas into native languages, and fused Christian and native beliefs and practices. Thus they spread Christianity among Indian peoples with far more effect than Anglo missionaries. The Christian Indian identity they forged emphasized pity and poverty as the conditions of existence to which Christ offered succor. It encouraged spiritual freedom, informed by dreams and experiential enthusiasms, which were deemed a danger to old patterns of authority and dogma. In the process they helped their communities survive, protecting lands, guarding autonomy, arranging for orderly exodus.

By the eighteenth century prominent Christian Indians like the Mohegan reverend Samson Occom left behind letters, diaries, hymns, sermons, and diatribes, which enterprising academics like Joanna Brooks have mined for meaning and published in recent years.[12] Born to "Heathens" and raised with "Heathenish Notions" and "Heathenish ways," Occom was inspired by the Great Awakening "New Lights" in 1741 and trained for missionary work at Eleazar Wheelock's Indian Charity School.[13] In 1765 Occom traveled to Britain on a fundraising tour for Wheelock and was disappointed when the moneys he acquired were diverted to non-Indian educational purposes: namely, Dartmouth College. "I am very Jealous that instead of your Semenary Becoming alma Mater, she will be too alba mater to Suckle the Tawnees," Occom wrote to Wheelock.[14] Setting off on his own, Occom became "elder, statesman, advocate, and spiritual advisor" to the nascent pan-tribal Brotherton Indian settlement, recognizing that "Indians must have Teach[ers] of their own Coular or Nation."[15] Over his thirty years as an active preacher Occom delivered jeremiads warning Indians of the evils of alcohol and whites of the evils of slaveholding, following in the homiletic footsteps of his friend George Whitefield. In 1786 Occom dreamed of the revivalist, who "put his face to my face, and rub'd his face to mine and said,—I am glad that you preach the Excellency of Jesus Christ yet."[16] Whitefield then "stretched himself upon the ground flat on his face and reachd his hands forward, and mad a mark with his Hand, and Said I will out doe and over reach all Sinners, and I thought he Barked like a Dog, with a Thundering Voice."¹⁷ When Occom awoke, he reflected about "the end of my Journey."¹⁸

The Letters of Eleazar Wheelock's Indians included missives in the mid-1700s from over a dozen of Occom's fellow Indians—Delawares, Montauks, Narragansetts, as well as Mohegans—who attended Wheelock's Charity School.¹⁹ The editor of this correspondence warned his readers, "The Indian of these letters is not the noble savage of eighteenth century poem and play. He is a dullard, often a drunkard, an unwilling pupil . . . , a consumptive, simple, and simple-minded," indeed, like "some captive animal performing his tricks."²⁰ Truly, the letters reveal subservient youths cowering before their martinet benefactor.

However, if we read the diaries and sermons of Joseph Johnson (Mohegan), who arrived at Wheelock's Charity School in 1758 at age seven and was granted a license to preach in 1774, we find a Christian Indian who transcended his "emotional dependency" and self-denigration to become "a religious and community leader" of the Brotherton Indians.²¹

Such Christian Indians of New England—especially Occom—took possession of Christianity without ceasing to embrace their Indian identity. For William Apess, a Pequot Methodist preacher, and the first Native American to publish his autobiography (*A Son of the Forest*, published in 1829), "becoming Christian and affirming being Pequot are essential to each other."²² His "militant consciousness" employed an Indian Christian judgment against white racism and hypocrisy.²³ His second major publication, *The Experiences of Five Christian Indians* (1833) explicitly attacks white Christians, and his sermon, a "Eulogy on King Philip," condemns "the evils repeatedly committed in the name of Christianity."²⁴ Nonetheless, Apess's most striking prose follows the tropes of sinfulness and redemption, as when in 1813 he heard a soothing voice tell him, "Arise, thy sins which were many are all forgiven thee, go in peace and sin no more!"²⁵ As a result, Apess wrote, "I enjoyed great peace of mind."²⁶

Contemporary scholars are intent on showing the independence of Christian Indian converts in making their life-changing decisions. Gathering the meager writings—a few dozen letters and a short diary—of Catharine Brown, a Cherokee Christian convert of the Brainerd Mission in Tennessee, whose pious life was popularly memorialized in 1825, Theresa Gaul calls her "the earliest Native woman author of published, self-written texts in the United States" and heralds her as "an agent, a leader, a figure of enduring Cherokee resilience and adaptability and—importantly—a writer."²⁷ Gaul does not want her readers to think of Brown as a "mere missionary pawn," but rather as an example of "*survivance*," "*intellectual sovereignty*," and "*communitism*."²⁸ Brown also did not cease to be a loyal Cherokee in the process of becoming a Christian.

The Mahican Christian writer Aupaumut constructed "a utopian tribal past" in his writings, claiming that Mahicans had always been the best of Christians, even before Christianity came to his people, through the English.²⁹ Hence, "by appropriating a Christian past for the Mahican people, Aupaumut challenge[d] the very basis of Anglo-American superiority."³⁰

By the mid-1800s, literary models existed for Indian-authored, evangelical conversion experiences. And by the turn of the twentieth century, literate Indian Christians had left more than their mark on the pages of history. The Tsimshian Methodist Arthur Wellington Clah, on the Pacific Northwest coast of Canada, left over fifty years of journals reflecting on his syncretic identity, while David Pendleton Oakerhater, Cheyenne, named a saint of the Episcopal Church in 1985, served as a deacon in Indian Territory in the 1880s.³¹ His letters are available in the Oklahoma State University Library.³² Likewise, Nez Perce and Dakota clergy in the late nineteenth century left their own records in Presbyterian archives.³³

The 1847 autobiography ("Life, History and Travels") of the Ojibwa George Copway cut a striking figure in the annals of Indian cultural change.³⁴ Copway (meaning "gahbowh," or "standing"; his whole Ojibwa name translates to "forever standing" or "standing firm"—i.e., "committed") portrayed his life as a meaningful progression. Born in 1818 and raised in eastern Ontario, he was fully enculturated in Ojibwa ways. A member of the crane clan, his father was a medicine man and hereditary chief. Copway learned to hunt, gained a guardian spirit through an empowering puberty vision, and engaged in the ceremonial patterns of his people. In his memoir Copway was able to evoke lovingly his traditional Ojibwa values; however, the emotional center of his narrative is located in 1830, when he underwent a conversion experience under the camp meeting influence of a Methodist missionary. From that moment on—at least as he presented it in his writing—he was committed to Christianity. He became a mission helper among the Ojibwas and attended a Bible school in Illinois. His dreams and his waking thoughts were devoted to evangelical ideals. Through a Christian lens he reevaluated Indians, and he found them to be poor, untutored, sometimes bloodthirsty and drunken, a people of broken spirit and economy whose only hope lay in Christian uplifting.

Through the same lens Copway perceived an American culture with which he identified vigorously. He married a white Christian Canadian,

Elizabeth Howells, in 1840. At the same time he faced up to Western civilization's faults. He saw its bigotry (including opposition to his mixed-race marriage), its insatiable hunger for Indian land, its dishonesty in the treaty-making process. He wondered if America could be transformed by the Christian ideals it supposedly claimed. Thus he became an evangelist in reverse: preaching to white Americans about their Christian duties to American Indians—not only to Christianize and educate them but also to provide them with a self-governing refuge from American expansion. With these goals in mind Copway went on the circuit of East Coast lecture halls, in which his life story served as a written exemplum.

Students have often found Copway's "Life" challenging in its internal contradictions. Here was an Indian man who seemed to identify himself more strongly with whites than with Indians, who appeared to want nothing more than to reform his fellows into pseudo-whites, much like himself. At the same time he romanticized Indian culture, finding in it the Christian values of family, honesty, sharing, and spirituality, which white Americans so often proclaimed but so rarely acted on. He wanted white America to save Indians; he also wanted to protect Indians from white Americans.

The greatest contradiction, however, was between Copway's idealized "Life" and the realities of his existence. In 1847, when Copway (surely with the editorial assistance of his wife) published his autobiography, he had recently been jailed and defrocked for financial irregularities. He claimed in his lecture tour to be raising funds for a future Indian school back home; however, the moneys went to support his growing family. An American celebrity, among his own band he was persona non grata.

Between 1847 and 1851 Copway promoted himself, lecturing widely, reprinting his "Life" in new editions; penning prose and poetry with the apparent help of his faithful Elizabeth and others. He promoted a plan for a sizable Indian territory (named Kahgega, meaning "forever"), where Indians could supposedly find permanent refuge from the ravages of white cultural aggression. On behalf of his plan Copway appeared before state legislatures; he appealed to liberal reformers; he lobbied Congress and the Indian Bureau in Washington, DC, but to no avail. At the same time he lost three of his four children to deadly disease. Then he lost his audiences, as the novelty of his message wore out. His marriage teetered and fell apart, as Copway's life devolved to drinks and schemes, and he was thought to have died by the early 1860s. An enterprising historian, Donald B. Smith, tracked down aspects of Copway's shifting career as a Union Army recruiter collecting bounties in Canada during the Civil War, and as an herbalist advertising healing arts in Detroit. Finally, he landed in a mission northwest of Montreal, where he claimed to be a pagan and received Roman Catholic baptism shortly before his death in 1869.

Copway's life and "Life" show us that Native American Christians can surely speak, and write, but also dissemble. Their lives are almost always more complicated than their oral and written expressions.

American Indian Catholic Voices

The *Jesuit Relations* of the seventeenth century include pious depictions of Indian converts to Catholicism. For instance, Rev. Jerome Lalement, SJ, described Joseph Chihouatenhoua, a Huron convert in 1640, who was attracted by the Spiritual Exercises of the Jesuits, shortly before he was martyred for his faith. Other Jesuits described all manner of Indian Catholic devotions—among captive Hurons in Iroquoia in the 1650s; among baptized Anishinabe in the 1660s, under duress from contagious diseases brought by the Frenchmen in the Great Lakes region; among pilgrims to Saint-Anne-de-Beaupré in the 1670s; and so forth.[35] Vivid depictions, but all the words belong to the Jesuits themselves.

In their *Relations* the Jesuits amply portrayed a Mohawk maiden of the late 1600s, Kateri Tekakwitha, arguably the most famous American Indian convert to Catholicism. Allan Greer terms her the most "fully and richly documented" indigenous person in the colonial Americas.[36] The "sources" of knowledge about her life—Jesuits Claude Chauchetière and Pierre Cholenec, primarily—were "incomparable," writes Greer, but "not transparent," because their writings were thoroughly hagiographic.[37] The Jesuits quoted Kateri's utterances—"I will love you in heaven," her last words in 1680 as she lay dying of her own self-abnegating zeal at age twenty-four—and we can read in Jesuit archives of her spectral communication to her beloved Indian companions: "Adieu, adieu, go tell the father that I'm going to heaven."[38] Nonetheless, the details of her baptism, her migration to the Christian Iroquois community of Kahnawake, her first communion, her vow of virginity ("I hate men") and intense austerities ("I shall be mistress of my own body"), all come from the Jesuits' pens. She herself was illiterate.[39]

All we have from her are small fragments of her bones, which have been judged by the Roman Catholic Church as capable of working miracles. The documents gathered by the Church were all *about* Kateri, without a word directly *from* her. The testimonies of the Jesuits were cogent enough on their own to produce a cult to Kateri among Indians and non-Indians alike. There is plenty of evidence of Catholic Indian devotion *to* Kateri, now a saint: an 1880 petition by Flathead Indians asking the pope to consider her canonization; twentieth-century exhortations, sermons, manifestos, and hymns honoring her holiness; dramatic reenactments and artistic renderings of her life story; testimonies by interviewed Indians of their reverence to the saintly Mohawk, and their desire to walk in her footsteps; celebrations of her miraculous cure of a Lummi Indian boy's necrotizing fasciitis in 2006.[40] In all these records Indian Catholics have their eloquent say; still, the historical Kateri herself remains mute. Even a contemporary Mohawk intellectual, Darren Bonaparte, intent on a "repatriation" of Kateri as an historical agent of Mohawk values who expressed her native culture through her Christian forms, must conduct his project without any fresh evidence from her mouth or hand.[41]

In the history of American Indian Catholicism we must wait until the 1800s to locate a primary text even putatively from the hand of a Catholic Indian. Pablo Tac, Luiseño, born in California's San Luis Rey Mission in 1822, accompanied a Franciscan friar to Europe when the missions of California were secularized. At the Urban College in Rome young Tac produced—or at least participated in producing, with a clerical linguist—a brief memoir, probably the earliest literary work by a California Indian, in 1835, before dying of smallpox in 1841. The document depicts a record of California mission routines: work, catechism, meals, and even native dances, but without much personal reflection.[42]

Later in the century, when Lakota chiefs petitioned President Rutherford B. Hayes in 1877 for Catholic priests and sisters to be sent to their reservations as teachers, one might also suspect the hand of others in the words' framing.[43] Sometimes the voices of Indian Catholics as captured on the pages of official documents seem stylized ("My Great Father"), perhaps even manipulated to express the desire of Catholic missionaries as much as that of the native signatories ("We would like to have Catholic priests and Catholic nuns").

Letters from Mississippi Choctaws between 1917 and 1920, expressing affection for their priest, have the ring of verity, as they ask questions about the Catholic rules prohibiting meat on Fridays or refer to local concerns.[44] So does the unsuccessful petition of Yankton Sioux parishioners in 1920, asking for the removal of the local priest for having infringed on their native leadership.[45] California Catholic Indians left writings of their own in the twentieth century, to be found in diocesan archives, including one from

Morongo Mission Indians to Pope Pius XII in 1952, protesting the departure of Franciscan friars and their replacement by other orders of priests.[46]

Among the Pueblo Indians it is nigh impossible to verify an unfiltered Indian Catholic voice—penned by a native hand, expressing clearly the desires of a native community—until the twentieth century, when we can locate archival letters, such as from Eugene Van Patten, president of the Tortugas Indians, in 1919, expressing his people's desire (to the head of the Bureau of Catholic Indian Missions) to maintain tribal autonomy over their local Pueblo church, as non-Indians encroached on their parish in South Texas; from Esther Naktewa (Zuni) in 1937, petitioning Santa Claus for gifts at Christmas; from Augustine Aguilar and other officials of Santo Domingo Pueblo, reminding the archbishop of Santa Fe in 1935 of the long-standing accommodation in which Pueblos avowed their Catholic identity and paid fealty to the church while maintaining their tribal customs, including their right to privacy from the prying eyes of Catholic officials.[47]

In a similar manner, in 1965 Isleta Pueblo Catholics evicted the appointed Catholic priest because of his campaign to eradicate tribal ritualism. Primary documents exist, attesting to the divisions within the Pueblo regarding this draconian expulsion. An Isleta Committee for Religious Freedom decried the eviction and the investiture controversy it engendered, calling, however, for the appointment of a new priest.[48] Hence, one can hear through the voices of Pueblo Catholics the continuing tensions inherent to dual religious participation, the valuing of both native and Catholic forms.

Petition constitutes one of the most frequent genres in American Indian Catholic writing, at least as found in Catholic archives. Asking state and church authorities for religious instruction, for protection, for redress, for gifts, for continuing services and accommodations regarding cultural prerogatives: these petitions demonstrate the unequal balance of power between white authorities and reservation Indians in the nineteenth and twentieth centuries. Swinomish Catholics petitioned the archbishop of Seattle in 1971, in vain, to keep their parish church open, and also to provide support for religious expression largely in keeping with their native values.[49] Another Swinomish parishioner in 1979 encouraged a Catholic Indian ministry grounded more in joyous celebration of creation than in condemnation of sin.[50] In the same year an Ojibwa Catholic woman in Milwaukee framed for the archbishop a concept for a pan-Indian urban liturgy, which was to become the Congregation of the Great Spirit a decade later.[51] Another Ojibwa woman wrote to the archbishops of Seattle, with the same notion of a special Indian Catholic ministry in the archdiocese.[52]

Twentieth-century Native American Catholic speeches and writings are ever present in archives: official and personal correspondence, autobiographical narratives, lecture notes, sound recordings of hymns and conversations, and more. In the past decades Mark G. Thiel, archivist at Marquette University's Department of Special Collections and University Archives, has produced and maintained a comprehensive set of guides, not only to Marquette's outstanding collections on "Christianity and Native America" but also to hundreds of archives throughout North America and Europe, with enormous resources concerning the encounter of Native Americans and Catholicism.[53]

Marquette's holdings include the archives of the Tekakwitha Conference, founded in 1939 as a priestly organization, but conducted since the 1970s as a movement for and of native Catholics—although under Catholic bureaucratic direction and support.[54] Its newsletters contain speeches and other declarations by Catholic Indian priests, sisters, deacons, and various laypersons, regarding all types of Catholic issues, including catechesis, cultural genocide, inculturation, and the overarching goal of the Conference: to make Indian Catholics feel at home, as Indians as well as Catholics, within the universal church.[55] The Tekakwitha Conference in 1995 formulated a Native Profession of Faith, which includes belief in "the Creator, the Great Spirit, Maker of Mother Earth and Father Sky," as well as "Jesus of Nazareth and the Holy Spirit."[56]

No documents at Marquette are more enticing than the records of "Medicine Men and Pastors Meetings."[57] Between 1973 and 1979 a theological dialogue took place on a biweekly basis on the Rosebud Lakota Reservation in South Dakota, featuring Jesuit priests and Lakota medicine men, most of them Catholics. Father William F. Stolzman, SJ, the organizer of the dialogues, taped and transcribed the entire proceedings, as the participants dwelt on all manner of cross-cultural religious formulations, including the nature of revelation, the purposes of ritual, the means of spiritual discernment, and the degree to which Catholicism and traditional Lakota religion were compatible and comparable. In my view the corpus represents the greatest documented example of Christian–Native American discourse on religious questions. For complete analysis the record awaits a fluent Lakota speaker with theological and anthropological expertise, for much of the dialogue took place in the Lakota language. The transcripts contain only the English translations, which are largely truncated summaries of the original speech.

Native American Perspectives on Indigenous Culture and Roman Catholicism

There has been ample native criticism of Catholic boarding schools as engines of cultural genocide, venues of cruelty and violence. For instance, the Lakota journalist Tim Giago has decried the treatment he and his fellows received at Holy Rosary Mission on the Pine Ridge Reservation in South Dakota. "We were separated from our cultural and spiritual teachers, our parents and grandparents," Giago writes.[58] "We were beaten physically, psychologically and emotionally for being Indian. Our culture, language and spirituality had to be stripped away so that we could become cheap imitations of our mentors, the Franciscan nuns and Jesuit priests, prefects and brothers." He asserts, "There are few Indian families who have not experienced the residual impact of the abuse heaped upon their friends and family members after they were victims of the rape and abuse they experienced at the hands of the missionaries sent out to save their souls. It was not only a sin, it was a crime." And yet, some Indian Catholics, such as an Apache man in 1981, had nothing but praise for the Franciscans who conducted his alma mater, St. John's Mission School, in Arizona, where he received what he considered "a sound education and thorough religious instruction," with enduring ethical values and character development, and he protested its scheduled closing.[59] The testimonial native judgment of Christian boarding schools ranges from condemnation to praise.

Some of the most famous of Christian Indian voices belong to those who have tried to walk both traditional and Catholic paths, or those who have reconsidered their relationship to the Christian faith and church. *Black Elk Speaks*, a book published in 1932, written by the poet and visionary John G. Neihardt, was based primarily on interviews conducted with Nicholas Black Elk and his fellow Lakotas in 1930–31. Probably the most popular book ever written about American Indians, still in print today—now in a "premier," critical edition, with annotations by scholar Raymond J. DeMallie—it focuses on Black Elk's childhood visions and his subsequent vocation as holy man, medicine man, ghost dancer, and nostalgist for the old Lakota ways.[60] Most—but not all—of the words in the book are Black Elk's, translated into English by his son and transcribed by Neihardt's daughters. The transcripts are intact and have been published by DeMallie, who has evaluated the original book's claim that Black Elk's words were "told through" John G. Neihardt.[61]

Not a word of *Black Elk Speaks* concerned Christianity, and there lies the rub, for Nicholas Black Elk was a Catholic convert, baptized in 1904 and for several decades a catechist and missioner for the Catholic Church. Black Elk was illiterate in English, but not in Lakota. He published many letters in a missionary newsletter, encouraging his fellow Lakotas to embrace and support Catholicism.[62] Thus his Jesuit associates were distressed when *Black Elk Speaks* was published in 1932, portraying the catechist they knew as an unreconstructed pagan. When Black Elk was injured and sought last rites, the Jesuits arranged for his signature on two documents—one typewritten, one handwritten (neither by Black Elk, it is certain, although perhaps he dictated the messages; his daughter, a staunch Catholic, surely played a role and affixed her signature to one of the statements)—in which he disavowed the contents of Neihardt's book, proclaimed his Catholic faith, and expressed regret for his apparent apostasy, telling his people, both Indian and white, to "stay in the right way which Christ and His church have taught us. I will never fall back from the true faith in Christ."[63]

Black Elk's recantations did not put an end to the fracas over his dual religious orientation. Over the past decades advocates for Black Elk's Catholic identity have argued publicly with defenders of Neihardt's portrayal of Black Elk's traditionalism, and scholars have weighed the nuanced evidence for Black Elk's complicated, combined religious practice and identity.[64] There is a strong possibility that more documents from Black Elk's hand will come to light in the years to come.[65]

Native American Roman Catholic Priests and Sisters

In the second part of the nineteenth century the first American Indian men were ordained priests in the United States. Rev. James Chrysostom Bouchard (Delaware-Comanche-French) was perhaps the first. Ordained a Jesuit in 1855, his spirituality reflected the widespread Indian tradition of fasting as a means of obtaining visions of protective spiritual guardians. Whereas traditional natives might receive visitations from cosmic forces or animal presences—Black Elk's visions are the most famous of these types—Bouchard recorded a dream in which members of the Society of Jesus served as his celestial guides. Bouchard hoped to serve among his own Indian peoples and was disappointed to receive orders prohibiting such a vocation, as his superiors feared that his proximity to native ways would draw him back toward paganism.⁶⁶

In Canada no man of Indian descent is more famous than the former seminarian Louis Riel of Manitoba, who led Métis-Indian military revolts against the consolidation of Canada in 1869 and 1885. His diaries and letters have been published, including manifestos written in exile in Montana in 1884–85, in which he preached an apocalyptic message of spiritualized politics. "Live as a saint, die as one of the elect," Riel wrote, with an eye both to heaven and earth. "Oh! Sacred Heart of Jesus, make us really understand that this world is simply the antechamber of eternity. . . . I hear the voice of the Indian. He comes to join me. . . . He is in the mood for war."⁶⁷ Riel was hanged for his revolutionary acts in 1885. His resistance and execution constitute the iconic foundation of Canada's myth of national origin.⁶⁸

The Ojibwa reverend Philip B. Gordon attended seminary in Rome, and upon ordination in 1913 sought assignment among his people. Instead he served as chaplain to Catholic students at the Haskell Indian School in Lawrence, Kansas, where he battled Protestant administrators and the YMCA. His letters reveal his Catholic stridency. When he was transferred to an Ojibwa parish in Wisconsin, he devoted his irascible energy to Indian politics, lobbying the Bureau of Indian Affairs in favor of Ojibwa land claims. His criticism of Catholic boarding schools placed him at odds with the Bureau of Catholic Indian Missions and teaching sisterhoods who ran the schools. By the 1920s he was perceived as an irredeemable troublemaker and was subjected to ecclesiastical and governmental investigations, then removed from his post. His correspondence captures the spirit of an Indian activist, identifying strongly with his Native American kinsmen. Even when assigned to a non-Indian parish, for two decades he continued to espouse a public, political Indian identity, as his correspondence attests.⁶⁹

Like the men, American Indian Catholic women sought to fulfill vocations in the church. There are extant letters from some of the Lakota novices and sisters in Rev. Francis M. Craft's Congregation of American Sisters in the early 1890s, including the vows of Mother Mary Catharine, Josephine Crowfeather Sacred White Buffalo, in 1892, and from Eskimo postulants in the Sisters of the Snows of Father John P. Fox, SJ, in the 1930s.⁷⁰ Sister Gloria Ann Davis, SBS, Navajo-Choctaw, like many Catholic women religious, tried to harmonize forms of native and Catholic spirituality, including those of the Native American church—that is, the peyote religion.⁷¹

The Historian's Task and Contemporary Native Christian Speakers and Writers

I must also make a pitch for the greatest archive of Christian Indian source material: living American Indian peoples themselves. If I may say so, it disappoints me to read so many books and articles about Indian responses to Christianity, which end in the faraway, without concern for native Christians of the present day. Some authors seem too timid or circumscribed to go beyond the archives and engage living Indians. Native Christians are our neighbors; they can speak. We should be listening. As Susan Elaine Gray says in her study of Ojibwa-missionary encounters in Manitoba, the Indian Christians who provided her interviews "injected life-breath into my work."[72] Indeed, some of the best recent books about American Indian encounters with Christianity have been built on testimonies of native Christians, for instance, J. R. Miller's history of First Nation residential schools in Canada, Kirk Dombrowski's study of politics and religion in Indian Alaska, Leonard Ortiz's survey of contemporary Indians in the United Methodist Church, and Sergei Kan's unsurpassed analysis of Tlingit culture and Russian Orthodox Christianity.[73]

Since the 1990s Marquette archivist Mark G. Thiel has conducted invaluable interviews with many native Catholics about their living faith. In their own words we can ascertain the contemporary forms of inculturation and syncretism in Indian Catholic communities, and the specific shapes of contemporary native worship.

I am not implying that today's Indians are repositories of orally maintained historical knowledge. Indeed, I have become increasingly skeptical of oral tradition as a source of accurate, verifiable data regarding the remote past. Contemporary Indians cannot speak for the primordial, or even the historical, past; they are merely authentic representatives of the present. I am speaking here of Christian Indian testimonies concerning their own experiences. I could not have produced significant work without meeting Indian Christians face to face, listening to their prayers and plaints, observing their liturgical forms, asking them questions, and trying to respond to theirs in sincere dialogue. Their professions of ambivalence, irony, forgiveness, and faith have been the guiding leitmotifs of my scholarship.

As I have traveled to Indian communities, from California to Maine, and into Canada, I have listened to native Catholics speak of their indigenous Catholic faith and the church with which they share an often ambivalent history. The late Sister Marie Therese Archambault once said, "As a native Catholic the very faith you embrace is one that was used to destroy you, that collaborated with the government in cultural genocide.... This is the terrible irony of being Native American and Catholic."[74]

On the other hand, I have met Catholics such as laypersons Eva and Norris Joseph Boudreaux of the Houmas of coastal Louisiana (she was Houma, he was Cajun; they are both deceased now), who seemed comfortable in their church, despite a long history of racist exclusion. On an autumn day in 1990 Mr. Boudreaux fashioned an enormous rosary out of netted rope and plastic corks; his wife was baking sweet potato pies for a St. Vincent Society raffle at their parish church. Past racism in the church? Mrs. Boudreaux exclaimed, "It's like it never happened. Those old people from then are dead now.... Now we all hug and kiss at mass.... Such a big change! ... God sees everything."[75]

I quote these voices. I picture the settings in which I heard these native Catholics speak. I realize, however, that their testimonies have become grist for my writing mill. For me, their voices still ring, living utterances of autonomous beings. But for my readers, these quotations are possibly no less problematic than Jesuit quotations of Indian converts in the 1600s, or anthropological accounts over the past century. I can only hope that I heard them right; one can never be sure.

Edward H. Spicer in 1940 cited a Yaqui Indian maestro in the semiautonomous Yaqui Catholic religion, telling a story about the Holy Family that demonstrates centuries of syncretism. In the narrative, Joseph cut down a tree, which was "really Mary, because Mary had turned herself into a tree. Jesus and God had planned this out long before.... So, when Jesus was crucified, he was crucified on a cross made of his mother, Mary. She holds him embraced in her outstretched arms."[76] When we read these accounts, do we regard them as accurate, authentic Indian Catholic voices?

When scholars have observed the ceremonial performances of native Christians, such as the Seminole Baptist churches of Oklahoma or the "indigenous Easter rituals" of Yaqui, Mayo, Opata, Papago, Tarahumara, Cora, and Huichol Indians of northern Mexico and the southwestern United States, they come to conclusions about the meanings of these acts to the indigenous Christians who have formed their distinctive brand of independent church life.[77] The scholars speak of a "unique intersection of two vastly different cultural traditions," or "the dynamism of syncretism and the role it plays in human adaptation and endurance"; however, it is not clear that such conclusions ring true to these native Christians.[78]

Nor is it clear that my own recordings of Indian voices can be held as authentic to anyone except perhaps myself. Hence, we must turn to native Christian authors, whose words are unfiltered through non-Indian writers and editors like me.

In contemporary America, Indian Catholics are not shy about portraying their particular forms of spirituality in words, song, and visual imagery. In Zuni Pueblo in New Mexico we can witness the artistry of Alex Seowtewa, who has painted the summer and winter divinities of the Zuni (with Jesus in the center, in traditional Zuni dress) on the interior walls of Our Lady of Guadalupe Church, as an expression of inculturated, or perhaps syncretistic, Zuni Catholic faith.[79]

Mohawk sister Kateri Mitchell, SSA, Turtle Clan, just like her forebear, Kateri Tekakwitha, composed (with an Oblate priest) a hymn, "In Her Footsteps," which employs a style of drumming and chanting—as well as a lyrical content—that combines native and Catholic forms of expression.[80] She served as executive director of the Tekakwitha Conference for twenty years.

Seowtewa and Mitchell are but two contemporary Indian Catholics who use their creativity to combine native and Catholic modes of expression.

James Treat, a Creek (Muscogee), whose father was a Baptist pastor to several Indian congregations, has aimed to make native Christians "a significant new collective voice on the North American religious landscape."[81] The Indian Christian authors whose writings he has anthologized ask, "Is it possible to be both native and Christian in any meaningful way?"[82] Like their spiritual forebears—Samson Occom, William Apess, et cetera—"they face a fundamental existential dilemma in attempting to resolve their hybrid identities into an organic unity."[83] Treat's bibliography lists major voices in "native Christian narrative discourse" over the last quarter of the twentieth century.[84]

In a speech Treat has delivered on occasion, "Tribal Visions of the Church Way," he amplifies and clarifies these Indian Christian articulations, as they reflect on "the oftentimes coercive ways in which their ancestors were converted to the faith," rue the fact that "competitive missionization has had a divisive effect among Indian communities," recognize that "some Indians are passionately Christian, others passionately traditional," affirm their ambivalent "bicultural identity," and refuse to "dismiss all native Christians as acculturated, anachronistic traces of religious colonialism."[85]

In 1999 Treat gathered some of the writings of Vine Deloria, Jr., Dakota, the most important American Indian public intellectual of the late twentieth century, who died in 2005. In *For This Land: Writings on Religion in America*, Treat introduced readers to a man once called one of the leading "shapers and shakers of the Christian faith."[86] Deloria was decidedly post-Christian, or what he called a "Seven Day Absentist."[87] Son and grandson of prominent Episcopal priests, of mixed Indian and white heritage, he attended a Lutheran seminary but then became more involved in law.[88] Yet he never lost interest in Christianity, and in religion in general, although his aim was primarily that of "critique," rather than expression, of Christian faith and institutions.[89]

Building on Deloria's critique, several other Indian Christian exponents—Osage-Cherokee George E. Tinker most prominently, and others—have espoused Native American values, apart from or joined with Christian structures of thought and behavior.[90] More moderated Christian Indians—such as Episcopalian bishops Steven Charleston, Choctaw, and Carol J. Gallagher, Cherokee—find a common ground for Christian and native religiousness in the values of kinship and responsibility.[91]

There are also evangelical Indian Christians today who exhort their fellow natives not to become Christians—because of Christianity's complicity in the "imperialist American" patterns that Indians so resent—but rather to "follow Christ," as Indians.[92] The late Richard Twiss, Lakota; Randy Woodley, Cherokee; and many of their evangelical colleagues throughout native North America have attempted to "demonstrate to Native peoples that there are alternative ways to express Christian faith that are not so complicit in colonialism."[93]

As part of the "long process of de-colonization," Randy Woodley calls on Indians to know "the real Jesus . . . not the one who was used to take our land and rob us of our cultures."[94] "Embracing" this Christ, this gospel, this God of Christianity, means that "forgiveness is essential in order to restore harmony and balance so our children can live in a better world," one in which "restoration is taking place between Native and non-Native people in America."[95]

In order for that to happen, Woodley declares, non-Indians need to listen to Native Americans, in their pain and on their Christ-like path.

Notes

1. The National Museum of the American Indian notes that "American Indian, Indian, Native American, or Native" are all "acceptable" nomenclature for indigenous Americans, who "prefer to be called by their specific tribal name." See "Did You Know?,"

National Museum of the American Indian, accessed September 3, 2015, http://www.nmai.si.edu/explore/education/did-you-know.

2. Christopher Vecsey, *Traditional Ojibwa Religion and Its Historical Changes* (Philadelphia: American Philosophical Society, 1983); Christopher Vecsey, *On the Padres' Trail* (Notre Dame, IN: University of Notre Dame Press, 1996); Christopher Vecsey, *The Paths of Kateri's Kin* (Notre Dame, IN: University of Notre Dame Press, 1997); Christopher Vecsey, *Where the Two Roads Meet* (Notre Dame, IN: University of Notre Dame Press, 1999); Marie Therese Archambault, Mark G. Thiel, and Christopher Vecsey, eds. *The Crossing of Two Roads: Being Catholic and Native in the United States* (Maryknoll, NY: Orbis Books, 2003); Mark G. Thiel, and Christopher Vecsey, eds., *Native Footsteps along the Path of Saint Kateri Tekakwitha* (Milwaukee: Marquette University Press, 2012).

3. See Reuben G. Thwaites, ed. *The Jesuit Relations and Allied Documents*, 73 vols. (Cleveland: Burrows Brothers, 1896–1901); Corinna Dally-Starna and William A. Starna, ed. and trans., *Gideon's People: Being a Chronicle of an American Indian Community in Colonial Connecticut and the Moravian Missionaries Who Served There*, 2 vols. (Lincoln: University of Nebraska Press, 2009); C. Daniel Crews and Richard W. Starbuck, eds. *Records of the Moravians among the Cherokees: Early Contact and the Establishment of the First Mission*, vol. 1, *1752–1802* (Tahlequah, OK: Cherokee National Press, 2010).

4. See James P. Ronda and James Axtell, *Indian Missions: A Critical Bibliography* (Bloomington: Indiana University Press, 1978).

5. Kristina Bross, *Dry Bones and Indian Sermons: Praying Indians in Colonial America* (Ithaca, NY: Cornell University Press, 2004); Laura Arnold Leibman, ed. *Experience Mayhew's Indian Converts: A Cultural Edition* (Amherst: University of Massachusetts Press, 2008); Hilary E. Wyss, *Writing Indians: Literacy, Christianity, and Native Community in Early America* (Amherst: University of Massachusetts Press, 2000), 5 ("bicultural"), 1 ("an alternative 'text' in the margins").

6. Phillip H. Round, *Removable Type: Histories of the Book in Indian Country, 1663–1880* (Chapel Hill: University of North Carolina Press, 2010), 75.

7. David J. Silverman, *Faith and Boundaries: Colonists, Christianity, and Community among the Wampanoag Indians of Martha's Vineyard, 1600–1871* (Cambridge, UK: Cambridge University Press, 2005).

8. Wyss, *Writing Indians*, 50.

9. Ibid., 16.

10. Bernd C. Peyer, *The Tutor'd Mind: Indian Missionary-Writers in Antebellum America* (Amherst: University of Massachusetts Press, 1997).

11. Edward E. Andrews, *Native Apostles: Black and Indian Missionaries in the British Atlantic World* (Cambridge, MA: Harvard University Press, 2013).

12. Samson Occom, *The Collected Writings of Samson Occom, Mohegan: Leadership and Literature in Eighteenth-Century Native America*, ed. Joanna Brooks (New York: Oxford University Press, 2006).

13. Ibid., 12 ("Heathens," "Heathenish Notions"), 121 ("Heathenish ways").

14. Ibid., 98. Here and below, all Occom quotations are presented exactly as they appear in Brooks's volume.

15. Ibid., 24, 133.

16. Ibid., 334.

17. Ibid.

18. Ibid.

19. James Dow McCallum, ed., *The Letters of Eleazar Wheelock's Indians* (Hanover, NH: Dartmouth College, 1932).

20. Ibid., 11.

21. Joseph Johnson, *To Do Good to My Indian Brethren: The Writings of Joseph Johnson, 1751–1776*, ed. Laura J. Murray (Amherst: University of Massachusetts Press, 1998), 15 ("emotional dependency"), 88 ("a religious and community leader").

22. William Apess, *A Son of the Forest and Other Writings by William Apess, a Pequot*, ed. Barry O'Connell (Amherst: University of Massachusetts Press, 1997), xvi.

23. Ibid., x.

24. William Apess, *On Our Own Ground: The Complete Works of William Apess, a*

Pequot,, ed. Barry O'Connell (Amherst: University of Massachusetts Press, 1992), lxix.

25. Ibid., 21.

26. Ibid.

27. Catharine Brown, *Memoir of Catharine Brown: A Christian Indian of the Cherokee Nation*, ed. Rufus Anderson (Boston: Samuel T. Armstrong, and Crocker and Brewster, 1825); Joyce B. Phillips and Paul Gary Phillips, eds., *The Brainerd Journal: A Mission to the Cherokees, 1817–1823* (Lincoln: University of Nebraska Press, 1998), 44, 48, 51; Catharine Brown, *Cherokee Sister: The Collected Writings of Catharine Brown, 1818–1823*, ed. Theresa Strouth Gaul (Lincoln: University of Nebraska Press, 2014), 2, 5.

28. Brown, *Cherokee Sister*, 15.

29. Wyss, *Writing Indians*, 117.

30. Ibid., 121.

31. Susan Neylan, *The Heavens Are Changing: Nineteenth-Century Protestant Missions and Tsimshian Christianity* (Montreal: McGill-Queen's University Press, 2003), 161–74; Susan Neylan, "'Eating the Angels' Food': Arthur Wellington Clah—An Aboriginal Perspective on Being Christian, 1857–1909," in *Canadian Missionaries, Indigenous Peoples: Representing Religion at Home and Abroad*, ed. Alvyn Austin and James S. Scott (Toronto: University of Toronto Press, 2005), 88–108.

32. K. B. Kueteman, "He Goes First: The Story of Episcopal Saint David Pendleton Oakerhater," 2006, From Warrior to Saint: The Journey of David Pendleton Oakerhater, Oklahoma State University Library, Digital Resources and Discovery Services, https://dc.library.okstate.edu/digital/collection/oaker/id/271.

33. Bonnie Sue Lewis, *Creating Christian Indians: Native Clergy in the Presbyterian Church* (Norman: University of Oklahoma Press, 2003).

34. George Copway (Kahgegagahbowh), *Life, Letters and Speeches*, ed. A. LaVonne Brown Ruoff and Donald B. Smith (Lincoln: University of Nebraska Press, 1997).

35. Archambault, Thiel, and Vecsey, *Crossing of Two Roads*, 75–83, 94–104.

36. Allan Greer, *Mohawk Saint: Catherine Tekakwitha and the Jesuits* (New York: Oxford University Press, 2005).

37. Ibid., viii.

38. Ibid., 17, 19.

39. Ibid., 142, 123.

40. Thiel and Vecsey, *Native Footsteps along the Path of Saint Kateri Tekakwitha*.

41. Darren Bonaparte, *A Lily among Thorns: The Mohawk Repatriation of Kátéri Tekahkwí:tha* (Akwesasne, QC: Wampum Chronicles, 2009).

42. Archambault, Thiel, and Vecsey, *Crossing of Two Roads*, 57–60.

43. Ibid., 118.

44. Ibid., 110–13.

45. Ibid., 125.

46. Ibid., 63–64.

47. Ibid., 20–22, 24–25.

48. Ibid., 37–38.

49. Ibid., 143–45.

50. Ibid., 150–51.

51. Ibid., 192–94.

52. Ibid., 153–54.

53. "Christianity and Native America," 2014, Special Collections and University Archives, Raynor Memorial Libraries, Marquette University, Milwaukee (hereafter SCUA), http://www.marquette.edu/library/archives/indians.shtml; "Guides to Catholic-Related Records about Native Americans in the United States," 2014, Teaching and Study Resources, SCUA, http://www.marquette.edu/library/archives/NativeGuide/Help/UserGuide.pdf.

54. "Tekakwitha Conference Records," Manuscripts, SCUA, accessed May 14, 2020, http://www.marquette.edu/library/archives/Mss/TC/TC-main.shtml.

55. Archambault, Thiel, and Vecsey, *Crossing of Two Roads*, 212–27.

56. Ibid., 237.

57. Ibid.; Vecsey, *Where the Two Roads Meet*, 290–324; Sandra L. Garner, *To Come to a Better Understanding: Medicine Men and Clergy Meetings on the Rosebud Reservation, 1973–1978* (Lincoln: University of Nebraska Press, 2016).

58. Tim A. Giago, Jr., *Children Left Behind: The Dark Legacy of Indian Mission Boarding Schools* (Santa Fe, NM: Clear Light, 2006),

frontispiece; Tim A. Giago, Jr., *The Aboriginal Sin* (San Francisco: Indian Historian Press, 1978).

59. Archambault, Thiel, and Vecsey, *Crossing of Two Roads*, 53.

60. John G. Neihardt, *Black Elk Speaks: Being the Life Story of Holy Man of the Oglala Sioux*, premier ed., ed. Raymond J. DeMallie (Albany: State University of New York Press, 2008).

61. Raymond J. DeMallie, *The Sixth Grandfather: Black Elk's Teachings Given to John G. Neihardt* (Lincoln: University of Nebraska Press, 1984).

62. Archambault, Thiel, and Vecsey, *Crossing of Two Roads*, 134–38.

63. Ibid., 139.

64. See Damian Costello. *Black Elk: Colonialism and Lakota Catholicism* (Maryknoll, NY: Orbis Books, 2005); Michael F. Steltenkamp, *Black Elk: Holy Man of the Oglala* (Norman: University of Oklahoma Press, 1993); Michael F. Steltenkamp, *Nicholas Black Elk: Medicine Man, Missionary, Mystic* (Norman: University of Oklahoma Press, 2009); Esther Black Elk DeSersa et al., *Black Elk Lives: Conversations with the Black Elk Family*, ed. Hilda Neihardt and Lori Utecht (Lincoln: University of Nebraska Press, 2000); Hilda Neihardt; *Black Elk and Flaming Rainbow: Personal Memories of the Lakota Holy Man and John Neihardt* (Lincoln: University of Nebraska Press, 1995); Clyde Holler, *Black Elk's Religion: The Sun Dance and Lakota Catholicism* (Syracuse, NY: Syracuse University Press, 1995); Clyde Holler, ed., *The Black Elk Reader* (Syracuse, NY: Syracuse University Press, 2000); Joe Jackson, *Black Elk: The Life of an American Visionary* (New York: Farrar, Straus and Giroux, 2016).

65. Holler, *Black Elk Reader*, 305–22.

66. Archambault, Thiel, and Vecsey, *Crossing of Two Roads*, 157–59.

67. Ibid., 108–9.

68. See Jennifer Reid, *Louis Riel and the Creation of Modern Canada: Mythic Discourse and the Postcolonial State* (Albuquerque: University of New Mexico Press, 2008).

69. Archambault, Thiel, and Vecsey, *Crossing of Two Roads*, 168–75.

70. Ibid., 178, 181–83.

71. Ibid., 49–51.

72. Susan Elaine Gray, *"I Will Fear No Evil": Ojibwa-Missionary Encounters along the Berens River, 1875–1940*. (Calgary: University of Calgary Press, 2006), xxi.

73. J. R. Miller, *Shingwauk's Vision: A History of Native Residential Schools* (Toronto: University of Toronto Press, 1996); Kirk Dombrowski, *Against Culture: Development, Politics, and Religion in Indian Alaska* (Lincoln: University of Nebraska Press, 2001); Leonard Ortiz, *The Preservation of Native American Practices in the United Methodist Church: A Case Study in Recent Protestant Missions* (Lewiston, NY: Edwin Mellen Press, 2008); Sergei Kan, *Memory Eternal: Tlingit Culture and Russian Orthodox Christianity through Two Centuries* (Seattle: University of Washington Press, 1999).

74. Vecsey, *Where the Two Roads Meet*, 281.

75. Vecsey, *Paths of Kateri's Kin*, 196.

76. Archambault, Thiel, and Vecsey, *Crossing of Two Roads*, 41.

77. Jack M. Schultz, *The Seminole Baptist Churches of Oklahoma: Maintaining a Traditional Community* (Norman: University of Oklahoma Press, 1999); Rosamond B. Spicer and N. Ross Crumrine, eds. *Performing the Renewal of Community: Indigenous Easter Rituals in North Mexico and Southwest United States* (Lanham, MD: University Press of America, 1997).

78. Schultz, *Seminole Baptist Churches of Oklahoma*, 78; Spicer and Crumrine, *Performing the Renewal of Community*, 518.

79. See Vecsey, *On the Padres' Trail*, 195–97.

80. Archambault, Thiel, and Vecsey, *Crossing of Two Roads*, 236–37; for studies of Christian Indian hymns, see Chad S. Hamill, *Songs of Power and Prayer in the Columbia Plateau: The Jesuit, the Medicine Man, and the Indian Hymn Singer* (Corvallis: Oregon State University Press, 2012); Luke E. Lassiter, *The Power of Kiowa Song: A Collaborative Ethnography* (Tucson: University of Arizona Press, 1998); Luke E. Lassiter, Clyde Ellis, and Ralph Kotay, *The Jesus Road: Kiowas, Christianity, and Indian* Hymns (Lincoln: University of Nebraska Press, 2002); Michael D. McNally, *Ojibwe Singers: Hymns, Grief, and a Native*

Culture in Motion (New York: Oxford University Press, 2000).

81. James Treat, ed., *Native and Christian: Indigenous Voices on Religious Identity in the United States and Canada* (New York: Routledge, 1996), 1.

82. Ibid., 2.

83. Ibid., 9.

84. James Treat, ed., *Writing the Cross Culture: Native Fiction on the White Man's Religion* (Golden, CO: Fulcrum, 2006), 241–48.

85. James Treat, "Tribal Visions of the Church Way" (lecture, Native American House, University of Illinois, January 31, 2005).

86. See Vine Deloria, Jr., *Custer Died for Your Sins: An Indian Manifesto* (New York: Macmillan, 1969); Vine Deloria, Jr., *For This Land: Writings on Religion in America*, ed. James Treat (New York: Routledge, 1999), 1.

87. Deloria, *For This Land*, 1.

88. Vine V. Deloria, Sr., "The Establishment of Christianity among the Sioux," in *Sioux Indian Religion: Tradition and Innovation*, ed. Raymond J. DeMallie and Douglas R. Parks (Norman: University of Oklahoma Press, 1987), 91–111.

89. Deloria, *For This Land*, 16.

90. George E. Tinker, *Missionary Conquest: The Gospel and Native American Cultural Genocide* (Minneapolis: Fortress Press, 1993); George E. Tinker, "Jesus, Corn Mother, and Conquest: Christology and Colonialism," in *Native American Religious Identity. Unforgotten Gods*, ed. Jace Weaver (Maryknoll, NY: Orbis Books, 1998), 134–54; George E. Tinker, *Spirit and Resistance: Political Theology and American Indian Liberation* (Minneapolis: Fortress Press, 2004); George E. Tinker, *American Indian Liberation: A Theology of Sovereignty* (Maryknoll, NY: Orbis Books, 2008); Clara Sue Kidwell, Homer Noley, and George E. "Tink" Tinker, *A Native American Theology* (Maryknoll, NY: Orbis Books, 2001); Homer Noley, *First White Frost: Native Americans and United Methodism* (Nashville: Abingdon, 1991).

91. See Steven Charleston, *The Four Vision Quests of Jesus* (New York: Morehouse, 2015); Steven Charleston and Elaine A. Robinson, eds., *Coming Full Circle: Constructing Native Christian Theology* (Minneapolis: Fortress Press, 2015); and Carol J. Gallagher, *Family Theology: Finding God in Very Human Relationships* (New York: Morehouse, 2012).

92. Andrea Smith, *Native Americans and the Christian Right: The Gendered Politics of Unlikely Alliances* (Durham, NC: Duke University Press, 2008), 85–86.

93. Richard Twiss, *One Church Many Tribes* (Ventura, CA: Regal Books / Gospel Light, 2000), 214–16; Smith, *Native Americans and the Christian Right*, 86.

94. Randy Woodley, *When Going to Church Is Sin and Other Essays on Native American Christian Missions* (Scotland, PA: Healing the Land, 2007), 167 and xiii.

95. Randy Woodley, *Living in Color: Embracing God's Passion for Ethnic Diversity* (Downers Grove, IL: InterVarsity Press, 2001); Randy Woodley, *Mixed Blood: Not Mixed Up: Finding God-Given Identity in a Multi-Cultural World* (Hayden, AL: Randy Woodley, 2004), 142–43.

Works Cited

Andrews, Edward E. *Native Apostles: Black and Indian Missionaries in the British Atlantic World*. Cambridge, MA: Harvard University Press, 2013.

Apess, William. *On Our Own Ground: The Complete Works of William Apess, a Pequot*. Edited by Barry O'Connell. Amherst: University of Massachusetts Press, 1992.

———. *A Son of the Forest and Other Writings by William Apess, a Pequot*. Edited by Barry O'Connell. Amherst: University of Massachusetts Press, 1997.

Archambault, Marie Therese, O. S. F., Mark G. Thiel, and Christopher Vecsey, eds. *The Crossing of Two Roads: Being Catholic and Native in the United States*. Maryknoll, NY: Orbis Books, 2003.

Bonaparte, Darren. *A Lily among Thorns: The Mohawk Repatriation of Kátéri Tekahkwí:tha*. Akwesasne, QC: Wampum Chronicles, 2009.

Bross, Kristina. *Dry Bones and Indian Sermons: Praying Indians in Colonial America*. Ithaca, NY: Cornell University Press, 2004.

Brown, Catharine. *Cherokee Sister: The Collected Writings of Catharine Brown, 1818–1823*. Edited by Theresa Strouth Gaul. Lincoln: University of Nebraska Press, 2014.

———. *Memoir of Catharine Brown: A Christian Indian of the Cherokee Nation*. Edited by Rufus Anderson. Boston: Samuel T. Armstrong, and Crocker and Brewster, 1825.

Charleston, Steven. *The Four Vision Quests of Jesus*. New York: Morehouse, 2015.

Charleston, Steven, and Elaine A. Robinson, eds. *Coming Full Circle: Constructing Native Christian Theology*. Minneapolis: Fortress Press, 2015.

Copway, George (Kahgegagahbowh). *Life, Letters and Speeches*. Edited by A. LaVonne Brown Ruoff and Donald B. Smith. Lincoln: University of Nebraska Press, 1997.

Costello, Damian. *Black Elk: Colonialism and Lakota Catholicism*. Maryknoll, NY: Orbis Books, 2005.

Crews, C. Daniel, and Richard W. Starbuck, eds. *Records of the Moravians among the Cherokees: Early Contact and the Establishment of the First Mission*. Vol. 1, *1752–1802*. Tahlequah, OK: Cherokee National Press, 2010.

Dally-Starna, Corinna, and William A. Starna, ed. and trans. *Gideon's People: Being a Chronicle of an American Indian Community in Colonial Connecticut and the Moravian Missionaries Who Served There*. 2 vols. Lincoln: University of Nebraska Press, 2009.

Deloria, Vine, Jr. *Custer Died for Your Sins: An Indian Manifesto*. New York: Macmillan, 1969.

———. *For This Land: Writings on Religion in America*. Edited by James Treat. New York: Routledge, 1999.

Deloria, Vine V., Sr. "The Establishment of Christianity among the Sioux." In *Sioux Indian Religion: Tradition and Innovation*, edited by Raymond J. DeMallie and Douglas R. Parks, 91–111. Norman: University of Oklahoma Press, 1987.

DeMallie, Raymond J. *The Sixth Grandfather: Black Elk's Teachings Given to John G. Neihardt*. Lincoln: University of Nebraska Press, 1984.

DeSersa, Esther Black Elk, Olivia Black Elk Pourier, Aaron DeSersa, Jr., and Clifton DeSersa. *Black Elk Lives: Conversations with the Black Elk Family*. Edited by Hilda Neihardt and Lori Utecht. Lincoln: University of Nebraska Press, 2000.

Dombrowski, Kirk. *Against Culture: Development, Politics, and Religion in Indian Alaska*. Lincoln: University of Nebraska Press, 2001.

Gallagher, Carol J. *Family Theology: Finding God in Very Human Relationships*. New York: Morehouse, 2012.

Garner, Sandra L. *To Come to a Better Understanding: Medicine Men and Clergy Meetings on the Rosebud Reservation, 1973–1978*. Lincoln: University of Nebraska Press, 2016.

Giago, Tim A., Jr. *The Aboriginal Sin*. San Francisco: Indian Historian Press, 1978.

———. *Children Left Behind: The Dark Legacy of Indian Mission Boarding Schools*. Santa Fe, NM: Clear Light, 2006.

Gray, Susan Elaine. *"I Will Fear No Evil": Ojibwa-Missionary Encounters along the Berens River, 1875–1940*. Calgary: University of Calgary Press, 2006.

Greer, Allan. *Mohawk Saint: Catherine Tekakwitha and the Jesuits*. New York: Oxford University Press, 2005.

Hamill, Chad S. *Songs of Power and Prayer in the Columbia Plateau: The Jesuit, the Medicine Man, and the Indian Hymn Singer*. Corvallis: Oregon State University Press, 2012.

Holler, Clyde, ed. *Black Elk's Religion: The Sun Dance and Lakota Catholicism*. Syracuse, NY: Syracuse University Press, 1995.

———. *The Black Elk Reader*. Syracuse, NY: Syracuse University Press, 2000.

Jackson, Joe. *Black Elk: The Life of an American Visionary*. New York: Farrar, Straus and Giroux, 2016.

Johnson, Joseph. *To Do Good to My Indian Brethren: The Writings of Joseph Johnson, 1751–1776*. Edited by Laura J. Murray. Amherst: University of Massachusetts Press, 1998.

Kan, Sergei. *Memory Eternal: Tlingit Culture and Russian Orthodox Christianity through Two Centuries*. Seattle: University of Washington Press, 1999.

Kidwell, Clara Sue, Homer Noley, George E. "Tink" Tinker. *A Native American Theology*. Maryknoll, NY: Orbis Books, 2001.

Lassiter, Luke E. *The Power of Kiowa Song: A Collaborative Ethnography*. Tucson: University of Arizona Press, 1998.

Lassiter, Luke E., Clyde Ellis, and Ralph Kotay. *The Jesus Road: Kiowas, Christianity, and Indian Hymns*. Lincoln: University of Nebraska Press, 2002.

Leibman, Laura Arnold, ed. *Experience Mayhew's Indian Converts: A Cultural Edition*. Amherst: University of Massachusetts Press, 2008.

Lewis, Bonnie Sue. *Creating Christian Indians: Native Clergy in the Presbyterian Church*. Norman: University of Oklahoma Press, 2003.

McCallum, James Dow, ed. *The Letters of Eleazar Wheelock's Indians*. Hanover, NH: Dartmouth College, 1932.

McNally, Michael D. *Ojibwe Singers: Hymns, Grief, and a Native Culture in Motion*. New York: Oxford University Press, 2000.

Miller, J. R. *Shingwauk's Vision: A History of Native Residential Schools*. Toronto: University of Toronto Press, 1996.

Neihardt, Hilda. *Black Elk and Flaming Rainbow: Personal Memories of the Lakota Holy Man and John Neihardt*. Lincoln: University of Nebraska Press, 1995.

Neihardt, John G. *Black Elk Speaks: Being the Life Story of Holy Man of the Oglala Sioux*. Premier ed. Edited by Raymond J. DeMallie. Albany: State University of New York Press, 2008.

Neylan, Susan. "'Eating the Angels' Food': Arthur Wellington Clah—An Aboriginal Perspective on Being Christian, 1857–1909." In *Canadian Missionaries, Indigenous Peoples: Representing Religion at Home and Abroad*, edited by Alvyn Austin and James S. Scott, 88–108. Toronto: University of Toronto Press, 2005.

———. *The Heavens Are Changing: Nineteenth-Century Protestant Missions and Tsimshian Christianity*. Montreal: McGill-Queen's University Press, 2003.

Noley, Homer. *First White Frost: Native Americans and United Methodism*. Nashville: Abingdon, 1991.

Occom, Samson. *The Collected Writings of Samson Occom, Mohegan: Leadership and Literature in Eighteenth-Century Native America*. Edited by Joanna Brooks. New York: Oxford University Press, 2006.

Ortiz, Leonard. *The Preservation of Native American Practices in the United Methodist Church: A Case Study in Recent Protestant Missions*. Lewiston, NY: Edwin Mellen Press, 2008.

Peyer, Bernd C. *The Tutor'd Mind: Indian Missionary-Writers in Antebellum America*. Amherst: University of Massachusetts Press, 1997.

Phillips, Joyce B., and Paul Gary Phillips, eds. *The Brainerd Journal: A Mission to the Cherokees, 1817–1823*. Lincoln: University of Nebraska Press, 1998.

Reid, Jennifer. *Louis Riel and the Creation of Modern Canada: Mythic Discourse and the Postcolonial State*. Albuquerque: University of New Mexico Press, 2008.

Ronda, James P., and James Axtell. *Indian Missions: A Critical Bibliography*. Bloomington: Indiana University Press, 1978.

Round, Phillip H. *Removable Type: Histories of the Book in Indian Country, 1663–1880*. Chapel Hill: University of North Carolina Press, 2010.

Schultz, Jack M. *The Seminole Baptist Churches of Oklahoma: Maintaining a Traditional Community*. Norman: University of Oklahoma Press, 1999.

Silverman, David J. *Faith and Boundaries: Colonists, Christianity, and Community among the Wampanoag Indians of Martha's Vineyard, 1600–1871*. Cambridge, UK: Cambridge University Press, 2005.

Smith, Andrea. *Native Americans and the Christian Right: The Gendered Politics of Unlikely Alliances*. Durham, NC: Duke University Press, 2008.

Spicer, Rosamond B., and N. Ross Crumrine, eds. *Performing the Renewal of Community: Indigenous Easter Rituals in North Mexico and Southwest United States*. Lanham, MD: University Press of America, 1997.

Steltenkamp, Michael F. *Black Elk: Holy Man of the Oglala*. Norman: University of Oklahoma Press, 1993.

———. *Nicholas Black Elk: Medicine Man, Missionary, Mystic*. Norman: University of Oklahoma Press, 2009.

Thiel, Mark G., and Christopher Vecsey, eds. *Native Footsteps along the Path of Saint Kateri Tekakwitha*. Milwaukee: Marquette University Press, 2012.

Thwaites, Reuben G., ed. *The Jesuit Relations and Allied Documents*. 73 vols. Cleveland: Burrows Brothers, 1896–1901.

Tinker, George E. *American Indian Liberation: A Theology of Sovereignty*. Maryknoll, NY: Orbis Books, 2008.

———. "Jesus, Corn Mother, and Conquest: Christology and Colonialism." In *Native American Religious Identity: Unforgotten Gods*, edited by Jace Weaver, 134–54. Maryknoll, NY: Orbis Books, 1998.

———. *Missionary Conquest: The Gospel and Native American Cultural Genocide*. Minneapolis: Fortress Press, 1993.

———. *Spirit and Resistance: Political Theology and American Indian Liberation*. Minneapolis: Fortress Press, 2004.

Treat, James, ed. *Native and Christian: Indigenous Voices on Religious Identity in the United States and Canada*. New York: Routledge, 1996.

———. "Tribal Visions of the Church Way." Lecture. Native American House, University of Illinois, January 31, 2005.

———. *Writing the Cross Culture: Native Fiction on the White Man's Religion*. Golden, CO: Fulcrum, 2006.

Twiss, Richard. *One Church Many Tribes*. Ventura, CA: Regal Books / Gospel Light, 2000.

Vecsey, Christopher. *On the Padres' Trail*. Notre Dame, IN: University of Notre Dame Press, 1996.

———. *The Paths of Kateri's Kin*. Notre Dame, IN: University of Notre Dame Press, 1997.

———. *Traditional Ojibwa Religion and Its Historical Changes*. Philadelphia: American Philosophical Society, 1983.

———. *Where the Two Roads Meet*. Notre Dame, IN: University of Notre Dame Press, 1999.

Woodley, Randy. *Living in Color: Embracing God's Passion for Ethnic Diversity*. Downers Grove, IL: InterVarsity Press, 2001.

———. *Mixed Blood: Not Mixed Up: Finding God-Given Identity in a Multi-Cultural World*. Hayden, AL: Randy Woodley, 2004.

———. *When Going to Church Is Sin and Other Essays on Native American Christian Missions*. Scotland, PA: Healing the Land, 2007.

Wyss, Hilary E. *Writing Indians: Literacy, Christianity, and Native Community in Early America*. Amherst: University of Massachusetts Press, 2000.

Chapter 8

NATIVE CHRISTIANS WRITING BACK?

The Periodicals of the Iglesia Filipina Independiente in the Early Twentieth-Century Philippines

Adrian Hermann

"The Period when newspapers begin to live in the history of any people is an important era. This diminutive messenger is sent forth to ascertain if that time has arrived among the native people of this country.... The paper will be addressed to the intelligent portion of the native community who are able to read, or have an interest in what is going on in the world beyond their own dwellings."[1] Thus we read in the first issue of the *Kaffir Express*, one of the earliest periodicals in colonial South Africa partly edited by members of the local Xhosa Christian elite.[2] This programmatic article published in the first issue reflects the importance that educated Christians placed on the newspaper as a vehicle of knowledge about global events and on the availability of a means of independent access to the wider world. A contemporary "letter to the editor" of Botswana's first native journal reflects a similar sentiment: "I hear that you plan to publish a small newspaper for Batswana in their language. How happy we will be if you do that! ... We are also tired of continually asking Europeans about the news of other nations."[3] The emergence of these and similar journals also points to a new situation in colonial Africa in which—mainly through the success of missionary schools—a Western-educated elite had emerged that then became available as a public to be addressed by such publications. More generally, periodicals and newspapers published by local Christian elites in colonial societies are a highly important but much too little researched source material for studying the voices of indigenous Christians in Asia,

Africa, and Latin America. In order to contribute to the development of a polycentric history of world Christianity,[4] this essay is interested in the ways in which the voices of native Christians can be discerned in these publications. In approaching this topic, I focus on a case study of the periodicals of the Iglesia Filipina Independiente (IFI) published in the Philippines in 1903 and 1904. My study draws on source materials and research prepared in the context of a comparative project on the development of a transregional indigenous-Christian public sphere around 1900 (with a focus on four regions: India, South Africa, West Africa, and the Philippines) and will present some results of the Philippine case study I myself am working on.[5]

I will begin with some general remarks about indigenous-Christian periodicals as neglected historical sources and then move on to the Philippine case study. Here, in introducing the *ilustrado* intellectual Isabelo de los Reyes (1864–1938) and his various journalistic, political, and religious activities culminating in the founding of the IFI, I will be drawing on the early periodicals published by the church. The case study is followed by a theoretical section on the emergence of a transregional indigenous-Christian public sphere and some additional short comments on the IFI's attempts at locating itself in this context. I will conclude with some remarks about the challenges in studying indigenous-Christian periodicals.

Indigenous-Christian Periodicals as Neglected Historical Sources

When talking about the ways we can discern the voices of native Christians in Africa, Asia, and Latin America, not enough attention has been paid to the journals and periodicals published by indigenous-Christian elites in the late nineteenth and early twentieth centuries. As interventions in the public sphere, they served to consolidate local Christian communities and the elite's visions of itself, but they also allowed indigenous Christians to raise their voices and constitute themselves as important and relevant members of their national communities. They were mediums of churchly, religious, and political commentary but also provided information about developments in other parts of the world and especially about the lives and struggles of indigenous Christians in other "mission fields" and colonial societies. Such periodicals mediated these various forms of mutual observation between different local Christian elites all around the world and served as a stepping-stone toward other indirect and direct contacts between indigenous Christians of different countries and regions.

In addition to the recent increased attention being paid to missionary networks and missionary channels of communication,[6] we should look at these publications—contributed to and often edited and published by indigenous Christians—and identify the ways they were involved in the emergence of what could be called a "transregional indigenous-Christian public sphere." Even though research in the history of Christianity in Asia, Africa, and Latin America has been booming in recent years, such periodicals and journals are not fully recognized in their importance for the history of world Christianity in the late nineteenth and early twentieth centuries.

Drawing on the work of Christopher A. Bayly, Mark R. Frost, Stephanie Newell, and others,[7] my case study presented below—as well as the larger comparative project of which it is a part—is interested in the possibilities for mutual awareness, indirect, and later direct contacts between indigenous-Christian elites that were made possible and encouraged by these publications. While a model case for such developments is the *Christian Patriot* in India,[8] studying the emergence of an independent Catholic church in the Philippines around 1900 through its early periodicals makes visible similar dynamics.

Isabelo de los Reyes and the Founding of the Iglesia Filipina Independiente

Next to its later archbishop Gregorio Aglipay (1860–1940), the Filipino intellectual Isabelo de los Reyes (1864–1938) was the central figure in the founding of the Iglesia Filipina Independiente around 1900. Born 250 miles north of Manila in Vigan (Ilocos Sur) in 1864, de los Reyes went to Manila in 1880 to study at the Colegio de San Juan de Letrán. In the following years, he earned a living working for different newspapers. Even though in 1887 he graduated with a notary degree from the Dominican Universidad de Santo Tomás, he continued to work as a journalist for a variety of newspapers and periodicals. He wrote for the bilingual *Revista Popular de Filipinas* (1888–89) as well as the *Revista Católica de Filipinas* (1888–89), for both of which he also served as editor. At the same time, de los Reyes founded two bilingual periodicals, *La España Oriental* and *El Ilocano*, published in Spanish and his mother tongue, Ilocano.[9]

At the end of the nineteenth century, Manila was a booming and expanding city. Contacts between the Philippines and the rest of the world (especially Europe) had increased substantially, and since the opening of the Suez Canal there were direct and regular steamship connections not only to Hong Kong but also to Barcelona and other European ports. In 1881, Manila had been connected to the telegraph network. Part of this boom had been the emergence of a large variety of periodicals and newspapers since the 1880s, now also printed outside the capital, since the printing press was no longer a monopolistic privilege of the religious orders.[10]

When he became involved in the founding of the IFI, de los Reyes already had been a journalist, folklorist, political activist, and organizer in the workers' movement.[11] The Filipino historian Resil B. Mojares describes him as "the country's most unorthodox intellectual. . . . [He] waged a campaign against Spanish and American rule; was incarcerated in Manila's central prison and Barcelona's infamous Montjuich Castle; consorted with anarchists and socialists; established a rebel church; and founded the Philippine labor movement. . . . He was as fecund in his private life. He married thrice (a *Tagala*, a Spaniard, a Chinese mestiza) and sired twenty-seven children. He is reported to have said: 'There is enough chaos in me for God to create another world.'"[12]

Studying de los Reyes and his work makes it possible to reconstruct how a member of the Philippine indigenous-Christian elite contributed to the emergence of an indigenous public sphere and was part of a complex network of international connections. Throughout his life he stood in close contact with Europe (especially Spain and Germany), but in the context of his work with the IFI he also established ties to American missionaries in the Philippines as well as Protestant groups in a variety of other countries. At the same time, in the 1900s the IFI developed contacts with independent Catholic movements in Ceylon and Europe (especially in Switzerland).

In the emergence of Filipino nationalism in the nineteenth and early twentieth centuries, the struggles of the indigenous clergy played an important role.[13] The founding of the IFI in 1902 represents an important late culminating point of these developments, coming after the execution in 1872 of three native priests who were accused of being involved in the Cavite mutiny that year, and the ensuing Philippine revolution at the end of the nineteenth century. The IFI soon became the most important Rome-independent Catholic church in Asia and still exists today, operating in close connection with the Episcopal Church in the Philippines and in the United States. It emerged out of a circle of indigenous *ilustrados* ("enlightened"), the cosmopolitan and internationally connected class of Philippine intellectuals that first demanded equal treatment under the law and later freedom from Spanish and American colonial domination.

The 1902 Founding of the Iglesia Filipina Independiente as Reported in Its Second Periodical in 1903

While the story of the founding of the IFI has been retold at different times and from widely different perspectives,[14] here I want to look at this founding moment and the motivations of the founders of the IFI through an examination of some articles published in the church's second short-lived periodical, *La Iglesia Filipina Independiente: Revista Católica* (*IFIRC*) (published from October 11, 1903, to December 15, 1904, over fifty-five issues), which had been preceded by *La Verdad* (published from January 21 to August 5, 1903, over twenty-nine issues).[15] Looking back at the proclamation of the IFI, the *IFIRC* in its second issue (October 18, 1903) (re)published an article detailing the moment of secession through a speech given by de los Reyes on August 3, 1902:

> In the name of the *Unión Obrera Democrática* I declare that we have come here to manifest our most vivid desire that not only the Spanish friars, but also the rest of the Spaniards of the secular clergy should be expelled from the Archipelago, because they also have helped and are helping in the disturbing enterprise—which they are carrying out with unbelievable impertinence and tenacity—of usurping the rights of the Filipino clergy and of [stealing from] the other natives the property they have inherited from our fathers. The principal culprit of this necessary decision is none other but the pope himself.[16]

This speech, which appears to have been reprinted from other Filipino newspapers in which it had appeared in 1902 after the proclamation of the IFI, refers to the secession as the last resort in the struggle of the Filipino clergy for recognition as being equal to the Spanish clergy.

A similar representation of the fight for the rights of Filipino priests against the unwillingness of the Roman Catholic hierarchy and the pope to acknowledge the importance of training and establishing a Filipino clergy, can be found in the "Doctrine and Constitutional Rules of the IFI," published in *IFIRC* in the first issue (October 11, 1903). In this document, the "purpose of the founding of the Iglesia Filipina Independiente" is described as follows: "It arises most primarily from the urgent need to reestablish the worship of the one true God and the purity of His most Holy Word in all of its splendor, which under the rule of obscurantism has been softened and disfigured in a way that is very distressing for any moderately enlightened Christian. ... And to shape and raise up [*dignificar*] a Filipino clergy who takes back all its rights and prerogatives that it has lost because of the pillaging and denial that it was and still is suffering."¹⁷

The IFI is presented here not only as a church that finally recognizes and realizes the rights of the Filipino clergy but, at the same time, one that claims to "reestablish the worship of the one true God" in its purity, reconstructing it and cleansing it from the obscurantism and distortions that the Roman church has caused over centuries. In the repeated publishing of reports about the new independent church's founding on its first anniversary, we can see that the motivation for the break with Rome is presented again and again in order to lend legitimation to the schism and put forth these arguments in the Filipino public sphere. These concerns and their close connection with the IFI's interest in engaging with contemporary scientific knowledge can also be found in a second speech given by de los Reyes in 1902. In its eighth issue (November 29, 1903), *IFIRC* reprints this speech from November 18, 1902, on the occasion of the inauguration of the public worship of the IFI. De los Reyes is reported to have said:

> My compatriots, we are done suffering abuses innocently and without hesitation we form our own Congregation, a Filipino church, preserving of Romanism all the good it has, but casting aside all the absurdities and superstitions that have been introduced to corrupt the most pure moral and most sacred doctrine of Jesus Christ.
>
> Our priests will be Christians, but pure Christians without sophistications of doctrine; priests that are not scared by the light of progress, but that illuminate the intellects with their science, with their altruism, and with their saintliness; but not priests that brutalize us, moving us away from the Divine Master, instead of moving us closer to his Holy Gospels so that we satisfy our thirst for science in the most pure fountains of his holy teachings.¹⁸

The declaration of schism and the inauguration of public worship were two central moments in the first year of the history of the IFI. The glowing reports cited above appeared in *IFIRC* one year later, highlighting the motivations for the founding of the new church and containing in a nutshell the theological program that de los Reyes, the editor of *IFIRC*, was envisioning for the young church. This program was not only to free the Filipinos from Roman domination but was also supposed to include a theological transformation through engaging with and drawing on contemporary theological and wider intellectual debates taking place in Europe at the time. *IFIRC* served to publicize these programmatic endeavors to the IFI community, claiming on its masthead that it was distributed "in all of the Philippines" (*en todo Filipinas*). In their quest for a religious modernity that allowed them to separate a Christian Filipino identity from the colonial Catholicism represented by the Spanish friars, the leadership of the IFI opted for a "religious nationalism grounded on logical and rational scientifism" as their starting point, as the Filipino historian Francis A. Gealogo argues.[19] In the rhetorical alliance with modern science they found the wedge that could be driven between an universal understanding of Catholicism and the Spanish-dominated Roman Catholic Church in the Philippines.

The Iglesia Filipina Independiente in a Colonial Public Sphere: Programmatic Aspirations

In order to take a closer look at the aspirations of the IFI's periodicals, I want to draw attention to two programmatic texts published in *IFIRC* that detail the IFI's motivation to have its own publications in the first year of the church's existence. The first of these texts appeared on the first page of the first issue of *IFIRC* (October 14, 1903), under the title "Nuestra Aspiración" (Our aspiration):

> We sincerely aspire to make a periodical that deserves the designation of Christian because of its love for God, because of its profound respect for the sacred things, because of the charity which can be felt in all of its lines, because of the elevation of its intentions and the supreme contempt toward human miseries. . . . It would be a vile deed if we were hoping that our success would lie in systematically fighting against the Romanists, exploiting the passions of our coreligionists and dividing our compatriots that profess different religions more and more. . . . On the contrary, we will show to our [faithful] that it is proper to each civilized and well-educated person to respect foreign creeds and that only gross men with bad principles will behave in other ways. . . . We therefore make a formal promise that if those of other religions do not throw the first stone, we will live in sacred peace with them; and that even if they do

fight with us, that we will know to contest them with measure and always with the charity that our Divine Master teaches us. A warning at the end: . . . The Iglesia Filipina Independiente is a union of free men and we therefore have the right to say very loudly that for nothing in the world will we give up our sacred freedom to express our loyal opinions. The natural consequence of this is that neither the Supreme Bishop nor anyone but we ourselves will be responsible for our writings. We send our respectful greetings to the principals of our Holy Church and the rest of the brothers, to the civil authorities, to the press, and to the general public.[20]

Here, the administration of the periodical presents *IFIRC* as a Christian press organ that will speak for the independent church in the public sphere, giving voice to its opinions and engaging in critical dialogue with the general public. At the same time, the IFI—in this text as well as in the whole print run of *IFIRC*—takes much care not to appear as a disturbance to the public order or even to be perceived as a revolutionary force. On the contrary, *IFIRC* stresses again and again that the IFI through its publicly expressed opinions wants to engage in a civil and friendly dialogue with the authorities as well as other religions, while at the same time asserting its right to speak for Filipino Catholics and the Filipino clergy.

One year later, in the fifty-second issue (November 1, 1904), *IFIRC* published a second programmatic article reflecting on the first year of life of the journal. It reads as follows:

Today the Revista Católica *La Iglesia Filipina Independiente*, the official organ of our community, celebrates one year of life. . . . In this collection are found the catechism and the rest of the doctrines, the rules, the history and the most solid defense of our church in all questions, and this organ has certainly arrived to fill a gap, not only to defend us immediately against all the intrigues of our implacable enemies, but also to contradict in an irrefutable way those who spread something of the sort that we do not have proper doctrines or rules, but only a ridiculous parody of Romanism or the sects. . . . Of our faithful brethren, especially the bishops, parish priests, Committees of Ladies and Gentlemen I request that they actively advertise our organ which we need very much, and I request every bishop, parish priest, Committee of Gentlemen, and Commission of Ladies that they at least subscribe to ten issues of propaganda for a price of four pesos a month.[21]

Once again, the programmatic look back across the first-year print run of *IFIRC* stresses the importance of the periodical as a public voice for the IFI that allows its leaders to share their *own* opinions and to counter the attacks under which they perceive themselves to be. At the same time, the Supreme Bishop takes this opportunity to remind the faithful and especially the clergy and various officials of the IFI to subscribe to the periodical so that it can fulfill its purpose for the community.

Indigenous-Christian Periodicals and the Emergence of a Transregional Indigenous-Christian Public Sphere

The short look above at the case study from the Philippines makes visible how the publishing of its own periodicals was an important part of the consolidation of the IFI in the Philippine colonial public sphere. In addition to making use of such publications to study the voices of native Christians on a local and regional level, however, these sources also allow us to explore an additional dimension of the polycentric history of world Christianity on a transregional and transcontinental scale. More than just being of local importance, the periodicals and newspapers edited and published by native Christians also contributed to the emergence of what in the context of our comparative research project we are calling a "transregional indigenous-Christian public sphere."[22]

The term refers to the communicative space established and continuously expanded by the rapid proliferation of newspapers and periodicals since the second half of the nineteenth century, which made possible mutual awareness and manifold forms of interaction between (formerly communicatively isolated) indigenous-Christian actors and groups from different regions or continents and in different missionary or colonial contexts. As the communicative horizon of an emerging transregional indigenous-Christian consciousness and a developing space of diverse encounters, it constitutes an independent dimension of the emerging global public sphere dominated by missionary and colonial voices, as our analysis of the material from four African and Asian regions shows. Subsequently, the indirect and direct contacts established between indigenous-Christian elites of distant regions or different continents in the context of the transregional indigenous-Christian public sphere could lead to stable interactions and far-reaching networks—for example, between actors in India and Japan as documented in the *Christian Patriot*,[23] and to the emergence of a variety of "Christian internationalisms."[24]

In theorizing this communicative space, the category of the "public sphere" is of central importance. Jürgen Habermas first introduced his understanding of this concept into English in a 1974 article as "a sphere which mediates between society and state, in which the public organizes itself as the bearer of public opinion."[25] After its translation into English in 1989, his work *The Structural Transformation of the Public Sphere* was widely discussed in the political and social sciences.[26] Habermas later adjusted his definition to understand the public sphere as "an intermediary structure between the political system, on the one hand, and the private sectors of the lifeworld and functional systems, on the other."[27] In doing so, he reacted to early critiques of his concept as too normative or universalistic, based only on his study of historical developments in Germany, France, and England.[28] The model of a "bourgeois public sphere" as a space of dialogue and rational debate had also been taken to task for paying too little attention to mechanisms of access and to the exclusion of different sections of the populace. His thesis of a modern decline also claimed that the equality and rationality of the early modern public sphere had soon been compromised by commodified public exchanges. Habermas's ideal vision of public discourse has been shown to conceal the constant presence of a plurality of publics and of various forms of contestation around public space.[29] In Nancy Fraser's words, "the bourgeois public was never *the* public."[30] Rather, on the basis of the simultaneous emergence of a variety of counterpublics, "including nationalist publics, popular peasant publics, elite women's publics, and working class publics," she describes the public sphere as being constituted as "always a plurality of competing publics."[31] Later revisions of the concept therefore led Habermas to describe the "public sphere" as "a highly complex network that branches out into a multitude of overlapping international, national, regional, local, and subcultural arenas."[32] He now saw it as differentiated into a variety of "publics" and into "levels according to the density of communication, organizational complexity, and range." Despite being differentiated in these ways, however, "all the partial publics constituted by ordinary language remain porous to one another" and can thus be bridged and extended.[33]

In his detailed exploration of "publics" and "counterpublics," Michael Warner argued that a public does not precede its being addressed as a *specific public* but rather is constituted by this act itself: "A public is a space of discourse organized by nothing other than discourse itself. . . . It exists *by virtue of being addressed*."[34] As a "relation among strangers,"[35] it "comes into being only in relation to texts and their circulation."[36] This form of an anonymous but reachable public, concretely addressable by virtue of specific media, constitutes a "modern" form of social community different from earlier "premodern" forms. Warner writes, "Without the idea of texts that can be picked up at different times and in different places by otherwise unrelated people, we would not imagine a public as an entity that embraces all the users of that text, whoever they might be."[37] As fellow members of a public that we are a part of, strangers "can be treated as already belonging to our world," placed on a "path to commonality." In modern societies, therefore, "strangerhood" appears as "the necessary medium of commonality."[38] In regard to the indigenous-Christian elites that are at the center of my interest here, this implies asking for the ways they actually constituted themselves *as* elites and *as* a specific public through their texts and periodicals. Locating themselves in wider local, transregional, and transcontinental Christian communities, they consolidated their group identities in and through print media. The *Christian Patriot*, for example, as Klaus Koschorke has pointed out,[39] saw its mission as representing and promoting "the views and . . . the interests of the Indian Christian community as a whole"[40] and wanted to further "the communal consciousness of Indian Christians, so widely scattered over India."[41] It also stated its purpose as bringing the different Indian Christian organizations at home and in the diasporas in contact with each other.

Habermas's notion of the public sphere also quickly became the subject of debates about the history of public life and the limits of modern conceptions of such spaces beyond the West. In 1991, Sandria B. Freitag, in the introduction to a special issue on the topic, asked about "the nature of 'the public' in colonial South Asia" and pointed to "important cultural differences in the ways 'public' is conceived."[42] Taking up these questions almost twenty-five years later, J. Barton Scott and Brannon D. Ingram draw on her work to call us to "provincialise 'the public,'" by treating it "less as a normative model for modern society than as a culturally peculiar notion caught up with the particular history of the North Atlantic region (i.e., 'the West')."[43] However, despite complicating "the public" and "the public sphere" as analytical categories, the essays collected by Freitag in 1991 already led her to draw our attention to the ways in which local concepts have often served "as the indigenous bases onto which western European notions of 'the public' could have become grafted or, perhaps more accurately, transmuted."[44] While notions of "the public" might differ depending on the cultural and historical context, modern understandings were widely adopted in South Asia since the nineteenth century, and this "easy transferability" itself presents a challenge for historians.[45] Therefore, while Western ideas about "the public" around 1900 might not be very helpful analytically in some situations, "we must nevertheless gauge the powerful appeal they exercised for people at the time."[46] Scott and Ingram underscore this point, highlighting how "the Anglophone term 'public' has, since the nineteenth century, become an integral part of the South Asian scene" and, just like the concept of "religion," should be understood as a "central term of modern thought."[47] It makes sense, therefore, not to treat it as a "Western concept" alien to South Asia, for example, but as having been produced as a *global category* over the last two hundred years through processes of "translingual practice."[48] This also includes the myriad ways in which print technology itself has had a decisive impact. In the "creation of a new kind of public"[49] and in refiguring relations between private and public, print media were involved in "the emergence of new and larger constitutive entities within which individuals situated themselves,"[50] as we have seen in the example of the *Christian Patriot* above.

Alongside these debates, some authors also wondered if something like a "colonial public sphere" emerged in those societies affected by European imperialism and attempted to analyze the characteristics of such a public. As part of his investigation of "Asia's maritime networks" in the nineteenth and early twentieth century, Mark R. Frost described the "region-wide publics of likeminded scholars, progressives or co-religionists" that Asian literati at the time could, mostly through the use of English, address as a coherent public.[51] For him, the "circulation of print between readers who were scattered across and yet united by the seas created transoceanic communities of text" held together and particularly consolidated by a large variety of periodicals.[52] The web of exchange of information and in particular the rapid development of postal services[53] in the British empire led to the emergence of what he calls a "colonial public sphere," not only on a local but rather on a transregional scale.

Neeladri Bhattacharya has argued in similar ways in his theorizing of the "colonial public" that the "public sphere" was not only a space for single individuals to represent themselves publicly but rather "a space where communities are forced to come together . . . to reconstitute themselves as a public."⁵⁴ If it was this public space that allowed the transformation of "community matters into public issues," public debate must be seen as a complex process: "In all these public debates, two audiences were addressed: one, the community, as it was being defined, and its constituent elements; and two, the wider public beyond the community that was implicated in the process as spectator and commentator, but as outsider. . . . It was a process through which the community opened itself to the outside world, just as it enclosed itself within harder boundaries."⁵⁵ At the same time, he draws our attention to the colonial public sphere as a "deeply segmented . . . space of struggle" between a variety of actors, particularly the colonial authorities and, in his case, Indian communities.⁵⁶ What does this segmentation amount to? Does it mean that the public sphere in colonial societies necessarily disintegrates into a plurality of segregated spaces?

If we follow Stephanie Newell's detailed exploration of native newspapers and their African editors in colonial West Africa, a more complex picture emerges.⁵⁷ We have to address, on the one hand, the segmentation inherent in the colonial context, and, on the other hand, the nature of contemporary evaluations of the emerging public spaces. Newell argues that rather than seeing the different publics in a colonial society as completely separate discourses and spaces (as described for the Indian case by Mrinalini Sinha)⁵⁸—and thereby excluding "the diversity of encounters made possible by colonial rule" by segregating "indigenous public spaces" from the colonial public sphere—a more inclusive understanding is needed.⁵⁹ She claims that in colonial West Africa, "newsprint made possible the imagination of a new type of public, conceived as anonymous, detached from personal and familial affiliations, and capable of expressing public opinion for the first time in the new public space constituted by African-owned newspapers."⁶⁰ While the critique of Habermas's concept of the public sphere laid out above is particularly valid regarding the limits of access and especially the various forms of censorship and control at work in the colonial public sphere(s), nevertheless the spread of newsprint also was a factor that made possible new imaginations of the public.⁶¹ African-owned newspapers were of particular importance here. In asserting the ideal of a public sphere as a space governed by liberties and social equalities, they adopted the utopian character of Habermas's model⁶² and "explicitly attempted to produce an egalitarian public sphere and to generate a form of civil society on paper that was activated through participation and debate and, crucially, through print."⁶³ The "colonial public sphere" should therefore be seen as a space where a "plurality of encounters *between* colonizer and colonized" was the norm.⁶⁴ In an "inclusive understanding" of the colonial public sphere, where imperial power is acknowledged as widely governing social relations, indigenous periodicals' power of articulation was crucial.⁶⁵ Their editors, according to Newell, were engaged in "utopian efforts to bring into being the very public sphere that was denied to the inhabitants of colonial societies by antidemocratic imperial governments."⁶⁶

In summary, taking these debates about the concept of the "public sphere" and particularly its use in relation to colonial societies into account, the following model for focusing on the role of periodicals and newspapers published by indigenous-Christian elites around 1900 emerges: while it is necessary to stress that there was a much larger *public space* and a plurality of *public arenas* as the context in which a public sphere emerges (as has been argued particularly in regard to the history of South Asia),⁶⁷ I propose to understand the *colonial public sphere* as the arena of debate produced and primarily maintained by print capitalism in the late nineteenth and early twentieth centuries, making use of the predominant colonial languages (English, but also Spanish or Dutch). It is flanked by and partly entangled and overlapping with other (public) spheres, particularly the communal spheres (the Islamic sphere, the Hindu sphere, the missionary sphere, the indigenous-Christian sphere, etc.) and the vernacular publics constituted by their vernacular (print) media.

The (indigenous-Christian) periodicals published in this colonial public sphere are characterized by a variety of publics being addressed. The South African indigenous-Christian paper *Inkanyiso*, for example, addresses not only an African readership ("it is published chiefly for the benefit of the Natives") but also the colonial government, the wider English public ("our English friends"), and the missionary audience.⁶⁸ At the same time, these local and emerging national colonial public spheres constituted by print and other new mass media are embedded in transregional and transcontinental exchanges, which were shaped by a large number of "international" newspapers and periodicals printed in the colonial centers, as well as by a variety of missionary publications with a transcontinental dissemination.

In addition, we should recognize that the emergence of a communicative horizon beyond local and regional dimensions predates the establishment of periodicals founded and conducted by native Christians. Even before indigenous-Christian periodicals emerged, a community consciousness among "native missionaries" already becomes visible, as detailed by Tolly Bradford with reference to nineteenth-century South Africa and Canada.⁶⁹

This public, its constitution as a community, and its being addressed in a transregional and transcontinental indigenous-Christian public sphere, is the main focus of our project and of the Philippine case study presented here.

Transcontinental Connections and the Periodicals of the Iglesia Filipina Independiente

As I have demonstrated elsewhere, the IFI already in its early period attempted to establish contacts with other Christian groups and was itself contacted by a variety of other independent Catholic movements in Europe, North America, and Asia.[70] Its early journals served to publicize these contacts to its constituency but also were sent abroad as informational material about the church. In addition to the important first phase of contacts with the Swiss Old Catholics in the 1900s, the failure of which has been reconstructed in detail by Wim H. de Boer and Peter-Ben Smit,[71] there were other attempts at establishing an early network of Asian independent Catholic churches that have not yet received much scholarly attention. These are primarily an exchange of letters with the "Independent Catholics of India, Goa and Ceylon" in 1903 that, while it did not lead to closer cooperation, demonstrates the existence of contacts between two independent Asian Catholic churches around the turn of the century.[72] The IFI also received letters from Joseph René Vilatte (1854–1929) in Chicago in 1903. At the time, Vilatte was archbishop of the "American Catholic Church," an independent Catholic church in the United States. All of those letters were publicized in the early journals of the IFI and point to the importance of these transcontinental contacts for the IFI. In being recognized as a legitimate church by their alleged peers all over the world in a transregional and transcontinental public sphere, the IFI saw its position in the colonial public sphere strengthened. A letter from Vilatte is described in the IFI journal *La Verdad* as "another evident proof of the sympathy that our holy and strong Iglesia Filipina, that prides itself on embracing all men of all races, enjoys in America" and is published for the IFI audience's perusal.[73]

The publication of such letters once again highlights the central role of these periodicals for the early history of the IFI. This is also attested to by a short fundraising letter, which seems to have been circulated by the Supreme Bishop Gregorio Aglipay in early 1906, after *IFIRC* had ceased publishing. In this printed mass letter dated February 1 (with a line at the top where the addressee's name could be filled in), Aglipay writes:

CHRISTIAN NATIONALISM

> The Iglesia Filipina Independiente understood and felt since its establishment the necessity of having an organ that would make public all those issues that affect it; and with this purpose first *La Verdad* saw the light of the day and later *La Iglesia Filipina Independiente*, some months after the first had disappeared. As the means that this Supreme Bishopric counts on to support the existence of the latter are limited to the help that its priests can offer, it didn't take long to cease to exist, a natural consequence of its languor. . . . And it is true, an entity with no organ of opinion cannot express itself, and he who says nothing does not speak either because he prefers to remain silent, or because he is inert. To this end, dear compatriot and brother, and because I consider it to be my duty to promote our common development, I turn to you, so that you, with regard to the growth of our country and its future destiny on which the force of the Iglesia Filipina Independiente has a positive influence, donate the sum of TWENTY-FIVE PESOS (₱25.00) to the same, and you will have your periodical as soon as possible.[74]

The letter is another expression of the importance that the IFI attributed to its periodicals as organs through which to voice its concerns and issues to the public. At the same time, the new church saw itself observed by the civilized world, which was not only watching closely but was also impressed by the early success that the IFI had had among Filipino Catholics. This public, on the other hand, could also read negative evaluations of the schism in many newspapers and especially religious periodicals all over the world. It was therefore important to the IFI—so the leadership appears to have thought—to (again) have its own periodical to be able to present its version of recent developments to the wider world. That this wider world not only represented a remote public but also (and not least *because* of these periodicals) stood in contact and was in direct correspondence with the IFI, is an additional dimension of the emergence of a transcontinental and transregional indigenous-Christian public sphere around 1900.

A Perfect Archive of Native Voices?

With reference to my case study of the IFI as well as to the larger project of which it is a part, it appears that we can still learn much about the discourses of indigenous-Christian elites in colonial societies around 1900 by looking at the newspapers and periodicals edited and published by them. This was, among other things, the starting point of our project, attempting to study in detail one of the little-researched mediums in which a native Christian voice—albeit mostly an elite voice—can be heard and recognized. However, as we found during the preparation and execution of the project, these voices are very diverse and often speak from very different contexts. In conclusion, I therefore want to highlight two important points that reveal the need for additional reflection regarding the specific characteristics of the medium of indigenous-Christian periodicals and the nature of the available sources.

The Limitations of Elite Native Voices

Indigenous periodicals, newspapers, and journals are a very important source of information about native Christians and their churches in the late nineteenth and early twentieth centuries and have so far received far too little scholarly attention. However, at the same time, especially when attempting to look at them from a comparative point of view, they appear as incredibly diverse in form, focus, lifetime, and level of native engagement. While they make it possible to discern the voices of native Christians, these voices are, in most cases, those of Christian elites, not only trying to speak to the public and other Christians but also at the same time attempting to establish and consolidate themselves *as* elites in a colonial public sphere. Likewise, the diversity of these journals makes it impossible to give a general assessment of their usefulness as source material for reconstructing native Christian voices without a detailed evaluation of individual journals in regard to the levels to which native Christians were actually responsible for the content of the periodicals, had to censor their expression in repressive colonial situations, and were producing their own visions, or only reproducing missionary viewpoints. In the case of *IFIRC* it remains an open question in which ways the theological concerns and programmatic statements published in the periodical actually resonated with and represented the attitudes of the larger IFI community.

The Reproduction of Colonial Archives in Digital Spaces

Regarding the state of archival research, one important aspect has to be highlighted: in our project one of the problems we regularly encountered—despite all the positive things to be said about recent initiatives at digitizing a large amount of archival material and especially historical newspapers—is that the logic of current digitization tends to reproduce the logic of colonial archives and many of the problems of a colonial perspective. The archives in which digitization is performed are mostly located in the former colonial centers (the United States, the United Kingdom, France, Germany) and their materials are often heavily biased toward missionary sources. The journals and periodicals our project was interested in, however, could very often only be found in the archives of the four regions themselves—for example, in the archive of the IFI in the Philippines. Only with the help of some local scholars have I been able to collect an almost complete set of the newspapers and journals on which this chapter is based. This is not a problem in and of itself; however, as more and more material becomes easily available on the screens in our offices, it becomes less and less likely that the historian of world Christianity actually goes to visit (and will be provided with the funds to do so) the local archives to supplement or even substitute the missionary perspective with a native one. We should be wary of this danger when attempting to trace the voices of native Christians in digitized printed materials.

Despite these two sobering points—and I hope my short glance at the early history of the IFI was able to illustrate this—a close examination of indigenous-Christian periodicals from the late nineteenth and early twentieth centuries will enable us to listen more closely to historical native Christian voices not yet heard enough in the continuously buzzing field of the study of world Christianity.

Notes

1. *Kaffir Express* 1 (October 1, 1870): 1 (printed in Lovedale, Cape Colony, South Africa).

2. See Les Switzer and Donna Switzer, *The Black Press in South Africa and Lesotho: A Descriptive Bibliographic Guide to African, Coloured and Indian Newspapers, Newsletters and Magazines, 1836–1976* (Boston: G. K. Hall, 1979), 269–70.

3. Anonymous letter from January 1883 printed in *Mahoko a becwana* 1: 2–3. See Part T. Mgadla and Stephen C. Volz, eds. and trans., *Words of Batswana. Letters to "Mahoko a becwana," 1883–1896* (Cape Town: Van Riebeek Society, 2006), 7.

4. Klaus Koschorke, "Transcontinental Links, Enlarged Maps, and Polycentric Structures in the History of World Christianity," *Journal of World Christianity* 6, no. 1 (2016): 28–56.

5. Together with a number of other scholars I have explored the history and importance of indigenous Christian periodicals from four regions (India, South Africa, West Africa, Philippines) in a research project under the title "Indigenous Christian Elites in Asia and Africa around 1900 and Their Journals and Periodicals: Patterns of Cognitive Interaction and Early Forms of Transregional Networking" (2011–15; principal investigators:

Klaus Koschorke and Frieder Ludwig; funded by the German Research Foundation). Its main results have been published in Klaus Koschorke et al., eds., *Discourses of Indigenous-Christian Elites in Colonial Societies in Asia and Africa around 1900: A Documentary Sourcebook from Selected Journals* (Wiesbaden: Harrassowitz, 2016); and Klaus Koschorke et al., eds., *"To Give Publicity to Our Thoughts": Journale asiatischer und afrikanischer Christen um 1900 und die Entstehung einer transregionalen indigen-christlichen Öffentlichkeit* (Wiesbaden: Harrassowitz, 2018). A second project, "Independent Catholic Movements in Late Nineteenth- and Early Twentieth-Century Asia: The 'Independent Catholics of India, Goa, and Ceylon' and the 'Iglesia Filipina Independiente' in the Context of Religious, Political, and Social Movements of Emancipation in Colonial Modernity" (2017–20; principal investigator: Adrian Hermann; funded by the German Research Foundation), focuses mainly on the Philippines and Goa / Sri Lanka.

6. See Xiantao Zhang, *The Origins of the Modern Chinese Press: The Influence of the Protestant Missionary Press in Late Qing China* (New York: Routledge, 2007); Felicity Jensz and Hanna Acke, eds., *Missions and Media: The Politics of Missionary Periodicals in the Long Nineteenth Century* (Stuttgart: Franz Steiner, 2013); Felicity Jensz and Hanna Acke, "The Form and Function of Nineteenth-Century Missionary Periodicals: Introduction," *Church History* 82, no. 2 (2013): 368–73.

7. See Christopher A. Bayly, "The Indian Ecumene: An Indigenous Public Sphere," in *Empire and Information: Intelligence Gathering and Social Communication in India* (Cambridge, UK: Cambridge University Press, 1996), 180–211; Mark R. Frost, "Asia's Maritime Networks and the Colonial Public Sphere, 1840–1920," *New Zealand Journal of Asian Studies* 6, no. 2 (2004): 63–94; Stephanie Newell, *The Power to Name: A History of Anonymity in Colonial West Africa* (Athens: Ohio University Press, 2013); Chandra Mallampalli, *Christians and Public Life in Colonial South India, 1863–1937* (London: Routledge, 2004); Benedict Anderson, *Under Three Flags: Anarchism and the Anti-Colonial Imagination* (London: Verso, 2005); Isabel Hofmeyr, Preben Kaarsholm, and Bodil F. Frederiksen, "Print Cultures, Nationalism and Publics of the Indian Ocean," *Africa* 81, no. 1 (2011): 1–22.

8. Klaus Koschorke, "'Absolute Independence for Indian Christians': The World Missionary Conference Edinburgh 1910 in the Debates of the Protestant Christian Elite in Southern India," *Annales Missiologici Posnanienses* 21 (2016): 37–52; Klaus Koschorke, *"Owned and Conducted Entirely by the Native Christian Community": Der "Christian Patriot" und die indigen-christliche Presse im kolonialen Indien um 1900* (Wiesbaden: Harrassowitz, 2018).

9. Megan C. Thomas, "Isabelo de Los Reyes and the Philippine Contemporaries of *La Solidaridad*," *Philippine Studies* 54, no. 3 (2006): 381–411.

10. Ibid., 382; Resil B. Mojares, *Brains of the Nation: Pedro Paterno, T. H. Pardo de Tavera, Isabelo de Los Reyes, and the Production of Modern Knowledge* (Quezon City: Ateneo de Manila University Press, 2006), 260.

11. William H. Scott, *The Union Obrera Democratica: First Filipino Labor Union* (Quezon City: New Day, 1992); Anderson, *Under Three Flags*, 9–25; Thomas, "Isabelo de Los Reyes and the Philippine Contemporaries of *La Solidaridad*"; Megan C. Thomas, *Orientalists, Propagandists, and* Ilustrados*: Filipino Scholarship and the End of Spanish Colonialism* (Minneapolis: University of Minnesota Press, 2012).

12. Mojares, *Brains of the Nation*, 255.

13. See John N. Schumacher, *Revolutionary Clergy: The Filipino Clergy and the Nationalist Movement, 1850–1903* (Quezon City: Ateneo de Manila University Press, 1981).

14. Pedro de Achutegui and Miguel Bernad, *Religious Revolution in the Philippines*, vol. 4 (Quezon City: Ateneo de Manila University Press, 1961); Lewis B. Whittemore, *Struggle for Freedom: History of the Philippine Independent Church* (Greenwich, CT: Seabury Press, 1961); Mary D. Clifford, "Iglesia Filipina Independiente: The Revolutionary Church," in *Studies in Philippine Church History*, ed. Gerald H. Anderson (Ithaca, NY: Cornell

University Press, 1969), 223–55; Schumacher, *Revolutionary Clergy*; Peter-Ben Smit, *Old Catholic and Philippine Independent Ecclesiologies in History: The Catholic Church in Every Place* (Leiden: Brill, 2011). See also Paul A. Rodell, "The Founding of the Iglesia Filipina Independiente (the 'Aglipayan' Church): An Historiographical Review," *Philippine Quarterly of Culture and Society* 16 (1988): 210–34, for an overview of the historical debate until the 1980s.

15. For a short introduction to the IFI and its early periodicals, see Adrian Hermann, "Introduction to the Early Periodicals of the Iglesia Filipina Independiente," in *Discourses of Indigenous-Christian Elites in Colonial Societies in Asia and Africa around 1900*, ed. Klaus Koschorke et al. (Wiesbaden: Harrassowitz, 2016), 339–44.

16. "Proclamación de La Iglesia Filipina Independiente: 3 Agosto 1902," *La Iglesia Filipina Independiente: Revista Católica* 1, no. 2 (October 18, 1903): 6–7; Koschorke et al., *Discourses of Indigenous-Christian Elites*, text 332. Unless noted as being previously published in *Discourses of Indigenous-Christian Elites*, all translations from the Spanish here and in the following are mine alone.

17. "Doctrina y Reglas Constitucionales de La Iglesia Filipina Independiente," *La Iglesia Filipina Independiente: Revista Católica* 1, no. 1 (October 11, 1903): 1; Koschorke et al., *Discourses of Indigenous-Christian Elites*, text 338.

18. "Discurso Que En Nombre Del Emmo. Señor Obispo Máximo de La Iglesia Filipina Independiente, Pronunció Isabelo de Los Reyes En La Inauguración de Los Cultos En El Arrabal de Santa Cruz (Manila, 18 Noviembre de 1902)," *La Iglesia Filipina Independiente: Revista Catolica* 1, no. 8 (November 29, 1903): 30; Koschorke et al., *Discourses of Indigenous-Christian Elites*, text 341.

19. Francis A. Gealogo, "Religion, Science, and Bayan in the Iglesia Filipina Independiente," in *From Wilderness to Nation: Interrogating Bayan*, ed. Damon L. Woods (Quezon City: University of the Philippines Press, 2011), 108.

20. "Nuestra Aspiración," *La Iglesia Filipina Independiente: Revista Católica* 1, no. 1 (October 11, 1903): 1; Koschorke et al., *Discourses of Indigenous-Christian Elites*, 320.

21. "Obispado Máximo de Filipinas / A Nuestros Amadísimos Hermanos," *La Iglesia Filipina Independiente: Revista Católica* 2, no. 52 (November 1, 1904): 205; Koschorke et al., *Discourses of Indigenous-Christian Elites*, text 321.

22. See the introduction and the sources collected in Koschorke et al., *Discourses of Indigenous-Christian Elites*. A more detailed evaluation of the concept of a "transregional indigenous-Christian public sphere" can be found in the chapter by Klaus Koschorke and Adrian Hermann, "'Beyond Their Own Dwellings': Die Entstehung einer transregionalen und transkontinentalen indigen-christlichen Öffentlichkeit," in *"To Give Publicity to Our Thoughts": Journale asiatischer und afrikanischer Christen um 1900 und die Entstehung einer transregionalen indigen-christlichen Öffentlichkeit*, ed. Klaus Koschorke et al. (Wiesbaden: Harrassowitz, 2018), 227–60.

23. Klaus Koschorke, "'What Can India Learn from Japan?' Netzwerke indigen christlicher Eliten in Asien und christliche Internationalismen um 1910," in *Jenseits der Grenze. Europa in der Welt in Zeiten der Globalisierung. FS R. Wendt*, ed. Jürgen G. Nagel and Michael Mann (Heidelberg: Draupadi, 2015), 19–42.

24. See Klaus Koschorke, "New Maps of the History of World Christianity: Current Challenges and Future Perspectives," *Theology Today* 71, no. 2 (2014): 190–91; Koschorke, "'What Can India Learn from Japan?'" 19–42.

25. Jürgen Habermas, "The Public Sphere: An Encyclopedia Article (1964)," *New German Critique* 3 (1974): 50.

26. Jürgen Habermas, *The Structural Transformation of the Public Sphere: An Inquiry into a Category of Bourgeois Society*, trans. Thomas Burger (Cambridge, MA: MIT Press, 1989).

27. Jürgen Habermas, *Between Facts and Norms: Contributions to a Discourse Theory of Law and Democracy*, trans. William Rehg (Cambridge, MA: MIT Press, 1996), 373.

28. Craig Calhoun, ed., *Habermas and the Public Sphere* (Cambridge, MA: MIT Press, 1992).

29. Oskar Negt and Alexander Kluge, *Öffentlichkeit und Erfahrung: Zur Organisationsanalyse von bürgerlicher und proletarischer Öffentlichkeit* (Frankfurt am Main: Suhrkamp, 1972); Michael Warner, *Publics and Counterpublics* (Cambridge, MA: MIT Press, 2002).

30. Nancy Fraser, "Rethinking the Public Sphere: A Contribution to the Critique of Actually Existing Democracy," *Social Text* 25–26 (1990): 61.

31. Ibid.

32. Habermas, *Between Facts and Norms*, 373.

33. Ibid., 374.

34. Michael Warner, "Publics and Counterpublics (Abbreviated Version)," *Quarterly Journal of Speech* 88, no. 4 (2002): 413.

35. Ibid., 417.

36. Ibid., 413.

37. Ibid., 414.

38. Ibid., 417.

39. See Koschorke et al., *Discourses of Indigenous-Christian Elites*, 15.

40. "Ourselves," *Christian Patriot*, January 10, 1903, 4; Koschorke et al., *Discourses of Indigenous-Christian Elites*, text 2.

41. "The Christian Patriot," *Christian Patriot*, February 19, 1916, 4; Koschorke et al., *Discourses of Indigenous-Christian Elites*, text 4.

42. Sandria B. Freitag, "Introduction," in "Aspects of 'the Public' in Colonial South Asia," special issue, *South Asia: Journal of South Asian Studies* 14, no. 1 (1991): 3, 6.

43. J. Barton Scott and Brannon D. Ingram, "What Is a Public?, Notes from South Asia," *South Asia: Journal of South Asian Studies* 38, no. 3 (2015): 358.

44. Freitag, "Introduction," 7.

45. Ibid., 6.

46. Ibid., 7.

47. Scott and Ingram, "What Is a Public?," 359, 370.

48. See Lydia Liu, *Translingual Practice: Literature, National Culture, and Translated Modernity—China, 1919–1937* (Stanford, CA: Stanford University Press, 1995).

49. Freitag, "Introduction," 9.

50. Ibid., 10.

51. Frost, "Asia's Maritime Networks and the Colonial Public Sphere," 87.

52. Ibid.

53. Mark R. Frost, "Pandora's Post Box: Empire and Information in India, 1854–1914," *English Historical Review* 131, no. 552 (2016): 1043–73.

54. Neeladri Bhattacharya, "Notes towards a Conception of the Colonial Public," in *Civil Society, Public Sphere and Citizenship: Dialogues and Perceptions*, ed. Rajeev Bhargava and Helmut Reifeld (New Delhi: Sage, 2005), 139.

55. Ibid., 140.

56. Ibid., 153–56.

57. Newell, *Power to Name*.

58. Mrinalini Sinha, "Britishness, Clubbability, and the Colonial Public Sphere: The Genealogy of an Imperial Institution in Colonial India," *Journal of British Studies* 40, no. 4 (2001): 489–521.

59. Newell, *Power to Name*, 37.

60. Ibid., 30.

61. Ibid., 33.

62. Ibid.

63. Ibid., 34.

64. Ibid., 37.

65. Ibid., 36.

66. Ibid., 42.

67. In addition to the essays following Freitag, "Introduction," see also Dietrich Reetz, *Islam in the Public Sphere: Religious Groups in India, 1900–1947* (New Delhi: Oxford University Press, 2006) for a useful model of public space in India, which I have partly adopted here.

68. "Native Thoughts," *Inkanyiso yase Natal* (March 12, 1891): 3; Koschorke et al., *Discourses of Indigenous-Christian Elites*, text 120.

69. Tolly Bradford, "World Visions: 'Native Missionaries,' Mission Networks and Critiques of Colonialism in Nineteenth-Century South Africa and Canada," in *Grappling with the Beast: Indigenous Southern African Responses to Colonialism, 1840–1930*, ed. Peter Limb, Norman Etherington, and Peter Midgley (Brill: Leiden, 2010), 311–39.

70. See also the sources I collected and translated in Koschorke et al., *Discourses of Indigenous-Christian Elites*, texts 427–33; see also Adrian Hermann, "Transregional Contacts between Independent Catholic Churches in Asia around 1900: The Case of the Iglesia Filipina Independiente and the Independent Catholics of Ceylon," in *Veränderte Landkarten: Auf dem Weg zu einer polyzentrischen Geschichte des Weltchristentums*, ed. Ciprian Burlacioiu and Adrian Hermann (Wiesbaden: Harrassowitz, 2013), 139–50; Adrian Hermann, "The Early Periodicals of the Iglesia Filipina Independiente (1903–1904) and the Emergence of a Transregional and Transcontinental Indigenous-Christian Public Sphere," *Philippine Studies: Historical and Ethnographic Viewpoints* 62, nos. 3–4 (2014): 549–65; Adrian Hermann, "Publicizing Independence: The Filipino *Ilustrado* Isabelo de Los Reyes and the 'Iglesia Filipina Independiente' in a Colonial Public Sphere," *Journal of World Christianity* 6, no. 1 (2016): 99–122.

71. Wim H. de Boer and Peter-Ben Smit, "Die frühen Beziehungen zwischen der IFI und der Utrechter Union," *Internationale Kirchliche Zeitschrift* 98 (2008): 122–44, 169–90. On the early negotiations with the Swiss Old Catholics and the Anglican bishop Charles H. Brent, see also Pedro de Achutegui and Miguel Bernad, "Brent, Herzog, Morayta and Aglipay," *Philippine Studies: Historical and Ethnographic Viewpoints* 8, no. 3 (1960): 568–83.

72. See Hermann, "Transregional Contacts between Independent Catholic Churches in Asia around 1900."

73. "Los Católicos Americanos, No Romanistas," *La Verdad* 1, no. 21 (June 10, 1903): 5; Koschorke et al., *Discourses of Indigenous-Christian Elites*, text 431.

74. Circular letter written by Gregorio Aglipay, February 1, 1906, Archive of the Iglesia Filipina Independiente, St. Andrew's Theological Seminary, Quezon City, Philippines; Koschorke et al., *Discourses of Indigenous-Christian Elites*, text 329.

Works Cited

Achutegui, Pedro de, and Miguel Bernad. "Brent, Herzog, Morayta and Aglipay." *Philippine Studies: Historical and Ethnographic Viewpoints* 8, no. 3 (1960): 568–83.

———. *Religious Revolution in the Philippines*. Vol. 4. Quezon City: Ateneo de Manila University Press, 1961.

Anderson, Benedict. *Under Three Flags: Anarchism and the Anti-colonial Imagination*. London: Verso, 2005.

Bayly, Christopher A. "The Indian Ecumene: An Indigenous Public Sphere." In *Empire and Information: Intelligence Gathering and Social Communication in India*. Cambridge, UK: Cambridge University Press, 1996.

Bhattacharya, Neeladri. "Notes towards a Conception of the Colonial Public." In *Civil Society, Public Sphere and Citizenship: Dialogues and Perceptions*, edited by Rajeev Bhargava and Helmut Reifeld, 130–56. New Delhi: Sage, 2005.

Boer, Wim H. de, and Peter-Ben Smit. "Die frühen Beziehungen zwischen der IFI und der Utrechter Union." *Internationale Kirchliche Zeitschrift* 98 (2008): 122–44, 169–90.

Bradford, Tolly. "World Visions: 'Native Missionaries,' Mission Networks and Critiques of Colonialism in Nineteenth-Century South Africa and Canada." In *Grappling with the Beast: Indigenous Southern African Responses to Colonialism, 1840–1930*, edited by Peter Limb, Norman Etherington, and Peter Midgley, 311–39. Brill: Leiden, 2010.

Calhoun, Craig, ed. *Habermas and the Public Sphere*. Cambridge, MA: MIT Press, 1992.

Clifford, Mary D. "Iglesia Filipina Independiente: The Revolutionary Church." In

Studies in Philippine Church History, edited by Gerald H. Anderson, 223–55. Ithaca, NY: Cornell University Press, 1969.

Fraser, Nancy. "Rethinking the Public Sphere: A Contribution to the Critique of Actually Existing Democracy." *Social Text* 25–26 (1990): 56–80.

Freitag, Sandria B. "Introduction." "Aspects of 'the Public' in Colonial South Asia," special issue, *South Asia: Journal of South Asian Studies* 14, no. 1 (1991): 1–13.

Frost, Mark R. "Asia's Maritime Networks and the Colonial Public Sphere, 1840–1920." *New Zealand Journal of Asian Studies* 6, no. 2 (2004): 63–94.

———. "Pandora's Post Box: Empire and Information in India, 1854–1914." *English Historical Review* 131, no. 552 (2016): 1043–73.

Gealogo, Francis A. "Religion, Science, and Bayan in the Iglesia Filipina Independiente." In *From Wilderness to Nation: Interrogating Bayan*, edited by Damon L. Woods, 108–21. Quezon City: University of the Philippines Press, 2011.

Habermas, Jürgen. *Between Facts and Norms: Contributions to a Discourse Theory of Law and Democracy*. Translated by William Rehg. Cambridge, MA: MIT Press, 1996.

———. "The Public Sphere: An Encyclopedia Article (1964)." *New German Critique* 3 (1974): 49–55.

———. *The Structural Transformation of the Public Sphere: An Inquiry into a Category of Bourgeois Society*. Translated by Thomas Burger. Cambridge, MA: MIT Press, 1989.

Hermann, Adrian. "The Early Periodicals of the Iglesia Filipina Independiente (1903–1904) and the Emergence of a Transregional and Transcontinental Indigenous-Christian Public Sphere." *Philippine Studies: Historical and Ethnographic Viewpoints* 62, nos. 3–4 (2014): 549–65.

———. "Introduction to the Early Periodicals of the Iglesia Filipina Independiente." In *Discourses of Indigenous-Christian Elites in Colonial Societies in Asia and Africa around 1900*, edited by Klaus Koschorke, Adrian Hermann, E. Phuti Mogase, and Ciprian Burlacioiu, 339–44. Wiesbaden: Harrassowitz, 2016.

———. "Publicizing Independence: The Filipino *Ilustrado* Isabelo de Los Reyes and the 'Iglesia Filipina Independiente' in a Colonial Public Sphere." *Journal of World Christianity* 6, no. 1 (2016): 99–122.

———. "Transregional Contacts between Independent Catholic Churches in Asia around 1900: The Case of the Iglesia Filipina Independiente and the Independent Catholics of Ceylon." In *Veränderte Landkarten: Auf dem Weg zu einer polyzentrischen Geschichte des Weltchristentums*, edited by Ciprian Burlacioiu and Adrian Hermann, 139–50. Wiesbaden: Harrassowitz, 2013.

Hofmeyr, Isabel, Preben Kaarsholm, and Bodil F. Frederiksen. "Print Cultures, Nationalism and Publics of the Indian Ocean." *Africa* 81, no. 1 (2011): 1–22.

Jensz, Felicity, and Hanna Acke. "The Form and Function of Nineteenth-Century Missionary Periodicals: Introduction." *Church History* 82, no. 2 (2013): 368–73.

———, eds. *Missions and Media: The Politics of Missionary Periodicals in the Long Nineteenth Century*. Stuttgart: Franz Steiner, 2013.

Koschorke, Klaus. "'Absolute Independence for Indian Christians': The World Missionary Conference Edinburgh 1910 in the Debates of the Protestant Christian Elite in Southern India." *Annales Missiologici Posnanienses* 21 (2016): 37–52.

———. "New Maps of the History of World Christianity: Current Challenges and Future Perspectives." *Theology Today* 71, no. 2 (2014): 178–91.

———. *"Owned and Conducted Entirely by the Native Christian Community": Der "Christian Patriot" und die* indigen-christliche Presse im kolonialen Indien um 1900. Wiesbaden: Harrassowitz, 2018.

———. "Transcontinental Links, Enlarged Maps, and Polycentric Structures in the History of World Christianity." *Journal of World Christianity* 6, no. 1 (2016): 28–56.

———. "'What Can Indian Learn from Japan?' Netzwerke indigen-christlicher Eliten in Asien und christliche Internationalismen um 1910." In *Jenseits der Grenze. Europa in der Welt in Zeiten Globalisierung. FS R. Wendt*, edited by Jürgen G. Nagel and Michael Mann, 19–42. Heidelberg: Draupadi, 2015.

Koschorke, Klaus, and Adrian Hermann. "'Beyond Their Own Dwellings': Die Entstehung einer transregionalen und transkontinentalen indigen-christlichen Öffentlichkeit." In *"To Give Publicity to Our Thoughts": Journale asiatischer und afrikanischer Christen um 1900 und die Entstehung einer transregionalen indigen-christlichen Öffentlichkeit*, edited by Klaus Koschorke, 227–60. Wiesbaden: Harrassowitz, 2018.

Koschorke, Klaus, Adrian Hermann, Frieder Ludwig, and Ciprian Burlacioiu, eds. *"To Give Publicity to Our Thoughts": Journale asiatischer und afrikanischer Christen um 1900 und die Entstehung einer transregionalen indigen-christlichen Öffentlichkeit*. Wiesbaden: Harrassowitz, 2018.

Koschorke, Klaus, Adrian Hermann, E. Phuti Mogase, and Ciprian Burlacioiu, eds. *Discourses of Indigenous-Christian Elites in Colonial Societies in Asia and Africa around 1900: A Documentary Sourcebook from Selected Journals*. Wiesbaden: Harrassowitz, 2016.

Liu, Lydia. *Translingual Practice: Literature, National Culture, and Translated Modernity, China, 1919–1937*. Stanford, CA: Stanford University Press, 1995.

Mallampalli, Chandra. *Christians and Public Life in Colonial South India, 1863–1937*. London: Routledge, 2004.

Mgadla, Part T., and Stephen C. Volz, eds. and trans. *Words of Batswana. Letters to "Mahoko a becwana," 1883–1896*. Cape Town: Van Riebeek Society, 2006.

Mojares, Resil B. *Brains of the Nation: Pedro Paterno, T. H. Pardo de Tavera, Isabelo de Los Reyes, and the Production of Modern Knowledge*. Quezon City: Ateneo de Manila University Press, 2006.

Negt, Oskar, and Alexander Kluge. *Öffentlichkeit und Erfahrung: Zur Organisationsanalyse von bürgerlicher und proletarischer Öffentlichkeit*. Frankfurt am Main: Suhrkamp, 1972.

Newell, Stephanie. *The Power to Name: A History of Anonymity in Colonial West Africa*. Athens: Ohio University Press, 2013.

Reetz, Dietrich. *Islam in the Public Sphere: Religious Groups in India, 1900–1947*. New Delhi: Oxford University Press, 2006.

Rodell, Paul A. "The Founding of the Iglesia Filipina Independiente (the 'Aglipayan' Church): An Historiographical Review." *Philippine Quarterly of Culture and Society* 16 (1988): 210–34.

Schumacher, John N. *Revolutionary Clergy: The Filipino Clergy and the Nationalist Movement, 1850–1903*. Quezon City: Ateneo de Manila University Press, 1981.

Scott, J. Barton, and Brannon D. Ingram. "What Is a Public? Notes from South Asia." *South Asia: Journal of South Asian Studies* 38, no. 3 (2015): 357–70.

Scott, William H. *The Union Obrera Democratica: First Filipino Labor Union*. Quezon City: New Day, 1992.

Sinha, Mrinalini. "Britishness, Clubbability, and the Colonial Public Sphere: The Genealogy of an Imperial Institution in Colonial India." *Journal of British Studies* 40, no. 4 (2001): 489–521.

Smit, Peter-Ben. *Old Catholic and Philippine Independent Ecclesiologies in History: The Catholic Church in Every Place*. Leiden: Brill, 2011.

Switzer, Les, and Donna Switzer. *The Black Press in South Africa and Lesotho:*

A Descriptive Bibliographic Guide to African, Coloured and Indian Newspapers, Newsletters and Magazines, 1836–1976. Boston: G. K. Hall, 1979.

Thomas, Megan C. "Isabelo de Los Reyes and the Philippine Contemporaries of *La Solidaridad*." *Philippine Studies* 54, no. 3 (2006): 381–411.

———. *Orientalists, Propagandists, and Ilustrados: Filipino Scholarship and the End of Spanish Colonialism*. Minneapolis: University of Minnesota Press, 2012.

Warner, Michael. *Publics and Counterpublics*. Cambridge, MA: MIT Press, 2002.

———. "Publics and Counterpublics (Abbreviated Version)." *Quarterly Journal of Speech* 88, no. 4 (2002): 413–25.

Whittemore, Lewis B. *Struggle for Freedom: History of the Philippine Independent Church*. Greenwich, CT: Seabury Press, 1961.

Zhang, Xiantao. *The Origins of the Modern Chinese Press: The Influence of the Protestant Missionary Press in Late Qing China*. New York: Routledge, 2007.

Chapter 9

"FOR YOU, MOST REVEREND FATHER, AND FOR OUR ARCHIVES"

Recovering the Voice of Bishop Aloys Bigirumwami in Late Colonial Rwanda

J. J. Carney

When I first began studying Rwanda over fifteen years ago, I had never heard of Aloys Bigirumwami (1904–1986), Rwanda's first indigenous Catholic bishop who led the Diocese of Nyundo between 1952 and 1974. (Perhaps more worryingly, neither had most of the experts I was reading.) Like most students, my initial exposure to Rwanda came through the lens of the 1994 genocide, a cataclysmic slaughter in which an estimated eight hundred thousand Rwandans lost their lives over one hundred days in a government-directed genocide against the minority Tutsi and some Hutu political opponents. As has been attested in a host of critical studies, tens of thousands of Tutsi died on the grounds of Catholic parishes, schools, and medical centers; a significant minority of Catholic priests, religious, and lay catechists actively collaborated in the killings; and the Catholic hierarchy was notable for its silence in the early weeks of the genocide.[1] Not surprisingly, my early studies of Rwandan church history focused on complicit churchmen like Monsignor Vincent Nsengiyumva (1936–1994), the Hutu archbishop of Kigali and close confidant of Rwanda's second president, General Juvenal Habyarimana (1937–1994). When I began delving more deeply into the history of the nation's majority Catholic Church, Rwanda's most influential Catholic religious order, the Missionaries of Africa or "White Fathers," emerged most prominently. One could read extensively on figures like Monsignor Charles Lavigerie (1825–1892), the French cardinal who founded the White Fathers in the 1860s to evangelize Africa, or Monsignor Léon Classe (1874–1945), the most influential White Father missionary and bishop in colonial Rwanda.[2] Even in the late colonial and independence periods that became the nexus of my doctoral studies, a figure like the White Father archbishop André Perraudin (1914–2003) was much better known than Bigirumwami.[3] If Rwandan voices emerged in historical narratives, they were typically political leaders like Gregoire Kayibanda (1924–1976), the former Catholic seminarian, journalist, and Hutu community activist who served as Rwanda's first president between 1962 and 1973. But with the exception of the Rwandan Catholic intellectual Father Alexis Kagame,[4] indigenous ecclesial voices from the colonial period tended to be overshadowed by their missionary patrons.

In light of this lacuna, Bigirumwami was the single most important indigenous Catholic voice to emerge in my dissertation research on Rwanda's late colonial period.[5] For in contrast to a missionary leadership that largely acquiesced to Hutu-Tutsi dualism, Bigirumwami offered an alternative vision of both ethnic discourse and Catholic politics. In essence, Bigirumwami's correspondence from the General Archives of the Missionaries of Africa[6] demands social justice without ethnic violence, castigating the missionary-aided ethnicization of Rwandan society and the ongoing salience of European racism in Rwandan church life. He also strongly contested the increasing rhetorical and political division of Rwandan society into "Hutu" and "Tutsi" identities. In the face of assumptions that "nobody in Rwanda in the late 1950s had offered an alternative to a tribal construction of politics,"[7] Bigirumwami reminds us that seeming historical meta-narratives are never inevitable, and they are often contested. We can be grateful for Monsignor Bigirumwami's commitment to writing, in his words, "for the archives," for his extensive correspondence reveals important and oft-overlooked complexities and tensions that marked intra-Catholic debates during Rwanda's critical political transitions of 1956–62.

Bigirumwami's Background and Early Years as Bishop

Aloys Bigirumwami was born in 1904, four years after the first Catholic White Father missionaries arrived in Rwanda. At the time of his birth, Catholic missions were struggling on the margins of Rwandan society. Missionaries were suspected by the royal court and generally scorned by

Rwanda's predominantly Tutsi elites. In contrast, many poor Hutu and Tutsi looked to the White Fathers as economic patrons. An exception to this early trend, Bigirumwami and his family came from noble heritage in the eastern region of Gisaka. He was a direct descendant of the Gisaka royal line through the king's Hutu son, although later in life Bigirumwami would be publicly classified as a Tutsi.[8] Bigirumwami's mixed ethnic heritage exerted no small influence on his later views of Hutu-Tutsi identities.[9]

Bigirumwami's Catholic bona fides were no less impressive than his noble pedigree, and his Catholic life would be one of many "firsts." His family was among the first indigenous converts to Christianity, and his 1904 baptism was one of the first at Zaza mission station in southeastern Rwanda. At the tender age of nine, Bigirumwami became one of the first Rwandans to enter the new Catholic minor seminary at Kabgayi. During these years, the White Father Laurent Déprimoz (1884–1962), the seminary's rector and future vicar apostolic (or bishop) of Kabgayi,[10] became his ecclesial patron and spiritual mentor. It was Déprimoz who shepherded Bigirumwami through the seminary system until his 1929 ordination to the priesthood. Déprimoz later appointed Bigirumwami as superior of Muramba mission and named him in 1948 as one of the first indigenous clergy to serve on the church's presbyteral council.

Greater things were in store for Bigirumwami. Since the Vatican's 1939 decision to appoint Uganda's Joseph Kiwanuka as the first black Catholic bishop in modern Africa, the White Fathers and the Vatican's missionary congregation, Propaganda Fide, had debated the idea of appointing an African vicar apostolic in Rwanda.[11] In 1952, the Catholic Church established a new vicariate based around the northwestern Rwandan town of Nyundo. Like Kiwanuka's Diocese of Masaka in Uganda, Nyundo would serve as a trial run for the broader indigenization or Africanization of the Catholic Church in Africa. Aloys Bigirumwami was tapped to lead the new Nyundo vicariate, becoming the first indigenous bishop in the Belgian African colonies of Rwanda, Burundi, and Congo.

The date of Bigirumwami's consecration to the episcopate—June 1, 1952—became a festive day of national celebration.[12] Twenty-five thousand Rwandans gathered for Bigirumwami's consecration at Kabgayi, including all of Rwanda's chiefs, official delegations from Burundi and Belgian Congo, and Uganda's Bishop Kiwanuka. Déprimoz formally consecrated Bigirumwami as a bishop and spoke of how this event fulfilled Lavigerie's nineteenth-century dream of "evangelizing Africa through Africa." In his own public remarks, Bigirumwami professed his fidelity to Rwanda and to the missionaries who had brought the gospel to his native land, stating that "they were and remain our fathers in the faith."[13]

Four years later, in March 1956, Bigirumwami symbolized this collaboration between missionaries and indigenous clergy by consecrating André Perraudin, a Swiss White Father, as vicar apostolic of Kabgayi. This became the first known instance in modern history of a black bishop consecrating a white priest to the Catholic episcopate. Coming in the midst of growing racial strife in South Africa and the American South, its symbolic importance was not overlooked. In Perraudin's words, "This is the first time perhaps in the annals of the world that a black bishop has conferred the plenitude of the priesthood on a white priest. . . . The church is in all the races, in the heart of all the races, unifying them from the inside."[14]

As so often is the case in Rwandan history, however, the public façade of unity masked deeper tensions between European and indigenous clergy. Correspondence housed in the General Archives of the Missionaries of Africa in Rome especially reveals these tensions. For example, prior to his own consecration as bishop, Father Perraudin, then rector of the Catholic major seminary at Nyakibanda, lamented a growing "critical spirit" among indigenous clergy that he attributed to the "psychosis of independence" associated with the consecration of Bigirumwami as a bishop.[15] For his part, Bigirumwami grew increasingly frustrated with European missionaries' refusals to serve under the leadership of indigenous Rwandan clergy.[16] He also opposed White Father plans to alter the boundaries of his vicariate and protested what he saw as the racist treatment of Nyundo seminarians.[17]

Even as he distanced himself from the White Fathers, Bigirumwami also moved to establish his independence from the political forces dominating Rwanda in the early 1950s. For example, Bigirumwami refused the offer of Mwami Mutara Rudahigwa, Rwanda's king, to serve on the royal advisory council,[18] and he was not close to the Belgian colonists. He generally kept his distance from Rwanda's embryonic political movements in the mid-1950s. His independent streak could leave him somewhat isolated. In the words of one Belgian colonial official, "[Bigirumwami] is too pledged to the politics of the White Fathers for the nationalist priests, too indifferent to indigenous public life for the chiefs and the sub-chiefs, too rigid from a disciplinary point of view and too heretical for the Hutu priests, too foreign for the chauvinist Tutsi, [and] a little old for the priests of the new school."[19] Bigirumwami never fit neatly in the ethnic and ideological categories that dominated late colonial Rwandan debates. As will be seen, this enabled him to present a more nuanced voice during a polemical period.

A Voice of Nuance: Bigirumwami and Ethnic Polemics in the Late 1950s

As the prospects for decolonization advanced in the late 1950s, political tensions accelerated in Rwanda. Increasingly these political disputes were framed in terms of Hutu and Tutsi identities. Reflecting the church's dominance among educated and political elites, Catholics were integrally involved on all sides of this dispute. Former Catholic seminarians like Gregoire Kayibanda and Aloys Munyangaju invoked the language of Catholic social teaching in leading calls for Hutu emancipation, perhaps most notably in their March 1957 "Bahutu Manifesto."[20] In the meantime, the Catholic Tutsi chiefs who dominated Rwanda's Superior Council also justified their political monopoly in part through Catholic ideas, especially medieval understandings of the "Thomist organic society" that underwrote a hierarchical vision of society.[21]

In the midst of these rising polemics, Bigirumwami offered a more balanced voice. Although he refused the offer to serve on the king's advisory council, Bigirumwami enjoyed good personal relations with Mwami Mutara and lavished praise on the king during twenty-fifth jubilee celebrations in 1957.[22] At the same time, he joined the other bishops of Rwanda and Burundi in drafting a 1957 pastoral letter on justice that was notably critical of social and structural inequality in Rwandan society. In the spring of 1958, Bigirumwami publicly rebuked local Tutsi chiefs for abusing their predominantly Hutu peasantry.[23] In the words of Father Guy Mosmans, the superior of the White Fathers in Belgium, "Monsignor Bigirumwami has many times taken the defense of unjustly condemned Hutu. This has strongly annoyed the Tutsi. The rumor has spread that monsignor was the bishop of the Hutu but not the bishop of the Tutsi."[24] Fearful of the social and political consequences of revolution, Bigirumwami believed that Rwanda's long-term stability and prosperity rested on the nation's treatment of the poor masses. In his words, "Well-treated, [the peasants] are grateful; poorly treated, they revolt."[25]

Bigirumwami's ethnic views were also more complex than those of many of his contemporaries. In September 1958, he penned an article titled "The Problem of Hutu, Tutsi, and Twa" in the Belgian Catholic weekly *Témoignage Chrétien*.[26] While admitting a growing crisis between what he termed the "'social' or 'racial' groups of Batutsi, Bahutu, and Batwa," Bigirumwami questioned the underlying social analysis and categorization at work here. Pointing to the discrepancy between his so-called Tutsi appearance and his mixed ethnic background, Bigirumwami derided what he called the "inanity of physical criteria" in determining Hutu and Tutsi identities. He also downplayed ethnic discrepancies in secondary schools, claiming that Hutu and Tutsi elites formed a privileged class over and against the impoverished masses of Hutu cultivators and thousands of poor Tutsi pastoralists. Democratizing education thus meant expanding educational opportunities for both Hutu *and* Tutsi peasants, not just implementing affirmative action for Hutus.[27]

In this sense, Bigirumwami also differed markedly from Archbishop Perraudin. In February 1959, Perraudin issued his most famous pastoral letter, "Super Omnia Caritas" or "Above All Things Charity." Here Perraudin argued that socioeconomic divisions in Rwanda broke down largely along a Hutu-Tutsi axis, which he described in racial terms: "In our Rwanda social differences and inequalities are for a large part linked to racial differences."[28] For Perraudin, it made no sense to leave out the word "Hutu" when Rwanda's entire social system was predicated on a Tutsi-Hutu hierarchy. Perraudin went on to write in support of the Hutu right to association, thereby offering tacit support to the rising Hutu political movements. Although generally mild in tone, the letter established Perraudin's public reputation as a social justice advocate and pro-Hutu partisan. He himself later described this letter as a "declaration of war against feudalism" and an appropriate application of Catholic social teaching to a "regime of servitude and humiliation for the large proportion of the population."[29]

As political and ethnic tensions accelerated in 1958 and 1959, Bigirumwami became increasingly concerned with the politicization of the Catholic press. Even as he publicly defended Catholic periodicals like *Kinyamateka* and *Temps Nouveaux d'Afrique* for their defense of the poor and marginalized, Bigirumwami's archival correspondence reflects deep frustrations with these newspapers' editorial biases. For Bigirumwami, Catholic journalists were "helping to create cold relations between Hutu and Tutsi" and had become "more destructive than constructive."[30] Writing in early 1959, Bigirumwami worried that the Catholic Church was sacrificing its ability to be a public moral arbiter due to increasing journalistic partisanship: "As for me, I have apprehensions for the direction given to our country. [Media] propaganda wants to destroy all that is Tutsi but does not say what the Hutu party should become. I myself imagine that we are indisposing thousands of our sheep by our *not neutral* politics. We should be making a Catholic and apostolic and peaceful politics."[31] Bigirumwami's pleas for moderation and balance could not withstand the more radical voices swirling in late 1950s Rwanda. Already a group of Tutsi chiefs were on record claiming that "the relations between us Tutsi and those Hutu has from all time been based on slavery; between us and them there is no foundation of brotherhood."[32] Meanwhile, a document penned by the Hutu Catholic activist Joseph Gitera exhorted Hutu peasants to rise up against their Tutsi oppressors: "Young men and young women of the Hutu movement: Liberty! Let's liberate ourselves from Tutsi slavery. We have had enough. Justice!"[33] In the midst of these polemics, Bigirumwami's efforts to chart a "Catholic and apostolic and peaceful politics" largely remained a dream deferred. As we will see, even his own voice would become more radical as Rwanda descended into revolutionary violence.

Aloys Bigirumwami and the Hutu Social Revolution of 1959-62

In the final months of 1959, Rwanda moved quickly toward the political and ethnic revolution that Bigirumwami had long feared. First, in July 1959, Rwandan king Mwami Mutara died suddenly in the care of Belgian physicians while seeking medical treatment in neighboring Burundi. Although Mutara's half brother, Kigeli V Ndahindurwa, was quickly appointed to succeed Mutara, the real political momentum lay with the emerging political parties. These included a Tutsi-dominated nationalist party, the Union Nationale Rwandaise (UNAR), which advocated for immediate independence from Belgium, a reduction of foreign missionary and clerical influence in society, and the continuation of Rwanda's traditional political hierarchy. Other key parties included Parmehutu ("Party of the Hutu Emancipation Movement") and APROSOMA ("The Association for the Promotion of the Masses"), both of whom vied to mobilize Rwanda's Hutu majority with an eye toward legislative elections anticipated in January 1960. After weeks of escalating incidents, large-scale violence broke out on November 1, 1959. Over the next two weeks, Hutu militias killed hundreds of Tutsi and drove thousands more from their homes, and hundreds of Tutsi chiefs and thousands of other fearful Tutsi fled Rwanda for neighboring Uganda and Burundi. In response, Mwami Kigeli V initiated a counterrevolution targeting Hutu political leaders in southern Rwanda. After largely ignoring the violence for two weeks, Belgian colonial forces reestablished a modicum of civil peace in mid-November. By the end of the month, the Belgians had replaced hundreds of displaced Tutsi chiefs with Hutu politicians, teachers, and business owners, arguing that they (the Belgians) should not thwart the will of the people. This helped lay the groundwork for the ultimate success of the Hutu nationalist movement that would retrospectively describe these events as a "Hutu social revolution."³⁴

Church leaders did not delay in responding. Whatever their analytical differences, Bigirumwami and Perraudin issued a joint pastoral letter on November 6 condemning the atmosphere of "mutual fear, hate, and vengeance" existing "between Banyarwanda" (significantly, this language referenced Rwanda's national identity and did not invoke more contested language of "Hutu" and "Tutsi").³⁵ Bigirumwami himself faced considerable risk in early November, accosted by angry crowds at two separate roadblocks before reaching his Nyundo church on November 12.³⁶ Perhaps reflecting these encounters, his November 15 circular letter forcefully condemned arsonists and pillagers: "Those who have chosen to participate in attacks, massacres, and fires are rendered gravely culpable, they are enemies of Rwanda, they have sinned against God and against their neighbor."³⁷

Later in November, Bigirumwami also spoke out against the Belgian handling of the growing Tutsi refugee crisis. Visiting a large group of internally displaced Tutsi at the northern Rwandan mission station of Janja, Bigirumwami described the colonial government's efforts to relocate internally displaced Tutsi to a refugee camp in the southern city of Nyamata as "deportations" and demanded that Belgium restore Tutsi lands and property.³⁸ As reflected in the White Fathers' archives, his private correspondence was even more forceful. In a November 28 letter to Monsignor Leo Volker, the superior general for the Missionaries of Africa in Rome, Bigirumwami accused the Belgian government of using "fire and blood and the massive destitution of all officials even to deportation" to achieve its political goals.³⁹ His attitude toward Parmehutu was no less scathing. Associating Kayibanda's party with "communist agents," he warned that Belgium was about to hand over Rwanda to the "the representatives of a single party destined to place the whole country under the tyranny of a popular dictatorship."⁴⁰

Archival correspondence also reveals an increasing deterioration in relations between the White Fathers and Bigirumwami. Not only did Volker refuse to acknowledge Bigirumwami's aforementioned letter, but he began conspiring against the bishop of Nyundo behind Bigirumwami's back. For example, in a January 1960 letter to the Vatican prefect for Propaganda Fide, Volker painted Bigirumwami as an ideological sympathizer of UNAR. "The anti-Christian racism of UNAR . . . is assured of the sympathy and favor of Monsignor Bigirumwami who, blinded by the interests of his race, does not see the deeper [communist] tendencies of this party."⁴¹ Volker's accusations went far beyond the views of both the Belgian colonial administrator in Nyundo and Alphonse Van Hoof, a local White Father missionary in Rwanda and frequent commentator on political affairs. In contrast to Volker, Van Hoof described Bigirumwami as an apolitical figure who "didn't understand anything about politics."[42]

As ethnic and political violence accelerated throughout 1960, Bigirumwami's criticisms of the White Fathers grew more pronounced. After issuing an unusually public rebuke of local missionaries in July 1960, Bigirumwami penned a stinging private censure in an August 1960 letter to Volker and the White Fathers in Rome. After recounting Rwanda's months of fire, expulsions, massacres, and surveillance, Bigirumwami wondered how so many missionaries could support such things in the name of what was termed "normal evolution," "justice," or "social vengeance": "I am suffering cruelly when I think that many Europeans and missionaries find this normal, indifferent, or perfectly good. I am more and more convinced that certain European and African conceptions are not the same, and I do not admit that evil means justify the end."[43] When Volker and the White Fathers failed to respond to Bigirumwami's letter, he requested a neutral arbiter from the Vatican to combat what he termed a "conspiracy of inaction."[44]

In a passionate January 1961 letter to Volker that he explicitly claimed was written "for you, most Reverend Father, and for our archives," Bigirumwami defended himself against missionary accusations while offering his own interpretation of Rwanda's recent history.[45] According to Bigirumwami, White Fathers in Rwanda had accused him of being a "communist, schismatic and nationalist." In response, Bigirumwami claimed that he had always "stood with the masses," spoken out against political abuses, and opposed the ethnicist ideology that underlay Rwanda's recent violence. For Bigirumwami, the November 1959 uprisings stemmed from the formation of ethnically based parties aided and abetted by sympathetic Catholic missionaries and a strident Catholic media that "incited hatred and division" in the pages of *Temps Nouveaux d'Afrique* and *Kinyamateka*. Bigirumwami argued that the White Fathers acquiesced to Hutu social vengeance in the name of social justice, lamenting that Rwanda's hopes for political democracy had degenerated into anarchy and violence. He also argued that missionaries and mission-sponsored newspapers were trying not to replicate the mistakes of their nineteenth-century predecessors in Europe. "Our journals have decided to defend the common people. Let it not be said that the church lost the masses in Rwanda-Burundi, committing the same error as the European clergy in the last century. I hope they do well and are in good faith in defending the Hutu to the detriment of the Tutsi."

This January 23, 1961, letter to Volker was one of Bigirumwami's last extended commentaries on church engagement with the political situation in Rwanda. Five days later, Kayibanda and nearly three thousand local Hutu legislators gathered for an impromptu national assembly at the central Rwandan town of Gitarama (located just three kilometers from Perraudin's residence at Kabgayi diocese). With the acquiescence of Belgian military commander Colonel Guy Logiest, himself a devout Catholic and social democrat, Hutu leaders declared what became known as "the *coup d'état de Gitarama*," proclaiming a new democratic republic and the official end to Rwanda's monarchy.[46] Twenty-five thousand supporters—including many White Father missionaries and sisters—rallied outside the hall where Hutu politicians were meeting. Eighteen months later, in July 1962, Kayibanda was installed as Rwanda's first postcolonial president.[47] Seeing the handwriting on the wall, Bigirumwami pulled back from public critique in 1961–62, issuing few circular letters and avoiding political commentary in his diocesan newspaper *Civitas Mariae*. Inside the church, however, he continued to challenge the White Fathers over the future of the Rwandan clergy, especially concerning the growing ethnic tensions in the Catholic major seminary. It is to that story that we now turn.

Bigirumwami's Showdown with the White Fathers at Nyakibanda Major Seminary

Since 1935, the Catholic Church had operated its major seminary—the final institution for the training of Catholic priests—in the village of Nyakibanda in southern Rwanda. The seminary had weathered several previous political storms, including a 1952–53 crisis between Rwandan, Congolese, and Burundian seminarians that led to the transfer of non-Rwandan students to seminaries closer to home. By the end of the 1959–60 academic year, Nyakibanda was showing the effects of the seismic political changes consuming Rwandan society. While Nyakibanda remained tense if relatively calm during the November 1959 Hutu uprisings,[48] twenty-nine of Nyakibanda's eighty-five seminarians departed Nyakibanda between November 1959 and July 1960. An additional sixteen seminarians quit during the first three months of the 1960–61 academic year. Many of these seminarians came from Nyakibanda's Tutsi majority and complained of alleged White Father bias in favor of Nyakibanda's Hutu minority. Others who left came from the seminary's Hutu minority, claiming they had no place in a seminary dominated by Tutsi students and Tutsi ideology.⁴⁹

The rector of the seminary, the White Father Paul Baers, lamented the divisions and expressed most concern about the loss of Hutu seminarians: "Without Hutu priests, what is the future of the church in Rwanda?"⁵⁰ This reflected Baers's general sympathy for the Hutu. In his words, Hutu seminarians had come to the belated realization that Rwanda's traditional society offered a "fallacious regime of unity and concord that required the Hutu to sacrifice his rights." Thanks to the "social doctrine of the church based on the rights of the human person," the Hutu were now rightfully demanding that Tutsi respect Hutu "valor and respectability."⁵¹ Ultimately, Baers advocated for the closing of Nyakibanda seminary "to bring about important purifications in the ranks of Tutsi seminarians."⁵²

In contrast, Bishop Bigirumwami saw the crisis as stemming from the "virus" of ethnicism introduced by scheming politicians and their missionary allies. Closing the seminary would only sacrifice the church to the "demons" that had already divided the Rwandan polity, obliterating an institution that had been the "the pearl of Africa" and the "joy and the glory of the White Fathers."⁵³ Accusing Father Baers of a failure of leadership, Bigirumwami called for the rector's resignation in November 1960 and repeated this request at a gathering of Roman Catholic leaders at Nyakibanda in late January 1961.⁵⁴ For Bigirumwami, it was not the Tutsi seminarians but Baers and his fellow White Fathers who threatened to undermine the mission of the seminary: "You [Baers] and your [White Father] brothers make much evil in mistreating the young men that God has confided to you. . . . Why should your Hutu and Tutsi seminarians regard themselves as dogs before a bone? Why have you not built unity between Hutu and Tutsi? Why do you not have peace in your seminary?"⁵⁵

For his part, Archbishop Perraudin ultimately sided with his fellow White Father Paul Baers. Attributing the "deplorable spirit" at the seminary to Bigirumwami's mistrust of Baers and the White Fathers, Perraudin called on the Holy See to intervene to "stop this situation from becoming catastrophic not only for the seminary, but also for the exterior."⁵⁶ In a private letter to Bigirumwami, Perraudin chastised the bishop of Nyundo for "gravely troubling ecclesiastical discipline," accusing Bigirumwami of making seminary education impossible through his attitude of "open mistrust and near systematic opposition to the seminary directors."⁵⁷ Even as Perraudin professed continued respect for Bigirumwami's "holy person,"

Perraudin promised to "save my own seminarians against the spirit that your attitude provokes in this house."[58]

Despite the White Fathers' appeals, the Holy See ultimately sided with Bigirumwami, reflecting the Vatican's general tilt toward Bigirumwami and Rwanda's indigenous clergy in the early 1960s.[59] Propaganda Fide announced in April 1961 that Father Matthieu Ndahoruburiye, a Tutsi priest from Bigirumwami's Nyundo diocese, would replace Baers, becoming the first African rector at Nyakibanda. Nyakibanda's new rector arrived in triumph on May 1, 1961, accompanied by Bigirumwami and twelve Nyundo clergy and welcomed by Perraudin at the doors of the seminary.[60]

The rest of 1961 played out as a sort of stalemate at Nyakibanda.[61] With Nyundo Tutsi priests installed as spiritual director and rector, Bigirumwami possessed the upper hand in his ongoing confrontation with Perraudin over seminary leadership. Yet the departures of dozens of Hutu seminarians and resignations of three White Father professors posed a continuing challenge to the seminary's viability. Ultimately Rwanda's bishops resolved the stalemate by agreeing to the construction of separate diocesan seminaries. Nyakibanda remained the major seminary for the Archdiocese of Kabgayi, and Bigirumwami's Diocese of Nyundo opened a new seminary, St. Joseph's, in October 1963. Nyakibanda's rector, Matthieu Ndahoruburiye, shifted into the same role at the new St. Joseph seminary in 1963, serving there until 1973 Hutu uprisings forced him out of the country.[62]

Conclusion: The Legacies of Aloys Bigirumwami

White Fathers like Archbishop Perraudin largely set the parameters of the church's postcolonial engagement with politics. Namely, Perraudin lamented political violence but never condemned ethnically based parties, preferring to blame Rwanda's revolutionary bloodshed on supposed "communist" agents associated with the Tutsi-dominated UNAR party. Perraudin also maintained warm personal relations with Kayibanda even after Rwanda's first president was implicated in the targeted killing of eight thousand Tutsi in Gikongoro province in southern Rwanda in 1963–64.[63] Perraudin set the tone for Rwanda's postcolonial Catholic bishops, a hierarchy notable for its consistent support of Rwanda's postcolonial Hutu governments all the way up to the 1994 genocide.

Bigirumwami reminds us, however, that there were alternative voices countering this dominant trend. Indigenous Rwandans had agency; they were not mere puppets for their missionary "fathers in the faith." In this sense, Bigirumwami also demonstrates that political and ecclesial alternatives to tribalism existed in late colonial Rwanda. Media and archival records conclusively demonstrate that the Hutu "tribal" construction of democratic politics was in fact a highly contested project within the Catholic Church. Bigirumwami in particular stands out for his repeated critiques of tribal or ethnic politics in Rwanda. Bigirumwami castigated Rwanda's political parties for dividing the country into partisan factions and inciting racial hatred. In turn, Bigirumwami recognized the inherent risks that political affiliation posed to Catholic identity, as reflected in his comments in a June 1960 pastoral letter to the Catholic faithful in Nyundo Diocese: "The height of calamities is that parties are introduced into our communities. We should not be for one or the other. The political parties have intruded in our words, in our walking, in our visits, in our agitations, and even in our sermons in which we name the gospel. . . . In this we give the impression of having joined the parties of Hutu and Tutsi, abandoning that which is of Jesus."[64] In this regard, Bigirumwami worried about the enthusiasm with which Perraudin and other church leaders were embracing Rwanda's new Hutu-dominated state: "I believe that the missions should no longer follow the trail of the government; this could cost them dearly."[65] In light of Rwanda's postcolonial history of church-state cohabitation and ethnic violence, Bigirumwami emerges in retrospect as a prophetic seer.

Second, Bigirumwami's voice offers a note of repentance in the midst of an overall colonial narrative of Catholic triumphalism. While all of Rwanda's late colonial church leaders expressed profound regret at Rwanda's ethnic violence, Bigirumwami probed further in exploring the deeper reasons for the violence. Rather than just blame one political party, the perennial bogeyman of "communism," or even what missionaries liked to describe as the "irresistible will of the Hutu masses," Bigirumwami pointed to the abuses of Tutsi chiefs, the machinations of Hutu provocateurs, years of destructive media propaganda, and sheer ignorance.[66] Bigirumwami also turned the critique on himself and the church, questioning the seeming failure of Christian discipleship in Rwanda. Far more than Perraudin, Bigirumwami saw Rwanda's violence as a direct contradiction of the nation's official consecration to Christ the King in 1946. Thus Bigirumwami wrote in January 1960 that the "worst calamity" in Rwanda's recent history was that "the propagators of evils of which I have spoken, were not pagans, nor notorious apostates who had abandoned Christianity, but rather Christians who were known as good models among others."[67] In this sense, it is not surprising that Bigirumwami saw Rwanda's revolutionary violence not just as a regrettable but inevitable political evil but as a deeper sign of the failure of Christian mission itself: "The true fires are not those of the thousands and thousands of burned huts and homes, but the true fires are those in the souls killed and scandalized by those who should console and love them. The true expulsions of Tutsi are not those who are confined to the interior of Rwanda and outside but those who are expelled from the chancel and nave of our churches."[68] Bigirumwami would not excuse his fellow Rwandans as illiterate peasants when they asked priests in the confessional if killing or wounding a Tutsi is a sin. Rather, he questioned how they had learned to think that way—and why church leaders had not already corrected such misperceptions. He challenged Rwandan Christians to resist categorizing themselves as "one who calls himself Tutsi" or "one who calls himself Hutu."[69] As revealed in missionary and diocesan archives, it is Bigirumwami's prophetic voice that emerges with particular resonance for a twenty-first-century Catholic Church still struggling to recover its moral authority and theological vision a generation after the 1994 genocide.

Notes

Although original in thematic focus and scope, this essay incorporates material previously published in J. J. Carney, *Rwanda Before the Genocide: Catholic Politics and Ethnic Discourse in the Late Colonial Era* (2014; repr., New York: Oxford University Press, 2016).

1. A sampling of the literature on the Catholic Church and the 1994 genocide would include Carol Rittner, John K. Roth, and Wendy Whitworth, eds., *Genocide in Rwanda: Complicity of the Churches?* (St. Paul, MN: Paragon Press, 2004); Timothy Longman, *Christianity and Genocide in Rwanda* (Cambridge, UK: Cambridge University Press, 2010); Saskia Hoyweghen, "The Disintegration of the Catholic Church of Rwanda: A Study of the Fragmentation of Political and Religious Authority," *African Affairs* 95 (1996): 379–401. For a balanced first-person account that neither exonerates nor scapegoats the church for the genocide, see André Sibomana, *Hope for Rwanda: Conversations with Laure Guilbert and Hervé Deguine*, trans. Carina Tertsakian (Sterling, VA: Pluto Press, 1998).

2. See, for example, François Renault, *Cardinal Lavigerie: Churchman, Prophet and Missionary* (London: Athlone, 1994); and Paul Rutayisire, *La christianisation du Rwanda (1900–1945): Méthode missionaire et politique selon Mgr. Léon Classe* (Fribourg: Editions universitaires Fribourg Suisse, 1987).

3. Part of this stemmed from controversy. Perraudin has been blamed for uncritically supporting Hutu politics from the late revolutionary period up to the 1994 genocide. See, for example, J. D. Bizimana, *L'Eglise et le génocide au Rwanda: Les Pères blancs et le négationnisme* (Paris: L'Harmattan, 2004). In his final years, Perraudin also worked to propagate his own narrative. See here André Perraudin, *Un évêque au Rwanda: Les six premières années de mon épiscopat (1956–1962)*

(Saint Maurice: Editions Saint-Augustin, 2003).

4. One of the great intellectuals of twentieth-century Africa, Kagame was the author of a host of books on culture, history, theology, and philosophy, including *La philosophie bantou-rwandaise de l'être* (Brussels: Académie Royale des Sciences Coloniales, 1956); and *Un abrégé de l'histoire du Rwanda* (Butare: Editions universitaires du Rwanda, 1972–75).

5. This dissertation was later revised and published as Carney, *Rwanda Before the Genocide*.

6. I will utilize AGMA to refer to the General Archives of the Missionaries of Africa in Rome; ADK to refer to the Archives of the Diocese of Kabgayi, Rwanda; and CML to refer to the Centre Missionnaire Lavigerie, the White Fathers' local archives in Kigali, Rwanda.

7. Philip Gourevitch, *We Wish to Inform You That Tomorrow We Will Be Killed with Our Families: Stories from Rwanda* (New York: Picador, 1998), 61.

8. Hutus and Tutsis had been traditionally delineated by occupation: the minority Tutsi were pastoralists and cattle-keepers while the majority Hutu were farmers. In precolonial Rwanda, local political leadership was distributed among both Hutu and Tutsi leaders. These social categories became more hierarchical in the late nineteenth century as many Hutu were forced to work on the land of prominent Tutsi chiefs. In the early twentieth century, Belgian colonial agents further hardened this divide by issuing ethnic identity cards and limiting higher education and colonial service to Tutsi. By the 1950s, nearly all Rwandan chiefs and subchiefs were Tutsi. This growing Hutu-Tutsi political inequality was a crucial factor in the revolutionary developments of the late 1950s and early 1960s. For a more extensive discussion of the historical development of ethnic identities in Rwanda, see Carney, *Rwanda Before the Genocide*, 10–15.

9. This biographical section draws on *Hommage à Mgr. Aloys Bigirumwami, premier Evêque rwandais: Témoignages recueillis à l'occasion du Jubilé de 50 ans de l'Institution de la Hiérarchie ecclésiastique au Rwanda (1959–2009)* (Kigali: Editions du Secrétariat général de la CEPR, 2009), 5–13; Alexis Kagame, "Le Page du Ruanda," *L'Ami* 82 (1952): 73; Ian Linden, with Jane Linden, *Church and Revolution in Rwanda* (Manchester, UK: Manchester University Press, 1977), 244; Aloys Bigirumwami, "Le clergé indigène du Rwanda," *L'Ami* 67–68 (1950): 130–31.

10. In the Roman Catholic tradition, the "vicar apostolic" served as the leader of a Catholic mission territory, overseeing a jurisdiction known as an "apostolic vicariate." After a lengthy period of development and growth, a church could be reclassified as a local diocese and would receive its own local hierarchy headed by a bishop or archbishop. But for all intents and purposes, the vicar apostolic was the equivalent of the bishop and received the same episcopal consecration.

11. Rome's advocacy of indigenization can be traced back to the founding of Propaganda Fide in the seventeenth century (Adrian Hastings, *The Church in Africa, 1450–1950* [Oxford, UK: Clarendon, 1994], 88–89). Establishing an indigenous hierarchy in the Catholic missions became one of the central goals of Catholic ecclesiology after Pope Benedict XV's 1919 apostolic letter *Maximum Illud*, considered to be the "charter" of Catholic papal missiology in the twentieth century.

12. This description of Bigirumwami's consecration stems from "Rapport du Vicariat du Ruanda du Juillet 1951 au Juin 1952," AGMA no. 542140; "Sacré de Son Excellence Monseigneur Bigirumwami 1 Juin 1952," *L'Ami* 91 (1952): 128–33, AGMA no. 542140; *Hommage à Mgr. Aloys Bigirumwami*, 14–20, AGMA no. 542140; "Souvenirs du Sacré de Son Excellence Mgr. Aloys Bigirumwami, Vicaire Apostolique de Nyundo," June 1, 1952, CML.

13. "Sacré de Son Excellence Monseigneur Bigirumwami 1 Juin 1952," 133. This echoed his comments at a 1950 jubilee of the first Catholic mission in Rwanda that "our [indigenous priests'] apostolic ministry is not only traced to the White Fathers but is absolutely the same" (Bigirumwami, "Le clergé indigène du Rwanda," 131). All French-to-English translations are mine unless otherwise noted.

14. André Perraudin, "Sacré," March 25, 1956, ADK. See also "Le Sacré de Monseigneur Perraudin," *Temps Nouveaux d'Afrique*, April 1, 1956, 4–5, ADK; "Byose bigengwe n'urukundo, Myr Andreya Perraudin umushumba wa Vikariyati ya Kabgayi, y ahawe Ubwepiskopi," *Kinyamateka* 25, no. 282 (1956): 1, 4–5, ADK.

15. André Perraudin, "Rapport du Conseil du Séminaire sur les Vacances des Séminaristes," April 9, 1953, AGMA no. 526268. In a separate circular, Perraudin instructed local priests to keep their distance from the seminarians (André Perraudin, "Circulaire au Prêtres," July 8, 1953, AGMA no. 526116).

16. Bigirumwami to Hellemans, April 11, 1954, AGMA no. 543229; Bigirumwami to Durrieu, April 15, 1954, AGMA no. 543228; Bigirumwami to Van Volsem, January 28, 1954, AGMA no. 543226–27.

17. Bigirumwami to Durrieu, September 1, 1952, AGMA no. 543198–99; Bigirumwami to Durrieu, January 24, 1953, AGMA no. 543200.

18. Mutara Rudahigwa had been appointed king after a Belgian and White Father–led coup against his father, Musinga (r. 1897–1931). Whereas Musinga never warmed to Christian missions and generally suspected the Belgians' and the White Fathers' political machinations, Rudahigwa became a Catholic catechumen in 1929 and was close to Monsignor Classe. He received Catholic baptism in 1943 and famously dedicated Rwanda to Christ the King in 1946.

19. Hove to Mosmans, "Climat du Ruanda Indigène en 1952," AGMA no. 540747.

20. This document can be consulted in Fidele Nkundabagenzi, *Rwanda politique, 1958-60* (Brussels: Centre de Recherche et d'Information Sociopolitique, 1962), 20–29.

21. Linden, *Church and Revolution*, 186.

22. "Les vingt-cinq ans de règne du Mwami du Ruanda," *Temps Nouveaux d'Afrique*, July 7, 1957, 8–9.

23. Aloys Bigirumwami, "L'Eglise a raison d'exiger plus de justice," in *Vérité, justice, charité: Lettres pastorales et autres déclarations des évèques catholiques du Rwanda, 1956–1962*, ed. Venuste Linguyeneza (self-pub., 2001), 50–56. For background, see Linden, *Church and Revolution*, 256.

24. Guy Mosmans, "L'avenir politique du Ruanda-Urundi," September 21, 1958, AGMA no. 720651.

25. Bigirumwami, "L'Eglise a raison d'exiger plus de justice," 51.

26. The article appeared in the September 5, 1958, edition and can be consulted in Nkundabagenzi, *Rwanda politique*, 38–42. For analysis, see Justin Kalibwami, *Le Catholicisme et la société rwandaise, 1900–62* (Paris: Présence africaine, 1991), 422–33; and Linden, *Church and Revolution*, 256.

27. Cf. Bigirumwami in Nkundabagenzi, *Rwanda politique*, 42.

28. André Perraudin, "Super Omnia Caritas," February 11, 1959, ADK. Perraudin's language is telling for its incorporation of racial discourse, reflecting the lingering power of the colonial Hamitic hypothesis. This theory purported to explain differences in Hutu-Tutsi physiognomy in terms of European concepts of "race," arguing that the taller and supposedly superior Tutsi descended from Middle Eastern tribes who traced their heritage to Ham, son of the biblical Noah. Hutu, on the other hand, were African Bantu who lacked the Tutsi's Middle Eastern heritage and more "Caucasian" features. On the Hamitic hypothesis, see Edith R. Sanders, "The Hamitic Hypothesis: Its Origin and Functions in Time Perspective," *Journal of African History* 10, no. 4 (1969): 521–32.

29. Perraudin, *Un évêque au Rwanda*, 194; André Perraudin, "Je rends grâce à Dieu," August 25, 1989, CML.

30. Bigirumwami to [Anon.], March 16, 1959, CML.

31. Ibid.

32. "Le dernier Conseil Supérieur du Ruanda: Lamentables débats," *Temps Nouveaux d'Afrique* 6 (July 1958): 5.

33. This quotation is taken from "The Voice of the Peasants," a June 1958 political manifesto written by the Hutu movement APROSOMA (the acronym represented the group's French title, which can be roughly translated as "Association for the Promotion of the Masses"). The author, Joseph Gitera, was a devout Catholic youth leader whose increasingly inflammatory rhetoric in 1958–59 led to strong rebukes from both Bigirumwami

and Perraudin. See Carney, *Rwanda Before the Genocide*, 91, 113.

34. On the revolution itself, see René Lemarchand, *Rwanda and Burundi* (New York: Praeger, 1970), 145–94. The best collection of primary source documents on the revolution can be found in Nkundabagenzi, *Rwanda politique*.

35. "Message de leurs excellences Monseigneurs Bigirumwami and Perraudin aux chrétiens du Ruanda," November 6, 1959, ADK.

36. *Civitas Mariae* 22 (1959): 4–5. I consulted this official newspaper of the Diocese of Nyundo in the Diocese of Kabgayi Archives, Rwanda (ADK).

37. Aloys Bigirumwami, "Vivre chrétiennement les événements," November 15, 1959, ADK.

38. Guy Logiest, "Communication no. 3 du Resident Militaire du Ruanda," December 10, 1959, ADK; Rudipresse no. 148, December 19, 1959, ADK; Van Hoof to Volker, January 19, 1960, AGMA no. 727126.

39. Bigirumwami to Volker, November 28, 1959, AGMA no. 740211.

40. Ibid.

41. Volker to Sigismondi, January 3, 1960, AGMA no. 739034. Volker's language is telling for its incorporation of racial discourse, again reflecting the lingering mythos of the colonial "Hamitic hypothesis."

42. Van Hoof to Volker, March 25, 1960, AGMA no. 727173; Van Hoof to Volker, April 14, 1960, AGMA no. 727177.

43. Bigirumwami to Volker, August 30, 1960, AGMA no. 740239.

44. Volker to Bigirumwami, November 29, 1960, AGMA no. 740244.

45. Bigirumwami to Volker, January 23, 1961, AGMA no. 740290–99. Subsequent quotations in this paragraph are taken from this letter. The quote referenced here is taken from AGMA no. 740292.

46. Mwami Kigeli V Ndahindurwa had already fled the country in June 1960.

47. On Rwanda's political history during the tumultuous 1959–62 years, see Carney, *Rwanda Before the Genocide*; Lemarchand, *Rwanda and Burundi*; Kalibwami, *Le Catholicisme et la société rwandaise*; Filip Reyntjens,

Pouvoir et droit au Rwanda: Droit public et évolution politique, 1916–1973 (Tervuren, Belgium: Musée royal de l'Afrique centrale, 1985); Donat Murego, *La révolution rwandaise, 1959–1962* (Louvain: Institut des Sciences Politiques et Sociales, 1975).

48. Cf. "Rapport de la Réunion annuelle des Ordinaires ayant des Séminaristes à Nyakibanda," November 6, 1959, AGMA no. 731351–58; Manyurane to [Parents], December 8, 1959, AGMA no. 741103; Nothomb to Volker, December 23, 1959, AGMA no. 731139–40.

49. Baers to Volker, April 4, 1960, AGMA no. 731163; Paul Baers, "D'état d'Esprit du Séminaire," November 12, 1960, AGMA no. 731485.

50. Paul Baers, "D'état d'Esprit du Séminaire," November 12, 1960, AGMA no. 731481; Baers to Bigirumwami, November 14, 1960, AGMA no. 731611. For similar sentiments, cf. Donat Murego, "La vie du Séminaire Vue et Vécue par les Séminaristes," December 1960, AGMA no. 731522.

51. Paul Baers, "D'état d'Esprit du Séminaire," November 12, 1960, AGMA no. 731478.

52. Paul Baers, "D'état d'Esprit du Séminaire," November 12, 1960, AGMA no. 731481.

53. Bigirumwami to Baers, November 14, 1960, AGMA no. 731502–3.

54. Aloys Bigirumwami, "Réflexions et commentaires de S. E. Mgr. Bigirumwami sur la situation du Grand Séminaire et la solution proposée," November 1960, AGMA no. 731615–16.

55. Bigirumwami to Baers, February 28, 1961, AGMA no. 731618.

56. Perraudin to Agagianian, March 7, 1961, AGMA no. 731623. The "Holy See" is the official diplomatic name for "the Vatican." I use both terms interchangeably in this essay.

57. Perraudin to Bigirumwami, March 7, 1961, AGMA no. 731624.

58. Ibid.

59. Alphonse Van Hoof complained about this perceived Vatican bias in 1961, wondering how long Rome would continue to support the local *abbés* despite their "Unarist sympathies." Van Hoof to Mondor, July 30, 1961, AGMA no. 727223.

60. See Volker to Perraudin, April 22, 1961, AGMA no. 731176; Van Hoof to Volker, May 2, 1961, AGMA no. 727197; Perraudin to Volker, May 10, 1961; *Civitas Mariae* 38 (May 1961): 2–6, AGMA no. 738203.
61. The following narrative is drawn from Perraudin to Sigismondi, July 25, 1961, AGMA no. 738231–32; Feys, Biname, and Vermeersch to Volker, July 26, 1961, AGMA no. 731181–83; Ndahoruburiye to Volker, October 17, 1961, AGMA no. 731184; and Feys to Volker, December 22, 1961, AGMA no. 731194–95.
62. "Rapport de la réunion annuelle des Ordinaires avant des séminaristes à Nyakibanda, 1961–62," June 30, 1962, AGMA no. 731418–21; Perraudin to Agagianian, June 8, 1962, AGMA no. 738272–73; Bigirumwami to Volker, July 18, 1962, AGMA no. 40301; Feys to Perraudin, November 25, 1962, AGMA no. 731209–10.
63. See Carney, *Rwanda Before the Genocide*, 176–84.
64. Aloys Bigirumwami, "Quel avenir?," June 1960, ADK.
65. Bigirumwami to Volker, January 23, 1961, AGMA no. 740295.
66. Aloys Bigirumwami, "La pire des calamités: Persévéré dans le mal," January 25, 1960, ADK; Bigirumwami, "Etre prudent et nous taire, ou parler à temps et à contretemps?," January 27, 1960, ADK.
67. Aloys Bigirumwami, "La pire des calamités: Persévéré dans le mal," January 25, 1960, ADK.
68. Bigirumwami to Volker, December 6, 1960, AGMA no. 740270.
69. Aloys Bigirumwami, "Echo à un pressant appel de Rome," June 10, 1960, ADK.

Works Cited

Bigirumwami, Aloys. "Le clergé indigène du Rwanda." *L'Ami* 67–68 (1950): 125–32.
———. "L'Eglise a raison d'exiger plus de justice." In *Vérité, justice, charité: Lettres pastorales et autres déclarations des évèques catholiques du Rwanda, 1956–1962*, edited by Vénuste Linguyeneza, 50–56. Self-published, 2001.
Bizimana, J. D. *L'Eglise et le génocide au Rwanda: Les Pères blancs et le négationnisme*. Paris: L'Harmattan, 2004.
Carney, J. J. *Rwanda Before the Genocide: Catholic Politics and Ethnic Discourse in the Late Colonial Era*. 2014. Reprint, New York: Oxford University Press, 2016.
Gourevitch, Philip. *We Wish to Inform You That Tomorrow We Will Be Killed with Our Families: Stories from Rwanda*. New York: Picador, 1998.
Hastings, Adrian. *The Church in Africa, 1450–1950*. Oxford, UK: Clarendon, 1994.
Hommage à Mgr. Aloys Bigirumwami, premier Evêque rwandais: Témoignages recueillis à l'occasion du Jubilé de 50 ans de l'Institution de la Hiérarchie ecclésiastique au Rwanda (1959–2009). Kigali: Editions du Secrétariat général de la CEPR, 2009.
Hoyweghen, Saskia. "The Disintegration of the Catholic Church of Rwanda: A Study of the Fragmentation of Political and Religious Authority," *African Affairs* 95 (1996): 379–401.
Kagame, Alexis. *Un abrégé de l'histoire du Rwanda*. Butare: Editions universitaires du Rwanda, 1972–75.
———. "Le Page du Ruanda." *L'Ami* 82 (1952): 73–75.
———. *La philosophie bantou-rwandaise de l'être*. Brussels: Académie Royale des Sciences Coloniales, 1956.
Kalibwami, Justin. *Le Catholicisme et la société rwandaise, 1900–62*. Paris: Présence africaine, 1991.
Lemarchand, René. *Rwanda and Burundi*. New York: Praeger, 1970.
Linden, Ian, with Jane Linden. *Church and Revolution in Rwanda*. Manchester, UK: Manchester University Press, 1977.

Longman, Timothy. *Christianity and Genocide in Rwanda.* Cambridge, UK: Cambridge University Press, 2010.

Murego, Donat. *La révolution rwandaise, 1959–1962.* Louvain: Institut des Sciences Politiques et Sociales, 1975.

Nkundabagenzi, Fidele. *Rwanda politique, 1958–60.* Brussels: Centre de Recherche et d'Information Sociopolitique, 1962.

Perraudin, André. *Un évêque au Rwanda: Les six premières années de mon épiscopat (1956–1962).* Saint Maurice: Editions Saint-Augustin, 2003.

Renault, François. *Cardinal Lavigerie: Churchman, Prophet and Missionary.* London: Athlone, 1994.

Reyntjens, Filip. *Pouvoir et droit au Rwanda: Droit public et évolution politique, 1916–1973.* Tervuren, Belgium: Musée royal de l'Afrique centrale, 1985.

Rittner, Carol, John K. Roth, and Wendy Whitworth, eds. *Genocide in Rwanda: Complicity of the Churches?* St. Paul, MN: Paragon Press, 2004.

Rutayisire, Paul. *La christianisation du Rwanda (1900–1945): Méthode missionaire et politique selon Mgr. Léon Classe.* Fribourg: Editions universitaires Fribourg Suisse, 1987.

Sanders, Edith R. "The Hamitic Hypothesis: Its Origin and Functions in Time Perspective." *Journal of African History* 10, no. 4 (1969): 521–32.

Sibomana, André. *Hope for Rwanda: Conversations with Laure Guilbert and Hervé Deguine.* Translated Carina Tertsakian. Sterling, VA: Pluto Press, 1998.

CONCLUSION

Arun W. Jones

Intercultural communication and interaction are, as noted in the introduction to this volume, foundational to the nature of Christianity. The preceding essays have explored a variety of ways in which such communication and interaction have taken place between African, American, Asian, and European Christians since 1500, during a long era of economic, political, and military dominance by various European nations and powers. The essays have provided valuable insights into how historians can discern some of the various voices in these intercultural engagements, especially the voices of indigenous persons in Asia, Africa, and the Americas. This conclusion will reflect briefly on what has been learned from this volume about the nature of intercultural engagement through Christian history, what dilemmas continue to haunt such a historical project, and what avenues of investigation can be explored in future scholarly endeavors.

Christians have related to one another (and to persons outside Christian communities) across cultural difference in a number of different contexts, with a variety of social arrangements and power relations. When cultural difference is noticed and accounted for in these interchanges, we can say that Christians relate to each other in a zone or space that allows for cultural difference to exist and be explored.[1] Christians have entered this zone through some combination of force and choice—great force in the case of most Native Americans, ample choice in the case of sixteenth- and seventeenth-century Japanese women. Yet the zone itself is a space where people acknowledge cultural difference and for any number of reasons begin, at least, to explore the nature of that difference, and what it might mean to inhabit the cultural world of the Other.[2]

This zone of intercultural interaction is a space and time for experimentation, as Vecsey and Mills illustrate well in their essays. The rules of one culture no longer completely control human interactions; they apply lightly and provisionally, as the rules, expectations, and norms of another culture are tried out and tried on in the course of human interaction. The experimentation is not restricted to individual intercultural exchanges: it can occur with communities in the public sphere, as in the case of the Iglesia Filipina Independiente (IFI) that Hermann helpfully discusses. By entering into conversations with disillusioned and independent Catholic communions in other countries, the IFI developed a network across the world of Catholics that had separated from Rome and were attempting a grand experiment in ecclesial and political life.

The experimentation involved in intercultural exchange entails a certain degree of unpredictability: Sebastian, quoting Spivak, writes about chance rather than choice governing verbal and other exchanges between persons. This zone of indeterminacy, although clearly circumscribed, is one without hard and fixed borders. The IFI demonstrates that: a national movement quickly developed international connections. Borders are fluid, flexible, and porous; various people come and go. Yet despite their permeability and elasticity, borders do exist, to protect and nurture the zones of intercultural activity from the areas of life—both secular and religious—where the prevalence of one particular culture is assumed, and its dominance and normativity cultivated.

Because it is a zone of experimentation and unpredictability, the space for intercultural communication also becomes a space for new criticism, argumentation, and conflict arising from the cross-cultural engagement. Different perspectives on what is good and right and acceptable may clash with one another, as Yannakakis describes in the case of Christians in seventeenth-century Oaxaca, Mexico. Intercultural communication even allows for minority and weaker cultures to confront dominant ones with some sort of authority and recognition. The result may well be critiques of the dominant culture by the weaker one. Thus, in the process of navigating African and European cultures, the beleaguered Bishop Aloys Bigirumwami of Rwanda criticized the attitudes of the European missionary White Fathers as well as African political leaders, as he imagined a new secular and religious politics for Rwanda.

The case of Bishop Bigirumwami leads to a broader insight: intercultural interactions can disrupt given and supposedly settled power dynamics. As persons set aside their established roles in order to engage the cultural world of their interlocutors, the ordering of power between the two sides is at least partially suspended, and new power arrangements emerge, however temporarily, for intercultural exchange to occur. Indeed, there are those who argue that setting aside one's power is a prerequisite to genuine intercultural interactions, although some of the cases in this collection have shown how this is not necessarily the case. Yet simply the desire to understand the Other on the Other's terms, whether one wishes to set aside one's power and authority or not, can change power dynamics. We see this unsettling of established power dynamics occurring with Japanese Christian women and male Jesuits; with Pedro de Mondragón as he operates in a Spanish Christian world; with African converts negotiating with European missionaries who are their sponsors and supporters.

In this zone of intercultural exchange, of indeterminacy, not only are certain dominant cultural rules suspended, but new ones can be written. As Mombo reveals in her essay, Quaker women in Kenya, through their experimentation of what could be permissible in Kenyan Christianity, introduced new dietary practices for Kenyan Christian women. For them, some of the old taboos—like that on eating chicken—would not be observed in their zone of intercultural exchange. In a similar vein, Mills argues that in Potosí, Peru, Pedro de Mondragón wrote a fresh script of what it meant to be a rich, mestizo Christian in the Spanish Empire at the turn of the seventeenth century.

Speaking more generally about the potential for creativity, in the process of experimentation, argumentation, and criticism, as power relations are (temporarily) refigured, zones of intercultural interaction can provide a space in which new (Christian) cultures can arise out of experiments with and critiques of old ones. Speaking of Lutherans in South India, Sebastian writes, "It is in this space that was neither fully European-Christian, nor fully Indian-Hindu, that the new minority community of the Protestant Christians takes shape." In the process of navigating pre-Columbian and newly imposed Spanish Catholic cultures, Mexican elites forged a new culture of Oaxacan Catholicism. Moreover, such new Christian cultures can be fashioned not just from two but several existing cultural influences and forces, as they converge, mix, and react with one another in the zone of intercultural engagement. In Rwanda and the Philippines, in addition to European Catholic and indigenous cultures, rationalism, nationalism, and other ideas and ideologies from the European Enlightenment played a key role in the emergence of new African and Asian forms of Christianity.

Because of their penchant to experiment, critique, and create, those engaging in intercultural communication and exchange risk forfeiting some of their authority to speak for their own people. By holding in abeyance their own cultural heritage in order to engage the world of the Other, they can be perceived as throwing into question the validity and authenticity of their own identity. So Native American Christian translators and authors in seventeenth-century New England found, in the words of Christopher Vecsey, that "they were 'caught in the middle of two cultures' with ambivalent loyalties to both. They possessed 'the power to write but . . . could no longer speak for their people.'" Yet paradoxically, in order to engage in intercultural movements, the participants had to be firmly rooted and grounded in their own cultural traditions, regardless of the perceptions of others.

It is this zone of intercultural engagement—a space of indeterminacy, of some suspension of cultural rules and hegemony, allowing for experimentation, critique, and invention—that makes possible the hearing of Native Christian voices. For even when documents are produced by Europeans, inasmuch as these Europeans are engaged in the dynamics of intercultural exchange, the texts allow for the voices and visions of local Africans, Asians, and Americans to be perceived, even if only faintly. As Sebastian writes, "A careful reading of these documents from the past, even if they are not written by the native Christian, can provide insights into the negotiating abilities and the agency of the early generations of . . . Christians." In the cases where documents and other historical evidence come from local Christians, the complexity and richness of their own perspectives can come into much clearer view. Carney describes Bishop Bigirumwami's voice as a "voice of nuance." This "voice of nuance" reminds us that the dominant ideological and even material structures in society can be suspended in the zone of intercultural communication and exchange—even if that zone is simply an archive. Writing for the archives, Bishop Bigirumwami refused to be controlled by the Hutu/Tutsi categories prevalent in his society and chose to examine his social and religious context with different categories.

The contingent nature of intercultural exchange calls into question the conceptual order and rules not only of the historical societies and persons being studied but also of us, the historians who study them. It calls into question the usefulness of the various theories to which we historians adhere. Theory in the writing and reading of history presents itself as both helpful and problematic, especially when studying intercultural history. It is useful because it arranges data—the historical record—so that certain patterns and narratives emerge from those data, and so that history can make sense to historians and our audience. Where would we be, for example, without theories of translation to describe the cross-cultural movement of Christianity?[3] But theory also disregards, displaces, and holds at bay certain data, so that that which does not fit well with the theory can be easily ignored or dismissed. One complaint against some postcolonial theory, for example, is that it tends to disregard religion as a historical force in the motivations and actions of various groups of people, especially the poor and oppressed sectors of society who, ironically, are often quite religious themselves.[4] And this is where simply looking at the data, and being surprised by them, especially when they do not fit our cherished theories and narratives, helps in the appreciation and understanding of intercultural history. So, Paul Kollman's unearthing of records regarding the rescued and converted African slave Suema upended the reigning narrative of her life, which in turn had been constructed using data and theories provided by a missionary in East Africa. It was Kollman's openness to being surprised by buried information that made possible a new—albeit far less romantic—apprehension of the life of an East African Christian. Theory is necessary but not sufficient to read intercultural exchanges. As historians we need continually to ask ourselves what our theories explain, and what they do not explain. And just as important, we need to pay constant attention to how information—whether new or neglected—can force us to rethink our categories and narratives.

This observation on the usefulness and problems of theory leads to the general observation that the intercultural activities of historical actors invite historians who are studying them into our own historiographical zones of intercultural thought and communication. There is a great deal of reading and writing going on among native Christians and Europeans—both among themselves and with each other—in the essays collected in this volume. The writing of indigenous Christians, which records both the authors' own thoughts and their observations of the world, is crucial to the work of historians who, even with the growing importance of other forms of material evidence, still rely heavily on the written word for the historical enterprise. The process of writing down and writing about the intercultural process—whether done by historical subjects or historians studying those subjects—of course supplies meaning to the author, for writing entails the ordering of thoughts, the arrangement of historical events and data—especially those that are surprising—so that they make sense. Writing can help historical actors and historians to start to understand, and even appreciate, on our own terms an order that we do not know and that we could not have anticipated. Yet writing also introduces us to new thoughts, new ideas, and new worlds. Through the writing that takes place as a result of intercultural interaction, meaning imposes itself on us from the outside, and words help us apprehend realms that we did not know existed, and ideas we never imagined to be conceivable. Then words are not simply the means by which we make meaning—they are also the means by which we receive meaning from the outside. Words flowing from intercultural encounters between Filipinos and Spanish, between Spanish and Mexicans, between Swiss and Rwandans, both establish and disrupt meaning for the historical actors, and just as importantly for the historians who are open to conceiving the world with new senses, borrowed from the worlds of those we study.

Turning from what we can learn from intercultural engagements to unresolved issues, one of the problems that this volume presents is that it consists of snapshots—or perhaps more accurately, video clips—of particular times and places. How do these fit into larger and longer narratives? Recently there has been a salutary criticism that world Christianity presents a plethora of local studies but little attention to global movements and phenomena that had profound consequences on the faith. As historian David Maxwell has put it, "There is much work still to do in the creation of a new history of Christianity.... While the growing diversity and multipolarity of the church does point to a remarkable set of religious transformations in global history, the process remains under-conceptualised."[5] Intercultural engagement promises to be both hindrance and boon to any grand narrative of Christian history. It is a hindrance because it insists on paying attention to how local actors are performing—often improvising—their parts on myriad local stages. It is a boon because it insists on drawing the local into more global constellations of people, materials, and ideas. After all, intercultural engagement presumes the meeting of two or more cultures. To change the image from story to painting, what is needed is a broad canvas that makes sense from a distance, yet allows for intense variation in details when these are examined up close. The different sections of this volume perhaps offer one way of putting together intercultural history: with a number of interweaving themes rather than one grand story or motif.

Finally, this volume gestures to new avenues of research in the history of Christian intercultural engagement and exchange. Of great importance is the incorporation of material evidence, as opposed to written evidence, in our explorations of the history of Christian interculture. This volume has focused on archives, with many satisfying results. Yet how can the learnings gleaned from here be helpful in the investigation of objects rather than written and spoken words? How must we come up with different ways of reading when dealing with material culture? And how can our reading in the archives be enhanced and changed when we examine other types of material evidence? Here Paul Kollman's suggestion that historians of archives can learn lessons from biblical scholars might be a starting point in dealing with material evidence, since biblical scholars have been incorporating archeological and other material into their historical analyses for a long time. Other religious historians have also paved the way in using evidence as varied as buildings, objects of art, gifts, and sartorial choices to construct their arguments and narratives.[6] Cultural exchange, after all, may happen more profoundly with things rather than words.

While materiality is being studied in new and exciting ways by historians, music and poetry also need to be investigated for our reconstructions of the past. Careful attention to aesthetics and the arts—for example, the composition and singing of songs, or the introduction, adaptation, and production of painting and fabrics—will pay great dividends in our understanding of the intercultural past.[7] Such avenues of research can only add to the complexity and richness of our apprehension and appreciation of Christians who have crossed cultural and religious boundaries to reassess, reform, and renew their faith.

Notes

1. For conceptualizing unique social and ideological spaces, see Edward Soja, *Thirdspace: Journeys to Los Angeles and Other Real-and-Imagined Places* (Malden, MA: Blackwell, 1996).

2. For similar perspectives in the field of New Testament studies, see Brian K. Blount, "The Souls of Biblical Folk and the Potential for Meaning," *Journal of Biblical Literature* 138, no. 1 (2019): 6–21. Blount begins his essay quoting W. E. B. Du Bois, who articulated how African Americans were forced into intercultural exchange and so developed a double consciousness that was not required of their white fellow citizens. See W. E. B. DuBois, *The Souls of Black Folk* (Greenwich, CT: Fawcett, 1961).

3. The pioneers in this theoretical approach have been Lamin Sanneh and Andrew Walls. See Lamin Sanneh, *Translating the Message: The Missionary Impact on Culture* (Maryknoll, NY: Orbis Books, 1989); and Andrew F. Walls, *The Missionary Movement in Christian History: Studies in the Transmission of the Faith* (Maryknoll, NY: Orbis Books, 1996).

4. See Gauri Viswanathan, *Outside the Fold* (Princeton, NJ: Princeton University Press, 1998), xiii–xiv.

5. David Maxwell, "Historical Perspectives on Christianity Worldwide: Connections, Comparisons and Consciousness," in *Relocating World Christianity: Interdisciplinary Studies in Universal and Local Expressions of*

the Christian Faith, ed. Joel Cabrita, David Maxwell, and Emma Wild-Wood (Leiden: Brill, 2017), 48.

6. For example, see Richard Eaton, *The Rise of Islam and the Bengal Frontier, 1204–1760* (Berkeley: University of California Press, 1993).

7. See Jeffrey Cox, "Sing unto the Lord a New Song," in *Europe as the Other: External Perspectives on European Christianity*, ed. Judith Becker and Brian Stanley (Göttingen: Vandenhoeck & Ruprecht, 2014), 149–63.

Works Cited

Blount, Brian K. "The Souls of Biblical Folk and the Potential for Meaning." *Journal of Biblical Literature* 138, no. 1 (2019): 6–21.

Cox, Jeffrey. "Sing unto the Lord a New Song." In *Europe as the Other: External Perspectives on European Christianity*, edited by Judith Becker and Brian Stanley, 149–63. Göttingen: Vandenhoeck & Ruprecht, 2014.

DuBois, W. E. B. *The Souls of Black Folk*. Greenwich, CT: Fawcett, 1961.

Eaton, Richard. *The Rise of Islam and the Bengal Frontier, 1204–1760*. Berkeley: University of California Press, 1993.

Maxwell, David. "Historical Perspectives on Christianity Worldwide: Connections, Comparisons and Consciousness." In *Relocating World Christianity: Interdisciplinary Studies in Universal and Local Expressions of the Christian Faith*, edited by Joel Cabrita, David Maxwell, and Emma Wild-Wood, 47–69. Leiden: Brill, 2017.

Sanneh, Lamin. *Translating the Message: The Missionary Impact on Culture*. Maryknoll, NY: Orbis Books, 1989.

Soja, Edward. *Thirdspace: Journeys to Los Angeles and Other Real-and-Imagined Places*. Malden, MA: Blackwell, 1996.

Viswanathan, Gauri. *Outside the Fold*. Princeton, NJ: Princeton University Press, 1998.

Walls, Andrew F. *The Missionary Movement in Christian History: Studies in the Transmission of the Faith*. Maryknoll, NY: Orbis Books, 1996.

List of Contributors

J. J. (James Jay) Carney is associate professor of theology at Creighton University. His research and teaching interests include Catholic history in the African Great Lakes area, the theology of reconciliation, political theology, and the intersection of sport and theology. Carney is the author of *Rwanda Before the Genocide: Catholic Politics and Ethnic Discourse in the Late Colonial Era* (2014), which was awarded the Bethwell A. Ogot Book Prize by the African Studies Association. He co-edited *The Surprise of Reconciliation in the Catholic Tradition* (2018). Currently he is working on two book projects: *Benedicto Kiwanuka and Catholic Politics in Uganda, 1955–1972* (co-authored) and *"For God and My Country": Catholic Leadership in Modern Uganda*. Carney holds a PhD from Catholic University of America.

Adrian Hermann is professor of religion and society and the director of the department of religion studies at the University of Bonn. His research focuses on theoretical and historical questions regarding the globalization of the concept of religion and on the history of religion as a media history. Hermann recently co-edited *Hijacked: A Critical Treatment of the Public Rhetoric of Good and Bad Religion* (2020), and he also is one of the co-editors of *Discourses of Indigenous Christian Elites in Colonial Societies in Asia and Africa around 1900* (2016) and *"To Give Publicity to Our Thoughts": Journals of Asian and African Christians around 1900 and the Making of a Transregional Indigenous-Christian Public Sphere* (2018). He is currently working on a monograph on an independent Catholic movement in the Philippines around 1900. In 2011 he received his PhD from the University of Basel.

Arun W. Jones is the Dan and Lillian Hankey Associate Professor of World Evangelism at the Candler School of Theology, Emory University. He explores how Christians have appropriated and spread their faith in Asian contexts, especially during the era of European and American imperialism. His current research focuses on the history of Christianity in Rajasthan, India, as well as other topics in the fields of world Christianity and missiology. Jones is the author of *Missionary Christianity and Local Religion: American Evangelicalism in North India, 1836–1870* (2017), which was named one of the ten outstanding books of 2017 for mission studies by the *International Bulletin of Mission Research*. He has served in a variety of capacities

LIST OF CONTRIBUTORS

in the American Society of Missiology, most recently as president, and is the secretary of the Society for Hindu-Christian Studies. He received his PhD from Princeton Theological Seminary.

Paul Kollman is associate professor of world religions and world church at the University of Notre Dame. His research focuses on African Christianity, mission history, and world Christianity. He is the author of *The Evangelization of Slaves and Catholic Origins in Eastern Africa* (2005) and co-author of *Understanding World Christianity: Eastern Africa* (2018). Kollman is currently working on a manuscript on the Catholic missionary evangelization of eastern Africa. He is the president of the International Association of Mission Studies and has served as the executive director of Notre Dame's Center for Social Concerns and the president of the American Society of Missiology. He earned his PhD from the University of Chicago Divinity School.

Kenneth Mills is the J. Frederick Hoffman Professor of History at the University of Michigan. He investigates the histories of the early modern Iberian world and colonial Latin America. In particular, his research explores religious and cultural transformations. Mills is the author of *Idolatry and Its Enemies: Colonial Andean Religion and Extirpation, 1640–1750* (1997; 2012) and co-author of *Colonial Latin America: A Documentary History* (2002). He recently co-authored *Lexikon of the Hispanic Baroque: Transatlantic Exchange and Transformation* (2013) and is currently writing a book about the journey of the Castilian Hieronymite friar Diego de Ocaña (ca. 1570–1608). He earned his DPhil from the University of Oxford.

Esther Mombo is associate professor, faculty of theology of St. Paul's University in Limuru, Kenya. Her research focuses on women's issues, evangelism, HIV/AIDS, and Christian-Muslim relations. Some of her recent work includes "Pray! Pray! Pray! Women and the Prayer of Persistence and Resistance," in *Listening Together: Global Anglican Perspectives on the Renewal of Prayer and the Religious Life*, edited by Mutharaj Swamy and Stephen Spencer (2020); and "The Singing Mysticism: Kenyan Quakerism, the Case of Gideon H. W. Mweresa," in *Quakers and Mysticism*, edited by Jon R. Kershner (2019). She co-authored *Mending Broken Hearts, Rebuilding Shattered Lives: Quaker Peacebuilding in East and Central Africa* (2019). She also co-edited *The Postcolonial Church: Bible, Theology, and Mission* (2016) and *Disability, Society and Theology: Voices from Africa* (2012). Her service includes mentoring young women for theological education and ministry. She has served as the co-chair of the Commission on Education and

Ecumenical Formation of the World Council of Churches, and is regional coordinator of the Circle of Concerned African Women Theologians. Mombo earned her PhD from the University of Edinburgh.

Mrinalini Sebastian is an independent scholar who also works as a mentor and site coordinator at the Grace-Trinity UCC Partnership Site of Harcum College. She currently explores the interaction between Protestant missionaries and Indians in South India, and the history of Indian Christians. Before moving to Philadelphia, she worked as fellow at the Center for the Study of Culture and Society, Bangalore. In 2013–14 she was international fellow-in-residence for the research project "Transfer and Transformation of Missionaries' Images of Europe in Contact with the Other, 1700–1970," at the Leibniz Institute of European History, Mainz, Germany. She earned her PhD from the University of Hamburg.

Christopher Vecsey is the Harry Emerson Fosdick Professor of the Humanities and Native American Studies and the chair of the department of religion at Colgate University. His research explores traditional American Indian religions, American Indian Christianity, and American music history, journalism, and religion. Vecsey is the author of *Jews and Judaism in the* New York Times (2013) and *Following 9/11: Religion Coverage in the* New York Times (2011). He holds a PhD from Northwestern University.

Haruko Nawata Ward is professor of church history at Columbia Theological Seminary. She investigates postcolonial histories of the age of Reformations, the Jesuits, encounters of cultures and religions in Christian missions, women and religious vocation, gender and theology in martyrdom and hagiography, and histories of Christianities in the early modern world. She is the author of *Women Religious Leaders of Japan's Christian Century, 1549–1650* (2009) and numerous essays including "Translating Christian Martyrdom in Buddhist Japan in the Early Modern Jesuit Mission" in *Global Reformations: Transforming Early Modern Religions, Societies, and Cultures*, edited by Nicholas Terpstra (2019). Ward received her PhD from Princeton Theological Seminary.

Yanna Yannakakis is Winship Distinguished Research Associate Professor of History at Emory University. Her research focuses on the social and cultural history of colonial Latin America, and the intersections of Mesoamerican ethnohistory with legal and religious history. She is the author of *The Art of Being In-Between: Native Intermediaries, Indian Identity, and Local Rule in Colonial Oaxaca* (2008), winner of the Howard Francis Cline

Memorial Award. She also co-edited *Indigenous Intellectuals: Knowledge, Power, and Colonial Culture in Mexico and the Andes* (2014) and *Los indios ante la justicia local: intérpretes, funcionarios y litigantes en Nueva España y Guatemala (siglos XVI–XVIII)* (2019). Yannakakis is currently working on a monograph, *Mexico's Babel: Native Custom and Imperial Law in Colonial Oaxaca*. She received her PhD from the University of Pennsylvania.

Index

abbot, 95, 99
abuse, 175, 194, 222, 226
accommodation, 173, 83–84
accounts, historical, 7, 9, 12, 20–25, 28, 33–34, 41, 45–51, 55, 87, 122, 131–36, 166, 179
accumulation, 34, 138, 141–42, 151
accusation, 90, 95, 99, 120, 192, 221–22, 224
Acosta, Jose de, 134, 138–39
adaptation, 3, 4, 89, 97, 107, 132–37, 152, 166, 168, 179, 239
adviser, 70, 84, 149, 167, 218
Africa, 1–12, 17–38, 63–78, 189–91, 197, 201–3, 214–37
African Record, 67
agency, human, 40–45, 54, 64–65, 70, 73–76, 166, 225, 236
agent, 18, 20–21, 67, 87, 132, 168, 172, 221, 225
Aglipay, Gregorio, 191, 203
agriculture, 52–54, 113
ally, 108–11, 114–15, 119, 121–22, 195, 224
alms, 130–34, 141–42, 152–53
Alpers, Edward, 21–23
ambivalence, 107–22, 166, 178, 180, 236
America, 4–5, 7, 10–12, 20, 26, 33, 87, 107–22, 130–53, 165–81, 190–92, 203, 217, 233, 235–36
American Friend, 67
Americans. *See* Euro-Americans; Native Americans; Mesoamericans
Amigidzi, Labeka/Rabeka, 71–72
analysis, 24, 40, 43, 65, 109, 174, 178, 197, 218
Anandapur, 52, 54
ancestors, 44, 53, 114, 119, 120, 122, 180
Andes, 138–53
anecdotal narratives, 49–51
Apess, William, 168, 180
apostasy, 85, 100, 176, 226
apostle, 51, 87, 94, 137, 176, 219–20
appropriation, 4, 75, 132, 167, 169
Archambault, Sister Marie Therese, 178
archives, 5, 7, 17–19, 21–31, 33–34, 40–44, 57, 63–76, 136, 165–67, 169, 171–74, 178, 204–6, 215, 217, 219, 221–22, 226–27, 236, 239
archivist, 21, 23, 174, 178,
art, 131–32, 135, 172, 180, 239
Ashgate Research Companion to Women and Gender in Early Modern Europe, 87
Ashikaga Shogunate, 82, 84–85

Asia, 1, 3–5, 7, 11–12, 83, 87, 149, 189–92, 197, 199–203, 233
assistant, 20, 29, 82, 91, 113, 115, 122
attacks, 168, 197, 221
attitude, 67, 84, 205, 221, 224, 234
Augustinians, 83–84
authenticity, 7, 19–21, 41, 166, 178–80, 236
authority, 74, 84, 109, 112–14, 120, 122, 133, 139, 143, 167, 227, 234–36
autobiography, 5, 40, 45, 47, 168–70, 174
autonomy, native, 115, 167, 173, 179
Aztec, 109–10

backsliding, 20, 112, 120
Bahutu Manifesto, 218
Baptist Church, 179–80
baptism, 22, 27, 32–33, 49, 53–54, 83, 91, 96, 108, 171, 216
Basel Mission, 41–56
battle, 85, 109, 112, 113, 114, 177
  See also combat; war
beatification, 122
benefactor, 26–27, 149, 168
bias, 7, 20, 24, 64, 87, 206, 219, 223
Bible, 1, 27, 42, 66, 71, 75, 87, 94, 99, 137, 166, 239
Bible School, 169
Bible Woman, 6, 47–48
Bigirumwami, Aloys, 7, 9, 12, 214–27, 234, 236
bishop, 7, 9, 12, 29, 94, 111, 120, 173, 181, 191, 196–97, 203–4, 214–27, 234, 236
Black Elk, Nicholas, 175–76
Black Elk Speaks, 7, 175–76
boarding schools, 175, 177
Bolivia, 8, 138
boy, 52, 56, 69–71, 98, 172
Brahmin, 10, 40
  See also Kaundinya, Anandrao (Ananda Row)
British (people), 22, 29, 53, 55, 67
Buddha, 95–96, 99
Buddhism, 82, 84–85, 87, 89–90, 92, 94–97, 99–100
Burundi, 216, 218, 220, 222–23

Cajonos Rebellion, 115, 122
Canada, 165, 169–70, 177–78, 202

INDEX

caste, 11, 40, 42, 48, 51, 56
catechesis, 22, 174
catechism, 92, 114, 119–20, 172, 196
catechist, 20, 30, 47–48, 53, 82, 84, 111, 113–15, 176, 214
categorical narratives, 47–48
Catholics, 9, 11–12, 17–34, 46, 81–100, 107–22, 130–53, 171–80, 191–96, 203–204, 214–27, 234–35
    See also Roman Catholics
celebration, 172–73, 196, 216, 218
ceremony, 122, 169, 179
Ceylon, 192, 203
Cheese and the Worms, The, 33
Chichimecateuctli, Carlos, 10, 109–17, 122
chicken, 72–74, 235
chief, 71, 169, 172, 216–20, 226
children, 28, 32, 46, 49, 52–55, 73, 85, 98, 170, 175, 181, 192
    See also boy; girl
China, 3–4, 82–83, 89
Christianity and Sexuality in the Early Modern World, 86
Christian Patriot, 191, 198, 199, 200
Christian village, 53–54
chronicler, 92, 130–31, 136–37
Cieza de Leon, Pedro de, 134, 136
Civitas Mariae, 223
clan, 116, 169, 180
class, social, 6, 10, 20, 48, 86, 88, 99, 107, 132, 192, 198, 219
Claudia of Alexandria, 92, 95–97
clergy, 11, 22, 87, 112, 169, 192–97, 214–31
    See also priest
clothing, 49, 53, 95
coercion, 114, 138, 180
coin, 141, 146, 149, 151–52
collaborators, 20, 81, 88, 109, 114, 179, 214, 217
colonial officials, 11, 27, 110, 113, 115, 118, 217
combat, 111, 114, 222
    See also battle; war
commentator, 145, 153, 201, 222
commentary, 90, 93, 190, 223
commoner, 116–17, 145
    See also peasant; villager
communist, 221–22, 225–26
composition, 83, 132, 134–35, 150, 180, 239
concubinage, 110–11, 115–17, 120–22
confession, 113–14, 119, 227
Confucianism, 84–85, 89, 93, 97
Congo, 216, 223
Congregation of the Holy Ghost, 22–29
Congress, United States, 170
conqueror, 108–9, 141, 149, 153
contract, 74, 141, 152

convention, 20, 113, 139
conversion, religious, 30, 40–41, 46–47, 49, 51, 54, 66, 83–84, 93, 114, 120, 153, 165, 169
converts to Christianity, 6, 9, 11, 17, 19–20, 23–24, 30, 32, 40–42, 47–48, 51, 54, 56, 66, 70–72, 74, 76, 82–84, 87, 89, 92, 114, 120, 166, 168, 171, 176, 179–80, 216, 235, 237
correspondence, 22–23, 31, 72, 168, 174, 177, 204, 215, 217, 219, 221
council, 1, 87, 111–12, 118, 138, 143, 216–18
    Council of Jerusalem, 1
    Council of the Indies, 112, 138
    Council of Trent, 87
court, 40–41, 83, 94, 108–9, 116, 121, 142, 149, 215
credit, financial, 141–42
crime, 96, 110–12, 116–17, 175
crisis, 218, 221, 223–24
Croesus, 147–52
curse, 43, 73
Cusco, 133, 141, 144, 145, 147
custom, 64, 72–76, 89, 93, 98, 111–12, 145, 173
Cyrus the Great, 148–49

dalit, 55
dance, 122, 172, 175
Dartmouth College, 167
darkness, 71–72, 97, 139
data, 33–34, 64, 178, 237
De los Reyes, Isabelo, 190–95
deacon, 169, 174
death, 27, 32, 40, 48–49, 64, 92, 95, 99, 113, 130, 134, 148, 171
debate, 28, 92, 195, 198–202, 215–16
deities, 85, 94, 119, 149, 180
Deloria, Jr., Vine, 180–81
demon, 122, 145, 153, 224
denunciation, 85, 111, 115
deportation, 84–85, 221
Der evangelische Heidenbote, 55, 56
description, literary, 18, 20, 25, 29, 46–49, 52, 75, 90, 92, 99, 138–39, 144, 146
devil, 99, 119
devotion, 88, 130, 133–34, 165, 171–72
dialogue, 84, 107–9, 118–19, 174, 178, 196, 198
diary, 167–68, 177
Dictionary of African Christian Biography, 34
diet, 10, 64, 72–74, 235
diocese, 22, 29, 30, 110, 113, 172–3, 214, 216, 223, 225–27
disciple, 48, 95–96
discourse, missionary, 19–20, 23–29, 32, 107–8, 120
discourse, native, 88–89, 108–9, 115, 121, 174, 180, 204, 215

discourse, public, 198–99, 201
disguise, 99–100
divinities. *See* deities
Doctrina Christiana en Lengua Castellana y Çapoteca, 119
doctrine, 2, 94, 118–19, 193–94, 196, 224
document, 7, 12, 19, 26, 31, 34, 40–42, 44, 47, 53, 55–57, 64, 68, 84, 117–18, 171–74, 176, 193, 198, 220, 236
documentation, 141–43
Dominicans, 7, 83–84, 100, 114–15, 119–20, 122, 138, 191
drama, 25, 131, 137, 172
dream, 94, 144, 167, 169, 176, 216, 220
dress, 90, 94, 98, 146, 173, 180
Dutch East India Company, 84–85

East Africa Yearly Meeting of Friends, 68
Echo, 39–40, 42–45, 52, 54, 57
edict, 83, 85, 96
Edict of Expulsion of Padres: 83
edition, 27, 82, 86, 170, 175
editor, 20, 91, 180, 201–2, 219
education, 28, 32, 42, 46, 54–56, 63, 66, 84–85, 93, 108, 114, 117, 119, 167, 170, 175, 189, 195, 218–19, 224
elder, 50–51, 167
El Ilocano, 191
elites, 7, 10–11, 51, 88, 108, 110, 114, 119, 121, 189–92, 197–99, 202, 204–5, 216, 218–19, 235
emperor, Japanese, 95, 96
empire, American, 181
empire, Asian, 4
empire, Aztec, 109
empire, British, 200
empire, European, 5, 25, 200,
empire, Japanese, 83, 86, 96,
empire, Roman, 1, 3–4, 93–96
empire, Spanish, 113, 121, 137, 234–35
Engendering Faith: Women and Buddhism in Premodern Japan, 87
England, 3, 65, 198
English (language), 27, 89, 174–76, 198, 200, 202,
English (people), 89, 169, 202
Episcopal Church, 169, 181, 192
equality, 57, 74, 173, 192–93, 198, 201, 218–19,
Ethiopia, 2–3
ethnicity, 20–21, 71, 73, 107, 143, 167, 215–26
ethnography, 25, 52, 143
Eugenio. *See* saint: St. Eugenia
Europe, 1, 3–6, 8, 11–12, 20, 25–26, 28, 30–32, 55, 81, 83, 86–87, 89, 91, 153, 172, 174, 191–92, 195, 200, 203, 215, 222, 233, 234–35

Europeans, 3, 5–6, 10, 12, 18, 22, 25, 33, 45–46, 48–49, 51, 63, 85, 91–92, 165, 189, 217, 222, 233, 234–37
Euro-Americans, 7, 10, 33, 66–67, 166, 169–70, 181, 192, 233
evangelicals, 181, 235
evangelization, 17–20, 24–25, 28–31, 66, 72, 82, 107–8, 119–20, 215–16
evangelists, 71, 167, 170
evidence, 1, 6, 11–12, 22, 24, 31, 33, 56, 64, 83, 87, 115, 131, 134, 136, 147, 167, 172, 176, 236, 237, 238, 239
evil, 107, 153, 167, 168, 222, 224, 226–27
exceptional narratives, 51
Excerpts from the Acts of the Saints, 82, 90–92
executions, 81, 83–84, 90, 96, 110–12, 177, 192, 205
exempla, 114, 120, 136–37
exemplary narratives, 48–49
exile, 83–84, 117, 177
Experiences of Five Christian Indians, 168
experiment, 4, 10, 82, 234–36
expulsion, 82–84, 120, 173, 222, 227
extirpation, 108, 114–15, 118, 120, 122
eyewitness, 22, 136, 139, 166

faction, 109–10, 117, 226
family, 26–27, 33, 40–41, 53, 70–71, 74, 91, 96, 100, 110, 141, 148, 170, 175, 179, 216
farmer, 50–51, 122
 See also peasant
father, 93, 95, 97–98, 141, 144, 147, 169, 171, 180, 193, 225
 See also parent
fear, 46, 136, 152, 221
fight, 193, 195–96
fire, 149, 221–22, 227
fishing communities, 55–57
First Jesuits, The, 87
Florentine Codex, 108
forgiveness, 22, 47, 168, 178, 181
form criticism, 27
For This Land, 181
fortune, 141, 144, 147–48, 151
France, 3, 21, 29, 198, 206
Franciscans, 83–84, 107, 111, 172–73, 175
freedom, 21, 44, 52–55, 57, 71, 150–51, 167, 173, 192, 194, 196
French (people), 9, 22–23, 28, 32, 171, 176, 215
French (language), 20–21, 27, 32, 89
friar, 7, 107–8, 110–11, 114–15, 120, 122, 130–53, 172–73, 193, 195
Friends Africa Mission, 68
Friends United Meeting, 66–67

INDEX

gender, 11, 21, 23, 43, 75, 81–100
genocide, 12, 174–75, 179, 214, 225, 227
German (language), 41, 55,
Germany, 28, 31, 192, 198, 206, 243
gift, 72–73, 95, 149, 173, 239
girl, 21–22, 56, 69–72, 74, 76, 81, 98
God, 25, 48, 57, 67, 72, 75, 89, 94, 96, 99, 118–19, 121, 139, 179, 181, 192–95, 221, 224
gods, *See* deities
Good to Eat, 74
gospel, 71, 181, 194, 217, 226
governance, 19, 51, 113, 117
government, 10, 40, 68, 83–86, 96–98, 112, 116–17, 177, 179, 202, 214, 221, 225–26
Great Expulsion, 82, 84
Guadalupe, 130–31, 133
Guadalupe, Virgin of, 122, 130, 133–35, 142, 180
guardian, 2, 133, 169, 176

Habermas, Jürgen, 198–201
hagiography, 18, 81–82, 85, 88, 171
hair, 94, 145
healing, 95, 108, 171
heaven, 49, 94, 97, 99, 131, 171, 177
hell, 138
heretic, 33, 111, 217
Herodotus, 138, 148–49
Hideyoshi, Toyotomi, 82–83
hierarchy, 54–55, 87, 89, 93, 114, 193, 214, 219–20, 225
Hieronymite, 130–53
historian, 1–3, 5, 7, 10–12, 18–19, 21, 23–24, 27–28, 32, 40, 44, 46, 86–87, 91, 131, 165–66, 170, 192, 195, 200, 206, 233, 236–39
historical-critical method, 27–28
Hole, Edgar, 66, 70
holy man 52, 175,
hospital, 22, 66
hostage, 83, 87
husband, 30, 72, 83, 93, 96, 116
Hutu, 9, 214–39, 236
hybridity, 89, 180
hymn, 99, 135, 167, 172, 174, 180

Iberia, 4, 84–85, 92, 120, 133,
ideology, 3, 63, 88, 74–75, 217, 221–23, 236
idols, 49, 94–95, 119–20
idolatry, 107, 110–15, 118–22
Iglesia Filipina Independiente (IFI), 190–97, 203–6, 234
illiteracy, 171, 176, 227,
image, 44, 56, 65, 85–86, 130–33, 180
Imitation of Christ, 3, 83
India, 2–3, 6, 11, 39–57, 84, 190–91, 198–99, 203, 235

Inkanyiso, 202
interpretation, 10, 19, 23–28, 30–31, 33, 43, 64–67, 76, 111, 151, 222
interpreter, 70–71, 116, 143
inheritance, 10, 96, 110–12, 141, 144, 193
initiation, 64, 70
Inquisition, 85–86, 109–12, 115, 118
interview, 30–31, 68, 172, 175, 178
Islam, 3–4, 120, 202
isolation, 31, 54, 85, 197, 217

Japan, 4, 7, 10, 81–100, 198
Japanese (people), 4, 7, 10–11, 81–100, 233, 235
Jesuit Relations, 20, 165, 171
Jesuits, 7, 10, 12, 20, 25–26, 46, 81–100, 134, 138, 171, 174–76, 179, 235
Jesus Christ, 1–2, 25, 48–49, 56, 66, 71, 82, 85, 94–99, 167, 174, 176–77, 179–81, 194, 226
Jews, 1–2, 120–21
journal, 20, 26, 29, 31, 50–51, 67, 169, 189, 190–91, 196, 203, 205–6, 222, 241
journalist, 175, 191–92, 215, 219
journey, 22, 29, 131–35, 137, 150, 168
judge, 113, 115–18, 120, 122, 143, 144, 147, 150
justice, 107–22, 215, 218–20, 222

Kabgayi, 216–17, 223, 225
Kaffir Express, 189
Kagame, Alexis, 215
Kaimosi, 66, 68–72
Kaundinya, Anandrao (Ananda Row), 40–42, 51–54, 57
Kayibanda, Gregoire, 215, 218, 221, 223, 225
Kenya, 11, 29, 65, 66, 67, 68, 70, 73, 235
king, 25, 53, 112, 116–18, 121, 131, 138, 142, 144, 148, 150–52, 168, 216–18, 220
Kinyamateka, 219, 222
Korea, 83
Koschorke, Klaus, 199
Kyoto, 84, 91–92, 95

labor, 29, 53–54, 73, 85, 98, 112–13, 138, 192
laborer, 52–53, 99
La España Oriental, 191
La Iglesia Filipina Independiente: Revista Católica (IFIRC), 193–97, 203, 205
laity, 11, 26, 82–83, 111, 113–15, 133, 174, 179, 214.
lament, 93, 99, 217, 222, 224–25
land, 31, 52–54, 116, 167, 170, 177, 181, 221
Latin, 32, 55, 89, 91–93, 108
Latin America, 11, 190–91
La Verdad, 193, 203, 204
Lavigerie, Charles, 215–16
law, 32, 40, 93, 96, 107–22, 181, 192
learning, 65, 69, 93, 99

letter, 12, 20, 22–23, 27, 33, 41, 52–53, 56, 72, 83, 142–43, 167–69, 172–73, 176–77, 189, 203–4, 218–19, 221–26
Letters of Eleazar Wheelock's Indians, 168
liberation, 8, 12, 66, 86, 100, 220
libraries, 67, 169,
Lima, Peru, 133– 34
literacy, 42, 66, 69, 88, 131, 166, 169
liturgy, 2, 30, 173, 178
loan, 141–44, 151
London, 29, 67
Lord's Prayer, 22, 119
Lungaho, Daudi, 70–71
Lungaho, Maria. *See* Maraga, Maria

machine, 20, 139–40, 142, 150
Madeleine. *See* Suema
magazines, 19, 46, 55, 64
magistrate, 85, 117, 143
    See also municipal officials
Mangalore, 40–41, 50–52
manifesto, 172, 177, 205, 218
Manila, 83–84, 191–92
Maraga, Maria, 65, 67, 69–76,
Marino. *See* saint: St. Marina
Marquette University, 174, 178
marriage, 27, 32, 64, 69, 70–74, 76, 93–96, 110, 113, 115–18, 121, 144, 169–70, 192
martyrdom, 7, 81–100, 122, 171
mass (liturgy), 113, 179, 203
massacre, 85, 221–2
mediation, 6, 10, 112, 166–67, 190, 198
medicine, 66, 91, 169, 174–75, 214, 220
memory, 12, 19, 52, 100, 136
mentor, 52, 75, 175, 216
merchant, 7, 91, 141, 150, 152
Mesoamerica, 107–8, 112
message, 11, 24, 45, 57, 149, 151, 165, 170, 176–177
mestiza/o, 85, 143–144, 151, 153, 192, 235
Metamorphoses, 43
Methodist, 168–69
Mexica. *See* Aztec
Mexicans, 11, 107–22, 130, 235, 238
Mexico, 4, 10, 12, 107–22, 165, 179, 234
Mexico City, 130, 134
middleman, 83, 141, 151
military, 3–4, 83, 85, 170, 177, 223, 233
mining, 138–39, 141, 147, 150–52
minority, 3, 51, 215, 233–235
miracle, 99, 133–35, 137, 139, 153, 171–72
mission station, 29, 31, 46–47, 55, 65–71, 216, 221
Missionaries of Africa. *See* White Fathers
Missionary Advocate. 67

mixed-blood. *See* mestiza/o
Mögling, Herrmann, 51–53
monastery, 94–95, 98
Mondragón, Juan de, 1
Mondragón, Pedro de, 7–8, 140–53, 235
money, 27, 141–43, 147, 149–52, 167, 170
monk, 82, 85, 95, 98–99
moral dialogue, 107–9, 119
Morisco, 120
mother, 22, 68, 70–73, 93, 95–97, 110, 133, 141, 144, 174, 177, 179
    See also parent
mountain, 94, 114–15, 121–22, 138–39
municipal officials, 11, 113, 115–16, 118, 143
murder, 22, 107, 115
Muslims, 27, 56, 120
Mutua, Rasoah, 66, 68, 72

Nagasaki, 83–85, 91
Nahuatl, 108–9
Naito Julia, 84, 87, 96
Narcissus, 39, 43–45
nationalism, 6, 192, 195, 198, 217, 220–22, 235
New England, 166, 168, 236
New Spain, 107–22
newspaper, 7, 10, 189, 191–93, 197, 201–2, 204–6, 219, 222–23
nobility, 25, 93, 95, 107, 108–12, 114, 116, 141, 144–45, 168, 216
North America, 12, 20, 26, 33, 87, 174, 180–81, 203
novice, 130, 177
nuns, 22–23, 84, 172, 174–78, 180, 223
Nyakibanda, 217, 223–25

Oaxaca, 12, 109, 113–22, 234–35
Ocaña, Diego de, 130–53
Occom, Samson, 167–68, 180
Ojibwa, 169, 173, 177–78
Old Law, 118–21
Ōmura, 86, 100
oral culture, 6, 64
oral history, 34, 46, 52, 68, 178
orality, 89
oral sources, 30–31, 130, 171
orders/societies, Catholic, 10, 22, 25–29, 31, 46, 81–84, 87, 91–92, 114, 173, 176, 192, 214
ordination, 177, 216
orphan, 71, 99
Our Father. *See* Lord's Prayer

padre, 50–51, 82–83, 98
    See also priest
pagan, 2–3, 96, 111, 171, 176–77, 226
parent, 69, 71, 98, 143, 146, 175

INDEX

parish, 29, 32, 108, 113–115, 173, 177, 214
Parmehutu, 220–21
pastor, 29, 66, 68, 72, 174, 180
patron, 91, 133, 153, 215–16
patronage, 82–84
Paulo, Yōfo, 90–97
peasant, 52–53, 85, 198, 218–20, 227
   See also farmer; villager
penance, 98–99
Perraudin, André, 215, 217, 219, 221, 223–26
persecution, 10, 12, 82–86, 96
persuasion, 41, 55–57, 84, 94, 107, 114, 132
Peru, 10, 130–53, 235
petition, 41, 55–56, 172–73
Philip III (king of Spain), 133, 151
Philippines, 4, 6–7, 10, 12, 83, 189–206, 235
pilgrim, 133, 137, 171
pillaging, 194, 221
poet, 148, 170, 175
polycentric History, 190, 197
polygyny, 110, 112, 115, 120
pope, 83, 87, 96, 122, 172–73, 193
   Cornelio/Cornelius, 96
   Gregory XIII, 83
   John Paul II, 122
   Paul V, 83
   Pius XII, 173
Portugal, 83, 85
Portuguese (language), 89, 92–93
Portuguese (people), 82–83, 92
Potosi, 133–34, 138–52, 235
prayer, 22, 71, 75, 96–100, 166, 178,
preacher, 50, 66, 91, 133, 153, 167–68, 170
predecessor, 133–34, 139–40, 222
prejudice, 148, 153, 166
priests, 22, 30, 82, 84–85, 91, 107–15, 119–22,
   172–76, 180–81, 192–94, 196, 204, 214–27
princess, 90, 93, 144
printing press, 82, 91, 192, 196, 219
   See also publication
prison, 28, 32, 95, 97–98, 192
propaganda, 197, 219, 226
Propaganda Fide, 26, 216, 221, 225
proselytization, 83–84
   See also evangelization
Protestant, 9, 20, 26, 29–30, 40–57, 87, 166–71,
   177, 192, 235
Psalms, 94, 99
public Sphere, 190–92, 194–205
publication, 24, 26–27, 30, 51, 68, 82, 85–86,
   166, 168, 189, 191, 195, 197, 202–3
pueblo, 173, 180
punishment, 81, 85–86, 96, 110–19

Quaker, 8, 10–11, 64–76, 235
Quaker Life, 67

race, 11, 153, 166, 170, 179, 217–19
racism, 17, 20, 168, 179, 215, 217, 221, 226
Ramos, Juan, 10, 116–18, 120, 122
rape, 95, 116, 118, 175,
rebellion, 52, 85, 96, 115, 122, 138, 192
rector, 216, 217, 224–25
redaction criticism, 28
reformation (of faith), 81, 87–88, 170, 239
refugees, 221
religious orders. *See* Orders
representation, 5, 17–18, 24, 43, 52, 89, 132, 142,
   144, 193
resistance, 10, 81, 96–100, 108, 148, 165–66,
   177, 227
revolution, 6, 177, 192, 196, 218, 220–26
Revista Católica de Filipinas, 191
Revista Popular de Filipinas, 191
rhetoric, 33, 93, 118, 121, 215
Riel, Louis, 177
rite, 64, 70, 73, 107, 176
ritual, 40, 108, 113–15, 119, 122, 174
Roman Catholics, 11–12, 17–34, 81–100,
   107–22, 130–53, 171–77, 214–27
Roman Catholic Church, 4, 12, 17–34, 171,
   192–96, 214–27
Rome, city of, 87, 92, 95, 172, 177, 217, 221–22
Row, Andanda. *See* Kaundinya, Anandrao
   (Ananda Row)
Rudahigwa, Mwami Mutara, 217–18, 220
rumor, 100, 142, 218
Rwanda, 214–27, 234–35, 238
Rwandans, 214–27, 238

sacraments, 27, 30, 32, 116, 118
saint, 81–82, 85–92, 97–99, 108, 122, 137, 169,
   171–72, 177
   St. Eugenia: 90–99
   St. Jerome: 90, 92, 130
   St. Marina: 90, 97–100
salvation, 48, 50, 99, 110
Sanjivi, 48
Sanneh, Lamin, 8
Sardis/Sart, 148–49
schism, 194, 204
scholars, 5, 18, 20–21, 27, 29, 32, 84, 131, 166,
   168, 175–76, 179, 200, 206, 239, 243
schoolteacher, 46, 48, 52
   See also teacher
schools, 32, 41–42, 46, 52, 56, 66, 69, 72, 82, 107,
   111, 167–70, 175, 177–78, 189, 214, 217, 219
   See also education

scripture, 1–2, 27, 66, 94–95, 137, 166
    See also Bible
seminarians, 33, 177, 215, 217–18, 223–25
seminary, 41, 177, 181, 216–17, 223–25
sermon, 114, 119, 133–34, 167–68, 172, 226
servant, 90, 94–95
service (to others), 25, 92, 117, 133, 135, 139, 142–43, 151, 173
servitude, 67, 75, 219
sexuality, 86, 110, 116–18, 122,
    sexual renunciation, 93–96
Shinto, 82, 89
Shogun, 82–86
signature, 55, 151, 172, 176
silence, 12, 21, 67, 95, 144, 204, 214
silver, 7, 138–39, 141–43, 146–47, 149–52,
sin, 47–48, 94, 98–99, 117, 118, 166, 168, 173, 175, 221, 227
sinner, 98–99, 167
singing, 69–72, 89, 99, 167, 180, 239
sister, 49, 71–72, 74, 111, 223
    See also nun
Sketches from the Dark Continent, 67
slave, 17, 21–25, 28, 32, 53, 66–67, 75, 87, 237
slavery, 21–25, 53, 55, 167, 220
Society of Jesus. *See* Jesuits
Solon of Athens, 148–50
Somaya (Stephanas), 52–53
son, 84, 91, 96, 107, 110, 141–42, 144, 175, 181, 216
Son of the Forest, A, 168
source criticism, 28
Spain, 7, 12, 83, 85, 107–13, 116, 118, 121–22, 130–32, 137–38, 141–42, 145–46, 150, 152–53, 192–93, 195, 202, 235, 238
Spanish (Language), 89, 92–93, 108, 118–20, 191, 202
Spanish (People), 7, 12, 108–12, 115–18, 120–21, 138, 143–44, 147–48, 150, 152–53, 192–93, 195, 238
Spiritans. *See* Congregation of the Holy Ghost
spirituality, 47, 75, 135, 167, 170, 174–77, 180
Spivak, Gayatri Chakravorty, 5, 17–18, 20, 39, 42–43, 45, 234
status, 29, 51, 55, 73, 99, 116–18, 121, 140
stereotype, 17, 19–20
Stewart, Tony, 8
Stoler, Ann, 19, 24
strategy, 11, 19, 24, 28, 31–32, 42, 107, 114, 118, 121, 133, 146
Structural Transformation of the Public Sphere, The, 198
struggle, 9–10, 12, 31, 68, 87, 93, 99, 110, 113–15, 190, 192–93, 201, 215

student, 32, 41, 46, 56, 66, 91–92, 177, 223
    See also seminarian
subalterns, 5–6, 18, 42–43, 45, 51–52, 54–57
Suema, 9, 21–23, 27, 33, 237
superstition, 67, 75, 107, 194
Supreme Bishop, 196–97, 203–4
Swiss (people), 41, 217, 238
syncretism, 89, 165, 169, 178–80,

taboo, 10, 72–74, 235
Tac, Pablo, 172
Tanzania, 21, 27, 29, 31–32, 66
tax, 85, 110, 112, 142
teacher, 20, 71, 172, 175, 220
    See also schoolteacher
Tekakwitha, Kateri, 171–72, 180
Tekakwitha Conference, 174, 180
temple, 46, 86, 94, 96, 98–100, 149
Temps Nouveaux d'Afrique, 219, 222
testimonial, 40–41, 49, 175, 47
testimony, 48, 69–70, 72, 111, 142, 165, 171–72, 178–79
Tetzcoco, 109–11, 122
text criticism, 27
Thiel, Mark, 174, 178
Tokugawa Shogunate, 82–85
Tokyo, 84
torture, 74, 85, 87, 90
trade, 22–23, 25, 83, 85, 141
    See also slavery
translation, 8–12, 20, 24, 27, 41, 51, 81–100, 107–22, 166, 174, 198, 236–37
trial, 33, 110–12
Turkey, 148
Tutsi, 9, 214–27, 236
Twa, 218

Uganda, 29–31, 216, 220
Union Nationale Rwandaise (UNAR), 220–21, 225
United Kingdom, 30, 65, 67, 206
United States of America, 20, 65–66, 165, 168, 176, 179, 192, 203, 206
    See also America
untouchable, 55
uprising, 28, 222–25

Valignano, Alessandro, 82
Vatican, 26–27, 216, 221–22, 225
vengeance, 221–22
Vicar Aspostolic, 216–17
Vilela, Gaspar, 91–92
Villa Alta, 115, 117, 120, 122
village, 51, 53–55, 69, 116–17, 223

villager, 55, 108, 113, 115, 122
    See also farmer; peasant
Villavicencio, Diego Jaimes Ricardo, 120–21
virgin, 90–98, 122, 171
Virgin of Guadalupe. *See* Guadalupe, Virgin of
vision, religious, 97, 107, 132, 169, 175–76, 180
Viswanathan, Gauri, 40–42, 44, 47
vocation, religious, 91, 93–94, 97, 175–77,
Volker, Leo, 221–23
vow, 25–26, 96, 130, 171, 177

Waliggo, John Mary, 30, 31
Walls, Andrew, 8
war, 7, 28, 82, 87, 94, 107, 110, 138, 144, 170, 177, 219
    See also battle; combat
Wheelock, Eleazar, 167–68,
White Fathers, 214–25, 234

Whitefield, George, 167
widow, 49, 95, 138
wife, 30, 41, 43, 71–72, 75, 92, 96, 110–11, 116, 170, 179
Women and Gender in Early Modern Europe, 86–87
worship, 53, 96–97, 178, 193–94
    See also mass

Xavier, Francis, 82

youth, 21–22, 40–41, 71–72, 91, 93, 95, 98, 111, 130, 133, 168, 171–72, 216, 220, 224

Zanzibar, 21–23
Zapotec, 7, 116–22
zone, 94–95, 233–37

www.ingramcontent.com/pod-product-compliance
Lightning Source LLC
Chambersburg PA
CBHW022047290426
44109CB00014B/1012